A Salvationist Treasury

Also by Henry Gariepy:

Portraits of Christ—Devotional Studies of the Names of Jesus (Fleming Revell, 1972)

Footsteps To Calvary (Fountain Press, 1977)

Study Guide: Footsteps to Calvary (Fountain Press, 1977)

Advent of Jesus Christ (Salvation Army USA Eastern Territory, 1979)

Study Guide: Advent of Jesus Christ (Salvation Army USA Eastern Territory, 1979)

100 Portraits of Christ (Victor Books, 1987)

Portraits of Perseverance—From the Book of Job (Victor Books, 1989)

Christianity In Action—The Salvation Army in the USA Today (Victor Books, 1990)

Wisdom To Live By—From Proverbs, Ecclesiastes, and Song of Songs (Victor Books, 1991)

General of God's Army, Authorized Biography of General Eva Burrows (Victor Books, 1993)

Challenge & Response—A Documentary on Christianity In Action in the Inner City (The Salvation Army, 1994)

40 Days With the Savior (Thomas Nelson Publishers 1995)

Light In A Dark Place —From the Prophets (Victor Books, 1995)

Guidebook for Salvation Army Writers & Editors (The Salvation Army International Headquarters, 1995)

Healing in the Heartland (The Salvation Army Arkansas and Oklahoma Division, 1996)

Songs In the Night (William B. Eerdmans Publishing Co., 1996)

A Century of Service in Alaska (The Salvation Army Alaska Division, 1998)

Mobilized for God—History of The Salvation Army, Volume 8 (The Salvation Army International Headquarters, 2000)

Contributor To:

Guidebook To Successful Christian Writing (The Salvation Army, International Headquarters, 1996)

The Salvationist Pulpit (The Salvation Army, USA Eastern Territory, 1991)

Discipleship (The Salvation Army, Canada, 1995)

Encouragement in the Word (The Salvation Army, Canada, 1995)

Genius of the New Testament Church (Charles W. Carter, 1995)

The Book of Jesus (Calvin Miller, Simon & Schuster, 1996)

The Christian Daily Planner (Word, 1996)

A Place Called Heaven (Chariot Victor Publishing, 1997)

Count Your Blessings (Victor Books, 1997)

Christmas Through the Years (Crest Books, 1997)

The Hunger of Your Heart (Partnership Press, 1998)

Easter Through the Years (Crest Books, 1999)

Called By My Name (Partnership Press, 1999)

NIV Reflecting God Study Bible (Zondervan and CHP, 2000)

Essential Practices (Bristol Books, 2000)

A Salvationist Treasury

365 Devotional Meditations
From the Classics to the Contemporary

Henry Gariepy

Crest Books
Salvation Army National Publications
Alexandria, Virginia

Published by Crest Books, Salvation Army National Publications
615 Slaters Lane, Alexandria, Virginia 22313
(703) 684-5500 Fax: (703) 684-5539
http://publications.salvationarmyusa.org

Printed in the United States of America

Unless otherwise noted, Scripture taken from the *Holy Bible, New International Version.*
Copyright 1973, 1978, 1984 by International Bible Society. Used by permission. All rights
reserved.

Layout and design by Kristin B. Griffin
Cover design by Henry Cao

Library of Congress Catalog Card Number: 00-105967

ISBN: 0–9657601–9–7

To quintessential Salvationists
and soldiers of Christ

Priscilla, Harold,
Sarah, Kathryn,
Carissa, Erin
(Burgmayer)

Foreword

There is a common theme that seems to weave through everything expressed in both thought and action that comes before us as we are in the first year of the 21st Century. The pace of change and the whirlwind of activity have a dizzying effect on all of us. In the midst of it all, a thought presented by Dr. Richard A. Swenson at a recent meeting I attended has much to say to us: "Our sense of the presence of God is inversely proportional to the speed of our lives."

The trained eye, the warm heart and the keen mind of Colonel Henry Gariepy (R) has distilled a lifetime of reading of Salvation Army literature into *A Salvationist Treasury*, which can help us practice the scriptural admonition, "Be still and know that I am God" (Ps. 46:10). In so doing, it will deepen our understanding of the rich heritage and ministry that is ours.

Covering 127 years of published material from the *Christian Mission Magazine* (1873) to *He Who Laughed First* (2000), Salvationists who discipline themselves to adjust the speed of their lives to take daily doses of this compilation of well–mined gold and silver will deepen their sense of the presence of God.

Commissioner John Busby
National Commander, The Salvation Army USA

Introduction

Over the years my spiritual life has been enriched by the devotional writings of a diverse and far-flung company of Salvationists. Ostensibly, an anthology of this genre could offer a salutary daily devotional book. With encouragement from my friend and colleague, Lt. Colonel Marlene Chase, I embarked upon this daunting project.

In this corpus of both notable and less celebrated works there lurked radiant gems of inspiration. Many of these volumes have long been out of print. Valued suggestions of authors and works came from around the Army world, including one package all the way from Pakistan, with both an inspiring content and a rare window on the life of the Army Founder.

The criteria for selection included (1) Salvationist authorship, (2) a published work, (3) well written, (4) adaptable to format and space, and (5) biblically-based with a devotional application. The anthology sought to be international insofar as research was practical. The School for Officer Training library in Suffern, NY especially proved to be a valued resource.

Readers will readily discern that the theme of holiness predominates the early writings, making its own statement. One would expect to find the passionate pleas of William and Catherine Booth, the homilies of Bramwell, the oratory of Evangeline, and the devotional lyrics of Herbert Booth. Such a compendium would also be incomplete without the polished prose of Arnold Brown and the persuasive eloquence of Albert Orsborn.

Germane to such an anthology are the scholarly offerings of Frederick Coutts, holiness articles of Samuel Brengle, rich insights of Shaw Clifton, picturesque prose of Marlene Chase, biblical discourses of Roger Green, lyrical lines of Flora Larsson, and the theological reflections of Paul Rader. Readers will also find their contemporaries in the polemics of Chick Yuill, the inimitable style of Joe Noland and A. Kenneth Wilson, and the unique insights of Keilah Toy and Richard Munn. Altogether, the reader will encounter the rich devotional insights of over 100 Salvationist authors, from the classics to the contemporary.

John Ruskin said that the highest reward for our toil is what we become from it. The review of this genre of Salvation Army literature has been an immeasurably enriching exercise. May it be so for the reader, and may each day's journey illumine our individual pilgrimages of faith.

Henry Gariepy

A Salvation People

Hebrews 2:3

We are a salvation people. This is our specialty—getting saved and keeping saved, and then getting somebody else saved, and then getting saved ourselves more and more, until full salvation on earth makes the heaven within, which is finally perfected by the full salvation without, on the other side of the river.

We believe in salvation! We believe in old-fashioned salvation. Ours is the same salvation taught in the Bible, proclaimed by prophets and apostles, preached by Luther, Wesley and Whitfield, sealed by the blood of martyrs—the very same salvation which was purchased by the sufferings and agony and blood of the Son of God.

We believe the world needs it, that this and this alone will set it right. We want no other nostrum, nothing new. We are on the track of the old apostles' salvation. The worst man that ever walked will go to heaven if he obtains it, and the best man that ever lived will go to hell if he misses it.

There is a hell. A hell as dark and terrible as is the description given of it by the lips of Jesus Christ, the truthful. And into that hell men are departing hour by hour.

Perhaps the most appalling aspect of this hell is its bondage. How devils and devilish habits rule it, and with what an iron yoke. Can these captives be delivered? Saved from sinning, saved into holy living and triumphal dying?

Ask the Salvationist and the answer will be, from both theory and experience, that the vilest and worst can be saved to the uttermost, for all things are possible to him who believes. Our redeemer is mighty to save.

We have salvation. We need it and we have it. There are think-so Christians, and there are hope-so Christians, and there are know-so Christians. Thank God we belong to the know-so people. We know we are saved. We know in whom we have believed, and the Spirit answers to our faith, and testifies in our hearts that we are the children of God.

Our work is salvation. Soul-saving is our avocation, the great purpose and business of our lives.

What is the business of your life? Not merely to save your soul and make yourself ready for paradise. Rescue the perishing. They are all around you. You are to be a copy of Jesus Christ. So consecrate every awakened power to the great end of saving others.

"How shall we escape if we ignore such a great salvation?" (Heb. 2:3).

William Booth, *Salvation Soldiery*

On the Windward Side of Grace

2 Corinthians 9:8

I have always been grateful for the phrase "turning over a new leaf" when thinking about new year's resolutions. There's not a new leaf to be found in January. Thankfully, they're all buried under a blanket of snow, and we'll not have to worry about turning over any new vegetation until at least March or April!

Like most people, I must confess to a certain reticence when it comes to change. Old routines and habits are comfortable, predictable. The unknown is unnerving, however bright a prospect might seem.

I suppose it's not so much change that bothers us as the certain dread that comes with something unfamiliar entering our lives. It's interesting to note the frequency of the phrase "fear not" in the Bible. From Genesis to Revelation, every time you turn over a new leaf of Scripture, it is "Fear not!"

How do we survive the unpredictability of life? The poet lamented, "O God, Thy sea is so great, and my boat is so small!" Perhaps our first step to victory is to recognize the finiteness of our present situation and to place our trust in the reliable and changeless—in God.

When we recognize that it is God who underlies the thoughts and movements and melodies of life, we learn to look at change in a new way. New possibilities, challenges, dreams. Some fresh wind or bright flower, some strain of music before unheard.

If ever there was someone pressed and oppressed by the exigencies of life, it was the Apostle Paul. He not only coped, he triumphed, for he had set his course on a fixed, immovable point—the glory of God whose very nature is victory. Witnessing to that fact, he advised: "God is able to make all grace abound to you, so that in all things at all times, having all that you need, you will abound in every good work" (2 Cor. 9:8).

No matter what comes into our lives, we don't need to wonder about our destination. "O God, Thy sea is so great, and my boat is so small." Perhaps the writer was not aware that God is in the boat with us. And there lies our victory.

If we've set our sails on the windward side of His grace, it is precisely His great sea that will bring us to safety—to a harbor where under each new leaf is some new treasure He has prepared for those who follow Him.

Marlene Chase, *The War Cry*

The Time is Now!

John 7:6

Do you sense that time is rapidly fleeting? Our entry into a new year seems to make this all the more apparent. Concerning this matter, I have a suggestion. Don't think of time as rushing by; think of the time that is yours now.

Jesus said, "Your time is always ready" (John 7:6 KJV). In the first part of that verse Jesus said that His time had not yet come. He, with God, knew what would happen and when it would happen. But His disciples were ordinary mortals, like you and me. The only time they had, and that we have, is now.

The time is now! This is so because we have no guarantee of any other time. It is not morbid to point to the slender cord of life which holds us in time; it is only to face a fact. James warned us not to take time for granted. He said that our life is "a vapor that appears for a little time, and then vanishes away" (James 4:14). Don't presume about tomorrow. Use today wisely; it is priceless.

The time is now! This is so because this very moment can be more important than any which have preceded it or any which may follow. See today as the living essence of time between a past that is gone and a future not yet come. Today we can take what has come from the past and, with God's help, transform it so that the future will be better and nobler. Today can be the time for new beginnings. What needs to be said? Say it. What ought be done? Do it.

The time is now! This is so because it is God's time. He has given us life, permitting us to participate in a segment of time. There are many necessary and important things to do with time, but nothing should prevent us from giving God His rightful place in today's schedule. This is God's time for us. Be sensitive to Him and His will so that we may effectively respond to the needs of the people around us. Today is ours because God has given it to us.

Another year has come, and we find ourselves swept up in its forward movement. But you and I are not fearful of time's relentless passage. We are not measuring a diminishing time but trusting the Eternal God. "Your time is always ready." Let us make the most of today, because the time is now!

Bramwell Tripp, *The War Cry*

The Word of Life

Psalm 1:2

God has most commonly and most powerfully spoken to me through the words of Scripture. Some of them stand out to my mental and spiritual vision like mighty mountain peaks rising from a vast, extended plain. The Spirit that moved "holy men of old" to write the words of the Bible has moved me to understand them, by leading me along the lines of spiritual experience first trodden by these men, and has taken the things of Christ and revealed them unto me, until I have been filled with a divine certainty as altogether satisfactory.

I am not sure that I lived so intimately with my darling wife as I have for many years lived with St. Paul. Far more constantly and intimately than he lived and traveled with his friend Barnabas and his young helpers, has he lived, traveled, slept and talked with me. Paul has been my greatest mentor.

If you want to hold the truth fast and not let it slip, you must read and read and re-read the Bible. You must constantly refresh your mind with its truths, just as the diligent student constantly refreshes his mind by reviewing his textbooks, just as the lawyer who wishes to succeed constantly studies his law books, or the doctor his medical works.

The "blessed man" of David is not only a "man that walks not in the counsel of the ungodly, nor stands in the way of sinners, nor sits in the seat of the scornful, but [notice] his delight is in the law of the Lord, and in His law does he meditate day and night" (Psalm 1:1–2 KJV).

The Bible is God's recipe book for making holy people. You must follow the recipe exactly, if you want to be a holy, Christlike person.

The Bible is God's guidebook to show men and women the way to heaven. You must pay strict attention to its directions and follow them accurately, if you are ever to get there.

The Bible is God's medical book, to show people how to get rid of soul sickness. You must diligently consider its diagnosis of soul diseases, and its methods of cure, if you want soul-health.

Jesus said, "Man shall not live by bread alone, but by every word that proceeds out of the mouth of God" (Matt. 4:4); and again He said, "The words I speak unto you, they are spirit, and they are life" (John 6:63).

Samuel Logan Brengle, *Helps To Holiness*

I Bring My Heart to Jesus

Proverbs 23:26

I bring my heart to Jesus, with its fears,
With its hopes and feelings, and its tears;
Him it seeks, and finding, it is blest;
Him it loves, and loving is at rest.
Walking with my Savior, heart in heart,
      None can part.

I bring my life to Jesus, with its care,
And before His footstool leave it there;
Faded are its treasures, poor and dim;
It is not worth living without Him.
More than life is Jesus, love and peace,
      Ne'er to cease.

I bring my sins to Jesus, as I pray
That His blood will wash them all away;
While I seek for favor at His feet,
And with tears His promise still repeat,
He doth tell me plainly: Jesus lives
      And forgives.

I bring my all to Jesus; He hath seen
How my soul desireth to be clean.
Nothing from His altar I withhold
When His cross of suffering I behold;
And the fire descending brings to me
      Liberty.

Herbert Booth, *The Salvation Army Song Book*

The Silences of Christ

Isaiah 53:7

We remark, and rightly so, on the virtues of Christ's speech, "His words were with authority." And so were His silences. The written word is wonderful, but what of the unwritten story which lies folded between the ordinary incidents of that wonderful life?

The things He did were wonderful; what of the things He did *not* do? All we know of Him is marvelous, but where were the springs of His character? Through what solitudes did He grow brave and strong?

I feel it to be true that people's attraction to the Master is in large measure attributable to those silent depths that were in Jesus.

No man can ever say that he has discovered the last beauty in that calm, deep character. That is why the multitudes are still studying, preaching, writing about and, in part, seeking to emulate the beauty of this at once simplest and profoundest character ever revealed to man.

When the Jewish ruler paid Him the high compliment, "You are a teacher come from God,"(John 3:2 KJV) the Master did not reply, "Thank you; which of My sermons impressed you?" He ignored the well-meant praise and went directly to the main business. Witnesses to God's message in this sin-stained world are not sent forth to court praise but to cry aloud "You must be born again."

Our Master's speech was admirable in its restraint. It may truly be said that we would be better understood if we said less. God will surely count a prudent silence unto us for righteousness.

In the midst of our activities we need a central place of rest, a place for meditation and prayer where the busy, fevered spirit can find sanctuary. It was ever so in the life of the Master. Again and again we come across those retirements and silences, still veiled with the sacredness of the secret place. We can never learn some of the sweetest things about Jesus, except by turning aside into the secret place to meet with God the Holy Spirit. The Son of Man had need of much meditation and private communion with His Father, and certain it is that no follower of His can keep up the rush and stress of life without following the Master's example.

Jesus lived above the world while yet He was doing His work in it, and He left us an example that we might follow in His steps. May it be yours and mine so to do by the grace of the Christ who was as wonderful in His silences as He was in speech.

Albert Orsborn, *The Silences of Jesus*

Reason to Celebrate

2 Corinthians 5:17

Tax gatherers in Judea in the time of Jesus were considered by their fellow Jews to be the arch betrayers of their nation. They were regarded contemptuously as collaborators with the Roman authorities for whose hungry coffers they extorted enormous taxes from those to whom they were bound by blood, race and history. Levi was such an individual.

He had sufficient resources to provide a "great feast" for "many" publicans, "many" sinners, and "many" disciples, and he was affluent enough to do it "in his own house" (Matt. 9:9–11). And what was it that Levi was celebrating? For one thing, a new name, in all probability bestowed by Jesus Himself. Hereafter he would be known as Matthew, "gift of God." With a new name there would be a new life, a life beyond all imagining.

It would be something of a wonderment if the stylus which, in the hand of Levi, had completed Herod's tax returns had, in the hand of Matthew, recorded the first words a reader would find 20 centuries later when opening his New Testament—copies of which would have been reproduced in the mega–millions and found in every corner of the globe!

At the feast given by Levi, the fraternization was incredible. "Why does your teacher eat with tax collectors and 'sinners'" (Matt. 9:11) was not merely the voice of curiosity. It was the voice of censure. But it did not go unanswered.

His answer would not soon be forgotten. It was a classic riposte that would echo through the centuries. "It is not the healthy who need a doctor, but the sick" (Matt. 9:12). His task was not to minister to the righteous, but to lead sinners to repentance.

Fare is provided for both soul and mind in pondering what we have come to call "the Feast of Levi," an event which began by celebrating Levi's entry into discipleship, and ended with a trenchant reaffirmation by Jesus of His evangelical mission. Levi had been given a new name. He had discovered a worthy vocation. He had found a new life. No wonder he rejoiced and wanted others to share his unbounded joy.

Like Levi/Matthew we, too, have been given a new name—one that is written in the Lamb's Book of Life. To have gained through Christ not only a new name but a new nature should provoke us more often than perhaps it does to invite our friends to join us in celebration and provide them with an opportunity to meet our Master.

Arnold Brown, *With Christ at the Table*

A Holistic Gospel

Micah 6:8

In our era, the road to holiness necessarily passes through the world of action," wrote Dag Hammarskjøld in his book *Markings*. Indeed, we have a whole gospel that is Christ-centered, holiness-summoned and justice-oriented.

The Christian's cross consists of two beams: the vertical beam of our relationship to God in His infinite love and forgiveness, and the horizontal beam of our relationship to others in the world. The two cannot be separated. They always intersect on the Christian's cross.

Holiness without social concern is a soul without a body; social concern without holiness is a body without a soul. One is a ghost, the other a corpse. Only when they are wedded together do we have a living organism.

Suffering and tragedy stalk our world every day. News media bring to our living rooms poignant scenes of the carnage of the innocent, the anguish of refugees, the sad spectacle of the millions who are hungry, homeless and hurting. The brokenness of our world constantly impinges upon us.

The evils of pornography and sexploitation relentlessly invade the mainstream of our culture. The traditional family may soon be added to the endangered species list from the infection of increased divorce rates, acceptance of same-sex marriages and the rise of dysfunctional families. Violence and murder now stalk our schools and churches as well as our streets. Terrorism fuels the fears of people worldwide. The silent holocaust of abortion claims 1.5 million lives each year in the United States and over 50 million worldwide. Our world is neck-deep in trouble.

Our nation was founded upon righteousness and reverence for God. The founders of this nation legislated for each session of Congress to open with prayer and inscribed upon our coins "In God We Trust." But we have strayed from those principles. We have outlawed prayer in our schools, made legal the killing of innocent unborn children and spawned a generation victimized by drugs, AIDS and the specter of nuclear holocaust.

The Christian faith is not an escape from the realities and problems of the world. The cross was the most eloquent demonstration of caring the world has ever known. Christ calls His followers to the costly implications of the cross, to the biblical authority of a vulnerable discipleship. Where the world is at its worst, there the Christian church ought to be at its best.

Henry Gariepy, *Reflecting God NIV Study Bible*

The Pragmatism of Holy Living

Hebrews 12:10

It was Evelyn Underhill, writing in the 1930s, but with lasting relevance, who said, "There is nothing high–minded about Christian holiness. It is most at home in the slum, the street, the hospital ward."

Holiness is for every day, hour by hour. It is for the workplace and the shopping center. It is for our dealings with all manner of people.

Most of all, and often most testingly of all, it is for our home life. None can overestimate the value to God's kingdom of a holy life lived out among one's relatives, especially when those relatives are unsaved and perhaps even skeptical about the gospel. There is no effective argument against the silent eloquence of holiness.

So many folk have a sadly mistaken notion of what holiness involves. They seem to think it's about pious conversation in serious voices. Far from it! Laughter abounds and a sense of humor is essential. A natural, healthy interest in the opposite sex is only to be expected, but lust is out and so too are all forms of sexual impurity. Holiness sharpens your mind and your opinions. You can speak your mind, but strife, self–indulgent anger or deliberately cutting words must go. Irritability as a mark of personality cannot coexist with the fruits of the Spirit, but natural tension and stress through tiredness are not sins.

The believer who has set out for holiness still needs to eat, but is no glutton. He needs to sleep, but is not addicted to indolence. He needs to earn and spend, but is not in love with money. He will dress appropriately, but undue pride in personal appearance or lack of modesty will have no place.

Holiness is not an exemption from temptation. It is not moral perfection or infallibility. Mistakes will still abound. Holiness does not make a man or woman all–seeing or all–knowing. Hence the believer needs to recognize that the holy life can still encompass error, and that our errors can still hurt others. In the holy life, "I am sorry, please forgive me" will be words readily upon the lips and frequently spoken.

The essence of holiness is that deliberately choosing to sin has stopped by the rich grace of God. Bramwell Tripp summed up the possibility of pragmatic holiness in three sentences:

> To say "I must sin" is to deny my Savior.
> To say "I cannot sin" is to deceive myself.
> To say "I need not sin" is to declare my faith in divine power!

Shaw Clifton, *Never the Same Again*

Between You and Me, Lord

Psalm 32:8

I see it clearly, Lord,
every single thing that happens
     is ultimately between You and me,
     just the two of us alone.
No matter who is sitting beside me,
no matter how many people crowd around
     or whether I am at home or abroad,
in the final analysis it is my relationship with You that counts.

There is the outside me that other people know:
     how I walk and talk,
     how I dress and eat,
     what I like and dislike.
Folk could write essays on all that
and yet I should find it difficult to accept
     for it wouldn't be the real me.

The real me only You know fully.
The inner person that only partially expresses itself,
     that struggles for life
against the bonds of the body encumbering it,
that flutters and strains for it hardly knows what,
striving for something greater than it can express—
This hidden self You know and understand,
and I am glad in that knowledge.

That is why all that happens is finally
     just between You and me.
For You are the only one who can truly judge me.
You are reality, the unchangeable truth,
and a spark of Your eternal spirit has been lit in my heart
     drawing me to You,
     linking me with You,
     invisibly and eternally.

Flora Larsson, *Between You and Me, Lord*

The Mind of Christ

Philippians 2:5

What is the mind of Christ? First, Jesus had a nonstop God-consciousness. God was part of every experience of His life. He did not split His life into two parts: the sacred and the secular, the religious and the ordinary.

When questioned about His miracles or His teaching He would reply humbly, "I do always the will of My Father," (John 8:29) or "I speak only what My Father tells me to speak" (John 12:50). Life was all of one piece, like the seamless robe He wore.

The awareness of God's presence and purpose was most perfectly seen in His obedience to God's will in the Garden of Gethsemane. As He prays beneath the olive trees lit by the Pascal moon, we hear His words in that sacred moment, "Not My will, but Yours be done" (Luke 22:42). Jesus was prepared to subordinate His own will, good and blameless as it was, to the will of God. So He rose from His knees and went forward to face the cross and become the world's Redeemer. That was the mind of Christ. Unquestionably obedient.

How obedient to the will of God are we? Does the world crowd in too much and put God to the margin of our experience? Let us ask the Holy Spirit to shape our attitudes to Christ's, to make us more aware of God's presence and ready to do His will above all else. Let this obedient mind be in you which was also in Christ Jesus.

Secondly, a beautiful characteristic of the mind of Christ was His awareness of others. He was never self-absorbed, but always concerned for the people He met among the crowds that milled around Him.

It is fascinating to watch Jesus in the Gospel stories, calling the children closer to Him when His disciples would chase them away, or noticing a poor woman quietly putting two coins in the temple treasury. He made friends with unsavory characters. His ear caught the faint cry of a blind man almost lost in the noisy crowd. His compassion reached out to each one. He was love personified.

The mind of Christ is a loving mind. Do we have a mind like that? That kind of love is costly. To have the mind of Christ is to love like that.

Eva Burrows, *The Salvationist Pulpit*

The Mind of Christ (cont.)

Romans 12:2

In response to Paul's challenge in Philippians 2:5, we address the question, "What is the mind of Christ?"

To have the mind of Christ is to love as He loved and serve as He served. Brigadier Josef Korbel was for ten years imprisoned in the communist labor camp in Czechoslovakia. He and the other prisoners were near starvation and issued but one piece of bread each day. When other prisoners devoured their food, Korbel divided his into three pieces. One he ate slowly and the other two he kept in his pocket. Later in the day as he ate his second piece, a fellow prisoner would eye him jealously and say, "Where did you get extra bread?" Korbel would reply, "Nowhere. I have kept some of my own back. Have a share of mine." Then, starving himself, he would give his last piece to the ravenous fellow prisoner. No wonder his selfless love made such an impression on others that many of his fellow prisoners came to accept the Christ whom Korbel loved and served.

Finally, the mind of Christ had an awareness of evil. Jesus saw the world as a battleground between the forces of good and evil. The more holy the life, the more alert is the mind to the approach of sin and wrong.

Besides the Lord's testing in the wilderness, Christ faced temptation throughout the whole of His life, right up to those agonizing moments when He hung on the cross, and the mocking Jews tempted Him to come down and prove Himself the Son of God.

As the power of the Holy Spirit enabled Him to resist every clever enticement of the devil, so the Holy Spirit will give us a conscience quick to feel the approach of evil, sensitive to the danger of rationalization, sensitive to the easy acceptance of the world's standards and to those sins which so easily beset us and trip us up, sensitive to wrong relationships, self–indulgence, pettiness, greed and pride.

Let us ask ourselves, am I as sensitive to evil as I should be? Do I have the mind of Christ to resist every approach of wrong? Let this sensitive mind be in you which was also in Christ Jesus.

We ask, how can I live like that? How can I have the mind of Christ—obedient to God, concerned for others, sensitive to sin? The Apostle Paul writes in Romans 12:2: "Be transformed by the renewing of your mind." It is the Holy Spirit's work to shape our thoughts to the thoughts of Christ, to align our will to His will, to shed abroad His love in our hearts. The Holy Spirit transforms our attitudes to those of Christ.

Eva Burrows, *The Salvationist Pulpit*

The Wind of God

John 3:8

Nothing in nature was more suitable than the wind as a symbol of the Spirit. "To anyone brought up in the Jewish tradition," J. S. Stewart explains, "it was natural, almost inevitable, to compare the Spirit of God with the wind. For in the Hebrew tongue the same term was used for both."

It was to a learned theologian that our Lord spoke of this simple, everyday occurrence—the blowing of the breeze. "Listen to the wind," He said. "Hear it rustling the leaves of the old olive tree. See the clouds scudding across the face of the moon tonight, driven by the wind." And then the parallel with spiritual realities: "Nicodemus, can you tell where it comes from, or where it goes? The Spirit is like that."

He is indeed like that. Unexplainable in human language, but known by what He does. He breathes into men the breath of spiritual life, regenerating, reviving, resurrecting the dead, doing what only He can do.

Harriet Auber sang, "All-powerful as the wind He came,/As viewless too." Viewless, but powerful! "Of all the forces of nature, wind is the greater Invisible," wrote David Read. "The painter or photographer can reproduce the sun and moon, the waves of the sea, the snow and the rain; but how do you catch the rushing mighty wind? Only by its effects."

Like a tropical hurricane, the Holy Spirit uproots deep-seated prejudices, overturns rigid bastions of self-righteous dogmatism, and sweeps the slum-like streets of our self-centered lives, ridding them of the debris which accumulate everywhere until He comes with His cleansing.

Where you see changed lives and transformed homes, you know the Spirit has been moving—invisibly, yes— but what He does provides evidence enough of His presence.

I remember the first time I saw a windmill. There it stood on a farm near our own, whirling steadily in the Nova Scotia wind. When I asked what it was for, someone explained that it harnessed the power of the wind to draw water for the cattle. This country lad was impressed! Now, it would be irreverent to speak of "harnessing" the Spirit, but it is true that to benefit from His ministry a believer must put himself in the path of His power.

The Wind is still blowing! God's Spirit is ceaselessly active, unseen but mighty, moving over the earth. Not for me to try to force Him to do my bidding but to put myself in the path of His power. Mighty Wind of heaven, move on me today!

Edward Read, *Burning, Always Burning*

Saints with Rosy Cheeks

2 Corinthians 4:7

My saints are not on pedestals. They do not look down at me condescendingly from stained-glass windows, or by their lofty words from behind rostrums fill me with awe. There they would be so still and cold, so remote, so apart from the good earth and the experiences that wring both tears and laughter from me.

My saints have rosy cheeks and warm, kind hands; they are jolly! They are near, too. Sometimes they are in the next office, in the shop around the corner or in the flat downstairs.

One of them all through her girlhood wrestled to control, by the grace of God, what seemed to be an uncontrollable temper. God and my saint were the victors.

"I hope," she said, "that I shall have a large family. I'll come with my six boys to see you and they'll tramp, tramp, tramp all over your immaculate house."

She had four children. Three were not the noisy boys who were to have invaded my home, but gentle little girls. Within a few days of each other two died; a few years later a third had left her.

My saint did not come out with placid face and unearthly calm. Her grief staggered us and ravished her strength. But God and my saint conquered again. She stole out to find other little children. She became a young people's sergeant-major establishing three Bible home companies, one for each dead child. One was formed from the Islamic population of a city, to whom the Christian message had never before been taken.

Some of my saints are young. One is only 14, a lad who tends his invalid mother at night and contends with a drunken father by day. Some are students with brows unduly furrowed by the effect of study accompanied by what, at times, must look like a losing battle with poverty. Some are mothers who never mention mystical experiences, yet have established the kingdom in their homes. Another of my saints is a Salvation Army officer, in an unromantic situation, who has not attained the recognition that many self-proclaimed "saints" demand, but in a faraway land to a great company of people, she is a light in the darkness.

Sometimes I wonder why my saints care to company with me. I expect it is because they do not know they are saints. And the world is rather slow in discovering it too. Can it be that we still prefer the stained-glass window kind with their white, solemn faces, smooth, untried feet and hidden hearts?

Catherine Baird, *Evidence of the Unseen*

Interpreting the Scriptures

2 Peter 1:19–21

What are the guiding principles by which we interpret the Scriptures? How shall we know that what we believe is true? A sound foundational method is needed, and I contend that our own Wesleyan heritage provides that method for us with what is termed the Wesleyan Quadrilateral. As the name suggests, it identifies four keys for establishing Christian truth and doctrine: the Bible first, and then the interpretation of the Bible by tradition, reason and experience.

John Wesley held that Scripture has the first and ultimate authority, as the Reformers had taught before him. However, people interpret Scripture from various perspectives, and Wesley believed that the three major perspectives should be tradition, reason and experience.

The tradition of the church is of vital importance in determining theological truth. We need to look not only to our own church history, and not only to Wesleyan history. We must look to the tradition and teaching of the historic, orthodox Church and learn from that tradition.

Reason is also of utmost importance. People are mistaken when they pit experience against reason, as though we can serve God with our hearts but not with our minds. God is the creator of our minds as well as our feelings. He has given us the capacity to reason, and our minds are redeemed at the moment of salvation just as much as any other aspect of us. Full intention of the Scriptures will never be realized without careful study and thoughtful interpretation.

Finally, our experience has a contribution to make. Not the primary contribution. Too often Christian people make experience the chief means by which they interpret the Bible, their touchstone of theology. In experience there is both a danger and glory. The danger is that our experiences and feelings come and go. They can beget all kinds of strange and wonderful thoughts, as well as strange interpretations of biblical texts.

The glory is that God works through our feelings and emotions and accepts them as part of the way we understand Him. He has implanted in us a heart with which to worship, a mouth to praise Him, hands to clap, feet to dance and imagination to create in rejoicing in God our Savior. We rejoice in our experiences when we recognize their place in our lives. However, we recognize that there is no sustaining power in experience without Scripture, tradition and reason.

Roger J. Green, *The War Cry*

The Victory of the Cross

Galatians 6:14

The central event in all human history is the crucifixion of Jesus at Calvary. It was here that the war between good and evil reached its climactic battle, and to the superficial observer it must have seemed that evil had triumphed beyond any possible doubt.

The strange and wonderful thing is that the New Testament writers, far from remembering the cross though a haze of tears, actually celebrate it as the place where Jesus ultimately triumphed over Satan. You would expect the leaders of a new religious movement to keep quiet about the fact that their founder had died a criminal's death. Those early Christians, in fact, gloried in the cross. What seemed at first glance to be a terrible tragedy was actually the key move in God's master strategy!

Jesus' willingness to go to the cross is all the more remarkable when we remember that He was the most sane, the most balanced, the most life-loving man who ever lived. When we read the story of Jesus in the Gospels we are not in the company of a religious fanatic with a death-wish lodged deep in His psyche.

This is the man who rescued the wedding celebration at Cana in Galilee by changing water into wine; this is the man who ruined every funeral He ever attended by raising the dead to life. And this is the man who, in the most poignant moment in the New Testament, pleads with His Father in Gethsemane that He might be allowed to take another road than that of the cross. Only the deepest conviction that the cross was the one way in which evil could be defeated could have led Him to say, "Yet, not what I want, but what You want" (Mark. 14:36, NRSV).

The cross is a place of victory because it demonstrates the justice and love of God. The daring assertion of the Gospel writers is that God turned the most evil act in history into the supreme act of righteous love.

The cross is a place of victory because it deals with the sin of mankind. The cross is the ultimate confirmation of the condition of humanity. But the paradox is that the cross is not only the place where our sinfulness is starkly displayed; it is also the place where God deals with that sinfulness.

The cross is a place of victory because it defeats Satan and the powers of evil. The victory has been won at Calvary. Insofar as we enter into the victory of Christ by faith we will share that victory.

Chick Yuill, *This Means War*

Holiness As the Will of God

Titus 2:14

We are told over and over again that God wants His people to be pure and that purity in their hearts is the very central idea and end and purpose of the gospel of Jesus Christ. If it is not so, I am utterly deceived.

In justification of this I have selected summing-up texts. "The will of God is your sanctification" (1 Thess. 4:3 KJV). There is, however, a sense, and an important sense, in which sanctification must be the will of man. It must be my will too, and if it is not my will, the divine will can never be accomplished in me. I must will to be sanctified, as God is willing that I should be sanctified.

"He gave Himself for us that He might redeem us from all iniquity, and purify unto Himself a peculiar people, zealous of good works" (Titus 2:14 KJV). And again, "Every man that has this hope in him purifies himself, even as He is pure" (1 John 3:3 KJV). Now, I say these are summing-up texts, and there are numbers of others to the same effect to show that the whole end and purpose of redemption is this: that He will restore us to purity; that he will bring us back to righteousness; that He will purge our consciences from dead works to serve the living God.

Now, I say, if this be not the central idea of Christianity, I do not understand it. This is not a sitting down and sentimentalizing and thinking of Christ in the heavens. It brings Him down, to all intents and purpose, into our hearts and lives here. These epistles represent a real, practical transformation to be accomplished in you.

I tell you, without it, you will not be able to die in peace. You will want to be cleansed before you can venture into the presence of the King of kings. You will want a sense of beautiful, moral rectitude and righteousness spreading over your whole nature, which will enable you to look up into the face of God, and say, "Yes, I love You, I know You, and You know me, and love me, and we are one. I love the things You love, and desire the things You desire."

You will want that, and nothing less, to die with. And why not have it? Why not let God work it in us? He can do it, and He promises to do it. Will you say, "Be it unto me according to Your Word?" (Luke 1:38 KJV).

Catherine Booth, *Godliness*

On a Wing and a Prayer

Job 5:9

꙳

Ian Knop for many years had his home in Perth, Australia. There he had a part in starting a new Christian congregation, and just as a hobby he kept half a dozen white ducks behind a wire netting fence in his backyard.

One day his wife warned him that he needed to clip the wings of the ducks, as some of them seemed to be trying to get over the fence. He said that he would do the job on Saturday when he was home from work. However, late on Friday afternoon as Ian was watching from his veranda, one of the ducks which happened to be a bit lame stretched its wings, flew over the netting and disappeared behind the house.

Somewhat surprised, Ian ran into the street, but the duck was nowhere to be seen. He went to the next street, but again there was no sign of the bird. Although he inquired of almost everyone he met no one had seen the rather improbable suburban sight of a white duck flying or walking about. Time went by and the mystery of the missing duck remained unsolved.

Almost a year later the truth came out, and what had happened to the lame duck became known. Ian had attended a Sunday night service when the theme had been on answers to prayer. As the weather was rough he offered a ride home to a woman in the congregation who lived four streets from where he lived himself and who had experienced a hard life with a drunken husband and their five children.

As they drove along, the woman kept up a stream of comments on this and that and then remarked on the lovely meeting they had shared thinking about answers to prayer. She said: "I know God answers prayer. Believe it or not, about a year ago on a Friday night I was standing on my veranda praying to God because I had little money with which to buy meat or other food for the family over the weekend."

"Suddenly, a white duck came out of the sky and landed just in front of me. It had a little bit of a limp but otherwise it was a lovely bird, and a real answer to prayer. In no time I had killed it and had it ready for the pot and we had all the meat we needed. Wasn't that wonderful!"

Ian resisted the temptation to reveal that it was his loss that had been her gain! God's servant of old reminds us, "He performs wonders that cannot be fathomed, miracles that cannot be counted" (Job 5:9).

Wesley Harris, *Truth Stranger than Fiction*

Prayer of Dedication

Philippians 3:10

Lord, I pray that I may know Thee,
    Risen One, enthroned on high;
Empty hands I'm stretching to Thee,
    Show Thyself to me, I cry.

        Show Thyself to me, show Thyself to me,
        That I may reveal Thy beauty;
          Show Thyself to me.

All that once I thought most worthy,
    All of which I once did boast,
In Thy light seems poor and passing,
    'Tis Thyself I covet most.

        Give Thyself to me, give Thyself to me,
        That I may show forth Thy power;
          Give Thyself to me.

Only as I truly know Thee
    Can I make Thee truly known;
Only bring the power to others
    Which in my own life is shown.

        Show Thy power in me, show Thy power in me,
        That I may be used for others;
          Show Thy power in me.

        Ruth Tracy, *The Salvation Army Song Book*

Face to Face

1 Corinthians 13:12

Could anyone question the assertion that there is a great deal more sorrow in the world than joy? A pall of sorrow covers the world. We learn from this statement of Paul, first, that no soul is left totally in the dark. Though as "through a glass darkly," (1 Cor. 13:12 KJV) yet we see. Abundant mercy has swung in the conscience a lamp which gleams in every man's path and has fastened a guiding star in the horizon of every man's soul.

Second, I learn in this "glass darkly" that this world's clearest and best vision is but a misty and imperfect one. How sadly too many have lost their hold of God simply because they could not trace the full meaning of His dealings, either concerning themselves or those dear to them. How much safer and better do we remember that it was within the planning of God's love that we should not know now, but know hereafter. This world is not our home—it is a place of sojourn.

Lastly, I see that there is to be an inestimable and indescribable difference between our present day and our eternal tomorrow. We are to enter into His presence; we are to look upon His countenance, nothing between—no glass, no cloud, no time intervening—but "face to face" with Jesus! Now the beclouded view, then a fadeless shining! Now the tumult and the strife, then the rest and eternal life! Now the weeping and the sighing, then the song and the tearless eyes! Now the children dying, then no more parting! Now the graves' hearts breaking, then the resurrection greeting! Morning with an eternity in it!

Oh, the transforming touch of that hour! We shall find our bereavements; they will meet us as reunions. We shall find our loss rebounding in eternal gain. We shall find our hidden struggles crowned in open victory. We shall find the complete fulfillment of every promise of the Bible, verifying the fondest dreams of the saints. The gates of strife will be closed behind us, the boundary crossed, the veil torn, the morning broken.

Sight unequaled, sound unparalleled, light unrivaled, as the heavenly orchestra catches the strain of the numberless multitude and bursts in with the chorus of the Hallelujah anthem. Oh, it is the "face to face" time! No one can describe the glory. The redeemed break out as every eye is cast on the wounded hands, the riven side, the thorn-pierced brow of the conquering Lord.

Evangeline Booth, *Love Is All*

Walk the Talk

Philippians 2:15

In the cut and thrust of business, entrepreneurs are constantly seeking that "winning edge." One corporation established as a requirement for its merchandise the following standard: "zero defects." The level of excellence was set; the company would not tolerate a blemished product on the market.

The very nature of Christian integrity is that it calls us toward zero defects. When our actions, thoughts, words or deeds become compromised, Christian integrity becomes blemished.

It is only by the grace of God that such integrity can be attained. This is an inner disposition rather than a coded set of behaviors. Such a high criterion, however, is possible, and when engaged it can be a witness to the grace of Christ.

General Arnold Brown has written of The Salvation Army: "If we are to hope that as a movement we will last through the next century, let alone the next millennium, then our byword and our hallmark must be integrity."

In due course, integrity will stand out in an influential way simply because it will be in contrast to so much else: "Become blameless and pure, children of God without fault in a crooked and depraved generation, in which you shine like stars in the universe" (Phil. 2:15).

The essence of integrity is utter honesty. The word literally means "not a fraction." In other words, there is wholeness between who we are and what we profess. It means we are for real. It answers the question, "What do you do when no one is looking?" There is a perfect match between our words and our deeds. In the language of the street, we "walk the talk."

One can sense the desperate need for people of integrity in the world today. Many among the generation of young adults have become cynical regarding the notion that politicians or even church leaders are people of honest principle.

Into this uncertain moral climate every Christian has an opening to be a refreshing agent of the gospel, in the privacy of home and in the openness of the workplace.

Richard Munn, *The War Cry*

Saints in Embryo

1 Thessalonians 5:23

John Wesley's teaching on holiness was both novel and radical—in fact revolutionary. Wesley followed in the wake of Luther's reformation. In Luther the pendulum had swung from "salvation by works" to "salvation by faith" but, as always the pendulum had swung too far in certain quarters. For some the wine had been too strong! "What a relief," they had said in effect. "Thank God we have been shown the evil of salvation by works! All we have to do is "believe" and everything will be well on the judgment day."

In pondering this sorry consequence of Luther's doctrine, Wesley realized that the fault lay in the narrow meaning which had been given to the word "salvation." In popular thinking "salvation" was simply a question of getting by on the day of judgment. It was strictly a heavenly matter.

Relentlessly Wesley stressed the need for personal holiness here on earth. Salvation was not a future question but a present concern. It was the duty and privilege of every Christian to live uprightly. Thoughts, motives, actions—all were within God's sphere of interest and influence. Holiness was not the concern of a handful of religious specialists; it was the very heart of religion—for everyone. Salvation and holiness were but two sides of the same coin. They could not be separated. Every "saved" man was a saint in embryo.

Wesley took Luther's doctrine one step further. Where Luther had said, "You are saved by faith," Wesley said, "You are saved and sanctified by faith."

The emphasis on holy living was long overdue. The preaching of entire sanctification as Wesley had taught it was an outstanding feature in the early revival days of our own movement. The doctrine is especially linked with two names: General Bramwell Booth and Commissioner Samuel Logan Brengle. Due to their influence The Salvation Army has maintained a dual emphasis: salvation and holiness. We go so far as to name our Sunday meetings by the doctrines that are taught in them. Wesley's teaching shook the church of his day, and there is little doubt that in Article 10 (1 Thess. 5:23) we have one of the most radical doctrines of holiness within the whole Christian Church.

John Larsson, *Doctrine Without Tears*

Confessions of a Teacher of Holiness

John 17:17

It is the privilege of all believers to be wholly sanctified." As a Salvationist teacher and preacher of holiness, I have heard that call and rejoice to proclaim it to others. Gladly I bear witness to its reality and redemptive power in my own experience. Still, I confess concerns as to the adequacy of my presentation of this grand truth and the extent to which we effectively embody it.

I wonder if we espouse a kind of holiness that is not tough enough. J. I. Packer speaks trenchantly of a modern preference for "hot tub religion," which soothes our troubled spirits and makes but few demands. Is our holiness far too fragile to see us through the traumas of life? We face a determined and powerful enemy who seeks to destroy us. We need an experience that makes us tough enough to triumph in life's inevitable encounters.

I also confess that I sometimes wonder whether our holiness is truth–centered enough, grounded firmly enough in the truth of Scripture, rather than based upon the experience of others. Jesus Himself said, "Sanctify them by the truth; Your word is truth" (John 17:17). It is our certainty of the truth that gives stability to faith and integrity to experience.

Further, is my approach to holiness total enough? Is our holiness too therapeutic in its emphasis? There are dangers of beginning with our human problems instead of God's purpose. Is my approach to holiness sometimes too cosmetic? Holiness deals with the essential inner orientation of the personality. The self dies hard. The cross is painful and total.

I must confess that I have sometimes had cause to wonder if the holiness I profess and proclaim has made me tender enough. The truth is that we live in an age that is seductively desensitizing us to evil. What once might have appalled and embarrassed us, perhaps even angered us, now only makes us sad. What would it take to make us cry out in indignation? What miscarriage of justice, what indifference to standards of integrity, what crass immorality would move us to tears and stir us to action? How much do I care about purity, justice and integrity?

Finally, is my holiness telling enough? Our age cries out for men and women of God whose lives stand in stark contrast to the darkness that surrounds us.

May the Lord direct our hearts to a holiness that is tough enough, truth–centered enough, total enough, tender enough and telling enough.

Paul A. Rader, The Salvationist Pulpit

The Father of Mankind

1 Corinthians 8:6

There is one head in a family, one chief in a village, one emperor in a country and one God who rules over heaven and earth. This true God has all wisdom and power. He is full of mercy and loves us as His children.

Alas, we often forget about His grace and blessings and think only of ourselves. This is a dangerous way of life. Even though we are taught about God we sometimes feel far from Him.

A friend of mine left his family in the country and came to Tokyo where he spent several years. He then called all his family to join him. The man's son, now eight years of age, was seen looking at his face in the mirror every day, and the father wondered why the boy was so interested in staring at himself. The boy replied, "I'm not sure whether you are my true father or not. I feel that you are, but I'm not sure. If you are my true father then I will bear some resemblance to you. So I look at my face in the mirror, and then I look at yours."

The illustration fits. If we have been far from God, our Father, it is difficult to identify our true Father and to see any likeness to Him. Yet if we take time to think about it we see that we have wisdom, as God has all wisdom; that we have discernment to judge what is right and what is wrong, as God Himself is all-righteous; and that we have a heart with which to love others, as God Himself is full of love.

Human beings were made in the image of God, and we are His children. Moreover, God has so richly blessed us that we cannot tell how great His grace to us has been.

The greatest scholar or scientist finds it impossible to create a cupful of water out of nothing. But God generously gives us the water with which to wash, to drink. No matter how hard the farmer worked, he alone could not produce enough rice. Or what if God did not cause the plants to grow, or withheld the rain? We might complain that the price of rice or wheat is too high or too low, but without the grace of God there would be no rice or wheat to complain about. As one grain of rice or wheat shows, we depend utterly on God's grace. To someone who strikes a match so that a man can see it is easy to say, "thank you." Then why should it be so difficult to say "thank You" to the God who by the sun provides light for the whole of the day? How understanding we need to be about such things.

Gunpei Yamamuro, *The Common People's Gospel*

Sorrows into Blessings

2 Corinthians 4:17

Do you ask how God can make sorrows into blessings? I will tell you. He can use them to soften the heart. A tender heart is a great treasure. What hard, unfeeling creatures men and women would become if they had one continual run of prosperity! In health and comfort and plenty, men grow careless about everyone's interests but their own.

Sanctified sorrow is favorable to humility. God hates pride; He beholds the proud man afar off. Trouble brings the lofty spirit to a true knowledge of itself and helps to lay it in the dust.

Sorrow makes men sympathetic to the sorrows of others. If I want sympathy I go to those who have suffered themselves.

Sorrow loosens our hold on the things of this life. The tendency of the human heart is to settle down and find its happiness in the things of earth. Sorrow weakens the cords that bind us to this world and draws the spirit to seek its heaven in the next. Sorrow opens the heart for the reception of all the blessed salvation of God. In prosperity, men can do without God—at least, many do not want Him. When affliction and bereavements and death come to them, they cry after Him.

Sorrow will work out far more precious things for us in the world to come. Of these momentary afflictions, Paul confidently says: "For our light and momentary troubles are achieving for us an eternal glory that far outweighs them all" (2 Cor. 4:17).

What must you do to turn your trials and sorrows to good account?

Ask God to forgive all the murmuring thoughts and words of the past. Give yourself up fully to obey His every command in the future—live a life of trust. Take hold of your Father's hand, and believe that He has hold of yours.

Tell Him that in the dark as well as in the light, in joy as in sorrow, you will trust Him to guide and lead you safely home. Sorrow may endure for a night, but joy comes in the morning (Ps. 30:5).

William Booth, *The Warrior's Daily Portion*

Christ the Door

John 10:9

You are The Door
But I'm afraid of You!
What shall I find
If I should
venture through?

The door to what?
To where?
I'd like to know.
The destination please,
And then I'll go!

Through You I shall find
Peace perhaps, or pain?
Through You I may know
Struggle, stress and strain!
But answers I have anguished
To find out
Shall be revealed
Through You
I have no doubt!

The Door to Hope,
To Love,
To all that's true,
The Door to God Himself
O Christ,
That's You!

John Gowans, *O Lord!*

The Spirit–Filled Life

Galatians 5:22

What is a normal Christian? What picture comes to your mind? Perhaps you picture a person who attends church, gives to charity every now and again, lives a respectable life, and goes about his business no different from the average man in the street. Sad to say, our society equates the nominal Christian with a normal Christian. But in fact, the nominal Christian lives a sub–normal Christian life.

What then is a normal Christian? A normal Christian is one who is filled with the Holy Spirit. The normal Christian, the Spirit-filled Christian, is one in whom the Spirit takes complete control.

At Pentecost, when the disciples received an outpouring of the Holy Spirit, they gave vent to this power in them. Onlookers were amazed and mistakenly thought the disciples were drunk. Peter had to repudiate that charge, saying they were exuberant because they were filled with the Spirit.

The Spirit–filled life overflows with joy. It characterized the early disciples; it was a hallmark of the early-day Salvationists. The Spirit of God enables us to have joy and give thanks always and in all circumstances.

"The fruit of the Spirit is love, joy, peace, patience, kindness, goodness, faithfulness, gentleness and self–control" (Gal. 5:22). This ninefold fruit of the Spirit expresses the Spirit-filled life. These qualities are found in the life of our Lord, so to be Spirit–filled is to live the life of Christ. A Spirit-filled person is a reproduction of, or a manifestation of, the life of Christ.

We value the fellowship with believers in the place of worship, but if our faith is to mean anything at all it has to be expressed in life's relationships outside the church as well. The effects of the Spirit-filled life are felt in our homes and in the society in which we live. It has its effects on the relationships of husband and wife, parent and children. Spirit-filled Christians apply Christian principles in the home, the office, the school, at work, in society.

For the Spirit to fill us, there first needs to be a self–emptying of self, sin and pride. Fullness comes at the point of full surrender. The Spirit of God, when He takes full control, revolutionizes us and the society in which we live.

Ah Ang Lim, *The Salvationist Pulpit*

The Thorn in the Flesh

2 Corinthians 12:7-10

Paul wrote of having been "caught up" to the third heaven, and for an indescribable moment was exalted to a rarified realm beyond time and space. There he heard "things that man is not permitted to tell" (2 Cor. 12:4). He did not wish to boast about his experience. All he could boast about was his own weakness, his own insufficiency and utter dependence upon the Lord.

It is against this astonishing background that Paul speaks of his thorn in the flesh. God permitted the affliction "to keep me from becoming conceited because of these surpassingly great revelations" (2 Cor. 12:7). Whatever it was, the affliction was so severe and disturbing, that on three different occasions the apostle "pleaded with the Lord to take it away" (2 Cor. 12:8).

As a lad I often wrestled with the meaning of the Lord's promise that, "Whatever you ask in my name … I will do it" (John 14:13–14). Does God really answer all our prayers? It appeared that some were overlooked! It was some time before I realized that praying "in the name" of the Lord means praying in tune with His will and purpose. When Paul pleaded with the Lord to remove his affliction, the answer was a positive refusal. "My grace is sufficient for you," the Lord replied, "for My power is made perfect in weakness" (2 Cor. 12:9).

On one occasion during my service as a World War II military chaplain I came perilously close to becoming a victim of self–pity. My battalion was camped on the edge of a forest. With 22 days of cold rain and submarines busy in the North Atlantic, mail was not getting through. A padre is supposed to help maintain morale, but how can you do that if your own morale is oozing through the bottom of your boots?

At long last mail arrived and there were over 20 letters from my wife Janet. I arranged the letters in order of dates on my rickety homemade desk, told the batman to keep my tent clear of visitors barring emergencies, then settled down to read the mail.

In one letter Janet told me about our six–year old son who got into such a tantrum that she had to order him down to the basement to cool off, where he whooped it up as loudly as he could. Close to bedtime he went to his own room. A few moments later she heard him talking. Tiptoeing to the door which was ajar, she peeped in. Clad in his pajamas, Donald was kneeling by the bed, having a conversation with God. She heard him say, "Dear God, help me not to cry when there's nothing to cry about, and make me a man!" How well I remember dropping to my knees in that dank, mildewed tent, and offering the very same prayer, word for word.

Clarence D. Wiseman, *The Desert Road to Glory*

Adorn the Doctrine

Titus 2:10

"Adorn the doctrine of God our Savior in all things" (Titus 2:10). To "adorn the doctrine" means that by his daily living the believer will seek to beautify that which is already inherently beautiful.

There are arts which make their own direct appeal to the beholder. The visual arts come under this heading. There are other arts, however, which demand an interpreter. Their beauty cannot be appreciated without one—music, for example. To the musically illiterate, a page of music is a collection of black blobs scattered indiscriminately over rulings of five lines and four spaces, and joined without seeming rhyme or reason to other short upright lines, a jumble of unintelligible markings. If these musical symbols are to live for me as they did in the mind of the composer before he committed them to paper, someone has to bring them to life.

This is the function of the performer. By virtue of his skill he can make the otherwise incomprehensible light up with meaning. When a genuine artist plays the passage in question he recreates it as a thing of beauty and joy. He has adorned the doctrine. By contrast, were I to try to play the same passage you might well tear out your hair and say I was murdering it. We will be agreed that by his capacity or lack of it, a player can enhance or diminish the beauty of a composer's work.

We have to accept the unwelcome fact that the Christian gospel is to some as meaningless as a page of music to the man who cannot read music. He hasn't a clue! The Christian faith needs interpreters, and this is where we come in. We can adorn the gospel or disfigure it. By our lifestyle we can make the "doctrine of God our Savior" positively appealing or utterly unlikeable. We can make it or mar it.

The Army Founder, in welcoming the Revised Version of Scripture in 1885, said: "If this revision throws any new light upon the precious volume, I accept it very gratefully. I am interested just now in a further translation. I want to see a new translation of the Bible in the conduct of men and women."

The character of our witness must be appealingly attractive. Not without reason do the Scriptures speak of "the beauty of holiness." The beauty of holiness is not a kind of external cosmetic, which is, as the saying goes, only skin deep. But Christian doctrine is adorned by the development of Christ's own character in the life of the believer.

Frederick Coutts, *The Splendor of Holiness*

My Bible

Psalm 119:11

Josef Korbel endured 10 harsh years in a communist prison camp, where despite severe punishment and constant threats of death, the Brigadier continued his Christian witness.

My poor fellow prisoners all over the forced labor camps and in the prison cells were often downhearted and even desperate, ready to commit suicide. It often happened that a verse from the Word of God, which I quoted to them from memory, was a source of help and encouragement. Then I had an idea, and much later in a forced labor camp I was able to realize it.

At that time we were working on buildings and so it was easy to get brown paper from cement sacks. Taking a clean part from such a sack, I made a little notebook, using a piece of thin wire to pin it together.

Although it was against the rules of the camp to possess a pencil, I had a little stump hidden in my jacket. With this I wrote many beautiful Bible verses I knew by heart. Soon my notebook was full and I started to lend it to fellow prisoners, who were sad and downhearted.

After a while my "Bible" was in such demand, that men had to wait for days until it was their turn to get it. Shabby, mended and worn out from hiding it under ragged jackets, this "Bible" was a source of much blessing.

"Joe, is your Bible back?" they would ask. "Remember it is my turn now to get it." I was so glad to see the eagerness in their eyes.

Once we got a hint that there would be a search of the camp. On such days the guards inspected every corner of the cells, including the ceiling and the floor boards, looking for knives, pencils, needles, notebooks, family photos and like articles that were strictly forbidden.

What should I do with my Bible? I wondered. At last I took it with me to the working place, hoping that we would have no personal inspection. I managed to get it safely there, and rolling it up I inserted it in one of the hollow bricks which were piled up.

"I shall take it out again tomorrow," I thought. However the next day the pile of bricks was not there any more. The night shift used them and so my "Bible" was somewhere in the wall of a newly built house and lost. I never had the opportunity of making another one, but the Lord's Word was kept hidden safely in my heart (Ps. 119:11).

Josef Korbel, *When the Gates Were Opened*

First Steps into Freedom

Deuteronomy 31:8

This was no dream. No, the beauty of this morning all around me was real, and the songs of birds and fragrance of flowers were real. How pleasant to be in this quiet and beautiful spot under the bushes where I spent my first night of freedom. How wonderful to know that I would never more be in a dark, narrow cell. No more starving, no more pain of separation from my beloved ones, no more heartbreaking loneliness.

I realized that it was time for me to get up, leave my hiding place and face my new life. I stood up straight, and took a deep breath of the fresh, fragrant air. My thoughts turned to my family. *"O Lord, soon, very soon I shall press them all to my heart, my beloved Erna and the children."*

For 10 long years like a robot I had been taught to obey without question the orders of my oppressors. I was afraid of people, of life and the future. But is it not 360 times written in the Word of God, "Fear not"? I would trust Him. My fear disappeared and in my heart rang the words:

> I will not care how dark the night,
> I will not care how wild the storm.
> Thy love will fill my heart with light,
> And shield me close and keep me warm.

With this determination I faced a new free life with a fervent prayer on my lips and in my heart to the Lord, that He would hold my hand and lead me as He did in the past. I felt the presence of the Savior gloriously, and overflowing joy came into my soul. Through fields and meadows I walked for many miles to the nearest railway station. From there I sent a telegram to my wife, asking her to meet me at the train, and with only our children. Now I wondered, how would they look, and how would they accept me? Ten years is a long time during which many things change, especially in the life of a child. It was hard for me to accept that the sweet years of their childhood were irrevocably lost for me.

"Prague!" The voice of the train conductor awoke me. I got up. My feet and legs were trembling. Pushing my way through the crowd I at last saw her—my beloved wife. In her simple dress she stood there quietly. She looked different from the flourishing young woman I was forced to leave ten years before. Her dark golden hair had turned grey. The fresh roses on her cheeks had been erased by pain and sorrow. Struggles and persecutions had left their mark on her sweet features. But in spite of all, out of her whole being another beauty radiated—the beauty of a soul purified by fire.

Josef Korbel, *When the Gates Were Opened*

The Power of Prayer

Ephesians 3:20

What a mystery prayer is! I wish I understood it better. But I do thank God that the power of it does not depend on being able to explain it, any more than the light in the office depends upon my knowing all about electricity.

Looking back on my own experience, I can see that my private prayer has come to be of two distinct kinds. The kind of praying I first learned was that definite closing out of all other doings and settling down to pray only. No one day can be complete without some such scheduled time.

The other grew out of the first. I mean that life of prayer which belongs to everything; that spontaneous lifting of the heart to God that becomes the habit of the soul. It would be difficult now to say which is the more precious, or which means the most to me. Both have to be cultivated.

In how many hearts has prayer been more a form than a life, more the performance of a duty than the expression of a desire, until the spirit of prayer was born in some dark night's struggle. Without doubt, in my own life the darkness of temptation and sorrow has taught me to pray—to wrestle before God until my soul found strength to go up to its Calvary.

Oh, never, never let the devil persuade you that your praying does not count! It does. And no heart need be without the proof of it, but it must be fervent, persistent, believing!

I am seldom helped by feelings in my own religious experience; but the times when I have been especially conscious of the presence and power of God have been chiefly during seasons of prayer for others. These seem to have brought me nearest to the heart of Jesus.

That other sort of praying is to my soul-life, more what breathing is to the body. The prayer that is breathed in a moment ensures the kind word, when, without it, the hasty one might so easily have been spoken; courage to act, when apart from it, an opportunity of witnessing or sowing might have been missed.

Yes, the silent prayer of an instant has preserved the integrity of the heart and saved the soul from the stain of sin again and again. And the strength of that continual communion with God, which becomes so natural that it is more like talking a matter over with one you love, has enabled so great a host of God's own children to be walking with Him in heavenly places, and has kept them in a heavenly spirit, when things round about were very earthly.

Catherine Bramwell-Booth, *Messages to the Messengers*

Does God Really Care?

1 Peter 5:7

⤳

Many questions well up from the heart of man, but none with greater urgency than: "Does God really care?" In our world, tragedy is written on the front page of every newspaper, etched in the faces of the people we meet, indelibly impressed upon our own memories because we too have known its terror and torment.

Does God look down with uncaring casualness upon man's calamities? Upon its answer depends not only our faith but our peace and even our sanity.

"Does God really care?" The fourth chapter of Mark's Gospel tells of an occasion when this question was asked of God Himself. The disciples of Jesus were crossing the Sea of Galilee in a little ship. A storm arose, and the water was whipped with such violence that the waves threatened to sink the vessel. Jesus was there but, exhausted by the day's ministry and teaching and healing, He had fallen asleep. The disciples awakened Jesus and, in voices that probably expressed irritation as well as fear, they asked, "Teacher, don't You care if we drown?" (Mark 4:38).

Storms are a natural occurrence on the sea. And just as surely, storms are natural to life and living. Disaster, misfortune, distress and violence are words which must be used to tell every day's story somewhere in our world. Life is a serious business.

Happily, the disciples found not only a reason for their question but also a response to it. The Bible goes on to say that Jesus arose, and rebuked the wind, and said unto the sea, "Quiet! be still!" (Mark 4:39). The wind ceased, and there was a great calm. Does God care? Without directly answering the question, Jesus responded in such a manner as to prove His concern for their safety and His sympathy with their fright.

Does God care? "Anyone who has seen Me," said Jesus, "has seen the Father" (John 14:9). And what witness to the deep concern of God would be complete without this sublime truth: "For God so loved the world, that He gave His one and only Son, that whoever believes in Him shall not perish, but have eternal life" (John 3:16).

The central truth of Christianity is that God cares. Because God loved, He gave His Son, who, in turn, gave Himself. Trust Him. Face life and all it brings with a positive faith in the reliability and compassion of God. Accept the Apostle Peter's invitation to "Cast all your anxiety on Him because He cares for you" (1 Pet. 5:7).

Bramwell Tripp, *To the Point*

God's Time

Ecclesiastes 3:1–8

Time flies, as the expression goes, and we're often left wondering where it all went. The clock ticks relentlessly on, defying our attempts to keep the pace. And if we get far enough behind schedule, time seems like some cruel, oppressive force keeping us in sheer frustration.

Do you spend time fighting the clock? Does it control your behavior patterns, set your limits, dictate your opportunities, keep you moving too quickly, rarely allowing you to stop, consider and perceive the deeper realities? Do you sometimes end the day feeling as if you have lost a race?

I've taken my fair dosage of the so-called Protestant Ethic in my time. I know what it means to be obsessed with the fear of wasting time.

The scientific western world has succeeded in quantifying time. It has been defined as a measurement: seconds, minutes, hours, days, months, years, decades, etc. Calibrated points on a continuum. The Bible has a much more interesting view. Since God transcends time, He doesn't need our means of time measurement to keep track. His time is different from ours. What is God's time like?

First, it is a gift. We don't have to "make time" in order to be good Christians. God the Creator is the only one who "makes time." He gives it to us as a gift. This means that we can relax from our obsessive-compulsive drive to fill up our time with scheduled activity. Instead, we can ask, "I wonder what opportunity God is giving in this moment, this day? How shall I respond to this gift?"

Second, God's time has content. In New Testament times the Greek language had two words for time. *Chronos* referred to measured time, the sequence of hours, days, years. *Kairos* implied much more: time with a distinct quality or purpose. It meant the right time for something to happen, the ripe time for events to come to fruition. God's time is *kairos*. Jesus began His public ministry with this the announcement: "The time (*kairos*) is fullfilled, and the kingdom of God is at hand" (Mark 1:15 KJV).

Third, God's time has purpose. It moves toward a goal. In the Bible, time progresses toward a definite goal set by God. The Book of Revelation describes this goal as "a new heaven and a new earth" (21:1). Today has meaning because it points toward tomorrow.

Let us then increasingly ask God rather than the clock or calendar what time it is, how God's tomorrow beckons our today. How's your timing?

Philip D. Needham, *The War Cry*

Christ of the Human Road

Luke 24:13–35

꩜

Following Christ's crucifixion, two crestfallen disciples were making their way down the dusty road to Emmaus, some seven miles from Calvary. Their sun had set at midday. Jesus had been impaled on a Roman cross and was now in a tomb. All their bright promise of tomorrow had been turned into the tragic frustration of yesterday. The word "finished" had suddenly been inserted by the hand of fate into the middle of what had promised to be the greatest story ever told.

There is a poignant and bewildering regret in their sorrowing words, "We had hoped that He was the one who was going to redeem Israel" (Luke 24:21). Their dream had been shattered and their bright hope had been nailed to an ignominious cross. They were mourning not only the loss of a cherished companion but the loss of hope itself.

The text has a special message for those for whom someone, or something, precious has been snatched away. When we walk the road of loss or sorrow, there is One who will come and walk beside us and bring hope.

"He opened the Scriptures to us" was the joyous exclamation of the two Emmaus travelers. What an exposition that must have been! The Light of the World illuminating the Word! He whose luster radiated from its pages, revealed its sacred mysteries. Under the illumination of the divine Expositor they now saw the cross in the light of ancient prophecy, and that inglorious tree gleamed with a glory of which they had never dreamed.

Christ wants to open the Scriptures to us. He wants us to see new things in the old Book. When we walk life's pathway with Christ the Bible becomes aglow with new meaning.

"Stay with us," they petitioned, "for it is nearly evening, the day is almost over" (Luke 24:29). If they had not offered that prayer, Jesus would not have lingered with them. Think of what they would have missed!

The stupendous truth of the resurrection was vouchsafed to these two ordinary, nondescript disciples—Cleopas and, what's his name, or her name? Jesus companioned with them until that seven miles of country road seemed as a golden path ending in a celestial city.

Still today, in our common ways of life, the Savior floods our prosaic paths with His peerless glory. The reality of the risen and reigning Lord on our road of life turns our Good Fridays into Easter Sundays!

Henry Gariepy, *The War Cry*

To Stand in the Gap

Ezekiel 22:30

W e read in the Bible that once God said, "I looked for a man" (Ezek. 22:30). Why was God looking? In this instance it was for the purpose of "building up the wall." The wall of Jerusalem had been a sacred monument of Israel's pride and glory. Within it the temple had proudly stood, the visible reminder of God's sovereignty and His election of a chosen people.

God's search for a man to be a builder was more than for a repair job with bricks and cement. He was looking for a man to be a leader for the rebuilding of the wall of faith and obedience in the hearts of His children. The invisible wall was the covenant of his promise and protection. Within it was the preservation of sound doctrine, the practice of pure worship, the execution of justice and the witness to God's goodness.

This man was not only to build the broken wall, he was also to "stand in the gap" (Ezek. 22:30). The gap in a city wall was vulnerable to the attacks of enemies. The gap in things of the spirit gives opportunity for the enemy of our soul.

God was, and still is, looking for a man or a woman to "stand in the gap," to help with the repair of those sacred things that have become broken, to be the watchman on the alert, to be the preserver of the faith.

During the June 4, 1989 massacre in Beijing, China, one lone man trying to make a point stood in front of an army of heavy tanks. His flesh and blood challenged the firing squad inside the metal monsters. He was indeed standing "in the gap" caused by an oppressive regime in his land. Few people in the world know his name, but his image has been etched deeply onto the hearts of millions. That man in China was a student. Behind him were tens of thousands of other students, all with the same goal, to bring freedom to China. I sensed the hopelessness on that day in front of the television set, watching the Chinese army open fire on the defenseless crowd. I never openly sobbed so much in my life.

What about the gaps in life all around us—in the lives of people, in our nation, in the world? Who will stand in these gaps for the Lord? Our Bible text reads: "I looked for a man among them who would build up the wall and stand before Me in the gap ... but I found none" (Ezek. 22:30). May we respond, "But Lord, there is someone! It's me. I am that man. I am that woman. I will stand in the gap for You and help rebuild the sacred things that are broken."

Check Yee, *The Salvationist Pulpit*

Jesus Is Lord

1 Corinthians 12:3

The New Testament word for "Lord"— *kurios*— is a word which carried deep significance. It is now almost commonplace to speak of the Lord Jesus Christ, but this title did not come to Jesus easily.

In Mark's Gospel, Jesus is referred to as Lord in the full theological sense on only two occasions. The same is true of Matthew's Gospel, while Luke utilizes the term some 17 times. It was, however, a favorite with Paul, who refers to Jesus as Lord 130 times in his epistles. It ultimately became the first Christian creed: "Jesus Is Lord."

Kurios was the word used to describe the Roman Emperor, who was considered supreme. The one demand the Romans made upon the people they conquered was that they must acknowledge Caesar as Lord—supreme or without rival. It was at this point the clash came between the Christians and the Romans, for the Christian would acknowledge no one but God as supreme.

Thus, to refer to Jesus as Lord means that He is without a rival. After hearing a minister preach on the coming again of our Lord, Queen Victoria said, "I wish He would come during my lifetime so that I could take my crown and lay it at His feet."

To acknowledge Jesus as Lord is a mark of the Spirit-filled life, "No one can say 'Jesus is Lord,' except by the Holy Spirit" (1 Cor. 12:3). We personalize this truth, when we exclaim with Thomas, "My Lord and my God" (John 20:28).

This submission will enable us to be effective witnesses in the field where God has called us to live and to work. We need to be reminded that the power of the Holy Spirit is not stored up in our little batteries; it flows in and through us as we maintain contact with God. We are transmitters of spiritual power, and need to be reminded of the truth declared by Edward Hale:

> I am only one,
> But still I am one.
> I cannot do everything,
> But still I can do something.
> And because I cannot do everything
> I will not refuse to do the something that I can.

Bramwell H. Tillsley, *Life in the Spirit*

The Psalmist's Soliloquy

Psalms 43:5

The Quakers have a phrase for something spiritually apt and timely. They say, "It speaks to my condition." Psalms 42 and 43 are like that; their message is relevant.

These Psalms present a man under pressure, airing his problems before God. The stress is situational. He can no longer attend the place of praise and prayer. Now, far from his homeland and the temple of the Lord, this exile feels the loss keenly. Perhaps for us, as with the Psalmist, something precious has gone out of our life and we must live on memories.

The stress is also relational. People taunt him (42:3,10); he goes about mourning (43:2). What hurts most is unrequited love. The child you've cared for turns from home and lives among the addicts whose lifestyle he adopts. The husband to whom you gave yourself proves unfaithful. Church leaders leave you disillusioned. A dear friend betrays you, an enemy speaks cutting words. A life partner dies, and the bereavement is grievous.

Added to all this for the Psalmist there is physical stress: "My bones suffer mortal agony" (42:10). Fear can debilitate even the most vigorous, anxiety can rob vitality, and discouragement can sap even the will to live.

What are the causes of stress in contemporary life? The list is long: unemployment, financial insecurity, an unpleasant work environment, feelings of isolation or inadequacy, an accident, loss of friends or loved ones and many more. Bereavements may follow one another until the earth seems a vast cemetery. One only has to hear the news to wonder why so many fellow humans are deprived of human rights, or why militarism and terrorism vie to make our world one madhouse.

These two Psalms speak to our human condition. But happily they do not stop with the problem, but move toward a solution. The power and beauty of this soliloquy is that the Psalmist exhorts his own soul: "Put your trust in God" (43:5). It is a powerful word to a generation that has learned to put its trust in man, to foolishly assert our autonomy. Look again at the Psalmist's affirmations: God is his rock (42:9), his stronghold (43:2), his joy and delight (43:4). God is our Savior (43:5). That makes all the difference.

Harry Read, *The Salvationist Pulpit*

God and Man

Psalm 8:4

Is there really a God out there? Is it reasonable to believe that, if He does exist, He could be interested in man—interested in a personal sense?

The great inventor Thomas Edison never thought of himself as a man of strong religious convictions, but he did believe in the existence of a Supreme Deity. Someone asked him, "Sir, do you believe in an intelligent creator, a personal God?" He answered, "I certainly do. If we but look at the natural laws of the universe, we would acknowledge the existence of the Great Engineer and His divine power."

The Psalmist cried out, "The heavens declare the glory of God; the skies proclaim the work of His hands" (Ps. 19:1). The mind of man can hardly comprehend the vastness and complexity of the cosmos, or the grandeur of the heavens. Scientists say that there are billions of stars in our galaxy. If that were not enough to stagger the imagination, the cosmologists say that there are billions of galaxies, and many have their own planetary systems! We, with the Psalmist, are compelled to exclaim, "What is man that You are mindful of him, the son of man that You care for him? (Ps. 8:4).

The more we learn about the enormous size of the universe, the less significant we view man to be. As our explorations enhance our comprehension of the measureless expanse and wonder of the heavens above us, we stand in awe of a God who is mindful of us.

The Creator, this governor of the universe, has clearly shown His love for His rebellious, erring, selfish creation, into which He breathed the essence of life. He cared enough to send His only Son to make possible man's salvation and his restoration. We have opportunity to respond to the love and beauty of the Creator. We may, if we choose, open our mind and heart to the living presence of the Spirit of God, as revealed by our Redeemer, the Lord Jesus Christ, God's resurrected Son.

Our God is the cosmic, creative Spirit who is ever at work throughout the vast universe and one whose presence can be experienced by faith. Repentance and faith in Christ as Savior and Lord can bring the God of outer space into the inner consciousness of the believer. The God of "out there" can truly become the God whose Spirit lives within us.

George Nelting, *The War Cry*

The Carpenter

Mark 6:3

⤳

The New Testament word for carpenter, *tekton*, denotes an artisan, a craftsman, one who is a builder.

The Scriptures reveal Christ as Carpenter of the universe: "Through Him all things were made" (John 1:3). The hands that held the hammer and worked the saw here on earth were hands that carpentered the fathomless galaxies and the infinite depths of creation. Those hands that shaved and smoothed the wood at the carpenter's bench in Nazareth also created the stars and the planets with their perfect design and precision.

The Cosmic Carpenter by the miracle of the Incarnation became the Carpenter of Nazareth. The question of our text asked by the disaffected Nazarenes is the only window in the Scriptures through which we may look on the years of His young manhood. These few words speak volumes to us about the silent years. This portrait of our Lord as a Carpenter suggests many things that would characterize His daily round of toil.

The absence of Joseph from the later gospel narratives suggest that the wise and humble father of that family had been laid to rest, and Jesus, as the elder brother, took over the support of the family by the trade He had mastered in His father's shop. Then finally, when the other brothers and sisters were old enough, He made His last yoke. After shaking the wood shavings from His tunic for the last time, He went out to build the eternal kingdom of God in the hearts of men.

This portrait of Christ as a Carpenter identifies Him with mankind. How reassuring it is to know that He who now holds a scepter in His hand once held a hammer and a saw. Often His hands were bruised and torn by the grain. As He worked day after day, making the wood obedient to His skill, His hands became as strong as a vise. They became roughened and calloused, the kind of hands strong fishermen would look at and know that they could follow Him with confidence. He knew the meaning of toil. He understands our burdens, our weariness, our tasks.

As the Carpenter, Christ forever sanctified human toil. Our tasks are given dignity by the One who worked amid the wood shavings at the carpenter's bench for the greater part of His life.

Today, the Carpenter of Nazareth who once smoothed yokes in His skillful hands, would take a life that is yielded to Him, smooth the coarseness of its grain, work out its flaws and imperfections, and fashion it into a beautiful and useful instrument of God's eternal kingdom.

Henry Gariepy, *Portraits of Christ*

To See the End

1 Peter 1:9

The world is always ready to sit at the deathbed of Christianity. From time to time it has confidently proclaimed the end of Christ and all for which He stands.

Sad, indeed, but far more sad when a disciple suffers a spiritual declension and sits down "to see the end" (Matt. 26:58). Not merely an eclipse, a temporary obliteration, but the dark, dismal and final end; the end of all the hopes that came suddenly to life on that bright morning when brother Andrew cried, "We have found Him!" (John 1:41). The end of the grand adventure, the miracles, the walking and talking, the confession at Caesarea Philippi, the holy transfiguration, the intimate supper, the tender prayer, "I have prayed for you" (Luke 22:32). The end! The collapse, the defeat, the final disillusionment.

The disciple becomes a spectator of the last act in the tragedy, before the curtain rings down upon unrelieved night. In and out of the entries and passages, along the narrow streets, the dejected and desperate Peter was drawn on. Fearing to advance, and unable to retreat, his fierce love and insatiable curiosity fighting against his failing faith, he went forward. The crisis held him, compelled him to go on and "see the end." Matthew 26 is a terrible chapter for Peter; from the 23rd verse on, he cannot get out of the story. There all his swift declensions and denials appear, until the terrible 75th verse, with its bitter tears.

First, he placed a distance between himself and his Lord. I find myself speculating about the measurement of those words, "afar off" (Matt. 26:58 KJV). How far? Then I remind myself that we do not measure spiritual distances in yards or miles, but in love and loyalties. How far is it from the embittered heart of a loveless husband to the empty heart of the disappointed wife?

Was it the second step in the disciple's collapse when he "went in" (Matt. 26:58 KJV) among the enemies of Jesus? Gripped in a dreadful reaction of despair, he went into dangerous company as he joined the coldly hostile crowd. Christians cannot be neutral. When we are told that he "sat down," we realize that his convictions are lost in the crowd.

It was nearly the end of Peter. The love of Christ saved this man—the love that knows no end. The love of Christ will save you and me. Indeed, I have no other hope, have you? The end? Not the end of Jesus, but the end of a chapter in a disciple's weakness, and the beginning of an experience which enables us to bow our heads for his apostolic blessing: "Receiving the end of your faith, even the salvation of your souls" (1 Peter 1:9 KJV).

Albert Orsborn, *The War Cry*

Engraved on His Hands

Isaiah 49:16

⌘

A Russian citizen imprisoned by the Nazis during the German occupation of World War II watched his young wife brutalized and killed after soldiers snatched her newborn child from her arms and gave it to a youthful officer whose wife was barren.

The prisoner gazed for the last time on the tiny lips and wide, bewildered eyes of his only child. Fearful of the days ahead and what cruelties might erode his fragile mental powers, the prisoner did a startling thing. With his knife he carved the name of the child on his right hand. Never would he allow himself to forget the object of his love.

"I will not forget you! See, I have engraved you on the palms of My hands" (Isa. 49:16). The stirring statement of Isaiah presents one of the most astonishing pictures in all the Bible of God's love for us. Those nail-scarred hands bear the marks of His caring, engraved with our names for time and eternity.

Such a bold cure was necessary for the deep wound mankind had sustained. The entrance of sin into the human heart had estranged us from our Creator, leaving us open for every sort of evil invention.

There may be times when the eventualities of life with their bitter qualities make us wonder if He has forgotten. The nation of Israel in Isaiah's day must have wondered if their God had turned His back on them. "But I will not forget you," God promised them and promises us.

Brigadier Josef Korbel was imprisoned by the despotic communist country of Czechoslovakia and subjected to unspeakable punishment. He tells of an occasion when he was tied to a barbed wire fence in the dead of winter and left for long hours because he dared to pass a bit of Scripture to a fellow inmate. In the moment of darkest despair, he testifies, he sensed a strange warmth. Looking up, "I saw a pair of beautiful hands covering my own—hands which bore unmistakably the marks of nail prints."

After the resurrection, Christ came suddenly into a room through no door at all—clad in His glorified body. But still He bore the nail prints in His hands. He will not forget us. Our names are engraved on His hands!

General Albert Orsborn penned the chorus as a memorial to this truth:

> He cannot forget me, Though trials beset me.
> Forever His promise shall stand.
> He cannot forget me, Though trials beset me.
> My name's on the palm of His hand.

Marlene Chase, *Pictures from the Word*

The Trinity for Us

Matthew 28:19

Trinity Sunday does not appear on our Salvation Army calendars, but that does not absolve us from the need to instruct our people in the meaning of our third Article of Faith. Our Handbook of Doctrine admits the difficulty of the task, saying that "It is impossible adequately to picture ... the complete truth concerning the mystery of the Godhead."

From the work of theologians, ancient and modern, guidelines can be singled out. Paul Tillich said that "Trinitarian monotheism is not a matter of the number three. It is a qualitative and not a quantitative characterization of God." That is to say, when we speak of the Father, the Son and the Holy Spirit, we are not making a mathematical statement. We are using the only language at our disposal to attempt to define what lies beyond definition, for in the Godhead there exists a richness of personality which is both beyond our conceiving and our describing. In the scriptural sense a mystery does not contradict reason though it may transcend it. No way can we describe infinity.

The doctrine of the trinity is more than a means of expressing what men have thought about God; it declares what God has revealed to men in history about His own nature.

In the fullness of time came the Incarnation, and in the life, death and rising again of Jesus the church of the New Testament saw God at work. Their experience of Jesus was nothing other than an experience of God. "The Word was made flesh and dwelt among us" (John 1:14 KJV).

More was to follow. Jesus told His immediate followers that it was expedient for them that He should go away, at which announcement sorrow filled their hearts. But their sorrow was turned into joy when the company of about 120 found themselves visited by the very Holy Spirit of God in their lives, both individually and corporately.

Yet the last truth must be that for all the unimaginable richness of His complex nature, God is one. The verb was, is and ever must remain, singular. The three persons share every act of thought, will and feeling.

How then does this affect my habit of prayer? Only to help me recognize that there is no activity on the part of the Father, the Son or the Holy Spirit that is not shared by the entire Godhead.

These revealed truths, even if apprehended only through a glass darkly in our personal experience, help us to appreciate the mystery and yet the reality of God as Father, Son and Holy Spirit.

Frederick Coutts, *In Good Company*

Valentine's Day

1 John 4:8–10

"Grandma, why do we give Valentines to each other?" The question sent me scurrying to find the answer. No use simply saying, "It is to show we love someone!" That would never satisfy the questing mind of this young lady!

We sat down on the rumpus room floor with books before us and began our search. We discovered, of course, that Valentine was a man and not a message of love. He was a young pagan priest in Rome during the reign of Claudius II. He hated the persecution the authorities had unleashed against the Christian community and he helped as many of these tortured people as he could, but he was found out and imprisoned.

During his imprisonment he was converted and became a Christian. He became a martyr, for he was clubbed to death on February 14, in the year 269 A.D. Actually, St. Valentine's day is consecrated to his memory.

While Valentine was in prison, he wanted most of all to tell his loved ones of his affection for them. Tradition has it that he could reach his arm through the prison bars and pick violets growing in the yard. He picked leaves and pierced a message on them, "Remember your Valentine" and sent them to his friends. The story says that eventually, he changed the wording simply to, "I love you."

The story of Valentine is but the faintest reflection of God's "Valentine" to us. God did not send a sentiment, He sent His Son.

"God is love. This is how God showed His love among us: He sent His one and only Son into the world that we might live through Him. This is love: not that we loved God, but that He loved us and sent His Son as an atoning sacrifice for our sins" (1 John 4:8–10).

Janet Wiseman, *Bridging the Year*

God's Valentine

John 3:16

꜊

The wedding of an older couple was the topic of a television soap opera conversation.

"I think it's wonderful," said Raquel.

"Wonderful?" asked Rita.

"Yeah. It's so romantic. Just think, at their age! There's hope for us all!"

Everyone loves a wedding, even if many of them do result in marriages that end in tears a few years later.

A wedding is always a time of hope. Never mind "for richer, for poorer, in sickness and in health." At a wedding everyone is optimistic. After all, the two participants are in love aren't they?

Love will certainly be on the agenda for a lot of people this Valentine's Day. Men and women around the world will be saying it with flowers, chocolates, cards, and helium-filled balloons, and personal classified ads in the newspapers. "I love you," they will declare.

And for a great many of them it will be a case of "at their age, too!"

Raquel is right. It is romantic. And there is hope for us all.

The world needs more love—love between individuals that will spill over into love for others, love even for the unlovely and the unloved, love such as that demonstrated in the life and teaching of Jesus.

Jesus was taken in by no one. He knew people's faults, but He also saw the good in them. And He loved them for it. And, as the New Testament records, time and again people responded to His love. They wanted to be what He showed them they were capable of becoming.

Valentine's Day is a good day to start following Jesus' example. As the song says, "You're nobody until somebody loves you." John 3:16 reminds us that God loves the world, each one of us: "For God so loved the world that He gave His one and only Son, that whoever believes in Him shall not perish but have eternal life." And that makes everybody a "somebody!"

On this Valentine's Day, when love for others is expressed, let us respond more than ever to that greatest love of all, the marvelous love of God for us, by committing more of our life to Christ. It's a gift that promises eternal and matchless returns.

That's why, as Raquel said, there's hope for us all!

Charles King, *The War Cry, U.K.*

Holiness to the Lord

Exodus 28:36

On January 9, 1885, at about nine o'clock in the morning, God sanctified my soul. I was in my own room at the time, but in a few minutes I went out and met a man and told him what God had done for me. The next morning, I met another friend on the street and told him the blessed story. God used him to encourage and help me.

That confession put me on record. It cut the bridges behind me. I could not go back now. I had to go forward. God saw that I meant to be true till death.

So two mornings after that, just as I got out of bed and was reading some of the words of Jesus, He gave me such a blessing as I never had dreamed a man could have this side of heaven. I walked out over Boston Common before breakfast weeping for joy and praising God.

Oh, how I had longed to be pure! Oh, how I had hungered and thirsted for God! He gave me the desire of my heart. He satisfied me. God has become my Teacher, my Guide, my Counselor, my All and All.

He has helped me to speak of Jesus and His great salvation in a way to instruct, comfort and save other souls. He has been light to my darkness, strength to my weakness, wisdom in my foolishness, knowledge in my ignorance.

When my way has been hedged up and it seemed that no way could be found out of my temptations and difficulties, He has cut a way through for me.

When my heart has ached, He has comforted me. When my feet have well-nigh slipped, He has held me up. When my faith has trembled, He has encouraged me. When I have been in sore need, He has supplied all my need. When I have been hungry, He has fed me. When I have thirsted, He has given me living water.

He has taught me that sin is the only thing that can harm me. He has taught me to hang upon Jesus by faith for my salvation from all sin, and to show my love by obeying Him in all things and by seeking in all ways to lead others to obey Him.

My whole being is His for time and eternity. I am not my own. He can do with me as He pleases for I am His.

"Holiness to the Lord" (Exod. 28:36 KJV) has been my motto. It has been the only motto that could express the deep desire and aspiration of my soul.

Samuel Logan Brengle, *Helps To Holiness*

A Glad Spendthrift

Luke 6:38

I want to be a spendthrift, Lord,
    a spendthrift of my time and strength,
    giving instead of withholding,
    sowing instead of wanting to reap.

Don't let me be a miser, Master,
    cuddling myself to myself,
    careful of every effort,
    counting each step,
    hoarding my physical resources
For the demands of a tomorrow that might never come.

Make me a glad spendthrift, Lord:
    joyously giving my love and care,
    opening the sluice-gates of my small reserves,
    pouring out what little I have to give
    without measure or stint,
    without anxious debate,
    and trust You for tomorrow.

Don't let me shelter myself in a glass case,
    fearful lest the light of day should fade me,
    dreading that the hand of time should touch me,
    shrinking from effort that might drain me,
    saving myself up ... for what?
    To look nice in my coffin?

Let me give what I have to give with open hands,
    offering myself to You each day for service,
    happy to be used as long as life shall last,
    living for You as a glad spendthrift.
    For at the end, Lord,
    You will not ask me what I have saved,
    but what I have given.

Flora Larsson, *Just a Moment, Lord*

Purity of Heart

Matthew 5:8

We all know what is meant by being pure. When we talk about the purity of things around us, we mean that they are clean and unadulterated. That is, that they are not only without dirt or filthiness, but have no inferior substance mixed with them.

Sin is spoken of in the Bible as filthiness or defilement of the body, mind or spirit. Purity in religion must mean, therefore, the absence of such things. In short, to be pure in soul signifies deliverance from everything which the Lord shows you to be opposed to His holy will.

We all like material purity. I am sure that everyone reading this letter prefers to have a clean body. You like clean clothes and clean linen, do you not? You like a clean home. See how the housewife scrubs and washes and brushes and dusts to keep the floor and windows and furniture clean.

You like a clean city. What a laborious and costly sweeping of the streets, carrying away of rubbish, and money spent on keeping our towns sweet and pure.

We like this sort of purity because it is pleasant to the eye and good for health. But all right-minded beings admire the purity of the soul far more than they do the purity of the body, or the clothes, the home or anything else; and that, because it is so much more important.

God loves soul purity. It is His nature to do so. I have no doubt, like us He prefers to see His children also outwardly clean. His dwelling place is pure. Its inhabitants are pure.

As the heart in your body is the great driving force of the natural man, so the heart we are talking about is the great driving force of the spiritual man. In this sense it is your heart that feels joy or sorrow. It is the heart that chooses between right and wrong. It is the heart that molds the character, guides the choice and masters all the course and conduct of a man's life. The heart is the captain of the ship. How important it is to each one of us that we should have a good—a right—a pure heart.

But what is a pure heart? A pure heart is a heart that has been cleansed by the Holy Spirit from all sin, and enabled to please God in all it does: to love Him with all its powers, and its neighbor as itself.

To those who know that they do not possess a pure heart, God is waiting to cleanse you. Now is the accepted time.

William Booth, *Purity of Heart*

The Salt of the Earth

Matthew 5:13

The follower of Jesus is "the salt of the earth" (Matt. 5:13). The metaphor used would have occurred to Him while watching the fishermen using salt to preserve their fish.

Salt is essential to life. The action of salt seems obscure, but it saves from putrefaction. It has the silent gentleness of divine strength. The morals of a Christian keep alive a sense of duty and a consciousness of right.

Salt preserves, keeps fresh and saves from corruption. It has sanitary powers. Christians are the antiseptics of society. Salt counteracts the moral pollution of the world and gives health to the soul amid the foulness of the sin around.

In ancient times salt was associated with offerings. Covenants were made over a sacrificial meal and salt was a necessary element; hence the expression, "a covenant of salt" (Num. 18:19).

Salt was also a sacrament of friendship, a symbol of an enduring compact, the seal of the obligation to fidelity. In Leonardo da Vinci's great painting of the Last Supper, Judas is picked out from all the others by having overturned the salt-cellar. The salt-cellar was a pledge of good faith. Overturned, it was an omen of coming treachery.

Our Lord used His picture of salt in relation to the Christian life. Nothing was more valuable than salt, but nothing more worthless if it had lost its flavor. It was fit only to be trampled down into the street. When once the Christian life has become tasteless, empty and futile, there is no way of making life worth living.

The new kingdom Christ inaugurated was to be radical and penetrating like "the salt of the earth." The members of the kingdom are covenanted not only to arrest the decay of morals in the world, but to preserve the high standards of Christian living, to flavor life with radiant happiness and buoyant good taste.

Christian character works secretly, penetrating a man's thought, influencing the atmosphere of life. Unseen and unapplauded, salt cleanses the elements around it. So the action of the follower of Christ is to disinfect the world, to bring those Christian antiseptics outlined in the Beatitudes to bear upon all around.

The Christian brings health to the life made foul by sin. We are "covenanted" to this sacrificial task. It is a "covenant of salt."

George B. Smith, *Meditations for the Ordinary Man*

To One Sorrowing

2 Corinthians 1:3–4

By the time this is in your hands, the first days of stunning grief will have passed. You will take up the threads of each day's duty, while you face afresh every morning, and take home to your heart every evening, that sense of emptiness which seems almost to swallow up the things that remain.

You must face life—life with that sense of emptiness in it—life with that other life gone out of it. But, my dear child, if God is to be glorified, you must face it in such a way that the shadow lies behind, and not ahead. Your spirit must not dwell in the darkness of the grave, but in the light of heaven. You must not walk through life holding death's icy hand, but holding to a living faith that, in the very presence of death, warms your heart with a hope that has its kindlings in the everlasting love of the unchanging Father.

Sorrows must come; we know that. We are reconciled even to the thought that to follow Jesus means a multiplying rather than a lessening of our griefs. How could it be otherwise when He was "a Man of Sorrows, and acquainted with grief" (Isa. 53:3 KJV)?

It seems to me that grief is like a furnace—it either refines or destroys; like a mighty wind, it either tears up by the roots the faith of years, or, sweeping over it, leaves it strengthened and established. You must decide which it shall be. The attitude of your soul, not the storm of sorrow that sweeps over it, will determine whether you remain rooted and grounded; the spirit in your heart, not the furnace of affliction through which it passes, will determine whether you come forth as gold.

If now you turn your eyes on yourself, on your loss, on your own broken hopes, you will walk in the shadow. But if you turn your eyes away from yourself to God, you will walk in the light, leaving the shadow behind.

I cannot explain why weeping with another dries my own tears, but it does; nor why sharing another's load should make me less conscious of my own, but it does; nor how putting out my hand to save someone else from stumbling in their sorrow keeps my foot from slipping, but it does.

Faith is the only soil in which a sorrow planted with bleeding hands and watered by bitter tears could ever spring up to blossom with new hope and joy for you, and to bring forth good fruit abundantly.

Catherine Bramwell–Booth, *Messages to the Messengers*

Can Anybody Live a Holy Life?

1 Peter 1:15–16

Nearly everybody means to get to heaven, and all who know what Christ teaches, as to the way there, believe that there is no admission for any who are not holy. And yet for anyone to profess to have attained holiness here and now is simply outrageous! Why?

Chiefly on account of that view of holiness almost universally prevalent, which confuses holiness with the perfection attained only by saints in their glorified state. God's people are required to be holy, and yet they are told that "If any man think himself to be anything ... he is nothing" (Gal. 6:3). How can these things be?

Children of God, shall we do less in these days of shame, than live a holy life? But what does holiness imply?

We all admit the reasonableness of presenting to God ourselves and all we have; but we generally fail to realize that a sacrifice must pass out of the possession of him who offers it.

One Being in the world's history is "the Holy One." This is the One who was always entirely God's from His mother's womb.

From all I conclude, to be holy is simply to be given up to God, and a man cannot become holy in any other way than by giving himself up, and not only wishing to become, but becoming wholly the Lord's.

Believer in Jesus, what does this blood that has washed away your guilt say as it streams from His side for you? Does it not cry, with the voice of God, "You are not your own ... you are bought with a price" (1 Cor. 6:19–20). You can be nothing higher, better than God's—dare you be anything less?

To be holy: that is how to glorify God. How glorious the life, the character, the destiny, the work, of every branch that abides in Jesus! Holy living is divine living, that is all.

Nobody can lead a holy life of himself, but Christ can live a holy life in anybody. Shall He live such a life in us?

George Scott Railton, *The Christian Mission Magazine*

Lent is for Now

Romans 12:2

H as Lent gone the way of rotary telephones and black–and–white television? Is it among the relics of a bygone era? If so, the Church will have lost part of her soul to the intrusion of secular values.

Early Lenten preaching taught mutual forgiveness and forbearance among church members. It encouraged prayer, biblical instruction in giving and strict abstention from food. Lenten disciplines reminded both the careless Christian and the devout: "Do not conform any longer to the pattern of this world but be transformed by the renewing of your mind" (Rom. 12:2).

Foregoing some pleasure as a voluntary act of self–denial symbolic of repentance was a standard expectation. "What are you giving up for Lent?" became a common conversation starter. It was the same spirit of sacrifice as a spiritual discipline that led the Salvation Army's Founder William Booth in 1886 to announce his plan to give what he would have spent on plum pudding toward the Army's mission around the world. Older Salvationists still refer to the now year–round world services effort to raise funds for world missions as "self–denial."

Is it too late to urge a renewed emphasis upon the spiritual disciplines of Lent? For the Roman Catholic, the ashes on the forehead, like the sackcloth and ashes of old, symbolize sorrow. Sorrow for sin characterizes the penitential nature of Lent. The 40–day period of reflection and repentance recalls the fasts of Moses, Elijah and Jesus. Lent calls us to reflect upon our guilt for which Christ's sacrifice atoned. The name "Lent," an Anglo–Saxon word for spring, reminds us of the regenerative nature of the spiritual disciplines encouraged during this season even as spring on the annual calendar is a season of rebirth and fresh growth.

If Christians are to be the light of the world and the salt of the earth, we must declare the significance of humility, penitence, sacrifice, devotion, righteousness, confession, prayer, reflection, piety, forgiveness and discipline in the face of winds that blow the other way.

More than words alone, that declaration must be a lifestyle of Christlikeness not limited to 40 days every spring. But we should be able to carve out a mere five–and–a–half weeks each year to give special emphasis to these disciplines through which God's grace flows to conform us to His likeness.

Donald Hostetler, *The War Cry*

The Call to Holiness

Ephesians 5:25–27

In the upper room our Lord prayed that His disciples should be sanctified. The next day He went to Calvary and died that it should be so. "Christ loved the Church and gave Himself up for her to make her holy, cleansing her by the washing with water through the word, and to present her to Himself as a radiant Church, without stain or wrinkle or any other blemish, but holy and blameless" (Eph. 5:25–27).

We cannot enter heaven with any sin in our hearts, for "Without holiness no one will see the Lord" (Heb. 12:14). Somewhere, and some time, our sinful nature must be completely destroyed. This may take place on our deathbed, or at the coming of our Lord, but God is able and willing to sanctify us now.

"But if anybody does sin, we have one who speaks to the Father in our defense—Jesus Christ, the Righteous One" (1 John 2:1). We dare not preach sinless perfection, for it is not taught in the Word of God. We can have an experience where it is possible not to sin, but we shall not, in this life, reach a state where it is not possible to sin.

To the sanctified man defeat will not be the rule, but the exception. He will show his holiness by humbly admitting his fault, and by putting things right with God at once, and if need be, with man also. We do not lose the blessing of sanctification by one act of sin or disobedience, provided we confess it at once and seek God's forgiveness.

A sanctified believer is always learning new lessons, growing in grace, and bringing forth more and better fruit. Perfection will be progressive. Thus a perfect bud may become a perfect flower, and then a perfect fruit. Even when the fruit is fully grown it will need to become perfectly ripe and sweet. Sanctified Christians too should become riper and sweeter as the years go by.

A cup of water can be perfectly filled, but it will not hold as much as a jug. A sanctified Christian should be always filled with the Spirit, but his capacity should increase, as it were, from that of a cup to that of a jug, then to that of a bucket, a tank, a reservoir. There is always more to follow.

We must ever be climbing higher up the mount of holiness, though we cannot reach the summit in this life.

Allister Smith, *Made Whole*

A Golden Daybreak

1 Thessalonians 4:16–18

No matter what our condition, the Bible speaks to it. For the distressed or depressed, God has a message of hope. Wrote James Stewart, "God does not mock His children with a night that has no ending; and to every man who stands resolute while the darkness lasts, there comes at length the vindication of faith and the breaking of the day."

The last chapter of the Old Testament, with its promise of the rising of the Sun of Righteousness, and the last chapter of the New Testament, with its announcement of the Bright and Morning Star, gives us God's Word about the breaking of the day. In that hope, we lift up our hearts.

The focus of our hope is the Lord Jesus, and the fulfillment of it was not completed during His first visit to earth. He will come again, and the hope of His return shines most brightly in times of darkness. In the gloom of this present era, let us keep our eyes on the eastern horizon, to watch for the dawn.

Jesus came to a world shrouded in darkness. Our world is still wracked by the anguish of its self–inflicted disease of sin. The Bible declares that the human race is fallen, corporately sinful and all alike condemned. Ours is a sad solidarity of weakness and wickedness, with separation from God as the consequence of our folly.

During World War II seven Jewish refugees were sheltered beneath the Cologne Cathedral in Germany at the invitation of the archbishop there. They hid for some time in that basement before they could flee. After they had left, it was found that during those grim days they had written messages on the walls of their shelter. Among the graffiti were these words: "I believe in the dawn, even though it be dark; I believe in God, even though He is silent."

I too believe in the dawn. I am confident of the eventual breaking of God's new day, the fulfillment of His program for the world. Today, men love darkness rather than light, and in the darkness we are beset by terrorism and war and violence. But when Christ comes again, he will bring light and peace.

Let us look beyond the darkness, and look with hope for the golden daybreak when Jesus will come in triumph and glory.

Edward Read, *I Believe in the Dawn*

When You Have to Say Goodbye

1 John 3:14

During my life I have been faced with many serious problems, but the most difficult thing I have ever faced was when I had to take my wife to a nursing home, and my daughter and I said goodbye to mother and wife. As we closed the glass doors behind us, she pulled on them, trying to open them and we heard her calling, "Open the door, I want to go with you!" But there was no handle on the inside.

My daughter and I tried to comfort each other. It couldn't have gone on any longer. We could still see her coming home that time in the police car. Somewhere along the way she had gotten lost and couldn't make herself understood to the people around.

The most difficult period was in the beginning. At first you don't realize what is happening; you are surprised by changes in behavior. Then you are amazed by attitudes and reactions which until then you had never seen. In the course of the illness we had tried everything. We tried to bring help in, but she wouldn't accept it. Sometimes she became aggressive, and then of course, no one would come back. Wietske was no longer Wietske; she had become another person.

When my daughter and I arrived back home we both sat and cried. We agreed that our loved one did not deserve such a goodbye. And we remembered the many times goodbyes were said in a dignified and warm manner. But at this goodbye there were no speeches, no flowers, no encouraging words. Was this how a faithful career as an officer in The Salvation Army was to end?

Of course I missed her. I visited her often. So many things were fading away. Sometimes we would sing the songs of years gone by. There was only one song she still remembered. It was our favorite song, and we sang it two or three times. The Dutch song seemed to be engraved on her heart. "Lord I Am Thankful That By Your Grace I Am Your Child." It broke our hearts to hear her trying to sing it, and yet, somehow, it comforted and encouraged us.

After all, one of the most essential truths of Christianity is that it is our faith that keeps us going. For a Christian doesn't live to die, but dies to live. Life with a capital L—a life in which there will be no more goodbyes.

Reinder Schurink, *The War Cry*

Hot Saints

Revelation 3:15–16

Hot saints have such a halo round about them that they reveal—make manifest sins in others. They do this by contrast. "What fellowship can light have with darkness?" (2 Cor. 6: 14). The light of God flashed from a hot saint onto the dark consciences of sinners makes them feel their sin.

A dark soul cannot dwell in the presence of a soul full of light without either repenting or opposing; if it does not submit, it will rebel. It was under the hot blaze of this light that the Jews round about Stephen "were cut to the heart, and gnashed upon him with their teeth" (Acts 7:54 KVJ). When intense spiritual light and darkness are brought in contact, their innate antipathy makes them reveal each other.

Heat cleanses, purges away dross. The burning fire of the Holy Spirit purifies the soul which is filled, permeated with it, hence, hot saints are pure. They purify themselves, as He is pure. They keep themselves "unspotted from the world" (James 1:27 KJV). They improve the moral atmosphere wherever they go.

Heat burns. Hot saints set on fire the hearts of other saints. They singe the consciences of sinners, melt the hearts of backsliders and warm up those who have left their first love.

Hot saints are mighty. The fishermen of Galilee produced more impression on the world in a few years than all the learning of the Jews had done in centuries, because they were hot in the love and service of God.

Hot people are not only able to work, but to suffer. They can endure hardness, suffer reproach, contend with principalities and powers, fight with wild beasts and hail persecution and death!

To be hot ensures opposition, first from the Pharisees. A formal, ceremonious, respectable religion they do not object to; but a living, burning, enthusiastic Christianity is still Beelzebub to them. To be hot ensures opposition from the world. The world hates hot saints, because they look with contempt on its pleasures, set at naught its maxims, trample on its ambition, ignore its rewards, and live altogether above its level. To be hot also ensures opposition from the devil.

Let me remind you, in conclusion, that to be hot ensures God's special favor, protection and fellowship, and final victory. "Be faithful unto death, and I will give you a crown of life" (Rev. 2:10 KJV).

Catherine Booth, *Practical Religion*

What Are We Worth?

Matthew 10:28–31

Sadly, life is cheap in America these days. The preservation of human life is no longer a primary value in contemporary culture, in spite of our Judeo–Christian heritage, which teaches us to value human life. What of the ongoing slaughter of unborn, innocent babies for reasons of uninhibited pleasure and personal and family convenience? No wonder Pope John Paul II in his encyclical proclaiming a gospel of life is constrained to describe modern culture as a "culture of death."

Jesus said that when a sparrow falls to the ground, God notes it. The birds of the air are incredibly precious to God. He made them. And ours would be a visually tedious and eerily silent world without them. The created universe and this beautiful planet of ours are of inestimable worth to God and therefore should be treasured.

Having said that, let us be clear: Precious as all created life is to God—and the environments and ecosystems in which it thrives—human persons are worth a great deal more to God. "You are worth more than many sparrows," (Matt. 10:31) says Jesus.

If we could focus as much compassion and creative energy on kids in our inner cities–blowing each other away with automatic weapons and self–destructing on crack cocaine–as we give to saving whales and the nesting sites of tufted titmice, we might accomplish a great deal for the peace and prosperity of our cities, not to mention the salvation of these kids! Perhaps we can, and should, do both! Look at the mass graves in Rwanda and read the painful reflection of horror in the eyes of the children there and you need not be persuaded that there is much to fear in our world.

Recognizing the value Jesus places on human life makes His words even more poignant and powerful: "Do not be afraid of those that kill the body, but cannot kill the soul" (Matt. 10:28). Many a martyr to totalitarianism within the past 50 years has sealed their testimony to that truth with their blood. There is something beyond human life, valuable as it is, that is of infinitely greater consequence. It is the soul.

It is the simple but liberating truth that God values us all as human persons. It is that love of God for us, not based upon our merit, but upon His grace toward us, that makes us infinitely worthy. This is such a crucial issue that God invested in it the life of His own Son. We can know ourselves loved, unconditionally. And we can respond to that love.

Paul A. Rader, *The War Cry*

Love and Hate

Romans 3:23

⤜

Stephen spoke. The council swore. Stephen preached. The council plotted. Stephen seized the opportunity. The council seized Stephen.

The high priest begins the interrogation saying, "Are these charges true?" (Acts 7:1). Instead of pleading the fifth amendment, Stephen takes the next 50 verses to remind them from whence they came. He preaches expositorily from their scriptures to set the record straight. Without mincing words, he methodically addresses the sins of "our fathers."

How did the Council react to these honest accusations? How would you react? Be honest. With rage? Fury? Hate?

And Stephen, being full of the Holy Spirit, surprised them again by gazing heavenward and saying, "Look! I see the heavens opened and the Son of Man standing at the right hand of God!" (Acts 7:56).

That was the proverbial straw that broke the camel's back, salt rubbed into an open wound, a modern day "in your face." With one accord, they cried out and cast him outside where they began to stone him.

Then Stephen did something amazing. The one who had "told it like it is" surprised them again by crying out with a loud voice, saying, "Lord, do not charge them with this sin" (Acts 7:60).

He had learned his lesson well. He was imitating the Master. This was the consummate example of love in action. Jesus taught him to hate the sin and love the sinner. Hating the sin is a sign of strength. Loving the sinner is an act of gentleness and greatness.

How does one distinguish between the sin and the sinner? Sometimes, as parents, we face the same dilemma. As parents of two active boys, my wife and I were often guilty of not being able to separate the soot from the son. Now you're supposed to hate the soot and love your son. You're supposed to separate your feelings toward the soot from your feelings toward your son.

It's a very thin and delicate line that separates the soot from the son. It is that same line that separates the alcoholic from the burned-out businessman, the sin from the sinner, you from yourself.

All of us have been guilty of "falling short" and missing the line. It is humanly impossible to separate the sin from the sinner, but it is heavenly possible to hate the sin and love the sinner. Christ recognized the difference when He spoke to the thief on the cross. Stephen understood it when he prayed within earshot of a young man named Saul. And with a little help from the Spirit, you too can keep on keeping on!

Joe Noland, *A Little Greatness*

Unfinished Business

Psalm 8:3–4

How many worlds
Did You make, Lord?
Not finished yet,
You say!
Still strewing stars
Like confetti
Out in Your
Milky Way?

Marvellous, Your creation.
Millions of stars I see;
Satellites of Your glory,
Studding eternity!

Standing in awe and wonder,
Answer me if You can:
With all the worlds to think of,
Why do You think of man?

Tell me, O Lord Creator,
(Promise You will not smile!)
Why in Your whole creation
Only mankind is vile?

I thought I heard You laughing?
How could I be so dim?
Where there's a man who'll let You,
You're still at work
On him!

John Gowans, *O Lord Not More Verse!*

Go and Do Something!

Matthew 25:35

One picture among the many that I cherish of my father explains a certain development in the history of the Army, and gives a glimpse of the deep fires that burned in the personality of William Booth. One morning, away back in the eighties, I was an early caller at his house. Here I found him in his dressing room. No "good morning how do you do" here!

"Bramwell," he cried, when he caught sight of me, "did you know that men slept out all night on the bridges?"

He had arrived in London very late the night before and had to cross the city to reach his home. What he had seen on that midnight return accounted for this morning tornado. Did I know that men slept out all night on the bridges?

"Well, yes," I replied, "a lot of poor fellows, I suppose, do that."

"Then you ought to be ashamed of yourself to have known it and to have done nothing for them," he went on, vehemently.

I began to speak of the difficulties, burdened as we were already, of taking up all sort of work, and so forth. My father stopped me with a peremptory wave.

"Go and do something!" he said. "We must do something."

"What can we do?"

"Get them a shelter!"

"That will cost money."

"Well, that is your affair! Something must be done. Get hold of a warehouse and warm it, and find something to cover them."

That was the beginning of The Salvation Army shelters, the earliest and most typical institutions connected with our now worldwide social work. But it also throws a ray of light on the characteristic benevolence of the Army's Founder. The governing influence of his life was goodwill to his fellows. His heart was a bottomless well of compassion, and it was for this reason principally that, although perhaps more widely and persistently abused than any other figure of his time, he was even more widely and tenaciously loved.

"For I was hungry and you gave Me something to eat, I was thirsty and you gave Me something to drink, I was a stranger and you invited Me in" (Matt. 25:35).

Bramwell Booth, *Echoes and Memories*

Our Human Weakness

2 Corinthians 4:7

The quest for the best is admirable in many ways, but it is not without its perils. Perfectionists are notably hard to live with because, in their passion for the highest, they may fall victim to the temptation of fussiness, become impatient with people less intense than they and arrogantly critical of others.

Perfectionists are often too critical of themselves as well. The noted translator, J.B. Phillips, confesses to this, "The tyrannical super-me condemns and has no mercy on myself." Seekers after holiness, conscientious as they invariably are, may blame themselves for feelings, weakness or shortcomings about which they have no choice and over which they have no control.

One of Satan's favorite devices with holiness seekers is to set standards so high that no one could attain them, and then to condemn the conscientious struggler for failing. Allister Smith counsels, "We must be careful not to excuse our sins by calling them faults, nor must we make the opposite mistake of regarding faults in ourselves or in others as sin." That requires that we make a distinction between iniquity and infirmity, without being either too easy or too hard on ourselves.

Come back to the simplicities. You did not save yourself, and you cannot sanctify yourself. Look to Christ who "is able to save completely those who come to God through Him" (Heb. 7:25).

Dr. Daniel Steele (one of Commissioner Brengle's early tutors) pointed out that infirmities are always involuntary, while sins are always voluntary. Paul makes the same point, writing, "But we have this treasure in jars of clay to show that this all-surpassing power is from God and not from us" (2 Cor. 4:7).

That the Spirit-filled man still has his weaknesses the Bible simply takes for granted. "The Spirit helps us in our weakness" (Rom. 8:26).

To be quite honest, we believers must admit to rebel emotions and unresolved conflicts. Given a complete dedication to Christ, the therapy and grace will begin quietly to work, and healing will proceed until it results in a beautiful wholeness. "He who began a good work in you will carry it on to completion until the day of Christ Jesus" (Phil. 1:6).

Edward Read, *Studies in Sanctification*

Temptation

James 1:12

We live in a world of temptation. Turn which way we will, we shall find something or someone ready and waiting to pounce down upon us with some kind of effort ingeniously calculated to lead us astray.

There is the world with its charms. The hermits of olden times fled into the desert to escape its attractions, but it followed them to their hidden caves and comfortless cells.

There is the devil with his heartless devices. We shall have little chance of getting very far away from him until we cross the Jordan.

But even if we could hide ourselves from the world and get out of the reach of Satan, we should still have our own selves to fight, and self is the worst enemy of the three.

Temptation is the common lot. Untried grace is said to be no grace at all. We have all to go through the furnace. No man has ever ascended the golden ladder and entered the pearly gates who has not passed through the ordeal of temptation, our blessed Lord being no exception, for we read that He was tempted in all points as we poor mortals are, although He was without sin.

Temptation is not sin. If a man offers you a bribe to tell a lie, that is a temptation. But if you refuse compliance, you have not sinned. Before temptation becomes sin the soul must consent to it. That consent refused, the temptation vanishes, leaving the soul as pure as though it had not been tested.

We must resist temptation with all our might. We cannot prevent the devil knocking at the door or looking in at the window, but we need not invite him to enter, offer him a chair, or engage him in friendly conversation! We should inform him plainly that he has got to the wrong house and bid him depart without delay.

If you will resist the devil and all his allurements boldly and perseveringly, victory is certain. Christ has purchased it with His blood. If you only fight on and keep believing, it is bound to be yours.

"Blessed is the man who endures temptation; for when he has been proved, he will receive the crown of life which the Lord has promised to those who love Him" (James 1:12 NKJV).

William Booth, *The Warrior's Daily Portion*

The Secret Place

Psalm 91:1

A secret is not common property. The best kept secret is the one that is kept only to oneself. "He who dwells in the secret place of the Most High shall abide under the shadow of the Almighty" (Ps. 91:1 NKJV). This secret place is different. Only you and God know of its whereabouts. It cannot be localized by time or space. It is a state of being. And only he who dwells in the secret place can invade it. It is peculiarly and privately his alone.

While this place is private, there is no dearth of such places. God deigns and desires to provide this secret place to every individual who would aspire to such lofty living.

The secret place was an Oriental phrase for the interior room or rooms of the house or tent, reserved for the master or chief whose abode was in the center of the camp. This was a place of honor and greatest safety. This then is a place where none but God can find him, where the enemy cannot reach him. It is a place not seen or known but by the eye of faith. In the words of a simple, uneducated saint, "It's better felt than telt."

Being in the secret place is no guarantee against trouble. Rather, we are likely to experience the onslaught of Satan there. But the Psalmist affirms, "Surely He shall deliver you" (Ps. 91:3 NKJV).

Paul epitomizes this lofty life in the words, "Your life is now hidden away with Christ in God" (Col. 3:3). This is not to be confused with some type of a monastic retreat, but more likely is most evident in the lives of those encompassed in a maelstrom of activity. The exercise of prayer is the heart and soul of the secret place, which has been described as, "quietly opening a door and slipping into the very presence of God, there in the stillness to listen to His voice."

McAfee captures the tenor of this mystical experience in the words:

> There is a place of quiet rest,
> Near to the heart of God,
> A place where sin cannot molest,
> Near to the heart of God.

Edward Deratany, *Refuge in the Secret Place*

The Rightful King

Luke 19:37–44

On what proved to be the first day of Passion week, Jesus entered His capital city. The road to Jerusalem would be crowded with thronging pilgrims on their way to the Passover feast, which commemorated the most important event in their national history, the exodus from Egypt.

Jesus chose to approach and enter the city riding on a donkey. The humble pilgrims acclaimed Him, shouting "Hosanna," but Jesus wept. Luke leaves us in no doubt as to the reason for those tears. He was foreseeing the dreadful consequences of the nation's rejection of Himself, knowing that their choice of revolutionary action would lead to disastrous overthrow, as indeed it did.

Jesus entered Jerusalem in such a way as to make an open and unmistakable claim to Messiahship. The time for reserve was over. He was throwing down the gauntlet. It was as though our Lord deemed it necessary to give the nation a final chance to accept its King, and made His entry in this way to remind the people of the prophecy in Zechariah: "Rejoice greatly, O daughter of Zion! Shout, O Daughter of Jerusalem! See, your King comes to you, righteous and having salvation, gentle and riding on a donkey" (Zech. 9:9).

As their rightful King, Jesus had claims, but force cannot command love. His kingdom had to be rooted in the hearts of men, so He appealed to them in a way unlike anything they expected or desired. All emblems of power and authority were laid aside; there was only His personal dignity to persuade them. Any man's acceptance of Christ must be free, completely unforced.

He, the Messiah, entered the capital of the chosen nation not on a war horse, but riding on a donkey, the symbol of humility and peace. Here was no political king, but the spiritual Lord of a spiritual kingdom. In the words of Henry Milman:

> Ride on, ride on in majesty!
> In lowly pomp ride on to die;
> O Christ, Thy triumphs now begin
> O'er captive death and conquered sin.

Harry Dean, *Power and Glory*

The Bread of Life

John 6:35

Eight times during His final year of earthly life, Jesus startled His listeners by using a mysterious phrase beginning with the words "I Am." Only the Apostle John records these cryptic, self-revealing declarations in his Gospel.

John sets the stage for Jesus' first declaration by recounting the only miracle recorded in all four Gospels: the feeding of the 5,000. After Jesus fed and addressed the multitude, He retreated to the nearby hills known today as the Golan Heights. His disciples sailed back to Capernaum.

By foot and by boat the people followed Jesus to Capernaum, where they cornered Him in the synagogue. Jesus ignored their shallow questions and bluntly challenged their motivation: "I tell you the truth, you are looking for Me, not because you saw miraculous signs but because you ate the loaves and had your fill. Do not work for food that spoils, but for food that endures to eternal life" (John 6:26–27). With these piercing words Jesus moved the conversation from their desire for physical nourishment to their need for spiritual sustenance. After Jesus described the spiritual bread that He offered, the crowd pleaded, "Sir ... give us this bread" (John 6:34).

The throng's approval plummeted when Jesus declared that He alone was the Bread they were seeking. Jesus proclaimed: "I am the Bread of Life. He who comes to Me will never go hungry, and he who believes in Me will never be thirsty" (John 6:35). It did not take long for the fickle crowd to turn their backs on Jesus. The Jewish leaders "began to grumble because He said, 'I am the Bread that came down from heaven'" (John 6:41).

The crowd came looking for bread, and Jesus offered them Himself—the Bread of Life. The cost of discipleship was simply too high for many to pay. Jesus illustrated the sacrificial cost with an unforgettable, startling metaphor: "I am the living bread that came down from heaven ... This bread is My flesh, which I will give for the life of the world" (John 6:51).

Sadly this discourse ended with many followers leaving Jesus. "'This,' they concluded, 'is a hard teaching. Who can accept it?' From this time many of his disciples turned back and no longer followed him" (John 6:60,66).

Thankfully, this is not the end of the story: "'You do not want to leave, do you?' Jesus asked the Twelve. Simon Peter answered Him, 'Lord, to whom shall we go? You have the words of eternal life'" (John 6:67–68).

Jesus' penetrating question resounds throughout the ages. His faithful disciples must ever follow Peter's example and response.

William Francis, *The War Cry*

Heaven's Joys

Revelation 22:3–4

Deep within most people there is a longing for heaven, for something after this life. Jesus compared heaven to a wedding banquet: "The kingdom of heaven is like a king who prepared a wedding banquet for his son" (Matt. 22:2).

Theologians and philosophers have often tackled the subject of afterlife and heaven. Thomas Aquinas in his *Summa Theologica* predicted: "Our scars will be seen as badges of honor; no one will rise in glory missing a limb; our senses will be enhanced, and we will be free of selfish passions." The Christian belief is that in heaven there is no self-centeredness—everyone thinks of the other before self.

Tom Harpur, Anglican priest and author of *Heaven and Hell*, describes heaven as "a place where one continues the journey of growing in spiritual enlightenment." St. Paul suggests that self-enlightenment will not be a process, but a part of the reality of heaven. On earth only certain things are revealed to us, but in heaven we shall know all things.

Will we simply be playing harps, or singing, all day and all night long? Mark Twain begged God to spare him from such boredom! There will undoubtedly be lots of surprises in heaven. No Internet will be necessary, for our search for knowledge will have been satisfied. We will have a heightened sense of spiritual identity, and God will fill our souls with ultimate joy.

We know that heaven will be a perfect place, and that there will be room for all who believe in Christ: "In My Father's house are many rooms ... I am going there to prepare a place for you" (John 14:2).

We also know it will be a place of peace: "He will wipe every tear from their eyes. There will be no more death or mourning or crying or pain, for the old order of things has passed away" (Rev. 21:4).

Heaven, as far as we can comprehend, is not so much above as beyond us. Anyone can reserve a place in heaven, but entrance is by God's grace alone. We must believe in Jesus Christ as our personal Savior. Once that belief is established, there must be a willingness to obey the leading of the Holy Spirit.

In heaven we will not only serve God, but the ultimate blessing will be to see his face: "The throne of God and of the Lamb will be in the city, and His servants will serve Him. They will see His face" (Rev. 22:3–4).

Beverly Ivany, *The War Cry*

Living in Two Worlds

Matthew 16:26

We live in not one, but two worlds. One is temporal; it is a world populated with people, in which we live and work. The other world is the one within us, an immensely private world, occupied by one's self alone.

Realizing that there are two worlds, the vital question is how does one live comfortably in both? On one side is the tangible life of mankind, dominated exclusively by material needs, instinctual reactions, intellect, economics, science and technology. On the other side, too often ignored, kept under wraps, is the actual world of the spirit. Excursions into that tiny corner of the heart where one tries to preserve immortal spiritual values are, alas, all too infrequent.

But how to live in both worlds with integrity? That is the question and the challenge. The schism between the spiritual and the temporal has deprived man of the nourishment he desperately needs. The undeniable truth is, however, that although the spiritual may have been repressed, there is still a great yearning for it.

The existence of the soul is of no concern at all to some. To others the very idea of its existence seems absurd. It is intellectual bigotry to assume that we can only believe what can be confirmed by laboratory proof. We all know that there are many things we've never seen that are real, the most priceless, according to Jesus, being the soul. To His disciples it could not have been made clearer. "What good will it be for man if he gains the whole world, yet forfeits his soul? Or what can a man give in exchange for his soul?" (Matt 16:26).

Many were surprised when the book *Care of the Soul*, by Thomas More, a noted psychotherapist, remained at the top of the *New York Times* best seller list for several weeks. What the author claims is that the enfeebling malady of the 20th century, affecting us individually and socially, is what he calls "loss of soul." He is speaking what the world should be hearing.

We care for the soul by honoring it, by living as much, or more, from the heart as from the head. When Christ is enthroned in the heart and life, the two worlds, the spiritual and the secular, are bridged. Sacredness then exists as much in the marketplace as in the monastery. By the grace of God all can live in both worlds, enriched within by His presence, and made influential for good in the challenging world without.

Arnold Brown, *The War Cry*

The Impossible Made Possible

Matthew 19:26

We have a God who specializes in things hardly possible. The Lord asks us to do the impossible and then He gives us the power to do it. It happened again and again during Jesus' lifetime.

Do you remember the man with the withered hand? Jesus came into the synagogue and said to him, "Stretch out your hand" (Matt. 12:13). He asked him to do the one thing that he couldn't do. But when the man stretched out his hand in obedience, he found the power was there.

Do you remember the paralyzed man at the pool, an invalid for 38 years? Jesus saw him and told him to do the one thing that was impossible. "Get up, take your mat and walk" (Mark 2:9). And he did.

Lazarus, the beloved friend of our Lord, had been dead four days when Jesus arrived at the tomb. Jesus called in a loud voice, "Lazarus, come out!" (John 11:43). To command a dead person to come to life was surely asking the impossible! But Lazarus came out of the tomb.

Then there was the occasion on the hillside when Jesus told a group of ordinary people to "go and make disciples of all nations, baptizing them in the name of the Father and of the Son and of the Holy Spirit and teaching them to obey everything I have commanded you" (Matt. 28:19–20). A small group of apostles to go to the uttermost parts of the world to make disciples of all nations? Surely this was mission impossible!

It is a principle, a Scriptural truth, that the Lord asks the seeming impossible thing and then gives us the power to do it. But there is a second principle. We have to initiate some action for that power to become available from on high.

If that man with the withered hand had held back from Jesus' command, there would have been no miracle. And the invalid man might have thought, "I've tried for 38 years to walk." But as he stepped out in faith, the power was there. And power was available for Lazarus also.

The great Augustine said, "Without God, we cannot. And without us, God will not." You have a God who asks you to do the impossible, but who gives you the power to do it. Keep your eyes on Jesus and you will find that the power will always be there.

John Larsson, *The War Cry*

Loving God

Deuteronomy 6:5

I desire to ask you a question that may possibly sound a little strange, but which nevertheless is very important. It is, "Do you love God?" I do not mean do you believe and talk and sing about Him, and admire Him; but do you really love Him, and that with all your heart?

Love to God is an essential part of religion, just as heat is an essential part of fire. You cannot have a living, sanctifying, enjoyable salvation without it. It does not matter what else you do; if you are without love, your religion is vain.

You can very readily tell whether you love God or not.

When any being is truly loved he will be very much in the thoughts. Last thing at night and first thing in the morning the heart will turn to the one it loves. Has God such a place in your mind, my comrade?

When anyone is truly loved, his interests will be cared for. When a father is loved by a son, the reputation and business and property of that father will be anxiously cared for by that son. So it is with your Heavenly Father. If you love Him you will assuredly care for His interests, and seek to promote them with all your heart.

When a being is really loved, the dearest object of life will be to do those things that will yield that being pleasure. What pleases that person and makes him happier will please and gladden you. If you love God you will delight in the doing of His righteous will, if for no other reason than that you will thereby give satisfaction to the heart of your Heavenly Father.

When any being is loved, there will be at least a measure of pleasure experienced in communion with that being. As the flowers turn to the sun, and the rivers run to the sea, so the heart ever turns to that one on whom its affections are chiefly set for comfort, and guidance, and satisfaction. To converse with that being and have his opinions regarding the men and things about us, to speak with him of our successes and failures, our hopes and fears, to hear him tell what his feelings are toward us and to tell him what our feelings are toward him, constitutes one of the chief delights.

Have you any such experience as this with respect to your Heavenly Father? Do you find pleasure in talking to Him, and hearing Him talk to you—on your knees, at your work, in your trials and in your joys?

Is this your experience? Do you feel after this fashion towards God?

William Booth, *The Warrior's Daily Portion, No. 2*

The Easy Yoke

Matthew 11:30

Farmers in Jesus' day knew that a good working team of oxen often stood between starvation and well-being.

My uncle had a team of horses that pulled the hay wagon and helped him clear heavily wooded areas. During our summer visits to the farm we loved to watch him work with Champ and Casper—sinewy, thick-haunched animals with amazing stamina. They were incredibly strong creatures, their muscles rolling and turning with the demands of their task. Often after a particularly difficult task was done, my uncle would jump down from the box and affectionately slap the horses' sweaty flanks. And they in turn would nuzzle his pockets for the treats he invariably carried for them.

Uncle Bill took special care with the wooden crosspiece and harness that bound Casper and Champ together. He'd sand away any rough spots in the wood and oil the leather parts until they were soft and pliable. And at the end of each day he checked the animals' flesh for sore or chafed spots. Casper and Champ were inseparable yokefellows, seeming almost to understand their common task and revel in it.

Paul used the word "yokefellow" to characterize people whose lives were bound together for a common mission (Phil 4:3). The Christian life was meant to be lived in community. Empowered by the same Spirit, it is the Christian's duty to labor not to develop private empires but to harvest souls for God's kingdom.

"Take My yoke upon you and learn from Me ... For My yoke is easy and My burden light" (Matt. 11:30) said Jesus. He never said the work would not be difficult, the nights long, the sun's heat intense and our energies tested. For some the hazards of being joined to Him would mean death.

What our Lord did mean to tell us is that His presence would make our service not only bearable but joyful and provide rest from our labors. "Come to Me, all you who are weary and burdened, and I will give you rest ... For I am gentle and humble in heart, and you will find rest for your souls" (Matt. 11:28–29).

With remarkable tenderness Jesus pours the ointment of His love and blessing upon us. He enables us to work for Him through gifts chosen especially for us, through the fellowship and sustaining of brothers and sisters. When pressed down with the weight of our toil or wounded in some desperate battle, He comes with His healing, with His presence, with His rest.

Marlene Chase, *Pictures from the Word*

The Splendor of Holiness

Psalm 29:2

The Psalmist has provided an appropriate matching word for "holiness." John Morley used to say that holiness was a word which defied definition. If splendor is used for a magnificence that beggars description, then the two are not unequally yoked in this four-word phrase.

Splendor is a poet's word which Wordsworth employed to convey the wonder of the sunrise on the Thames as seen from Westminster Bridge. But splendor is also a word which Christian hymn writers have applied both to the person of God and His handiwork. Robert Grant described Him as "pavilioned in splendor," and our own Will Brand wrote of "the splendor of the clear unfolding" of the name of Jesus. With good cause splendor may be joined in divine matrimony to holiness—and this for three reasons.

First of all, the phrase restores to the experience of holiness that breath-catching sense of wonder, that gasp of the heart's astonishment, as if this possibility was almost too good to be true.

Further, the union of splendor with holiness demonstrates afresh the appeal of the experience. True goodness both looks good and is good. We must not forget that our vocation is so to practice virtue that men are won to it.

Finally, this phrase about "the splendor of holiness" reawakens in our hearts a sense of the desirability of the experience. I must have given many hours to a consideration of this subject—to my own confused thinking on the matter, to listening to speakers on Salvation Army platforms, not to mention my own earlier and mixed-up dissertations on the same level. But it was a long time before I realized that any seeker was not so much to be argued into the experience as convinced by its inherent attractiveness.

Some Sunday mornings I was urged to remember that the experience was biblically based, with chapter and verse quoted in support. This could not but be agreed. On other occasions I was reminded that there was a divine command, binding on all God's children. Again, this could not be denied. Yet rarely did these approaches raise the pulse beat of desire because, "the beauty of holiness" was veiled from sight.

Now beauty in any form at once captures our attention. In the language of the New Testament, what is holiness but to be conformed to the image of the Son? This is surely desirable. More than that, it is gloriously possible. Thanks be to God!

Frederick Coutts, *The Splendor of Holiness*

Breaking the Power of Addiction

Romans 7:14–19

In Christ we have been released from what once kept us enslaved. People who have experienced this liberation testify with passion to the power of Christ that freed them from bondage. That which once enslaved them is now rendered powerless.

Addiction has been the curse of our age. In reality, however, the enslaving power of sin has always been part of the human predicament. It was in recognition of this that Paul wrote: "I do not understand what I do. For what I want to do I do not do, but what I hate I do ... the evil I do not want to do—this I keep doing" (Rom. 7:15–19).

The addictive capacity that we each have is powerful. Recognizing our inability to suppress or escape the enslaving power of sin propels us with abandon to the grace of Jesus Christ.

Addiction is defined as any compulsive, habitual behavior that limits the freedom of human desire. We attach our desires to specific objects and become completely consumed by the habitual behavior. It controls us. We want to break away from the object of our craving desires, but we cannot. It rules us. It torments us.

The cruelest dimension to addictive behavior is found in those substances that cause personal physical destruction or injury to other people. For the lives of innocent people—so often children or spouse—to become shattered because of addiction is similarly wicked.

Abstaining from harmful substances and behaviors is not only a decision of principle, it is also sheer common sense. A lament of the addict is the regret that they experimented in the first place.

"I will abstain from alcoholic drink, tobacco, the non-medical use of addictive drugs, gambling, pornography, the occult and all else that could enslave the body or spirit." In making this commitment, Salvation Army soldiers strengthen themselves in a very tangible way for spiritual warfare. They engage in the action unfettered and alert.

Richard Munn, *The War Cry*

Ladies of the Night

Matthew 22:9–10

Alida Bosshardt, of the Netherlands, is a legend in her lifetime. For many years she worked as a Salvation Army officer in the Red Light district of Amsterdam, the confidant of prostitutes and the means of helping many to find a different way of life. Even members of the Dutch royal family have been among her friends.

One day she was approached by a prominent Christian lady who wanted to go into the homes of poor people and also some of the bars and brothels regularly visited by Alida to see for herself what life was really like both for the poor and the "ladies of the night." There was some reluctance about the proposal on the part of Alida because the area of Amsterdam to which they would have to go could be dangerous. She consulted her colleagues in The Salvation Army and the idea was finally agreed upon.

The day came when the lady climbed the stairs to Alida's flat where the two had a cup of tea and then shared a reading from the Bible and a time of prayer. Because the lady's face was well-known, it was decided that she would go in disguise. The two set off, arm in arm.

They visited some poor homes and then they made for the pubs and brothels. The lady was amazed that Bosshardt got in without difficulty and prostitutes and others greeted her so warmly.

All was going well until in one bar photographer Peter Zonneveld recognized the lady with Alida and was able to take a quick picture before the two managed to escape by a side door. They jumped into a taxi and at one-thirty in the morning Bosshardt and her companion arrived back at their starting point. Back in Alida's room it was time for coffee again. Then at four in the morning the lady rang for a car to take her back home after what she described as the most fascinating experience of her life.

The next day *De Telegraaf*, one of Holland's most popular morning papers, carried a large photograph on its front page of Alida in the Red Light area of Amsterdam. But it was not the picture of the Salvation Army officer at work that gave Peter Zonneveld the scoop of his career. It was the lady next to her, snapped in the act of distributing copies of *The War Cry*, for she was none other than Her Royal Highness Crown Princess Beatrix, heir to the throne of the Netherlands and now that country's queen!

"Go to the street corners and invite to the banquet anyone you find. So the servants went out into the streets and gathered all the people they could find, both good and bad, and the wedding hall was filled with guests" (Matt. 22:9–10).

Wesley Harris, *Truth Stranger Than Fiction*

My Father Wrote a Book for Me

Psalm 119:105

My father is a writer. He wrote a book for me. My father's life has been very colorful. He aspired to be a writer and by the age of 17 became a newspaper editor in his homeland, China. The communists blacklisted him as an "intellectual," which in effect placed him on a "hit list." Upon learning this information, his family slipped a few dollars into his pocket, put him on a train that same evening, and he disappeared into the night just ahead of his persecutors.

He found his way to Hong Kong, eventually marrying a church girlfriend. He then emigrated to North America, became a Salvation Army officer and retired after 35 years of faithful ministry. Through it all, he wrote. He wrote letters, newsletters, devotional columns, hundreds of articles for Chinese newspapers, several books and sermons with fresh insights from God every week of his 35-year ministry.

Through the years his readers would comment to me, "Oh, I love your father's writing." "Your father's book touched my heart." "Your dad wrote about you this week in his newspaper column." I would smile and nod.

I never read my dad's writing. Everything he wrote was in Chinese, his native language. English is my native language. So I asked my dad to write a book for me. "Dad, tell me your story, so I won't forget." As a result, he wrote the book *For My Kinsmen's Sake*. It is the account of my family's heritage. Now I have one book my father has written in English that I can read, understand, cherish and know his mind.

It is one of my most precious possessions. There is only one other book that is more precious to me than the book my dad wrote.

I discovered it in my young adulthood when I reached an exceptionally painful time in my life. It was then I discovered that this book I had never before appreciated was the greatest love letter of all time. My incredible discovery was that it was written to me. I couldn't read enough about the fact that God loves me immeasurably, and has plans for my future.

It was as if I gained new vision, the true lens through which life could be accurately viewed and interpreted. Despair lost its hold on me as I became aware of God's love and plans for me.

God's Word is my love letter, my mirror, my map, my lamp, my instruction manual. It is nourishment for my soul. It is my window into God's heart. It is the story of my spiritual heritage.

My heavenly Father is a writer. He wrote a Book for me, and for you.

Keilah Toy, *The War Cry*

The Prelude to Calvary

Matthew 26:30

On the holy night in the Upper Room with Jesus and His disciples, we listen to His immortal words that float as music through the night air, and finally to His moving prayer. As we put our ears and our hearts up close to the door of that room, there is one more sound that falls on our ears. Suddenly, all those in the room rise and burst into song. Matthew and Mark both record this moment for us: "When they had sung a hymn, they went out to the Mount of Olives" (Matt. 26:30; Mark 14:26).

If only we knew the words they sang as the shadows grew heavy in the dim light of that Upper Room. Those words would be forever sacred. We would want to ponder them, meditate upon their timeless truth and make them a part of our own devotional experience. If only we knew what Jesus sang with His disciples there on that night of nights.

But we *do* know the very words Jesus and His disciples sang. At the Passover meal, the Hallel Psalms were sung—Psalms 113–118. They were psalms of praise that every Jewish boy had to memorize. Psalms 113 and 114 were sung near the beginning of the observance, saving Psalms 115 through 118 for a later point. At the end of the feast, the great Hallel Psalm 136 rang out from grateful hearts.

It is a salutary devotional exercise for the Christian to read these psalms and consider the words that were actually on the lips of our Lord as He prepared to go out to Calvary. Together He and the disciples stood and sang words of courage: "The Lord is with me; I will not be afraid. What can man do to me?" (Ps. 118:6). "The Lord is my strength and song, and He has become my salvation" (Ps. 118:14). In confidence they sang, "This is the day the Lord has made; we will rejoice and be glad in it" (Ps. 118:24). And in gratitude they exclaimed, "Give thanks to the Lord, for He is good! His love endures forever" (Ps. 136:1).

The music of these psalms was the prelude to Calvary. With these words of praise and confidence, Jesus went on His way to the cross. The medley of praise which the Lord with His disciples sang is one of the hidden highlights of inspiration in the Bible.

Music is to the soul as air is to the body. It was Bach who said the purpose of his music "should be none else but the glory of God," inscribing at the top of his manuscripts *Soli Deo Gloria* (to God alone the glory). Our Lord knew the devotional expression of music, and for Him it was a source of strength and inspiration as He journeyed to the cross.

Henry Gariepy, *Forty Days with the Savior*

The Way of the Cross

Luke 2:49–52

It was a rocky road to Bethlehem!
The precious parchments of the patriarchs
had set the scene on history's holy page.
The sacred signs were there. Messiah's Day
would dawn when God's own time had fully come.
A star proclaimed The Hour and angels sang
"Good News! The Peasant Prince is birthed in straw!"

It was a winding way near Nazareth!
A village youth at work among the shavings of
the shop where wooded things were hewn once paused
to stretch his arms as shafts of light etched out
His silhouette upon the farthest wall.
The shadowed shape traced not a carpenter
but victim, cast upon a cross of shame!

It was a pleasant path by Galilee!
The Rabbi from obscurity strode down
the dusty road beside that sea so prone
to trouble workers on the wave. He marched
into the mart where wondrous words would hold
the throngs enthralled and grasping for God's news—
the gospel of a kingdom near at hand.

It was a craggy course, discipleship!
He called his own, as rabbis do, out from
the ordinary and bland—the fishing and
the taxing, too. He molded, melded them,
and minded them to down their nets, take up
their cross to follow Him. No turning back,
no wav'ring on the way ahead for them.

Lucille L. Turfrey, *The War Cry*

The Way of the Cross (cont.)

1 Corinthians 15:55–57

It was a torturous trail, throughout this land
where steadfastly He strode toward His goal.
His wisdom at a village well brought peace
to one so wrong and wronged. He offered draughts
of living water, quenching all soul thirst.
The bland, the lame, the leprous, wasted ones
found hope and wholeness in His healing touch.

They were such stately streets, Jerusalem's!
Downtrodden by the alien force of Rome,
the city also suffered men so holy to
themselves but far from God in Temple veils.
His challenge to the blasphemies, the sins,
injustices of priests and king, would take
Him to a cross, the rugged frame of death.

It was a treach'rous track to Calvary!
The shouldered beam, the bloodied back bent low
from lashings cruelly cast, the thorny crown,
the grief of pains more deep than soldiers made.
He bore our griefs, our pains of sin, and laid
them in the tomb of God's forgetfulness,
those sins of ours, releasing us to life!

It was a radiant road of joy from out
the empty tomb so near that knoll,
Golgotha's ghastly face—that "Calvary."
The Resurrection dawn extends its glow
upon this precious path. So where, O Death,
is now your sting, your conqu'ring, gaping grave?
The victory is Christ's, the Lord of Life!

Lucille L. Turfrey, *The War Cry*

I Was There

Galatians 6:14

The great difference between the historical fact of Easter and all others in the long record of events upon earth is that I feel that I was in the deepest sense a participator in it. I do not feel this way regarding any other fact in history, striking and moving as many of them are.

At the lovely Cathedral of Canterbury I was taken into those cool, shadowed cloisters and shown the place where the blood of a famous cleric ran down upon the gray stones. "This is the spot," my guide said to me, "where Thomas Becket, the proud and powerful prelate, was at prayer when five of the king's knights came upon him with drawn swords." Becket was kneeling before the altar when they struck him, and his blood ran down upon the sacred stones. The story touches my heart. Its drama, struggle and tragedy come vividly before me. But I do not feel that it has anything to do with me. I come away from Canterbury grateful for a history lesson. But that is all.

I go to the place, dear to many, where Mary, Queen of Scots was beheaded. I ponder over her restless life with its continual storms blowing upon her until she had to die with the axe upon her slender neck. But I do not feel that her life and death have anything to do with me. I say, "Ah, yes! I remember the story." And to me it is only a story.

But I go home from a meeting, late in the evening, and I feel I would like to hear a little music. So I put on my player a record by the International Staff Band, and I hear men's voices singing the old spiritual, "Were you there when they crucified my Lord?" And I feel deeply and inescapably that the question is for me. I reply, "Yes! I was there! Indeed, I was there!"

This matter has to do with me as no other fact in history. Why do I feel like this? It is not because of an emotional reaction to an oft-told story. This matter goes deeper than that. I am brought to Calvary by my sin, by my need of forgiveness, by my identity with the human race in its need of a Savior.

We must all come near to the cross, with our guilt, our hopes and fears. Here we will find the answer to our deepest needs. It must be a personal approach that we make to Calvary. Until we can say "I was there!" we cannot know the true meaning of the central fact in all history.

Albert Orsborn, *The War Cry*

Why Me?

Isaiah 6:8

Find someone else!
Your files are full
Of super-gifted saints
Who'd love to do this job for you,
No groans and no complaints!
It's just not fair,
When You must have
A million men or more,
Your finger falls on me again,
Does no one keep the score?

Forgive me, Lord.
It's not by chance
You want me for this task.
Just call me any time You like,
You only have to ask.
With You there's no "coincidence,"
But only good design.
No doubt You have Your reasons
Why the name You name
Is mine!

John Gowans, *O Lord Not More Verse!*

Consider Him

Hebrews 12:2–4

We often look back along our own little thorn-set pathway and say, "If I had known it all beforehand, I could not have walked this road, but God mercifully hid it from me. He led me step by step, gave me hourly grace, held fast my hand all the way, and so I have come."

But Jesus, as His feet drew near Calvary, knew beforehand its unspeakable terrors. He knew that He would go out from that quiet garden to hours of hatred and scorning, which should only end on the awful cross. He knew each pang for His body, each crushing reproach for His heart, the weight of human depravity to be poured out upon His innocent soul, knew the utter loneliness, the sting of desertion, the failure of human love, and yet He went forth. "Jesus, therefore, knowing all things that should come upon him, went forth" (John 18:4 KJV).

The writer of Hebrews entreats: "Let us fix our eyes on Jesus, the author and perfecter of our faith, who for the joy set before Him endured the cross ... Consider Him" (12:2–3). But what joy could be seen across the immense stretch of horror and desolation between Him and the far side of the cross? The joy of having His human will entirely lost in the Divine will. The joy of the salvation for others. These lasting joys He saw by faith, still working out salvation for God's Church, still bearing great fruit of joy in two worlds.

This is the joy of which Jesus spoke to His disciples, "These thing have I spoken unto you, that My joy may remain in you, and that your joy may be full" (John 15:11 KJV). Full-brimming, satisfying, heaven-like joy—the very joy of God! He bring us to and keeps us in His presence, where, as David tells us, "is fullness of joy" (Ps. 16:11 NRS).

Perhaps you know already where your hill of Calvary rises, and you see the somber cross awaiting you. But you lack power to go forth–your flesh and your heart fail you. Then "consider Him," until you can believe His love, trust His providence. You have long dwelt on your own sorrows—the hardness of your lot. Now, "Consider Jesus."

You do not know what is before you. God does. God calls you to His presence, to union with Him, to radiant light, to a joy that can endure the cross.

Jesus went forth for you, went forth to bear all that flesh cannot endure, to take once for all, every bitter drop from the cup of life, and leave there only the living water.

Elizabeth Swift Brengle, *Half Hours with My Guide*

If My Feet Have Faltered

Psalm 27:4

Savior, if my feet have faltered
    On the pathway of the cross,
If my purposes have altered
    Or my gold be mixed with dross,
O forbid me not Thy service,
    Keep me yet in Thy employ,
Pass me through a sterner cleansing
    If I may but give Thee joy!

All my work is for the Master,
    He is all my heart's desire;
O that He may count me faithful
    In the day that tries by fire!

Have I worked for hireling wages,
    Or as one with vows to keep,
With a heart whose love engages
    Life or death, to save the sheep?
All is known to Thee, my Master,
    All is known, and that is why
I can work and wait the verdict
    Of Thy kind but searching eye.

I must love Thee, love must rule me,
    Springing up and flowing forth
From a childlike heart within me,
    Or my work is nothing worth.
Love with passion and with patience,
    Love with principle and fire,
Love with heart and mind and utterance,
    Serving Christ my one desire.

Albert Orsborn, *The Beauty of Jesus*

Musings in the Upper Room

Luke 24:36–41

Lord, how You frighten me,
coming through walls, suddenly appearing,
all shining, unearthly. Can it be
You're the smiling One I remember
bouncing children on Your knee?

I remember Your hillside stories,
so terrible and wonderful,
but all their awe-inspiring glories,
their woundings and their soothings were
gentled by some calm or ease
we felt with You. We marked the real
way Your lips formed words and sighs,
the way dust clung to Your heel
when you walked the village roads, the arch
of muscle and bone when You stooped to kneel.

And when You died, Your blood was red.
It matted Your hair, fell on Your chest.
Your chest ... I could see it pound. I fled
when I knew that You were innocent,
that you were dying for me instead.
They put You in a human tomb.
Women wept, as women do,
 as many touched with grief and gloom.
(Once, Lord, I saw You weep
tears like rain in the silent room.)

Resurrected, now You stand
too wonderful for me to look,
too high, I cannot comprehend
our majesty, Your holiness.
But suddenly You extend a hand.
I can't believe the marks I see,
the ugly wounds, ragged gashes,
marks of experienced humanity!
Why have you allowed these to remain
in your splendid, glorified body?

Reminders always of mankind's son?
Marks of earth You choose to wear?
Can it be when all is said and done
these bloody badges forever prove
that You and I are inexplicably one?

Marlene Chase, *The Officer*

A Resurrection Religion

1 Corinthians 15:51–56

~⚘~

I drove my jeep out of the empty camp and onto the main road that led into the city of Da Nang, South Vietnam. I happily anticipated the events of the day with Seabees, who comprised the scattered 800-man battalion I served as a Navy chaplain, coming together to celebrate Easter.

The sun had already risen over the South China Sea, and the temperature promised to soar above 100 degrees. The hot road was unpaved.

Halfway between my camp and Da Nang, I saw her—a small Vietnamese woman kneeling at the side of the road. As I drew closer I could see that she was convulsed with sobbing. Her head rested on a little red wooden box.

I pulled the jeep off the road, stopped and walked toward her. Wanting to help but not knowing how, I knelt beside her. "Can I help you?" I asked. She turned her tear-streaked face toward me, and noticing the cross on my lapel, she lifted the lid of the box and invited me to look inside. There lay the body of a small child.

Exercising my sparse knowledge of Vietnamese, I discovered that she was trying to make her way to her ancestral village where her child would be entombed. But the day was too hot, and the box too heavy for her. I was glad when she accepted my offer of help. After overseeing my placing of the box on the jeep's back seat, she climbed into the vehicle and directed me to the tomb where the body of her child would rest beside her ancestors.

While I had witnessed the horror of violent death before and would again, no experience during my tour of duty was sadder than that. It was a moment of death, defeat and utter sadness.

During that same tour of duty, a Roman Catholic priest and fellow chaplain joined me in conducting an Easter sunrise service for our Seabees and Marines who had slogged across the rice paddies to join us for worship. Following the celebration of Mass, I led the group in singing songs of Easter and preaching its message of the empty tomb.

I am still gripped by the contrast between the Vietnamese woman who grieved for her dead child and that of the servicemen who celebrated the risen Lord. The first experience was one of death and defeat, the second, of life and victory. "Christianity," writes John Stott, "is in its very essence a resurrection religion." Resurrection—Christ's and, through Him, our own—is the living center of Christian faith. Having made that discovery, we may leave death and defeat, and embrace eternal life and victory.

Kenneth L. Hodder, *The War Cry*

The Ultimate Bottom Line

1 Corinthians 15:3–4

The "bottom" line in the world of commerce is the last line of a financial statement showing net profit or loss. It is the deciding or crucial factor, the ultimate result. Could it be that Easter is the ultimate bottom line of man's search to find meaning in life?

There are those who simply consider Easter to be a continuation of what mankind has witnessed through time—a celebration of the coming of spring. To them, Easter heralds the return and renewal of life in nature.

The Salvationist, called to balance an evangelical ministry with social concerns, lives in a pragmatic world. He lives among the people, feels their hurts. Philosophic thought has to take second place to getting the job done.

He tries to fullfill Jesus' injunction in Matthew 25 to feed the hungry, clothe the naked, visit the prisoner, be aware of the needs of mankind, doing it in the name of the Christ who rose again on that first Easter morning. The substance of what we do hinges on the actuality of that great moment when Jesus came forth from the dead.

We need to know, these twenty centuries later, whether the promises of that first Easter morning are still in effect. We need to know if that great resurrection day can still supply the dynamic for men to live above themselves in our troubled world. Does the living presence of the Lord Jesus Christ, working through us, still meet the needs, aspirations, hopes and plans of modern man?

Two millennia later the witness remains the same. Salvationists can say that the Risen Christ motivates our ministry around the world.

Now, these near seventy generations later, the personal as well as the institutional relationship of the resurrection is a glorious reality. It is a joy to witness to the indwelling presence of Christ in the human heart.

The bottom line of the Christian life is that Christ lives in us. The hope of glory is Christ living in and through us. It does not mean that we are free from weakness, nor that we are doing all that we should. But it does mean that we have His presence, His Spirit and His guidance. We exclaim and exult with Charles Wesley, "Christ the Lord is risen today, Hallelujah!"

The might, majesty and magnificence of His resurrection leads us to kneel before our risen Lord and thank Him for His resurrection power in our lives. His triumphant resurrection is the bottom line. It is the deciding factor. It is the ultimate result.

Andrew S. Miller, *The War Cry*

The Strongest Force in History

Luke 24:4,12

꜒꜠

Sorrow and love sleep lightly. As a result, it was early in the morning when the women found their way to Jesus' tomb. In their hands they carried, as a representation of the love in their hearts, spices to anoint the body of Jesus. When they came to the tomb they found the stone rolled away. Luke tells us that "While they were wondering about this, suddenly two men in clothes that gleamed like lightning stood beside them" (24:4).

Guilt and shame also sleep lightly. Peter had spent sleepless nights as he thought about his failure in denying and deserting Christ. When the word reached him that the stone had been rolled away and the tomb was empty, he rushed to see if it was true. Luke tells us, "He saw the strips of linen lying by themselves, and he went away, wondering to himself what had happened" (24:12).

Jesus challenged the two foes that people in all their strength cannot handle—sin and death—and conquered them both. The empty tomb stands as the strongest force in history. There is a power in the resurrection that gives deep meaning and purpose to life.

Wondering minds, then and now, begin to see from the signal event in history that truth is stronger than a lie. The claim of the resurrection is so great that, if true, nothing else matters, and if not true, it is the biggest deception ever.

Most of the disciples died violent, agonizing deaths. While men may die for what they think to be true, they will not die for what they know to be a lie. Truth is stronger than a lie.

The whole existence of the church rested on the strength of the resurrection. After the crucifixion, the disciples found themselves despondent and despairing. But after seven weeks and Pentecost, a very different Peter preached to a mob.

A new sense of power was experienced. Apart from the resurrection, there would be no church. If the enemies of Jesus had succeeded, that which is false would have been shown to be stronger than truth.

Wondering minds, then and now, begin to see from the strongest force in history that life is stronger than death.

The resurrection is the strongest force in history, for it shows us that truth is stronger than a lie, love is stronger than hate and life is stronger than death.

John Busby, *The War Cry*

Power in the Blood

Ephesians 1:7

During Holy Week, our corps sponsored a blood donation drive. Being eager to set a good example for the troops, I gave a pint of my best type O+. They asked me all manner of questions concerning my health and past medical history. After being tested and screened, they laid me down on the table and siphoned off a pint of the precious, life–giving fluid. Eventually my blood would be used either whole for transfusion or in parts for platelet and plasma. It brings a certain comfort to imagine that my blood will be used to save the life of an accident victim or to sustain life during surgery.

There is something special about blood. We have been taught that it is the conduit that carries oxygen and nourishment to every cell of the body while carrying off toxic waste products. We have a deep reverence for this sacred body fluid. Without it, we would quickly die.

No one from the Red Cross asked Jesus if He was healthy enough to give blood. They didn't use a sterile needle to extract an even pint. A Roman soldier used a whip made of many leather strands, each tipped with a piece of stone or metal that literally tore skin and muscle off the bone. Another shoved a crown of thorns on His brow. No one was there to give Jesus orange juice and cookies or present Him with a donor's button. No one asked if it was all right as His blood fell drop by drop into the dust of Golgotha. There on that Good Friday, as the High Priest offered a lamb for the sins of Israel, the sinless Lamb of God gave His life as a ransom for us, to pay the price and penalty of our sin.

My blood may be used to save a life. Yet in spite of all that science and medicine can do, the patient will eventually die. Jesus gave His blood, gave it to save lives from hell so that they will never die spiritually. "He was pierced for our transgressions, He was crushed for our iniquities ... and by His wounds we are healed" (Isa. 53:5).

My blood will come through intravenously in a hospital for a stranger I will never know. Jesus' blood was shed for people He knew and loved–you and me. He died not just for a transfusion, but for a transformation of stubborn, rebellious, selfish, willful sinners into God's children. All who will accept Jesus Christ receive the gift of His life, His own shed blood to redeem us from sin. This is a gift that truly keeps on giving.

A. Kenneth Wilson, *The War Cry*

He Showed Himself Alive

Luke 1:3

The Apostle Paul declared that the entire structure of the Christian faith rests upon the fact of the resurrection of Jesus Christ.

Referring to Jesus, Luke wrote in the first chapter of the Acts of the Apostles, "He showed himself alive!" (Acts 1:3 ASV). These words are the key to the amazing events which Luke describes. Indeed, were it not for the appearance of the risen Lord, there would have been no "Acts of the Apostles" to describe.

"He showed Himself alive." To whom? To those who saw Him die. It was imperative that those who saw Him die should also see Him alive again. He had not been a brave but deluded fanatic dying vainly for a lost cause. He had not died as a political pawn or a condemned criminal. He had died as the divine agent in God's supreme act of love.

And "He showed Himself alive" to those whose hopes were dead. We cannot fully understand the disappointment and dejection and despair of the followers of Jesus in those days after Calvary. We catch some of their hopelessness in the sad faces and despondent tones of the two who spoke with the "stranger" on the Emmaus road that first Easter Sunday afternoon. "We had hoped," they said, "that He was the One who was going to redeem Israel" (Luke 24:21). "We had hoped!" The inference was plain. They spoke of hope as being something in the past.

But they didn't remain that way. Read in that twenty-fourth chapter of Luke the joyous record of "burning hearts" and running feet and jubilant witnesses. And all because "He showed Himself alive" to those whose hopes were dead. There is no other way to explain the transformation of the grieving into the joyful, the doubting into the confident, the frightened into the bold. "He showed himself alive," and the invigorated, invincible disciples became one of the leading proofs of His resurrection power.

And here is the final truth for you and me: "He showed Himself alive" to those who were dead in sin. To the Corinthian church, Paul wrote, "He appeared to me also, as to one abnormally born" (1 Cor. 15:8). Even those who did not actually see the risen Lord were beneficiaries of His appearing.

"Christ is risen! Hallelujah" Believe in the historical fact of the resurrection of Jesus. Believe in the spiritual fact of the risen Christ, who will "show Himself alive" to you. Accept not alone the evidence of the empty tomb. Accept the irrefutable and incomparable evidence of the indwelling Christ.

Bramwell Tripp, *To the Point*

Turning Tragedy into Triumph

1 Corinthians 15:55

Never in history did such tragedy visit one life in a single day as on that dark Friday when Jesus stumbled to Calvary bearing the cross, carrying the world's sin and guilt.

Crucifixions were reserved for the outcasts of earth. But Christ was no ordinary victim. He was the One of whom it was written, "Through Him all things were made; without Him nothing was made that has been made" (John 1:3).

The tragedy of this ignominious crucifixion of Christ, even in this day, causes the heart to cry out, "Why?" Why such blindness to the Spirit–filled, God–indwelt character of the Savior? But through the tragic darkness of that Friday shone a glorious light of salvation, purchased at tremendous cost.

The continuing tragedy is that there are still those who remain blind to the cross of Christ, who do not see the Light, but continue to live in the darkness of sin and doubt.

John 3:16 is a truth certified by Jesus when He gave himself on the cross, so that "whoever believes in Him shall not perish, but have eternal life." Today there are millions of Christians who not only can recite that familiar text, but can relate it to a personal Easter experience. The sacrifice of Jesus wraps John 3:16 around them in loving assurance.

"Where, O Death, is your victory? Where, O Death, is your sting?" (1 Cor. 15:55). Paul's joyous exclamations to the Corinthians are echoed by all Christians during Easter, when it is realized anew that Jesus conquered death. What consternation there must have been among His enemies when the stone was rolled away in the garden, and Christ stepped out from the tomb to reveal Himself, first to Mary, and later to other followers.

Having experienced such a shattering tragedy, how could His followers accept the truth of a resurrected Christ? The darkness of their spirits would be difficult to penetrate. But when Jesus visited them, giving proof of His triumph, a glorious light dispelled the darkness. They knew without doubt that Jesus had turned tragedy into truth and truth into triumph.

Hallelujah! He is still doing it in the hearts of men and women, who with the poet exult:

> The head that once was crowned with thorns,
> Is crowned with glory now!

John D. Waldron, *The War Cry*

Three Crosses—Three Results

2 Corinthians 5:19

That barren hill outside Jerusalem's wall will not be forgotten. Its name, Golgotha, will always bring a shudder to our mind and heart. There were three crosses on that ugly hill; three lives ended on those cruel instruments of torture and death. One was the Son of God.

The attitude of the one malefactor on the right of Jesus seems portentous and the foreshadowing of the position taken by skeptics through the ages. The word that might well have been mounted on the cross above this man is "rejection."

The Scripture records: "One of the criminals who hung there hurled insults at him: 'Aren't You the Christ? Save Yourself and us!'" (Luke 23:39). Men of this character find it hard to accept anything but the material world. Accept only the things that are tangible and sensate, live for today.

The attitude and demeanor of the criminal to the left of Jesus differed significantly. He shouted above the din, "We receive the due reward of our deeds; but this man has done nothing amiss." And then to Jesus he said: "Lord, remember me when you come into your kingdom." The word that might well have been mounted on the cross above this man is "realization."

This man's values and activities may have been quite like that of the other thief. He makes no boast of goodness but expresses regret and shame. How lovingly the Master replies. His words convey the message of forgiveness and acceptance. Even for those who have lived shamefully, rejected Him openly, there is forgiveness. The realization that Christ was and is the Son of God makes a tremendous difference, not only for the world that is yet to be, but in this present world as well.

On the center cross, in agony and shame, hung our blessed Lord. The sign that might have been placed above this cross is the word "redemption." This was the atoning Christ who suffered death for every man. By this perfect sacrifice upon the cross, Jesus abolished death for every believer. The Scripture states, "God was reconciling the world to Himself through Christ" (2 Cor. 5:19). That was the purpose for His ignominious suffering and death—it was for our redemption, to atone for our sins and set us free from guilt and death.

May our attitude toward Christ's suffering and death, be that of the realization of sins forgiven, and faith in a living Lord whose death and resurrection brings us the assurance of redemption and life abundant.

George Nelting, *The War Cry*

Wagging Heads

Matthew 17:39

Recording the crucifixion, Matthew's Gospel says, "They that passed by reviled him, wagging their heads" (Matt. 27:39 KJV). Pondering this scene of the thorn-crowned head of Christ and the shaking heads of the scornful spectators, one remembers Job's words about the reversal of jeering judgments: "I also could speak like you, if you were in my place; I could make fine speeches against you and shake my head at you" (Job 16:4).

He hung on a cross by the wayside. He was lifted up within sight and sound of the motley crowd. Men trample and push as they look, point, jeer and talk within the shadow of the cross. Maybe some few would weep, or recall His kindness, as the crowd went home to sup and to sleep.

As the most impressive part of the human body, the head plays a leading role in expressing man's reactions to life. Doubt, questioning, agreement, denial, refusal, rejection and, indeed, almost the whole range of feeling and opinion may be conveyed without a spoken word by the head alone. These gestures at Calvary were the language of contempt.

And so the crowd passed by. They wagged their heads contemptuously at the Man whose ideals of love were so unworkable that they brought Him to a cross.

The cross says to man, "This is the way God loves and forgives." The wagging heads say, "Love us if you like, but do not ask us to kneel and be forgiven." It was the language of dismissal. God must keep His distance and not interfere in human affairs.

With the same mind and the same verdict of scorn, the world today parades past the cross. Without complete repudiation, is our impersonal view of the Savior declaring that though at times we think Him interesting, we do not really regard Him as relevant or important to the main business of living? Do we give Him a nominal acknowledgment without the least intention to own up that our sin had anything to do with Calvary?

One of the persistent follies and sins of mankind is the refusal to take Jesus Christ seriously—to wag the head and say, "A most interesting figure in history, but what a pity He was so idealistic, so set upon dying!"

The head laid in the manger, bending over the carpenter's bench, anointed with spikenard, hurt by a traitor's kiss, beaten with hand and rod, defiled with the persecutor's spittle, crowned with thorns, bowed in death, will be raised in power and crowned with glory.

Albert Orsborn, *The War Cry*

If I Be Lifted Up ...

John 12:32

It is not, Lord, that we would bring You down,
Take hold of holy things with hasty hand
And bear them low, and lower, till they reach
That sunken place, where unrepentant stand
The sons of men.

It is not, Lord, that we would force men's faith,
And in unconsecrated bread and wine
Bring You to them, and press unwilling lips
To taste, at least, communion divine.

It is not, Lord, that we would lure men to
Their highest good, or coax them to the cross,
Or bribe them with the promise of great gain,
Flaunting the profit, covering the loss.

But we would lift You up, that seeing You
Men shall be drawn to leave their self-made slum,
And toss their tawdry treasures to the dust,
And claim their right, through Your power, to become
The sons of God.

John Gowans, *O Lord Not More Verse!*

He Is Not Here!

Matthew 28:6

The empty tomb, its vacancy, shook the people who made their way through the garden to the place where Christ had been buried—and it shakes us still. It all seems too good to be true.

The biblical account tells us that the angel rolled back the stone and sat upon it with a kind of cheerful insolence. "He's not here!" said the divine messenger. "Have a look!" It seemed important that the world should see just how empty the place was.

The message must have become crystal clear to His staggered disciples. The Master whom they thought was done for was up and about again—as ready as ever to comfort, to guide, to direct and correct, to help and to heal. Love was liberated. The rocky walls of His "container" could not contain Him. What can one say but "Whoopee!" or, perhaps more appropriately, "Hallelujah!"

Our world needs to know about this. Every Christian ought to stand by the door of Christ's empty tomb and whisper or shout as may be appropriate: "He is not here!"

Ever since Christ moved out of His grave, people have been trying to get Him back inside. They have attempted to imprison Him afresh—in history, in literature, in tradition—but in each case the cry rings out: "He isn't here!" They try to wrap Him up in the shroud of regimented religion and the angels must laugh as they sing out, "He isn't here, either!" Regular attempts have been made to bury him in the past, but He is more modern than the latest revelation or man's way-out technology. Don't look for Him among dead things. You won't find Him there.

"Then where is He?" you ask. The simple answer is, "Everywhere!" His presence is totally unrestricted, as His disciples soon found out. He seemed to be everywhere at once and He still is. He is here with the fellow setting out for college and the girl going to her first job. He is here with the new mother cuddling her contented child. He is at the bedside of the seriously ill and on the road beside the recently unemployed. He is here with the laughing crowd at the Super Bowl and at the Olympic Games. He is here with the lonely and the depressed and especially the bereaved, and a simple prayer will make His living, powerful presence felt.

He is the Christ of the human road.

John Gowans, *The War Cry*

From Darkness to Light

Luke 24:33–34

The tomb is empty! Christ is risen! From the newly hewn tomb in Joseph's garden this victorious cry of the gospel has emerged, crossing oceans and continents to encircle the world.

Its message brought the disciples from the dark night of the tomb into the bright sunshine of the first Easter day. Its reality confirms for all believers, "Because I live, you also will live" (John 14:19).

It is upon the hinges of the resurrection that the doors of Christianity swing open. It is the core of Christian theology, the basic tenet of the Christian faith.

Yet, at the close of the first Easter day, the light of truth had only penetrated the darkness within a few hearts. It had reached Mary Magdalene and her sister in sorrow. It had been revealed to John the Beloved, as well as to a lone fisherman who had denied his Master.

It had also touched two disciples who rehearsed the joyful news of their unexpected encounter with their Master as they hastened from the city of Emmaus to tell the others. Finding the Eleven gathered, and others with them, they announced, "The Lord has risen and has appeared to Simon" (Luke 24:34). As the group pondered these things, some doubting, some half persuaded, some believing, but all sorrowing and depressed, remembering how they had failed their Lord, suddenly He appeared in their midst. His presence changed the darkness of their perplexity into the sunlight of peace.

One cannot help but contrast the lives of the disciples before and after the resurrection. Often during their walk with Jesus they had failed to comprehend His words. He spoke of meekness; they spoke of might. He spoke of servanthood; they thought of self. He spoke of a heavenly kingdom; they could only comprehend an earthly one.

However, following the resurrection, these same men now became stamped from a different mold, with their spiritual eyes opened and their understanding enlarged. They feared neither punishment nor death. Nothing could stop them from proclaiming the good news of the gospel.

The same transformation, from the darkness of the tomb to the light of the risen Lord, may permeate the hearts and lives of all who receive Him today. He brings gladness into all hearts and lives when He enters, and we too can state with confidence, "The Lord is risen indeed!"

Willard S. Evans, *The War Cry*

Easter Is Exciting!

1 Corinthians 15:57

What makes Easter so exciting is its cosmic quality. Easter has less to do with one man's escape from the grave than with the victory of seemingly powerless love over loveless power.

I personally believe in the resurrection of Christ for two reasons. The first is the documented enthusiasm of the disciples. A historian may find little objective evidence to support the story of the empty tomb, but no historian will dispute the fact that, after Easter, the disciples became ten times the people they were before. Promise-making, promise-breaking Peter, that fearful fellow we remember on Good Friday, suddenly after Easter was so aflame with faith that he gladly lived and bravely died for the Master he had thrice denied.

In fact so great was the enthusiasm of all the disciples that we can say Christianity really began at Easter. Had there been no resurrection of Christ, there would have been no gospels, no epistles, no New Testament, no Christian Church, including The Salvation Army.

But Easter was not a function of the disciples' faith; their faith was a function of Easter. They were convinced Christ had risen from the dead. Christ was a real presence. What is clear is that the disciples recognized Christ's identity, His personality and His character. Instead of death, they beheld a metamorphosis. As it is written in the preface of the Roman Catholic Requiem Mass: Life is changed, not ended.

But the historical reason is only a buttress for my second reason for believing in the resurrection. I, like so many throughout the centuries, have experienced in my own life the presence of the risen Christ and the Holy Spirit. I experience the risen Christ as a mirror to my humanity, showing me what human beings should be about. I experience the risen Christ as a window to divinity, revealing as much of God as is given mere mortal eyes to behold. I experience the risen Christ as strength above my own, as joy deeper than the heart's understanding. Best of all, I experience the risen Christ as that love which indeed does "make the world go round," the love that binds us, one to another and all to God.

What is beyond the grave we may not know, but we do know Who is beyond the grave. Life is eternal and death is only a horizon, and a horizon is nothing but merely the limit of our sight. What then shall we declare but, "Thanks be to God who gives us the victory through our Lord Jesus Christ" (1 Cor. 15:57).

Peter & Grace Chang, *The Gift of God*

The Revealing Cross

Colossians 1:20

The story of the cross hardly needs repetition. Read it once more in any one of the Gospels. Never were words used with such economy and force. Ponder prayerfully the succession of bitter events.

As we ponder, we must beware of feeling no more than pity, a reaction that Jesus Himself discounted. "Weep not for Me, but weep for yourselves, and for your children" (Luke 23:28). His wounds are not His main appeal to us, for His sorrow was more than physical pain. His great agony was the knowledge of what men were, the realization of how deeply sin was entrenched in human hearts, sin from which He had come to save them.

The cross reveals the power of the love of God that cannot be shattered, because it is indestructible. It reveals the power of the holiness of God by revealing the way our sins—everyday sins that crucified Christ—appear in His sight. It reveals the power of the mercy of God, for by means of the cross He pledges His forgiveness to all who truly repent.

But why was such an extremity of shame necessary to divine revelation and redemption? Simply because God is love, and love knows no limits. Jesus understood what God was like, and His knowledge enabled him to face "even the death of the cross" (Phil. 2:8 KJV).

The cross was a parable in flesh and blood. The truth which Jesus had sought to convey by His life, teaching and work, He confirmed by His death. Mere words could not describe God, and even if they could, they would have been open to misunderstanding and misinterpretation, for they lack compelling power. If words had been equal to the task, a book could have saved mankind.

The truth about God had to be demonstrated unmistakably. His love had to be put beyond all shadow of doubt. So the cross speaks the unutterable truth. We need always to remember that what the cross reveals is eternally true about God.

The moral victory of Christ's way of love stands before us as the ideal which must become established in the real. In the presence of His utter self-giving can we not find the courage to follow? Dare we pray to be stripped of all false values and for grace to welcome the cross into the center of our lives?

Harry Dean, *Power and Glory*

What If?

1 Corinthians 15:20

What if His practiced and ruthless executioners were deceived? What if He never really died after the tortuous hours endured in measureless agony on the cross? What if Jesus had planned all along to dupe His loyal disciples into believing Him to be the victor over death, finally fleeing away to somewhere in the Himalayas to live out His days in obscurity? The grave clothes discovered by Peter as if His body had simply evaporated? That memorable early morning encounter with Peter and his friends on the shores of Galilee, and even Thomas' confession wrenched from his cynical soul: "My Lord and my God!" (John 20:28). What if it were all a dream?

The resurrection was the consistent testimony of the Gospels, the defining affirmation of the apostles and the early Church. This was the central theme—an inescapable, incontrovertible, indispensable fact: Christ is risen from the dead. To this they bore their testimony with their blood!

Doubt it if you will. The consequence is a gutted gospel, powerless to offer the peace of God or the possibility of transformed lives. And a never-ending stream of witnesses will rise up joyfully and irrepressibly to declare with the Apostle Paul: "But Christ has indeed been raised from the dead!" (I Cor. 15:20).

We heard the thousands of believers crowded into a Beijing church on an Easter morning sing it: "I know that He is living whatever men may say. He lives, Christ Jesus lives today. You ask me how I know He lives; He lives within my heart!" Fifty years of determined denial had not quenched the fire of their faith.

Because Christ is now risen from the dead, we live in the "now" of God's salvation—the day of His grace and favor (2 Cor. 6:1-2). His presence can be real to us. His power can be released within us, by faith.

So many of us are boxed in by circumstances. We are paralyzed by the impossibility of our situation. We have long since exhausted our options. We are in the grip of a "fatal attraction." Addictive behaviors are sapping our strength and destroying our will to freedom. Why dream any longer of what cannot be? There is no way out. No hope.

But now hope lives again in Jesus. Christ is now risen from the dead! The power that burst the bonds that held Him and broke open His tomb to the brilliant light of an Easter morning can open again the airless grave where your dreams may have been entombed.

Paul A. Rader, *The War Cry*

The Magnetism of the Cross

John 1:12

꙰

John records in his Gospel that before yielding up His Spirit, Jesus said, "It is finished!" (John 19:30). In the Greek this is one word, "accomplished."

This is perhaps the boldest exclamation mark in all of Scripture. Nothing more to do—finished! Nothing more we can do—accomplished!

Feel the earthquake. See the splitting of the rocks. Notice the darkness. Witness the separation of the veil of the Temple so all may come directly into the presence of God through Jesus. Finished! Accomplished! His task completed. Philip Bliss has penned it eloquently:

> Lifted up was He to die;
> It is finished! Was his cry!
> Now in Heav'n exalted high;
> Hallelujah! What a Savior!

Magnetic forces are all around us in these days—drugs, alcohol, sexual permissiveness, power plays, the clamor for material things. But the magnetism of the cross pulls men and women from the abyss of sin. This power is triggered by our free will and the surrender of our hearts. He does not violate our freedom to choose.

Jesus speaks of the parish of the cross when He says, "I ... will draw all men" (John 12:32). No geographical limits. No ethnic, racial or socioeconomic barriers. No degree of depravity is beyond Calvary's drawing power. "Yet to all who received Him, to those who believed in His name He gave the right to become children of God" (John 1:12).

We too can be His children in this special way. God says, "I created you, but I want to come into your heart and forgive you, and make you a new creature in Christ so that you can know that promise as your personal experience." Such indescribable suffering and unconditional love requires a response from us. Failure to accept this free and full salvation is like making a visit as nothing but a disinterested tourist to that hill in Jerusalem, allowing all the distractions to claim our attention, thus missing the real purpose of the cross.

At the center of The Salvation Army's crest is the cross, pointing people to the Savior who died upon it. It also symbolizes that all of our service rendered around the world is done in the name and servanthood of Christ.

Robert A. Watson, *The War Cry*

Ressurection Power

Philippians 3:10

Power is a dominating theme of our age. We talk about nuclear power, money power, political power, people power. Men in the corridors of power play the power game, manipulating men and nations. Yes, human power is great. But it fades into insignificance when we consider the power of Christ.

The Scriptures give us a picture of His power. All things were made by Him. By His creative power He gave the hills their shape, the landscape its color and beauty and the animal kingdom its rich variety. He demonstrated His power over nature when He stilled the storm and calmed the raging sea. He showed His power over human nature when He opened the eyes of the blind and made the lame to walk.

But mightiest of all was His power over death when on that first Easter morning He burst the shackles of the grave and overcame death with resurrection power. The words of Paul shared his longing: "I want to know Christ and the power of His resurrection" (Phil. 3:10).

Such power is irresistible. It takes no account of obstacles. Jesus emerging from the tomb found the heavy stone no barrier. He left the grave clothes behind undisturbed. He ignored the Roman guards.

Doesn't life at times seem to hem us in with all kinds of obstacles? Immovable barriers and insurmountable limitations? We just can't be the kind of people we want to be. Sinful habits keep coming back to thwart us. Frustrations and difficulties weigh us down and we feel we can't cope. There is no way we can break through.

But wait! Resurrection power can touch your life. It doesn't have to be defeat and despair. Just as the women who went to the garden in that pre–dawn hour found the massive stone rolled away from the tomb, you can find the resurrection power to overcome your setbacks, your sins.

Symbolically that quiet power, so unlike the world's noisy, explosive variety, we see at work in springtime each year. New life, color, beauty and glory come unobtrusively to the earth after the cold barren death–like time of winter. So the resurrection power of Christ, His quiet force, can bring new beauty and loveliness to your life. As John Gowans has reminded us:

> Out of my darkness He calls me,
>> Out of my doubt, my despair,
> Out of the wastes of my winter,
>> Into the spring of His care.

Eva Burrows, _Salvationist_

From Tragedy to Triumph

1 Corinthians 15:58

The incredible Easter miracle, the bodily resurrection of Jesus Christ, is either the greatest fact of history or it is the greatest fraud ever perpetrated. Our belief in the resurrection is at the very heart of our Christian faith. It is the resurrection that interprets the cross. It transforms what initially appeared to be an irreversible tragedy into a brilliant triumph, the power of God unto salvation.

Unbelievers and opponents have through the centuries attempted to discredit the truth of the resurrection. Of all the theories introduced to disprove it there is none further from the truth than that suggesting it was a hoax perpetrated by the disciples and followers of Jesus. That overlooks one indisputable fact. The followers of Jesus were themselves amazed and astounded by the resurrection, and had to be persuaded that it was true.

Mary Magdalene came first to the tomb. She approached the tomb with concern for a proper burial. She was horrified to find an open tomb. According to the scriptural account, Mary stood outside the tomb weeping. Jesus appeared. Mary did not recognize that the One who spoke to her was Jesus, until He intoned her name. When our name is uttered by the one we love, the source can never be mistaken. When Jesus said, "Mary," she immediately knew it was Jesus. Tears of sorrow changed to tears of joy. All doubts were dispatched and belief in the resurrection instantly infused.

As the disciples met at night behind locked doors, Jesus, no longer bound by earthly limitations, came and stood in their midst. All is changed when Jesus comes. As soon as the disciples saw Jesus they rejoiced and believed. Thomas, absent that night, eight days later came to the inescapable belief when Jesus honored his presumptuous request to see the nail prints in His hand and to put his hand into His side.

The evidence is irrefutable. The overwhelming truth of the resurrection is that it was not planned by men, it was of God. The further resurrection miracle was that out of disillusioned, despondent, defeated and divided disciples was fashioned a force that turned the first century world upside down, that established a church so strong it has endured two thousand years and is a growing, dynamic influence in the world today.

With resurrection faith, we too determine to be "steadfast, unmovable, always abounding in the work of the Lord, for as much as we know that your labor is not in vain in the Lord" (1 Cor. 15:58 NKJV).

James Osborne, *The War Cry*

Try and Try Again!

Hebrews 12:1

Perhaps the story of every winner of fame and fortune in the wide, wide world might be written in these words: "He succeeded because he tried and tried and tried again."

I often try, and fail at the onset. I cannot see, nor hear, nor feel, nor even imagine conquest; more frequently I imagine the very opposite to conquest. The devil or something whispers to me of defeat rather than triumph. But I try again and again, and again, and then I see, I hear and rejoice when the thing is done. So I say, "Go on, my brother; try, my sister. Try again, and you shall conquer."

My comrade, you want a clean heart. You did try for the treasure once. You went to the altar and tried to understand, tried to consecrate, tried to believe, tried to feel, tried to keep hold of God, but you did not succeed; at least, you thought you did not get the blessing, or if you had it you thought you lost it again, and now you say to yourself, "I failed." There is only one thing for you to do and that is to give up reasoning about it, and try again.

You want to see that soul saved—father, mother, brother, sister, son, daughter, husband, wife—someone who is very dear to you. You made an effort on their behalf once; you talked to them, wrote to them, prayed, believed for them, or thought you did. Anyway, you tried hard, really hard, and yet not so very hard, nor so very long, after all, compared with what your Savior did for you. Still, you did try, and you failed; and yet I won't let you call it failure. How do you know what you accomplished? Well, they are not saved. What ought you to do?

There is only one thing you can do. Try again.

Look to your aim. Is it in God's plan that you should have it? Is it for the welfare of someone else? Is it within the circle of the atoning blood? Is it a pleasing object to the Almighty? Then make your resolution, see to your faith, sharpen your sword, throw away your scabbard, summon heaven and earth to your help, make a death-struggle of it, and try, and try, and try again, and again, and again, and you shall overcome as Jesus overcame and sit down with Him on the Conqueror's Throne and wear the victor's crown.

William Booth, *The Warrior's Daily Portion*

"Peace Be With You"

John 20:21

To describe life as bleak and gloomy would have been an understatement. For the followers of Jesus the future seemed completely hopeless. Their Master had been put to death.

Then the Bible states: "On the evening of the first day of the week Jesus came and stood among them and said, 'Peace be with you'" (John 20:19). What the disciples needed more than anything was reassurance and peace of mind and heart.

To that greeting Jesus added a significant gesture: He showed them His hands and side, the hands that had been wounded by the nails at His crucifixion, the side that had been pierced by the spear of the Roman soldier. The gesture was a sign of identification, but it also carries another message. It speaks about the basis, the foundation upon which the peace of Jesus is built, the peace which He offers to His followers. It speaks of the price at which that peace was bought.

We are promised the peace of Jesus, founded on His perfect work, His life, death and resurrection. What a foundation! Nothing can shake it!

When a Christian lives daily in the atmosphere of constant trust and obedience, he will experience the blessing of our Lord's peace. The Apostle Paul wrote: "Let the peace of Christ rule in your hearts, since as members of one body you were called to peace" (Col. 3:15). The word translated "rule" could also be rendered "to be a referee." So when a Christian is in difficulty or a dilemma, it is his privilege to call on the peace of Christ to be the referee of his troubled heart.

"Peace be with you," was the greeting Jesus gave His fearful disciples. In fact, He uttered those words twice. When He repeated the greeting, He added a commission: "As the Father has sent Me, I am sending you" (John 20:21).

The peace He offered His followers was not given for their selfish enjoyment. A great task awaited them. They were to be His witnesses to the world. Most of them would be martyred for His sake. In order to be strong and faithful they needed a stabilizing force in their lives. They needed His own peace, the peace that filled His own heart, in life's varied testings.

The peace of Christ, won through a fierce battle, is promised to His followers for the battle against evil, the battle for the kingdom of God. Let us open our hearts and lives and receive the gift of His peace, and then fearlessly go forth with the good news: Jesus lives and saves!

Jarl Wahlström, *The War Cry*

Knowing Jesus

Colossians 2:2–3

What an astonishing thing that we can know Jesus! This is an age of specialists, when men devote their lives to the pursuit of special departments of knowledge. One learned professor will give fourteen hours a day for forty years to the study of fish, another to the study of birds, and yet another to that of bugs. Another, more ambitious, devotes his life to the study of history and the rise and fall of nations, and yet another to astronomy, the origin and history of worlds.

But to know Jesus Christ is infinitely better than to know all that has been learned or dreamed of by these professors, for He it was who made the worlds, and "without Him nothing was made that has been made" (John 1:3).

Personally, I am inclined to think that to know Edison would be worth more than knowing one or all of his works, and so to know Jesus Christ is the first and best of all knowledge.

The knowledge of the naturalist, the astronomer, the historian, may be of passing value, but in due time it will be antedated and fail. But the knowledge of Jesus Christ is of infinite value and will never pass away. It is profitable for this world, and for that which is to come, and only by it does a man come to the knowledge of himself, without which it would be better never to have been born.

In this knowledge of Jesus is hidden the germ of all knowledge, for Paul tells us that in Him "are hidden all the treasures of wisdom and knowledge" (Col. 2:3). Am I eager for learning and knowledge? Let me then constantly seek to know Him, and in due time, in this world or in the next, I shall know all that is of value for me to know.

In this knowledge lies true culture of both head and heart, especially of the heart. How then shall we come to the knowledge of Jesus?

We must utterly and forever renounce sin and seek forgiveness for past bad conduct. But we must not only renounce our sins, we must also renounce self. Jesus gave Himself for us; we must give ourselves for Him.

This knowledge, to be maintained, must be cultivated, which is done by communion with Him. Secret prayer must often bring the soul face to face with Him, and the Bible, God's record of Him, must be daily, diligently and lovingly searched and faithfully applied to daily life. Thus shall we know Him.

Samuel Logan Brengle, *Heart Talks on Holiness*

Supper in Emmaus

Luke 24:32

George Eliot called it "the loveliest story in the world." But what is it that makes the Emmaus story so beautiful?

First, you have a country road and a country village. You have two ordinary people—not members of the Eleven. Only one of them, Cleopas, is named. You have an earnest invitation to share in a very frugal meal. And that is all. Yet out of these commonplace threads is woven a story that has thrilled people for 2,000 years.

Walking down that Emmaus Road were two dispirited travelers. For them the thoroughfare could not be measured in miles; it stretched from bewilderment to heartbreak, from bitter disappointment to disillusionment.

As Cleopas and his companion trudged homeward, the death of Jesus, which was certain, and His possible resurrection, which was manifestly uncertain, were the only subjects of discussion. And while they reasoned on them, "Jesus Himself came up and walked along with them" (Luke 24:15)

The first thing He does for these two who thought their precious dream had faded, that death had taken charge, was to open to them the Scriptures. During the walk, not only the Scriptures, but hearts, were opened. "Were not our hearts burning within us while He talked with us on the road and opened the Scriptures to us?" (Luke 24:32).

It was an experience that His listeners did not want to end. The day was melting into evening and they begged Him to stay. In these twilight moments, while the three supped together, the room was suffused with burning glory. Suddenly the two villagers were dazzled by the awareness that the stranger to whom they had offered hospitality was none other than the risen Lord! Truly alive! As quickly as they recognized their royal guest, so quickly did He vanish from their sight. Pieces of the broken bread were still there on the table. And while the two sat in stunned silence, the room still echoed the sound of His blessing.

The appearance of the resurrected Jesus had to be reported at once to the Eleven in Jerusalem. While only hours earlier their footsteps had dragged along a weary road, now their feet fairly flew. They were bearers of the best news of all: "He is risen!"

The most commonplace walk, the dustiest road, the lowliest home and the most ordinary people can be filled with radiant glory, if the living Lord draws near and takes preeminence. The burning heart, surely, is a supreme need of every individual who names the name of Christ.

Arnold Brown, *With Christ at the Table*

The Light of the World

John 8:12

The world needs light. It cannot exist or survive without it. The world without Christ is a world of darkness. Without Christ the world is in philosophical darkness. He alone is the fulfillment of the philosopher's quest. Without Christ the world is in sociological darkness. He alone teaches the higher laws of love that contribute to true brotherhood and peace. Without Christ the world is in spiritual darkness. He alone can save man from the dark night of sin.

Light is the great revealer. The most beautiful flowers, the most majestic mountains are obscured in inky blackness until they are rescued from the night and bathed in the sunlight.

At the Academia in Florence, Italy, are Michelangelo's great works of sculpture, including his magnificent *David*. Also on exhibit are unfinished statuary which revealed by their chisel marks the method of Michelangelo's sculpting. His concept was that he unveiled what was already in the marble, cutting away the superfluities, giving to the world his *Pieta* or an angel that he saw in a rough piece of marble. Christ releases from its imprisoned splendor the divine qualities within a life and reveals by His light the otherwise hidden glory and beauty of the divine imprint.

Light permeates. It travels at its phantom speed of 186,000 miles a second. It is unhindered by space and time. Christ transcends the barriers of time and space. He is nearer than our dearest one on earth.

Light is pure. Water may start out as a pure spring but too soon it becomes impure when it comes close to man's habitations. The wind and air become contaminated with man's toxic chemicals. But light may shine through the most foul medium and yet remain impeccably pure. Christ mingled amid earth's moral pollution and yet remained pure.

Jesus said to His disciples, "I am the light of the world," (John 8:12) and "You are the light of the world" (Matt. 5:14). How do we reconcile these two sayings?

Every student of astronomy knows that there are two orders of luminaries. There is that which is its own source of light. The sun is of this order. Then there is the luminary which catches and reflects light from another source. The moon is that kind of luminary. Without the light of the sun it would be a sterile, dark ball in a midnight sky. But catching the radiance of the sun, it becomes a glowing, luminous body up in our sky.

Our light is a borrowed ray from the Son of Righteousness. And our lives can catch His radiance and reflect it in a darkened world.

Henry Gariepy, *Portraits of Christ*

Send Out Thy Light

Psalm 43:3

Send out Thy light and Thy truth, Lord,
 Into my heart let them shine;
Here while I'm waiting in faith, Lord,
 Hark to this pleading of mine.
 Search now my heart, do not spare it,
 Pour in Thy Spirit's pure light;
Tell me the truth I will bear it,
 Hide not the worst from my sight.

Savior, my all I will bring;
 How can I offer Thee less?
Widely the doors now I fling,
 Come and Thy temple possess.

Send out Thy light, let it lead me,
 Bring me to Thy holy hill;
When from all sin thou hast freed me,
 I shall delight in Thy will.
Jesus, Thy wounding is tender,
 Kind is the light that reveals,
Waiting until I surrender,
 Pouring the balm then that heals.

Fullness of joy in Thy presence,
 Bliss at Thy side evermore,
This is the life that I enter,
 Now that my struggles are o'er.
When with Thy Spirit's rich treasure
 My earthen vessel is stored,
Mine is the service of pleasure,
 Thine all the glory, dear Lord.

Ruth Tracy, *The Salvation Army Song Book*

The Christian Armor

Ephesians 6:10–18

Paul's passion heats up in the closing chapter of Ephesians. He is about to end his letter and must make one last strong attempt to convey his message. What image will best explain the Christian's duty in God's divine plan?

The chain that binds Paul to the guard is cumbersome, allowing the prisoner to take only a few short strides in either direction. Perhaps he pauses at the end of the chain's reach and gives the soldier a penetrating glance. There it is, the metaphor that will clinch his argument: "Put on the full armor of God so that you can take your stand against the devil's schemes" (Eph. 6:11).

Paul describes two distinct spheres: first, the dark world, malevolent forces on the attack from within. These could include the temptations of money, sex and power. The second realm is a heavenly one. Paul implies that Satan himself would war against the Christian. He alludes to the devil's ability to dwell beyond the confines of this world. Either sphere portends danger and calls for the Christian's full protection. The full armor of God is not for special occasions only; it is an everyday necessity.

"Stand firm then, with the belt of truth buckled around your waist," (Eph. 6:14) Paul writes. He likely lists it first to underscore that we need the truth because our enemy is a liar and the "father of lies" (John 8:44).

The breastplate reminds us that Christ's righteousness can guard our hearts from all evil. Paul's metaphor leaves out any protective gear for the soldier's back. There can be no retreating from the war, only steady advance, shielded by faith. "Take the shield of faith," writes Paul, "with which you can extinguish all the flaming arrows of the evil one" (Eph. 6:16).

Training his gaze on the soldier's gear, Paul calls his readers to stand firm "with your feet fitted with the readiness that comes from the gospel of peace" (Eph. 6:15). The "helmet of salvation" (Eph 6:17) referred to reminds us that salvation provides not only forgiveness for past sins but also strength to deal with all future attacks of sin.

Now Paul comes to the greatest weapon of all, prayer. Paul makes it clear that the twin disciplines of prayer and Bible study will enable the Christian to advance into the battle for righteousness and to be protected in enemy attack. "Take the ... sword of the Spirit, which is the Word of God. And pray in the Spirit on all occasions" (Eph. 6:17–18). Let God's armor protect you in the fight!

Marlene Chase, *The War Cry*

Four Ground Rules

2 Timothy 2:5

No new believer ever progressed to any great extent without paying attention to some basic rules. Years ago a young Christian minister called Timothy was reminded of this. More experienced in the faith than his young friend, the Apostle Paul wrote to him a few basics of the Christian life. He likened it to running as a training athlete in a race: "If anyone competes as an athlete, he does not receive the victor's crown unless he competes according to the rules" (2 Tim. 2:5).

God's chief way of communicating His will for you is through the Scriptures. A Christian who neglects the Scriptures will soon grow spiritually feeble. The Bible is God's instrument for speaking truth to you. At the same time, it is a sword in your own hand to use in battle when your soul is besieged by the forces of evil and the world (Eph. 6:17).

For this reason, carve out time on a regular basis to read it. Read it prayerfully, first asking God to speak to you as you read and to enlighten you by His Holy Spirit. Remember there is a difference between reading the Scriptures for inspiration and studying them for information. Both approaches are valid.

Prayer is exercise for the soul. It keeps you spiritually fit. Neglect it, and you grow flabby and listless. Jesus was a man of prayer. If He needed spiritual exercise through praying, how much more do we! We can approach God at any hour, day or night. The whole tone of a Christian's life should be a prayerful one.

It is important that you become part of a Christian worshipping community. This gives you a setting for regularly worshipping God, hearing the Scriptures read and explained through the preaching, praying in the company of other believers and drawing strength through good fellowship. It also gives you an opportunity to make a contribution to the life of the church, the body of Christ on earth.

Everyone I have met who has just come into a new knowledge of the Lord has expressed an instinctive desire to do something for Him. Nothing could be more natural. It is a loving and grateful response to the realization of all that Jesus has done for us at Calvary to save us from our sins.

Shaw Clifton, *Never the Same Again*

A Crisis and A Process

Philippians 3:12

The question is sometimes debated whether the experience of holiness is gained instantly or gradually. The answer is that the life of holiness is both a crisis and a process. There can be no experience without a beginning, but no beginning can be maintained without growth.

First there must be a beginning. There arises an awareness of personal need which draws a man on to an act of full surrender. The forgiven soul awakes to the truth that forgiveness is not enough. Blessed is the man whose iniquity is forgiven—but that act of divine grace arouses in him a longing to be like the One to whom he owes his forgiveness.

Or the beauty of holiness as seen in another life may awaken this desire. Here is the magic of Christian love shining in other eyes and the light of Christian joy illuminating another face. What could be more inviting? True Christian living not only *is* good but *looks* good. Grace and charm are never far apart.

The life that is wholly forgiven needs to be wholly possessed. And to be fully possessed requires a full surrender. Need, of which I am made conscious by a variety of reasons, may drive me to my knees in total surrender.

God's answer is to grant me of His Spirit according to my capacity to receive. In faith believing I receive of His Spirit. That is the beginning.

The beginning, but not the end. This is the commencement of the life of holiness, not its crown. And a start loses all meaning unless there is a continuance.

The crisis must be followed by a process. In the initial act of surrender I receive the fullness of the Spirit according to my capacity to receive. But that capacity grows with receiving—as a bandsman's facility to play grows with playing, or to speak with speaking or to follow his craft by practicing it. I learn by doing, not less in matters of the heart than of the hands. A full surrender is the beginning of the life of holy living; the end of that experience I do not—I cannot—see. There's a long, long trail a-winding between start and finish.

At no point is the believer ever as good as he can be. Ever must there be growth in grace, and every day of growth will prepare the way for days of further growth. Just as the longer a musician practices his art, the more sensitive becomes his ear to any untunefulness, so the closer a believer draws to Christ, the more sensitive will he become to anything un-Christlike.

Frederick Coutts, *The Call To Holiness*

Perfect Love

1 Thessalonians 3:13

There are various titles for holiness, that experience between man and God. We sometimes call it "entire sanctification," "filled with the Spirit," "full salvation." The description that I like is "perfect love."

Love is a tremendously important ingredient in the living of life. Psychiatrists and psychologists tell us that until we know how to rightly love one another, and to rightly be loved, we're warped, bent out of shape. You listen to today's song lyrics and you'll often find the word "love" mentioned. I agree sometimes it's distorted, sullied love, but it's echoing the cry of the human heart for that which God would plant within every one of us.

It's very evident that human love isn't meeting the need today. We often hear of "man's inhumanity to man." You don't have to go to some far–flung battlefield to find the inhumaneness of man. It's all around us. Pick up your newspaper; listen to the news.

Only the perfect love of God will meet every need and longing of the human heart. The perfect love of God is the absolute solution to interpersonal problems of every kind—husband and wife, parents and children, brothers and sisters, in the fellowship in the church, in the neighborhood where you live, in the place where you work, where you go to school.

Our Lord says, "A new command I give you: love one another. As I have loved you, so you must love one another" (John 13:34). How do you achieve that? Don't you earn it? Don't you merit it? Ah, we must remember that our love could never do that, never. It's His love that we must have; that will enable us to do it. So what He is commanding is that we be filled with His perfect love. And then we too will love one another, regardless of how we're treated. For we read, "God has poured out His love into our hearts by the Holy Spirit" (Rom. 5:5).

God's Word tells us something strange about this perfect love. Paul, in writing to the Christians in Thessalonica, lets them know that this perfect love can be increased: "May the Lord make your love increase and overflow for each other" (1 Thess. 3:12). Now, if something is perfect, and it has filled your soul, how can it increase? And yet that's what the Scripture is saying. For the Lord has a miraculous way of increasing the capacity of the soul to be more and more filled with His love.

As we walk with the Lord, and as we grow in grace, and as He develops our spiritual capacities, He keeps filling us with His perfect love.

Clifton Sipley, *The Salvationist Pulpit*

What Things?

Luke 24:18–19

Cleopas on the Emmaus Road is astonished that anyone coming from the direction of Jerusalem should be in ignorance of the trial and death of Jesus, with the defeat of His cause. Almost petulantly he answers the inquiry about the cause of his sadness. "Don't you know the things that have happened?"

The question is like the despairing gesture of a defeated, disillusioned and hopeless man. All was lost. Their leader was fallen. Their hopes had gone with him into the grave. How can anyone come from the scene of such tragic events and yet know so little of their grief and disappointment? But the third traveler who had joined them did nothing to allay the incredulity of the other two, when He quietly countered, "What things?" (Luke 24:19).

Yet He was in fact the principal sufferer, the cause and the center of "the things which had come to pass." He was Himself the pain–racked sufferer at the heart of "these things." Yet, with the empty grave behind Him, the agony past, and a vision that put time and eternity in true proportion, He quietly put the sufferings in the light of His victory, with the wonderful words, "What things?"

Was there ever a more astonishing and glorious question? With simple dignity, and yet supreme authority, He takes hold of the dictates of evil and thrusts them into the background. The leers and jeers, the barbaric cruelties, the scorching lashes, the mockery, the crimson robe, the ridiculous reed, the spiteful crown, the heavy cross, the shrieking maledictions, the stripping and the shame, the death walk of the condemned, the nailing and the railing, as He went down into death! "What things?" Yes, indeed, who knows the answer but He who suffered "these things."

All too often, we who are His disciples permit ourselves to be dominated by the things that happen. These little words tyrannize us and make our lives a journey along heartbreak road.

As we journey along the road, running away from the world of our broken dreams, One draws near and walks with us. We tell Him the things that are troubling us. Quietly, strongly, with the tones of boundless love and limitless power, our Lord replies, "What things?" and just that direct and simple question dispels our fears, restores our peace.

On your Emmaus Road, you will find Him walking by your side. As He speaks, instead of being obsessed by "these things" you will, as those of old, go forth with a living word of witness, "We have seen the Lord!" (John 20:25).

Albert Orsborn, *The War Cry*

There's A Price Tag

Luke 14:27

～

Remember the Mother Goose rhyme about Simple Simon? He's the one who met the pie man and asked for a sample. The pie man said, "Show me first your penny." Or as we might say, "There's a price tag on it."

Jesus said this about Christian discipleship. "No one can be My disciple who does not carry his own cross and follow Me. But don't begin until you count the cost" (Luke 14:27, 28 TLB).

There's a price tag on life. Whether at its beginning or end or at any point in between, life costs something. The world offers many desirable, fascinating things. Impulsively we say, "That's for me! I'll have a big helping of that!" Then comes the unavoidable demand, "First your penny!" Health, peace, liberty, reputation, all of these and much more demand prior and continuing payment. There's a price tag on everything.

There's a price tag on achievement. To master a musical instrument, or to sing well requires long hours of diligent study and patient practice. To get a good education, to excel in some sport, to be a leader in a profession or in the arts, every worthwhile thing demands payment in industry, self–discipline and perseverance. Some of us do no more than window shop. We see the price tag and don't want to pay what it costs.

There's a price tag on religion. Jesus dispelled any illusions of an easy, cheap, pie–in–the–sky sort of discipleship when He said, "If any man would come after Me, he must deny himself and take up his cross daily and follow Me" (Luke 9:23). A satisfying relationship with God will cost the surrender of every known wrong, every conflicting love, every doubtful practice. Time and effort must also be spent in cultivating the things of the Spirit. Salvation is of such surpassing value that whatever it costs us it is still a gift. It cost Heaven's best, the self–giving of the Son of God.

Whether we choose the best or the worst, we pay for it. The best Christian you know chooses to be a servant of Jesus Christ and pays for it. Some people choose to be slaves to their appetites and they pay for it. We take what we want and pay for it.

May we so live as to be satisfied and benefitted with what we are paying for.

Bramwell Tripp, *To the Point*

Sanctified Wholly

1 Thessalonians 5:23

It seems to me that there is a large amount of uncertainly abroad among us on the subject of holiness. I have no new truth to set forth; the doctrine is as old as the Book.

Holiness to the Lord is to us a fundamental truth; it stands in the front ranks of our doctrines. We inscribe it upon our banners. Holiness in its broad significance means separation from all unrighteousness and consecration to God. It means that the soul is brought into a state in which it has both the liberty and the ability to serve God as He desires and that it constantly does so.

In the early stages of Christian experience this deliverance is only partial. Although the soul is delivered from the domination and power of sin, and is no longer the slave of sin, still there are the remains of the carnal mind which trouble the soul, often lead it into sin, and which, if not continually fought against and kept under, bring the soul again into bondage. Nevertheless in this state the soul, when faithful, has peace with God, the guidance, energy and witness of the Holy Spirit, which together create in the soul a blessed certainty of salvation, and a joy which is unspeakable and full of glory. All this is, however, perfectly compatible with the conscious existence of sin in the soul.

There are three broad relations in which a man can stand toward sin. He can be, firstly, under sin; secondly, over sin; and thirdly, without sin.

He can be under sin. He is not only exposed to the penalty which God has in infinite wisdom and benevolence attached to the transgression of that law, but he is under its power. Even when enlightened to see its cruel and ruinous character, and yearning for deliverance, he is powerless to free himself from its iron grip. He is a slave to the tyrant; he is under sin.

He can be over sin. It may be that the pride, anger, lust or whatsoever other evils ruled him with a rod of iron before, may be there. Bruised and broken and faint they may be, but still they exist; but the Master has taken them from the throne of the soul and has been given power over them. He is now no longer under sin, but under grace. The old habits and tempers and tendencies can still make their presence felt, but they are no longer the masters.

But there is another state, and that is without sin. In this experience, Paul's prayer for the Thessalonians (1 Thess. 5:23), and through them for all saints, is answered. The God of peace sanctifies wholly, and the whole body, soul and spirit are preserved blameless.

William Booth, *Salvation Soldiery*

Divine Fire–Power

Acts 2:3

ॐ

We learn to have a healthy respect for fire from an early age, recognizing just how powerful it is. Primitive people regarded it with awe and reverence. Perhaps this underlies the fact that in Scripture fire is used as a symbol of God the Holy Spirit.

The first occasion we read of God's making His presence known through fire is when He appears to Moses as a flame coming from the middle of a burning bush (Exod. 3). As a shepherd, Moses had perhaps seen tinder–dry brushwood burst into spontaneous combustion in the blazing heat. But this bush was different because it did not burn up.

Having used this unusual fire to make Moses aware of Him, God revealed His plan for the children of Israel under Moses' leadership. Then, as they traveled through the wilderness, God announced His presence with them each night by a pillar of fire.

Further in Israelite history, when their loyalty to God was under test, He revealed Himself on Mount Carmel as the true God. As he did so, flames burnt up the water–drenched sacrifice that Elijah had prepared.

So when John the Baptist announced that one was coming who would "baptize you with the Holy Spirit and fire," Jewish listeners would have understood the symbolism.

It is from the Greek word for fire that the English word "pure" is derived. In industry fire can be used in the refining and purifying processes. Anyone who has had a splinter in his finger knows that it needs a little persuasion to come out. So it's into the sewing box and out with the needle! But first the needle should be sterilized, purified—by holding it in a flame.

When Isaiah had his vision of God in the Temple, he soon realized that he was sinful and that his life needed purifying. Burning coals were lifted from the altar and placed on his lips to symbolize the purification of his life. As with Isaiah, God wants to use us as His messengers, to bring others into His kingdom. But first of all we need to be purified.

The quality of our spiritual life depends on the fire of the Holy Spirit within us. At Pentecost, what looked like tongues of fire rested on each of the disciples' heads. This divine fire–power cleansed them and clothed them. It gave those ordinary men and women extraordinary power.

Quite simply, there is no power other than the Holy Spirit's which can turn men inside out and the world upside down!

Nigel Bovey, *Salvationist*

A Prayer of Turning

Isaiah 52:7

Father of mercies, God of peace, You have sent me, as my Lord was sent, into a world sick with hate. He proclaimed peace. He put hostility to death through the cross. I too would dare to be a peacemaker. Forgive me of my indifference.

The subtle savagery of racism is consuming my brothers and sisters. I have been silent at their suffering, the inequities, the humiliations, the murder of their children's dreams.

You have ever stood by me, but I have not stood by them. I have not fought against their exclusion and exploitation. I have not struggled to my own hurt. Nor have I embraced the underclass of strangers: the mentally infirm, the disabled, the AIDS afflicted, the incarcerated, those I tend to distrust, to disdain or ignore.

Father of mercies, faltering and weak my labor has been. Have mercy.

Jesus, Son of God, Savior, You came into our neighborhood to bring good news to the poor, to bind up hearts that are broken, to proclaim liberty and favor with God. I too would be a mender of broken things. By your wounds we are healed, and by them we heal.

Jesus, You know the torment of the sinned–against. The refugees of our cursed wards, the famished, the maimed, the dispossessed, the 25,000 who die daily for want of clean drinking water, the one hundred million street children. You keep company with the defenseless among the poorest, the lowliest and the lost.

And I? Faltering and weak my labor has been. Jesus, forgive.

Holy Spirit, Pursuer of the prodigal, insistent Friend, I too would be a winner of souls. Blow into a flame the gift of God within me.

Missionary Spirit, faltering and weak my labors have been. Forgive.

Fit me for soldiership in an Army fully alive in Christ, pure in heart, united in purpose, aflame with a passion for God and souls, ready to take a stand for truth and justice, empowered by the Spirit.

Lyell M. Rader, Jr., *The War Cry*

God's Shepherds

1 Peter 5:2–4

꙳

The Gospel narrative records that "When [Jesus] saw the crowds He had compassion on them, because they were harassed and helpless, like sheep without a shepherd" (Matt. 9:36).

The picture of the shepherd with his sheep is woven into the Bible's language and imagery. Flocks of sheep blanket Judea's central plateau that stretches 35 miles from Bethel to Hebron. In biblical times, as today, the most familiar figure of the Judean uplands was the shepherd.

The shepherd's life was hard. He was never off duty. No flock ever grazed without a shepherd. The shepherd's lonely task was constant and dangerous. Besides protecting his sheep from physical danger, the shepherd had to guard against wild animals. And there were always thieves ready to steal the sheep. The shepherd maintained constant vigilance, fearless courage and patient love so his flock would survive and prosper.

God entrusts church leaders, whether lay or clergy, as shepherds of His people. The Greek word for shepherd, *poimain*, reveals that the shepherd is one who feeds and nurtures the flock. Peter admonishes Christian leaders to be shepherds and examples to the flock.

First century shepherds had four indispensable pieces of equipment. Essential to the shepherd was his script—a bag made of animal skin in which he carried his food, typically bread, dried fruit, olives and cheese, all needed to remain physically strong.

Each shepherd treasured his custom-made sling. In the hands of a competent shepherd, a sling became a lethal weapon. This versatile device served as an instrument of offense and defense.

The third essential tool was the shepherd's rod, a short, wooden club often studded with nails. The rod aided the shepherd in defending himself and his flock against beasts and robbers.

The shepherd's final requisite equipment has become symbolic of his vocation—the staff. With his staff he could retrieve any sheep that had strayed from the flock.

The biblical picture of the shepherd illustrates the Christian leader's responsibility to love, nurture and guide those under his or her care. The trustworthy leader of God's children follows his Lord's example, the One who for each of us became the Good Shepherd.

William Francis, *The War Cry*

The Message of Hope

1 John 3:14

In one of the most sensitive moments of my life, I learned the glory and strength of Easter. My mother, a brave little Salvation Army warrior, went to be with the Lord early in April of 1946. I was still in the United States Navy, looking forward to discharge and returning to my calling as a Salvation Army officer.

A well-meaning comrade said to me, "Andrew, it must be very sad for you that your mother would have been promoted to Glory right at Easter time, just before your own return to service as an officer." Then it was that I knew the reality of all the theology I had been taught about the meaning of Easter.

Her promotion to Glory helped me understand and unlock for myself the mystery, marvel, strength and compassion of the Savior's willingness to die for me and to live again so that I could always understand the rich meaning of the resurrected Christ. I knew then, as I know now, that death does not conquer the Christian, but that through Christ, the Christian conquers death.

I knew then, as I know now, that we who love the Savior are born again, never to die, but to live eternally.

The glorious, practical message of Easter is not only that Christ Jesus came into the world and lived a perfect life and gave us precept and example, not only that the Master was willing to share His very life so that our sins might be forgiven, but an even greater message, that the Savior rose again. And because He rose, we, too, can live—not simply live out the days of our years, but live eternally with Him. Our souls, our spirits, will never die. This eternal message of Easter was implanted that day in my heart.

I wept as I bowed my head at that funeral service, but not as those without hope. I wept with joy that the lady I had called mother would always live and live forever by the tender mercies of a loving, heavenly Father who taught us this lesson by the sacrifice and resurrection of His Son for all mankind.

"But Christ has indeed been raised from the dead" (1 Cor. 15:20). Jesus Christ rose! Jesus Christ lives! Because He lives, we too shall live, eternally! Hallelujah!

Andrew S. Miller, *The War Cry*

The Second Coming of Christ

Acts 1:11

Astronaut James Irwin, Commander of Apollo 15, shared that while walking on the moon and looking out at planet Earth, suspended in space like an iridescent jewel, the thought came to him that this moment, man walking on the moon, was the greatest event in the history of the world. Then he adds that the Lord whispered to his heart, saying, "I did something greater than that—I walked on the earth!"

Stand with me on the tiptoes of your mind and contemplate the awesome wonder of the God whose power is flaunted by orbiting spheres, unveiling His love in the Babe of Bethlehem. Think of it—God, walking the earth in sandals!

The coming of Christ into the world is the most stupendous event of human history. That first Advent of our Lord is the marvel of the ages.

When we hear the news of our day, we say, "The worst is yet to come." But when we read the Bible, we say, "The best is yet to be." God's Word declares that the most colossal event of history is yet to come!

The promise of the Second Coming of our Lord runs as a golden thread throughout the Bible.

We put our ear and heart close to the door of the Upper Room on the night before the crucifixion. The immortal words of our Lord float as soft music through the night air. "Do not let your hearts be troubled ... I will come back and take you to be with me" (John 14:1–3). Jesus, in His last will and testament to His followers, bequeathed the precious promise that He will return and take us to be forever with Him.

Further on in the New Testament narrative, we read where, on the Mount of Olives, without the aid of booster rockets or computers, our Lord defies the law of gravity and ascends into the heavens. As 500 onlookers stand in wide-eyed wonder, the angelic messenger announces: "This same Jesus, who has been taken from you into heaven, will come back in the same way you have seen him go into heaven" (Acts 1:11).

Throughout the New Testament no less than 318 references, one of every 30 verses, assert the return of Jesus Christ. We turn to the very last page of the Bible, and read the final recorded words of Jesus to His followers of all ages. No fewer than three times He affirms the peerless promise (Rev. 22:7,12,20), His final words being, "Yes, I am coming soon."

The Second Coming is the most precious promise yet to be fulfilled for the believer. Jesus is coming again! Let us be ready.

Henry Gariepy, *The Salvationist Pulpit*

A Portrait of Love's Obedience

Revelation 13:8

In a commanding voice the Lord instructed Abraham to offer his only son Isaac as a burnt offering (Gen. 22:1–15). The message was clear and has significance for us as a portrait of love's obedience.

If ever an account so clearly parallels the sacrifice of Jesus Christ, it is this. Significant beyond its time, the record was not kept simply as a trial of faith for one man. Affirming the historical and religious importance of that event is, in the midst of a mosque in Jerusalem, the rock upon which Isaac lay beneath the point of Abraham's dagger.

Isaac was Abraham's life, the heir apparent to his father's treasures. "Take now your son," (Gen. 22:2) said the Lord. No comforting preamble, just a succession of statements, ending with one command. Isaac must be sacrificed!

The burnt offering of Hebrew animal sacrifices became known as the "holocaust"—an offering totally consumed and ascending in the smoke of its altar fire. Such an offering connotes complete consecration to God.

Steadily up the steeps of Mount Moriah, Abraham ascended toward the rocky summit. That moment is symbolic to Christ's walk toward His crucifixion. Abraham and Isaac simply prefigured the provision by God as Christ became "the Lamb that was slain from the creation of the world" (Rev. 13:8).The experience of both Isaac and Jesus is filled with holocaustal meaning. Each walked on a Via Dolorosa (Way of Sorrow). Each would have its peculiar altar and fire, offerer and victim. But in Abraham's case the angel of the Lord, satisfied with Abraham's obedience and Isaac's submission, halted the process by saying, "Do not lay a hand on the boy ... Now I know you fear God, because you have not withheld from me your son, your only son" (Gen 22:12).

In Jesus' case God the Father, satisfied with His Son's gracious love, accepted Him, with no one else to stand in His place. Jesus' life was offered with the only words that would finalize the essential act: "It is finished!" (John 19:30).

The crucifixion event culminates in the verse: "For God so loved the world that He gave His one and only Son, that whoever believes in Him shall not perish but have eternal life" (John 3:16).

David Laeger, *The War Cry*

Our Words and God's Word

Romans 1:17

It is a source of joy to remember that in the midst of our humanity God's word breaks in on our words and grips us in a way that human words do not.

Our initial relationship to the Bible is that of faith. By faith we accept the Bible as the Word of God to us. I have a simple definition for faith which has been helpful to me through the years. Faith is taking everything you know about yourself and committing it to everything you know about God. Every time we pick up the Bible to read it, we are acting on faith.

Martin Luther's life well illustrates this commitment of faith. Luther, above all, wanted to find God, and he began his journey as a monk, trusting falsely in salvation by works. In 1510 he traveled to Rome by foot, a distance of 800 miles, and in the basilica of St. John Lateran he ascended on his knees the sacred stairs believed to have been trod by Jesus in Jerusalem. Surely, he thought, he would find God in Rome by such acts of contrition. But Luther left Rome a disappointed and disillusioned man. He next turned to scholasticism, and then to ruminations about the doctrine of election, still without assurance.

But in 1514, reading in Romans, his eyes fell on 1:17: "The righteous will live by faith." Luther's tortured pilgrimage ended. All was settled. He knew himself as a child of God by grace. God's Word spoke to him clearly through the Bible. Luther came to know both himself and his Christ through the Word of God, and he was obedient to that Word.

The heart of our relationship to the Bible is our realization that Jesus Christ is the center of Scripture and the focus of the Christian faith. The lasting value of the written Word, the Bible, is that it points as an everlasting sign to the enfleshed Word, Jesus Christ, the center of Scripture.

What results from our relationship with the Bible? One word will do—obedience. The sure mark of the Christian is not spirituality. Martin Luther and John Wesley demonstrated intense spirituality before they were saved. The clear sign that we are Christians is that we obey the Word of God. William Booth wrote: "I want to see a new translation of the Bible into the hearts and conduct of men and women."

We approach the Bible by faith. The heart of our relationship to the Bible rests in the recognition that Jesus Christ is the central Word in God's Word. And the result of our relationship to the Bible is to act out obediently and ethically the mandate of that Word.

Roger J. Green, *The Salvationist Pulpit*

Hedges

2 Corinthians 5:15

I saw it so clearly, Lord,
Through the words of one of your servants.

I have built hedges around my life
    without realizing it.
    Higher and higher they have grown
    without my knowledge.

These hedges have shut others out and myself in.
    It was comfortable, so comfortable and cozy.
    Less demanded of me,
    less expected of me, only myself to consider.

I have hedged about my time. My time!
Did I create time to be my own?
Have I sovereign right to twenty-four hours a day?
Is not each hour a token of Your grace?

I have hedged about my leisure,
    My free time is my own, I have said,
    and I have miserly gloated over it,
    resenting any encroachment upon it.

I have hedged about my love.
    These, and these only, I care for,
    my nearest, my dearest, my friends,
    all precious because they are mine.

Forgive me, Lord. Forgive my selfish living,
    my disregard of others.
Help me to tear down the high hedges I have built
and in their place to plant an open garden.
    Then I can look out
    and others can look in
and we shall be drawn nearer to one another.

Flora Larsson, *Just A Moment, Lord*

Apples of Gold

Proverbs 25:11

My "country aunt" was my favorite when I was a child. Not that her city counterparts weren't wonderful people whom I loved, but Aunt Dina embodied a kind of natural beauty and order that I found especially attractive.

The time-honored practice of sitting down to the table at mealtime was a habit she refused to abandon, even in later years when that custom was challenged. She brings to mind a white linen tablecloth stretched and ironed to perfection, real cloth napkins carefully folded, and clean, sparkling dinnerware. Aunt Dina's table always featured some centerpiece of grace and beauty.

Her favorite centerpiece was a silver basket-like bowl reserved for special occasions. From one of the several fruit trees on the farm she chose five of the most perfect golden apples, polished them with beeswax and placed them artfully in the bowl. Generally, the top apple retained a pinkish blush and two or three of its own dark green leaves. The effect was one of perfection and simple elegance.

"A word aptly spoken is like apples of gold in settings of silver" (Prov. 25:11). Whether the writer of Proverbs had such a centerpiece in mind when he wrote his delightful simile, one cannot be sure. The image at once summons the idea of beauty and good taste. Coupled with its allusion to the apt word, the picture engenders some rather significant insights.

The word is the right word to speak when it is the true word. Silver and gold, to which the writer refers, are both precious metals, costly substances, that must be refined. The purer the gold or silver, the greater the price. The truth is often costly, but precious and enduring.

For the person who follows Christ, the true word is the natural word, springing from a heart that has been purified at great cost. "Surely you desire truth in the inner parts," the psalmist wrote, knowing that the inner part determines the direction of the outward behavior (Ps. 51:6).

We will be responsible for our words as well as our deeds. People who cherish truth will heed the injunction: "Do not let any unwholesome talk come out of your mouths, but only what is helpful for building others up according to their needs, that it may benefit those who listen" (Eph. 4:29).

What a different world we would know if everyone did "speak truthfully to his neighbor" (Eph. 4:25). It would be a world as beautiful as "apples of gold in settings of silver."

Marlene Chase, *Pictures from the Word*

How to Study the Bible

Psalm 119:18

Read and study the Bible as two young lovers read and study each other's letters. As soon as the mail brings a letter from his sweetheart, the young man grabs it and without waiting to see if there is not another letter for him, runs off to a corner and reads and laughs and rejoices over it and almost devours it. If he is a particularly demonstrative lover (may the Lord make us demonstrative lovers of our Lord Jesus Christ) he will probably kiss it and carry it next to his heart till the next one comes.

He meditates on it day and night, and reads it over again and then again. He carries it to town with him, and on the street car appears very quiet and thoughtful, until at once a twinkle comes into his eye, out comes the letter and choice portions are read over again. He delights in that letter. Read in Acts 17:11 KJV what the disciples in Berea did: "They received the Word with all readiness of mind." A frank and noble mind is open to the truth, and wants it more than gold or pleasure or fame or power.

"They searched the Scriptures daily" (Acts 17:11 KJV). Precious things are deeply hidden. Pebbles and stones and autumn leaves abound everywhere, but gold and silver and precious stones are hidden deep in the bowels and rocky ribs of the earth; shells cover the seashore, but pearls are hidden in its depths. And so with truth. Some truth may live on the surface of the Bible, but those that will altogether satisfy us and make us wise unto salvation are found only after diligent search, even as for hidden treasure. "Search the Scriptures," (John 5:39 KJV) said Jesus.

"They searched the Scriptures daily." Daily, not spasmodically by fits and starts, but daily, habitually. They dug into the Word of God.

Read and study the Word not to get a mass of knowledge in the head, but a flame of love in the heart. Read it to find fuel for affection, food for reflection, direction for judgment, guidance for conscience. Read it not that you may know, but that you may do.

Finally, do not be discouraged if progress in the knowledge of the Word seems slow at first. It is like learning to play an instrument or master a trade. Keep at it, keep at it, keep at it!

Happy shall we be, if, like David, we can say, "Your Word have I hid in my heart, that I might not sin against you" (Psalm 119:11 KJV).

Samuel Logan Brengle, *Heart Talks on Holiness*

Footprints in the Morning

Mark 1:32–37

～

That evening after sunset the people brought to Jesus all the sick and demon-possessed. The whole town gathered at the door, and Jesus healed many who had various diseases. (Mark 1:32–34).

Early morning in Capernaum the earth around Peter's house was marked by many sandals. Last night's events could be read in the footprints. The trail of a single shoe dragged along. The distinct imprint of a stick accompanying each footstep. The uneven markings of a blind person, indicating a groping movement toward one spot. Hundreds of sandal marks, some in patterns of four where men had carried a stretcher. Some bare footprints. All were the footprints of those searching hard for a miracle, for deliverance. Last night in this very spot around Peter the fisherman's cottage, they found what they were looking for.

That morning Peter gazed at one distinctive pair of footprints cutting across the patterned terrain. A long time before daybreak Jesus had made these footprints as He moved toward some chosen spot of quiet rendezvous with His Father. Perhaps He was now in the crevice of a rock on the seashore, the constant rhythm of the sea on the beach accentuating His communal words.

It was this morning as it would be throughout the next three crowded years. People would follow Him with such anxious yearning, such intense needs, that He would have few undisturbed hours for meditation or reflection. The footprints of Jesus were those of a man who had much to do, and not much time in which to do it as He constantly crossed and crisscrossed the crowded ways of life.

He also walks across our crowded ways. If only people knew of His availability. The lonely soul in some spiritual Sahara would discover a relationship that would transform loneliness into shared companionship. Out of the crowded corridors of life would emerge one who would be there, not always to silence the turmoil of our despair, but to breathe tranquility into our sound-soaked settings.

When Peter found Him that morning, he said, "Everyone is looking for You" (Mark 1:37) Jesus knew then, and knows now, that the strength He had already gathered before sunrise would be shared with that waiting world, available to all who need and call upon Him.

Arthur R. Pitcher, *The War Cry*

The Christian Hope

John 14:1–3

⤳

Jesus left many bequests free and clear, requiring only the acceptance by the beneficiary. However, He left one special gift in the form of a testamentary trust (a trust formed under the terms of His will).

Jesus looked into the troubled eyes of His disciples and responded to their unspoken grief with sympathy and reassurance. "Do not let not your hearts be troubled," He said. "Trust in God; trust also in Me. In my Father's house are many rooms ... I am going there to prepare a place for you" (John 14:1–3).

The Christian hope is not a wish; it has substance. We can depend on it. Faith is personal, an attitude which we can choose to have—or not to have. The Christian hope exists independent of our attitudes.

If there is one distinction which separates the Christian faith from other religions, it is the Christian hope. Without what the Church fathers called "the sure and certain hope of the resurrection," the Christian faith crumbles. It becomes a lovely, impractical dream. When Jesus presented Himself as the hope of the world, and proved the validity of His promises through His resurrection, He made it possible for the common, unremarkable person to live an uncommon, remarkable life. This is a life of victory with the sure and certain knowledge that our Lord has not forgotten us, but will one day return to claim us as His own.

As a beneficiary, I am able to draw from His trust freely, day by day, even moment by moment whenever the need arises, without diminishing the assets. This daily draw-down on the Christian hope makes it possible to move ahead in faith, knowing that God can fashion beauty from ashes when they are given over to Him.

The Christian hope rescues us from grieving over what might have been—or what we might have done better—and challenges us with all that God has yet for us to accomplish in His name. The Christian hope keeps us from wrapping ourselves in the encumbering robes of self-pity and despair. It sets us free to praise and honor the Lord in word and works, in spite of what happens in the world.

Sharon Robertson, *The War Cry*

An Anchor in a World Adrift

Hebrews 6:19

As we network the globe with the wonders of the World Wide Web and probe the secrets of distant planets, the molested bodies of small children are exhumed in Belgium and victims of genocide are uncovered in mass graves in Bosnia and Rwanda. Teenage militia roam the streets with automatic weapons ablaze. Little children are exploited as cannon fodder, marched in waves across mine fields ahead of their older comrades.

Sadly, the lives of children are cheap. Millions of unwanted children are ripped from their mothers' wombs in the most prosperous nations. The horrors of sexual abuse of small children is but the tip of the iceberg of moral degeneration. Land mines lodged in the landscape of warring nations are the tragic legacy of conflicts that have already exacted a horrific toll. Eight hundred persons a day have been killed by them and thousands more maimed—often children.

Society is paying the consequences of the pollution of our moral ecosystems with pornography and permissiveness and more subtle but powerful messages that incite to morally outrageous behaviors. When we have forgotten the worth God sees in us and abandoned the purpose God has for us, then the glory of human persons is abdicated. When the *Shekinah* of His glory fades, life becomes cheap.

Meantime, the fragile ecosystems of our planet home are increasingly threatened by indifference and greed, and the irreplaceable resources of the human family are recklessly squandered.

We enter a millennium that will be remarkable for its mind-boggling technological achievements, but without moral direction. We must speak to a generation searching for a place to stand, someone to trust, searching for a place to lodge faith's anchor, to find meaning, a place to invest one's life for a purpose grander than achieving financial security and self-gratification.

We have just such an anchor! Against the drift of the tide of meaninglessness and despair, "We have this hope as an anchor for the soul, firm and secure" (Heb. 6:19). The question is whether we have taken hold of the hope offered us in Jesus Christ. And whether we are prepared to offer it to others, and to say, "Master, for just this, we are here, in this time, in this place, in our kind of world—a world adrift, a world in moral danger of self-destructing. Master, for You, for that world, we are here."

Kay F. Rader, *The War Cry*

Seedtime and Harvest

Galatians 6:7

Seedtime and harvest. They are inseparably linked, but always occurring at different times and under differing conditions. Seedtime speaks to us of the spring, while harvest speaks to us of the fall. Springtime is fertility; autumn is fruition. The inexorable springtime and autumn, seedtime and harvest, point to a vindication of faith in the process of natural growth which fulfills God's purpose and promises.

Who is the mastermind who can define the process which transforms a black, ugly, twisted mass of autumn roots into the roses of springtime? Who can explain how a seed falls into the bosom of springtime and dies, only to reproduce itself a thousand times in the golden grain of harvest?

Springtime and harvest, uncompromising, follow the law of identical harvest. If the earth receives seeds of wheat, the harvest will be wheat. If corn is received, the harvest will be corn. The law of identical harvest says that one reaps what one sows. Whatever you put into the ground, into your body, into your mind, into your heart—is what you will get back.

I have heard advice given to young people today that all should have the opportunity to "sow their wild oats." Personally, I am not too attracted to wild oats, and I find this kind of thinking to be fallacious double-talk. Instead, these young people should hear that if one chooses to sow wild oats, one must bear the responsibility of reaping them as well. The law of identical harvest is: what we plant, we reap.

Every person continually sows and plants. Each of us puts seeds of one kind or another into the ground of our character by the choices we make. The seeds dictate the nature of the harvest. In the holy presence of God one must examine the nature of seeds already planted and find ways to pluck them from our lives.

God is not mocked. What we plant is what we reap. We get back more than what we put into life, whether it be good or evil. What seeds are we sowing in our life? Psychologist Abraham Maslow said, "The test of any person is does he bear fruit. Is he fruitful?"

So what will the harvest be in your life? My father once wrote: "Let us plant the memories, the traditions of yesterday; let us water them with our tears and warm them with the sunshine of devotion and service, and may God grant to us a rich harvest of souls." Those are the seeds we must all sow and the harvest we must all seek.

Robert L. Docter, *The Salvationist Pulpit*

Watching Daily

Proverbs 8:34

One beautiful moment in my life was a visit to a Moslem mosque where I sensed the deep reality and seriousness of the people's worship. It was a dim mosque, lit with rows of lamps and filled with solemn white-clad figures, rising and falling in prostration as they worshipped. We stood and listened to the chanting of the call to prayer: "God is most great."

These people were worshipping Allah, their God; Mohammed was his apostle. For me this did not take away from the beauty of their act, but it did make me feel somewhat ashamed. We worship the true and living God, and Jesus His Son, but how many of us are as devout as these people who pray five times a day? Their prayers were so intense as their voices rose in a kind of wail: "Allah! Allah!" One could feel the urgency in the cry.

The privilege of prayer should be one of life's most cherished experiences. I am convinced that God does hear our prayers of faith and answers as He wills for our good. Sometimes the answer is yes, sometimes no, but whether He gives or withholds, He knows best.

What a blessed release it is to be able to take our needs to our Lord. There are times when pain or illness afflict the human frame; even death has to be faced. What confidence comes to those who hear His voice and know that He hears their cry.

Once following a powerful prayer meeting we entered the waiting elevator. The door that should have closed automatically remained ajar and nothing happened. Quickly, someone stooped down, picked up a handkerchief that was against the door, and exclaimed, "That cuts the beam!" He then went on to explain how the electric beam from both sides had to meet to produce the power to close the doors.

How often the power of prayer in a life is cut by some obstruction. There are occasions when you sincerely enter into the attitude of prayer, you want to be lifted to higher heights in your spiritual experience, but something enters and cuts the beam, bringing prayer to a standstill.

The prophet Isaiah tells of the people offering prayers and sacrifices, but God was not pleased. Their evil ways made Him exclaim, "I will hide My eyes from you, when you make prayers I will not hear." The beam of power was cut, for their own greed came between them and God.

Prayer is vital to spiritual health. "Blessed is the man who listens to Me, watching daily at My doors" (Prov. 8:34).

Janet Wiseman, *Watching Daily*

The Dynamics of Discipleship

Luke 14:26–27

In examining the New Testament standard for discipleship, it would appear that Jesus had many believers and followers, but few disciples. Luke 14:25–33 records three principles of discipleship given by Jesus.

First, there can be no rival in the life of the disciple: "If anyone comes to Me, and does not hate his father and mother, his wife and children, his brothers and sister—yes, even his own life—he cannot be My disciple" (Luke 14:26). Such a statement sounds strange especially to those of us who come from close families. But what Jesus is stating is that our love for Him must be supreme and all other loves secondary. We have a divine paradox here, for when we love Christ to this degree, we love father, mother, wife and children even more.

We must recognize that Jesus holds one of three places in the life of every believer. He is either present, or prominent, or preeminent. He is present the moment you are born again. He becomes prominent when you become deeply involved in His service. Until Jesus becomes preeminent and reigns supreme, we may be His followers, but we cannot be His disciples.

The second principle of discipleship is that there can be no refusal to bear the cross: "Anyone who does not carry his cross and follow Me cannot be My disciple" (Luke 14:27). Note that it is a cross of which Jesus is speaking and not a burden. Sometimes people say, "If only you knew the cross I have to bear," and begin to talk of problems of finance or health or family. But these are not crosses; they are burdens. A burden is something we bear because we must. A cross, however, is voluntary. Until we are prepared to take up the cross, and thus experience a voluntary death to the old life and the life of the world, we may be believers, but we cannot be His disciples.

The third principle of discipleship is that by God's grace there must be no return: "Any of you who does not give up everything he has cannot be My disciple" (Luke 14:33). Everything must be surrendered and nothing kept back. This principle became the motivating force in the life of the Apostle Paul: "I consider everything a loss compared to the surpassing greatness of knowing Christ Jesus my Lord" (Phil. 3:8).

Can we say that in our life there is no rival in our love for Christ, no refusal to bear the cross, and by God's grace there will be no return?

Bramwell H. Tillsley, *The Salvationist Pulpit*

The Search for Justice

Isaiah 1:17–18

Isaiah 1:18 has long been a favorite text for evangelistic sermons. These are great words to sound in the ear of every sinner who is hungry for forgiveness: "'Come now, let us reason together,' says the Lord. 'Though your sins are like scarlet, they shall be as white as snow; though they are red like crimson, they shall be like wool.'" But this verse has an added dimension in its context. God's people need to "seek justice, encourage the oppressed. Defend the cause of the fatherless, plead the case of the widow" (1:17).

I believe that God's people today are still deficient in the area of social justice. We too have neglected the fatherless and the widow. We too have failed to stand alongside the oppressed. We too must come under God's awesome judgment for our complacent, self-satisfied religion. But, thank God, we too receive His invitation to reason with Him, to discover why the concern for justice must lie at the heart of our Christian life and witness.

It is the calling of every Christian to be holy, to reflect the very character of God. And it is the character of God which gives us reason for our involvement. Our God is not aloof and distant, untouched by human suffering. From the burning bush God said to Moses: "I have indeed seen the misery of My people in Egypt ... I am concerned about their suffering" (Exod. 3:7). Our holiness must go far beyond a concern for our personal piety. Our hearts should burn with a love for justice; our consciences should be troubled about the suffering in our world.

Just as the character of God gives us the reason for our involvement, so the incarnation of Christ guides us as to the manner of our involvement. The Word becomes flesh, infinity dwindles to infancy, the hands that flung stars into space are nailed to a cross. God deals with sin and suffering and injustice, not by force, but by the power of costly, redemptive love.

This is the kind of involvement to which we too are called. Jesus still gives to the Christian both the mandate for his involvement and the manner it which it should be undertaken: "Whoever wants to become great among you must be your servant ... For even the Son of Man did not come to be served, but to serve and to give His life as a ransom for many"(Mark 10:43).

Chick Yuill, *The Salvationist Pulpit*

Homeless

Matthew 25:40

He has no home except this grimy street
Which wears the winter like a shapeless shroud.
He has not friend, except the witless one
Who walks beside him through the thoughtless crowd.

He has not food but what his fingers find
Among the garbage which the dogs disdain.
He has not hope to help him through the day,
No one to ease the lonely night of pain.

Does no one care? Is not one moved enough
To throw a blanket round his bony form?
Will no one put some bread into his hand,
Protect his head against the stinging storm?

I care! ... says Christ. I know what "homeless" means.
I'm with the hungry in the line for beans!
I know the pitted pavement of the street,
And Skid Row bears the imprint of My feet.
I've often had no place to lay My head;
At Bethlehem they borrowed Me a bed!

You want to find Me? Then you'd better come
And face the stinking of the slum,
Where men live daily wishing they were dead,
And give away their dignity for bread.

You have the gall to ask Me if I care?
Come down to Desp'rate Street, you'll find Me there!
And grasp this truth, for it could set you free:
All that you do for them, you do for me.

John Gowans, *O Lord Not More Verse!*

The Divine Christ

Titus 2:13–14

Let me try to put before you what I conceive to be the true representation of the Christ of God. We say that He meets the whole world's need—that He comes to it walking on the waves of its difficulties, sins and sorrow, and says: "I am the Bread of Life; take Me, appropriate Me, live by Me, and you will live forever. I am the Christ, the Savior of the world." This is the Deliverer, whom philosophers have longed for, and which all the world, more or less, groped after as some dim figure.

The Christ of God is divine. We see at the outset that man needed some being outside of himself, above him, and yet able to understand him in his guilt and helplessness, able to inspire him with a new life, to impart light, love, strength and to do this always and everywhere, in every hour of temptation and danger. Humanity needed an exhibition of God, not merely to be told about him, but to see him. God's expedient for showing this to man was to come in the flesh. Truly, no man as he is by nature can see God and live. He promised a Savior who should reveal Him in all the holiness and benevolence of His character and in His plenitude of power to save!

Christ is the nearest to the divine of anything we can conceive. And this perfect being claimed to be divine, and He claimed it unmistakably and persistently. His divinity is the central fact around which all His doctrines and teachings revolve. Then, if He were so near an approach to perfection, as even unbelievers admit, how was it that He allowed such an impression of His teachings to go abroad, if He were not divine? How could He say, "If you believe not that I am He you shall die in your sins" (John 8:24 KJV), if He had not known Himself to be the Christ of God?

Take this mystery out of Christianity, and the whole system utterly collapses. Without a divine Christ it sinks into a mere system of philosophy and becomes powerless.

As He came walking over the sea of Galilee to the men of His day, He comes now to you, walking over the storm raised by your appetites, your passions and sins. He offers to pronounce, "Peace, be still" (Mark 4:39 KJV) and end this tempest of your soul forever. Will you let Him?

Because of His vicarious sacrifice, God waits to pardon your guilt, transform your character, beautify and utilize your life. Let this divine Christ reign over you as sovereign of your heart and life.

Catherine Booth, *Popular Christianity*

Communion with Jesus

Psalm 46:10

Three kilometers from Jerusalem lay the village of Bethany and the home of Jesus' friends, Mary and Martha and their brother, Lazarus—a convenient place for Jesus to pause, an oasis of true friendship. A few hours within this home's peaceful confines would provide the quiet interval that His body and spirit needed before proceeding to the thronging city of Jerusalem.

In describing this stopover, Luke mentions only the two sisters, Mary and Martha, and the brief narrative revolves around the fact that a special meal was intended for their revered visitor. The two sisters have much in common. But they were quite different in temperament.

It was Martha who was in charge of the preparations for dinner. "Martha was very worried about her elaborate preparations" (v. 50 PH), or as the King James Version has it, Martha was "cumbered about [with] much serving" (Luke 10:40). Joseph Scriven's famous hymn, asks: "Are we weak and heavy laden, Cumbered with a load of care?" What today's meteorologist calls "cumulus clouds" are those rounded masses heaped upon on each other, and at once we see analogies: "the work is all piled up"; "it is just one thing on top of another!" In such terms Martha's feelings are described. She was pulled away from fellowship with Jesus by the distractions of the kitchen and by her anxiety to provide an impressive table.

Hospitality is good. Even culinary achievements in their own way can be good. But something is better. Nothing can compare with, or take the place of, communion with Jesus. To hear His voice is better than all other sounds that can fall on the ear of the soul. To listen to His instruction is better than all the knowledge that a secular world can impart. Outside of the presence of Jesus we are soon inevitably enveloped by the cumulus clouds of care. In His presence all is at peace.

In this frenetic age it is not easy to find the time for communion with Jesus. Tremendous forces are at work to keep His followers from spending quiet periods in His presence. We have only to think of the chaotic atmosphere that dominates many homes and many lives. In the morning the house is a panic zone, with members of the family scrambling in all directions as they rush from ablutions to breakfast to the bus. The pace only quickens by noon. In the evening fatigue takes over.

Let us, in the rush of life, not neglect our communion with the Master.

Arnold Brown, *With Christ at the Table*

Cleansing For Me

1 John 1:9

Lord, through the blood of the Lamb that was slain,
Cleansing for me;
From all the guilt of my sins now I claim
Cleansing from Thee.
Sinful and black though the past may have been,
Many the crushing defeats I have seen,
Yet on Thy promise, O Lord, now I lean,
Cleansing for me.

From all the sins over which I have wept,
Cleansing for me;
Far, far away by the blood–current swept,
Cleansing for me.
Jesus, Thy promise I dare to believe,
And as I come Thou wilt surely receive,
That over sin I may never more grieve,
Cleansing for me.

From all the doubts that have filled me with gloom,
Cleansing for me;
From all the fears that would point me to doom,
Cleansing for me.
Jesus, although I may not understand,
In childlike faith now I stretch forth my hand,
And through Thy word and Thy grace I shall stand,
Cleansed by Thee.

From all the care of what men think or say,
Cleansing for me;
From ever fearing to speak, sing or pray,
Cleansing for me.
Lord, in Thy love and Thy power make me strong
That all may know that to Thee I belong;
When I am tempted, let this be my song,
Cleansing for me.

Herbert Booth, *The Salvation Army Song Book*

The Twofold Work of the Spirit
Psalm 84:7

The ceaseless activity of love as expressed in the life of Jesus is the distinctive element in the Christian experience of holiness. Therefore Christlikeness is holiness. Where Christ is enthroned, there is holiness. Christian holiness will spring from the inward possession of that same Holy Spirit who was in Jesus and by whose power He wrought and taught.

So the blessing of holiness is never an "it." No one should say: "I've got it!" for the experience is personal and the source of the experience is personal. Things and places can never be holy because of any intrinsic virtue which they may be held to possess.

The work of the Spirit was perfectly exemplified in Jesus. He can make us like Him, not through any outward conformity but by the workings of inward grace.

Finally, if it be asked whether this experience is the work of a moment or a matter of years, the answer is—both. For example, I was commissioned as an officer of The Salvation Army on May 3, 1920. But I have been learning ever since how better to do my work as an officer, and that task is never–ending. There will always be some fresh truth to be discovered. Perfection in any full and final sense will never come my way.

I can yield my forgiven life to God that He may bestow upon me as much of His Spirit as I am able at that moment to receive. That may take place at a moment of time. But the work of the Holy Spirit in my life will never be ended, for it is the greatest of the saints who have been the most conscious of their imperfections. Those who live closest to Jesus are most aware of how far they fall short of His glory. Their sense of their shortcomings is not due to His absence but to His presence.

Here then is the twofold work of the Spirit. He can purify, but He will reveal what more remains to be purified. He can provoke us to that disinterested service for God and man which is love in action, but He will make us long to serve more selflessly still. His work will never be done though His first coming may have been at a recognizable moment.

Though the presence of the Holy Spirit does not guarantee immunity from temptation or exemption from failure, He will give us grace to grow.

Frederick Coutts, *Essentials of Christian Experience*

What's On Your Mind?

Philippians 4:8

Jesus said, "love the Lord your God with all your heart, and with all your soul, and with all your mind" (Mark 12:30). Paul, writing to the Philippians, urged that we should use our minds to meditate and reflect on whatsoever things are true, honest, just, pure, lovely, gracious, virtuous and praiseworthy. Said Paul, "Think about these things" (Phil. 4:8).

A great preacher of the nineteenth century, Thomas Chalmers, preached a memorable sermon on the topic, "The Expulsive Power of a New Affection." In this discourse he sought to prove that the best way to cast out a wrong affection is to invite a right one. In the same way, we can drive out a low thought by putting a high one in its place. Banish the unclean by entertaining the pure.

We should think on these higher, nobler things, too, because thinking is the manipulation of memories. The brain is a memory machine. We cannot think of things that we do not have some memory of. Even so-called new thoughts, or insights are, at best, rearrangements of patterns of ideas or experiences stored in our memories.

How important it is, therefore, that we store up the proper memories. We turn to the storehouse of memory and find that our stock of the true, the honest, the just and the pure is low because we failed to build up our resources.

Reading the Bible and other good books, attending church, seeking the company of good people are some of the ways we can go about storing up worthy memories. If you want to bring forth good things, see that your treasured memories are of the best.

Thoughts are the basis for action. Solomon wrote in his proverbs, "For as [a man] thinks in his heart, so is he" (Prov. 23:7 NKJV).

Let us face the truth, then, that we cannot think low thoughts and expect to perform high actions. Paul admonished: "Be transformed by the renewing of your mind. Then you will be able to test and approve what God's will is—His good, pleasing and perfect will" (Rom. 12:2).

We all have recollections of moral failures and wrong choices. But such memories can lose their guilt-ridden, peace-destroying power if we will confess them to God and believe in His loving willingness to forgive. Then, with Paul, we can say, "Forgetting what is behind and straining toward what is ahead, I press on toward the goal to win the prize for which God has called me heavenward in Christ Jesus" (Phil. 3:13).

Bramwell Tripp, *To the Point*

A Practical Faith

1 Corinthians 1:28

During one year, 1882, the number of soldiers of The Salvation Army who were known to have been knocked down or otherwise brutally assaulted in the United Kingdom was 642. More than one-third of them were women. In addition, 23 children suffered. Some of these people were injured for life. And all because they attended religious meetings in their own buildings or in the open air. In that same year 60 of our buildings were practically wrecked by the rabble. There was no redress. We could obtain neither protection nor reparation.

The most persistent and unrelenting opposition that The Salvation Army had to encounter in what we sometimes call the lawless years came less from the drinking saloons than from the parsonages. The children of this world were for once outdone in malevolence by the children of light! Always the chief opposition to the Army was from the churches. Every conceivable calumny was spread abroad against us. And men tripped up our processions, insulted and assaulted our women, threw sticks and stones, not to mention dead cats and dogs, refused us even the peaceful burial of our dead, invaded our halls and smashed our furniture.

The denunciation reached its height of absurdity when the great Earl of Shaftesbury solemnly stated that, as the result of much study, he had come to the conclusion that The Salvation Army was clearly the Antichrist.

Our officers were refused admission to well-known places of worship at the hour of service, because they were accompanied by poor, unkempt and broken creatures whom Christ came to save. The trouble with the Army was that it was not respectable. A deeper reason for the obloquy which met us was that we were intruders, disturbing the unruffled calm of lip-service which many nice people had mistaken for the religion of Jesus.

Ours was a practical faith. It offered a spiritual charter to the ecclesiastically disfranchised. Because we were what we were, religion which mistakes refinement for abundant life in Christ, or thinks that fine preaching or good music and ornate ceremonies can somehow be a substitute for surrender to God and the service of others—that religion was bound by its very nature to oppose The Salvation Army. And it did. "God has chosen the foolish things of the world to put to shame the wise, and God has chosen the weak things of the world to put to shame the things which are mighty" (1 Cor. 1:27 NKJV).

Bramwell Booth, *Echoes and Memories*

Moments of Spiritual Breakthrough

Romans 5:5

A spiritual experience is something that is felt. "God has poured out His love into our hearts by the Holy Spirit whom He has given us" (Rom. 5:5), exclaims Paul.

Even the cerebral Pascal had to exclaim with astonishment, "Feeling! Joy! Peace!" Anyone who insists on not mixing emotion with his religion diminishes greatly the possibility of personal experience of the divine. It is like trying to fall in love without becoming emotionally involved.

In his autobiography Dwight L. Moody recalls: "Right there on the street the power of God seemed to come upon me so wonderfully I had to ask God to stay His hand."

Charles Finney, whose writings greatly influenced William and Catherine Booth, in his memoirs describes in vivid terms his experience: "The Holy Spirit descended upon me in a manner that seemed to go through me, body and soul. I could feel the impression, like a wave of electricity, going through me. It seemed to come in waves of liquid love. I wept aloud with joy and love."

Stanley Jones describes the infilling which transformed his ministry: "The divine waves could be felt from the inmost center of my being to my fingertips. My whole being was being fused into one, and through the whole there was a sense of sacredness and awe—and the most exquisite joy."

But moments of spiritual encounter are not only felt, they are moments of insight. The mind perceives truth in a supernatural way, it is illumined in a way which defies description but which is real beyond doubt.

Illumination came to Martin Luther through a sentence of the Creed: "I saw the Scriptures in an entirely new light; and straightway I felt as if I were born anew. It was if I had found the door of paradise thrown wide open."

A further aspect of that which is perceived in spiritual experience is the sense of affinity, harmony or even unity which emerges between the experiencer and the created world. The created world often seems suffused with a new glory as a result of a divine revelation.

The actual moments of revelation are usually brief. Having entered into a new dimension, the presence of the Lord is sensed in a new way, not perhaps with the intensity of the original moment of glory, but nevertheless quite differently from anything known prior to that experience.

John Larsson, *Spiritual Breakthrough*

While on the Way Home

Luke 24:32

Two disciples from Emmaus were on the road home, having been in Jerusalem for the Passover celebration. They had been with their fellow believers who, with them, had their hopes in Christ as the Messiah crushed by His arrest, trial and crucifixion. It all had happened so quickly and with such finality. What remained there to do but to go home?

The long walk gave Cleopas and his companion time to discuss their disappointment. They had hoped that their Lord would redeem Israel and usher in a new golden age, only to see the might of Rome march Him to Golgotha and nail Him to the cross.

As they walked, a stranger suddenly drew near and walked with them. He discerned their state of mind but still solicited their story, which they related in detail. The stranger reminded them of their prophets who had foretold that Christ would suffer but also enter into eternal glory. He opened to their understanding the teachings of the Scripture and how they were fulfilled by the events of recent days. The word of the prophets of old were illumined by a new light, and that dusty road to Emmaus became as a royal road to life's deepest meaning.

Wanting to hear more, and with evening fast approaching, the disciples invited the unknown traveler to stay with them. Then at their evening meal, in the simple act of the stranger breaking bread, there was a flash of discovery. It was the Lord, risen and alive! Their burning desire on the walk to Emmaus was now fulfilled by the wonderful realization that Christ had triumphed over death.

Their new-found hope sped them back to Jerusalem to share the glorious news with the other believers. Disappointment and discouragement were replaced by joy and a now unshakable faith.

The good news is that it can be the same for us. We are all on our journey home. We are only passing through on this earthly pilgrimage. And we can discover the reality of our Lord and Savior as we travel toward our eternal home. May His presence and power, as with those disciples of old, cause "our hearts to burn within us," (Luke 24:32) as the risen Lord deigns to walk and talk with us on our road of life.

Edward Fritz, *Salvationist*

The Ministry of Comfort

2 Corinthians 1:3–4

Comfort is a great biblical word. Presumably the word appears often in Scripture because our frailty requires that we be reassured and strengthened so frequently. It is significant that the Greek word which is translated "comfort" in the New Testament shares the same root as the name for the Holy Spirit, who is so often known as "the Comforter" (John 14:16). The Holy Spirit is much more than a Comforter, but He is that, and He fulfills the role wonderfully well.

The Greek word means "calling to one's side," and it is the Holy Spirit in all His power, and with all His resources who draws alongside us. He comes to strengthen us, help us to handle our problems and stresses.

James Moffatt's translation of verse is helpful because he moved from the statement that the Father is the "God of all comfort" to the personal affirmation, "who comforts me in all my distress." Sooner or later the pressures of life require that we stand firm when others crumble or would, at least, be perplexed or resentful. The reason for our strength and stability is the fact that the comfort which God alone can give is available to us, and we have learned how to draw on Him as our prime resource. He "comforts me in all my distress."

Who can better comfort another than the person who has been comforted? Those people who have walked the dark, lonely road of grief and learned that through the Holy Spirit Christ has been a comforting companion on the way are well qualified to give support. Credibility is a vital element in helping others. We listen to those who have experienced suffering and sorrow—the people who "do understand" because they are familiar with the doubts, darkness, pain and, wonderfully, the comfort of God.

Paul was writing out of deep personal experience as he shared with the Corinthians. He had the mindset which enabled him to turn difficulties into opportunities and blessings, and he knew that he was qualified to comfort other people because he himself had been comforted. He recognized this as an important ministry both for himself and others to exercise.

When we belong to Christ, we belong to God and we belong to each other. This special relationship means that comfort and encouragement are lovely ministries that we can, and should, fulfill.

Harry Read, *Words of Life*

The Privilege of Stewardship

Galatians 4:7

Get a bunch of Christians together to talk about stewardship and their conversation flows naturally into the language of obligation: "It is giving back to God what we owe Him."

This is true. But stewardship is rooted in the rich soil of privilege, not the rocky soil of obligation. The Apostle Paul wrote, "So then, you are no longer a slave, but a son. And since you are His son, God will give you all He has for His sons" (Gal. 4:7 GNB).

This is where stewardship begins: in the family of God into which we have been adopted in Christ, in the realm where gifts are more important than obligations. In this soil true stewardship thrives. It is a matter for sons and daughters, not slaves.

God responded to man's hopeless condition by coming in the person of Jesus. It was the supreme act of love, with the cross as proof. Did God want us to feel obligated because of what He had done? Of course not. He wanted us to feel loved, and He trusted in the strength of His love to draw us to Him. How we invest our lives (our stewardship) is not firstly how we respond to divine orders, but rather how we are drawn by love.

Yes, God is the owner and we are the managers (stewards) of His resources. But that reality is contained in a greater reality: God is our Father and we are His family. He is not interested in asserting ownership and squeezing the last ounce of legal obligation out of us. He is interested in having us in the family where we can find fulfillment.

Stewardship is the forfeiture of ownership and therefore the way to true happiness. It opens the door to one of the greatest privileges of the Christian life: freedom from the power of possessions. Christian stewards have this freedom because they have a family that shares and a God who gives.

Consider also what activates the Christian's labor: the needs of others. This motivation characterizes the family of God. You will remember that in the early Jerusalem Church, "There was not a needy person among them ... for [distribution was made] to anyone as he had need" (Acts 4:34,35).

The most important thing to say about this matter of stewardship is that it is a splendid privilege granted to God's own: the privilege of owning nothing—and therefore having everything, and the privilege of giving to others.

Philip D. Needham, *The War Cry*

God's Sixfold "I Will"

Psalm 91:14–16

The summit experience of the blessing promised in the last three verses of the 91st Psalm are exciting. The crescendo note reverberates when the Almighty declares: I will ... I will ... I will.

> Because he loves Me, says the Lord,
>   I will rescue him;
> I will protect him, for he acknowledges My name.
> He will call upon Me,
>   and I will answer him;
>   I will be with him in trouble,
>   I will deliver him and honor him.
> With long life will I satisfy him
>   and show him My salvation.

This auxiliary verb is used no less than six times, introducing a total of eight action verbs and sung in a majestic major key. It is as though, having reviewed the onslaught of Satan and the injustices of men, God becomes actively involved with His saint.

By this positive set of declarations God ensures He will ultimately bring into being His plan for that individual who has sought to live for His honor and glory. The purpose of God is that our whole nature be brought under His reign. The full application of God's ultimate will is reserved only for those who have reached, by constant devotion and dedication, "the secret place." This involves a perfect union of the will of man with the will of God.

We tend to confuse the work of God with the will of God. There is such a thing as "the barrenness of busyness."

The ultimate will of God is to be realized only if, with the Psalmist, we earnestly affirm, "I will say of the Lord, He is ... my God" (v. 2). It has been said, "He must be Lord of all or He is not Lord at all." This does not come easy for most of us unless we have been refined in God's crucible. Our obedience and response to the will of God is often very slow. God's plan is to recreate man in His own image and thereby reveal His glory through our life and service.

Let us be surrendered to the will of God so as to be among those who know the rich blessings of this Psalm.

Edward Deratany, *Refuge in the Secret Place*

A General's Resource

2 Corinthians 4:16

As a lad in Australia, I was converted as unexpectedly as was Saul on the Damascus road. My life was turned upside down and inside out by the convicting and saving power of the Holy Spirit. Responding to the voice that spoke in my soul I yielded, thus taking the first step in a career which has grown more and more dependent upon the guidance of God as it has developed beyond my wildest imaginings [George Carpenter was General of The Salvation Army from 1939 to 1946].

Were I not able to ask for this strength and guidance, and to receive it, I should never have the resolution to face the demands which any one day now brings to me. But as I awake in the morning I can, and do, know the sense of God's presence. So I come to my desk to spread my affairs before God, and throughout each day I am conscious that His Spirit is with me.

He illuminates the Word of God. As I read, my heart is suddenly warmed, my mind sees deeper import in a truth with which I have been familiar for years. Often one word or text is, as it were, carried before me through the hours.

He gives me to see the inward significance of my daily business. Perhaps more than any would suppose, I am called upon to deal with matters not usually regarded as spiritual matters of business, finance, property and personal affairs. But the Holy Spirit reminds me that all these things are tools to be used skillfully and reverently for the building of the kingdom of God. He gives me patience with myself, with others and with the unending frustrations of each day. He warms my heart, averting the ever-present danger of a cold professionalism.

To His glory alone I would say that He does direct, control and suggest each day. Sometimes I want to get on more quickly, to see the road ahead. Especially do I find need for patience and faith because of war-time hindrances to make contact with our worldwide forces. By day and by night I seek for wisdom in the matters to which God has called me.

He keeps before me the vision which won my heart as a youth. I cannot thank Him enough for this constant renewing. Let no one imagine that, because of divine aid, life for me is merely like riding on an escalator up to mansions in the skies. Life is warfare. I have to struggle. I know the effects of unceasing strain upon brain and heart and body. The flight of time appalls me; the battle with human sins and frailties burdens me. But in the darkest hour there is still the unquenchable conviction that if I trust God and seek only to do His will I shall come out all right.

George Carpenter, *War Cry*

What Holiness Is Not and Is

Hebrews 12:10

First of all, holiness is not necessarily a state in which there is perpetual, rapturous joy. Isaiah 53:3 tells us that Jesus was "a man of sorrows, and acquainted with grief," and Paul tells us that he, too, had continual sorrow and great heaviness.

Joy is the normal state of a holy man, but it may be mingled with sorrow and grief and perplexities and heaviness on account of manifold temptations. The low-water mark, however, in the experience of a holy person is one of perfect peace; the high-water mark is up in the third heaven somewhere; however, this third heaven experience is not likely to be constantly maintained.

Holiness is not a state of freedom from temptation. This is a world of trial and conflict with principalities and powers, darkness and terrible evils, and the holy soul who is in the forefront of the conflict may expect the fiercest assaults of the devil. Our blessed Lord was tried and tempted for forty days and forty nights by the devil, and the servant must not be surprised if he is as his Master was.

Holiness is not a state of freedom from infirmities. It does not produce a perfect head, but rather a perfect heart.

Holiness is not a state of freedom from affliction. The saints of all ages have been chosen "in the furnace of affliction" (Isa. 48:10). It is not God's purpose to take us to heaven on flowery beds of ease. That would not develop strength of character.

Holiness is not a state in which there is no further development. When the heart is purified it develops more rapidly than ever before.

Holiness is not a state from which we cannot fall. It is only those who endure to the end who shall be saved. But while we may fall, thank God holiness is a state from which we need not fall.

Finally, holiness is a state of conformity to the divine nature. He [the believer] is like God, not in God's natural perfection of power and wisdom and omnipresence, but in patience, humility, self-control, purity of heart and love. As the drop out of the ocean is like the ocean, not in its bigness, but in its essence, so is the holy soul like God.

Samuel Logan Brengle, *Heart Talks on Holiness*

The Wind Beneath Our Wings

Isaiah 40:31

Isaiah, in chapter 40, lyricizes the grand themes of the majestic attributes and works of God, and his mighty manuscript here heralds the coming of the Suffering Servant on the stage of world history.

"All men are like grass, and all their glory is like the flowers of the field" (40:6) declares the poet–prophet. Indeed, man is but a transient being whose life quickly fades away like the grass, and his glory is short-lived like the flowers of summer.

In contrast, "the Word of our God stands forever" (v. 8). Man is transient; God's Word is timeless. Man is ephemeral; God's Word is eternal. Man is fleeting; God's Word is forever. Man is impermanent; God's Word is imperishable. Thus Isaiah's message comes to us with the divine imprimatur upon every verse and promise. It is the cosmic compass by which we can chart life's direction and destiny.

Isaiah proclaims in lofty lyrics the unique and incomparable God of creation, compared to whom the nations and empires of earth are like a drop in the bucket or as dust on the scales (vv. 12–15). He satirizes the manufacturers of idols and eulogizes the glory of God who stretches out the heavens like a canopy. "Lift your eyes and look to the heavens," summons Isaiah. "Who created all these? He who brings out the starry host one by one, and calls them each by name ... not one of them is missing" (vv. 22,26).

All the revelations of modern science but add to our awe of God as Creator of the fantastic wonders of the universe. Isaiah calls us to an adequate theology and to a recovery of the awesome transcendence of God. If we can be assured of God's sovereignty over the universe, then surely we can trust Him with our finite lives.

This magnificent chapter culminates with one of the most inspiring passages of the Bible. God's penman compares the believer who trusts in God to an eagle that soars with unwearying grace and strength. The eagle's noble inheritance is the heights of the heavens. It builds its nest in lofty crags where man has not set his foot. It plays with the winds and currents of the air. This majestic specimen is king of the birds.

The eagle soars to great heights not by the power of his wings, but by surrendering himself to the currents and power of the wind. So it is with the believer. We soar and reach the heights of the spiritual life not by our own finite power, but by surrendering to the mighty power of the Holy Spirit, who is the wind beneath our wings.

Henry Gariepy, *Light In a Dark Place*

An Undivided Consecration

Romans 12:1

I am free to confess that about this state of holiness there may be difficulties and perplexities. I simply insist that it is described in the Bible, and that the descriptions of the Bible have been verified by the experience of thousands of saints. It means a clean heart, being cleansed from all filthiness of the flesh and of the spirit, sanctified wholly, being made perfect in every good work.

Holiness implies: (1) full deliverance from all known sin, (2) the consecration of every power and possession to God and His work, (3) constant and uniform obedience to all the requirements of God.

Now, don't let us get into confusion. We don't say without imperfection, both physical and mental. We still suffer as the consequence of the fall from disease and are liable to mistakes and errors.

Nor is it without temptation. If the inside enemies have been cast out there are those without, and they will become all the more fierce and furious, and cunning too, in their attempts to regain possession.

It is not without the possibility of falling. The angels of heaven, who kept not their first estate, and Adam, who unquestionably was sinless in paradise, fell. This side the celestial city it is a debatable question whether any condition can be reached from which we may not fall.

No, it is not without temptation or trouble or error; it is still a condition of conflict and suffering and danger, but without sin.

I now ask you what you ought to do with regard to holiness. I reply: get it. It must strike every Christian as a pearl of great price.

But how? To this question I reply by asking two others. The first is, what is it that you want, to be made clean and happy and holy? Then your first work is to bring all that you want thus sanctified to God. In other words, you must separate yourself in choice and purpose, and, so far as you have power, from all known sin, or even that which is doubtful, and present all before God for the purpose of being sanctified.

Do you want to be a holy man? Holy in thought, feeling, conversation, business, holy always? Come then, bring your all to God. It is no use crying to God to cleanse you wholly while keeping something back. For a full salvation you must bring an undivided consecration.

Reservation is one secret of the weakness prevalent among God's children, and the cause of three–fourths of the failures in this higher walk of the divine life. Let us make a clean sweep and offer all.

William Booth, *Salvation Soldiery*

The Doctrine Adorned

Titus 2:10

A good plan for helping the kingdom forward is found in this sentence which Paul wrote: "But showing all good fidelity; that they may adorn the doctrine of God our Savior in all things" (Titus 2:10 KJV). There is nothing which commends an apple tree so much as the sight of ripened fruit hanging from the branches. So nothing sets people longing for holiness like the living exhibition of it.

To "adorn" is to set off to advantage, to add to the attractiveness, to beautify, to decorate as with ornaments. Now that is exactly what the apostle meant, and the application is that you and I must set off to advantage, add to the attractiveness of the gospel which we believe.

Jesus Christ meant that when He said, "Let your light shine before men, that they may see your good deeds and praise your Father in heaven" (Matt. 5:16). This also was the idea in Paul's mind in that verse to the Philippians, "Shine as lights in the world" (Phil. 2:15 KJV).

There are people who know very little of what you call "the body of doctrine," who yet in all simplicity hold the truth of God and live up to it. Tens of thousands have "crossed the river" who could never give you a definition of any doctrine; but they accepted the simple truths in their hearts, were ornaments to their profession, and are now in Glory.

Our trumpet has no uncertain sound. We not only talk about the pardoning mercy of God but about the all–cleansing Blood of Jesus Christ. We not only point out how the rebel can be transformed into a child, but we show how a man's heart can be made pure and his natured renewed by the indwelling Spirit. Delivered from the love of sin and from its pollution in his heart, he can be kept from sin and sinning and be enabled to rejoice evermore, to pray without ceasing, and in everything to give thanks. Think what a commendation of the doctrine it would be if you all adorned the truth and showed in your daily lives the power to live in holiness.

Talking about holiness has small effect unless it is to be seen in your disposition, in your ordinary life, in your loving consideration for other people, or in your patient endurance of injury. If you want to adorn this doctrine, there must be the beauties of a happy, consistent character and life, otherwise it goes for nothing.

T. Henry Howard, *Standards of Life and Service*

Never Despair

Hebrews 12:1

"Never despair," says the natural world. A little drama was played out in my garden. Two birds made five attempts to rear a family. The first nest was forsaken when a cat attacked the sitting bird. When the next two nests were built, the hen was again set upon, was blinded in one eye, and had a wing damaged. In the fourth, again tragedy came, for two babies were found dead on the grass. For a few days the parent birds flew about in obvious distress, and then began building their fifth nest. Nature is like that! It does not admit defeat. Only man loses heart and despairs.

Who can tell how the history of Scotland might have been altered but for the perseverance of the little spider associated with the thirteenth-century story of Robert the Bruce, the greatest and best known of the Scottish kings. In a hut in a dark forest lay a young man in despair. He had tried his utmost to free Scotland from its English enemies, and had failed again and again. Almost ready to abandon the struggle, he caught sight of a spider above his head trying to swing by its slender thread from one beam to another. The tiny creature missed its goal six times, the exact number of Bruce's lost battles. "If it can try again," he said to himself, "then surely so can I." He watched the spider swing once more–and win! Robert the Bruce rose to fight again, and became the hero of his people.

The hopefulness of nature is seen in all her ways. Disturb an ant colony and, as though trained in military discipline, each ant will accept its responsibility and carry an egg to safety, so that within a couple of minutes not one of the precious things is left in sight.

Part of man's trouble is the wrong use of his imagination. He observes the dark clouds and forgets that they have a silver lining. Like Christian in Bunyan's *Pilgrim's Progress*, he sees the lions in the way and does not notice that they are chained.

No one would guess from the writings of the Scottish author Robert Louis Stevenson that most of them were produced while he was fighting a desperate battle with ill health. When he started to write his delightful and beloved *Child's Garden of Verses*, which has in it the words, "I'm sure we should all be as happy as kings," one of his lungs as well as his eyes became badly affected. What kept him going? Courage, and faith in God.

God will show us the way if we seek His guidance. A situation is desperate only when all hope is abandoned.

James Morgan, *Nature Speaks*

Good Grief!

1 Thessalonians 4:18

Christians are not immune from grief. They suffer loss and feel the pain as deeply as anyone. What are the reasons for the power of grief?

First, we grieve because we are concerned over our departed loved one. Death is sin's final blow, and we can't help feeling, when we lose loved ones, that they have been deprived.

Paul declares that "The dead in Christ will rise first" (1 Thess. 4:16). They will meet the Lord before any of the living will.

But knowing this doesn't put grief to an end. We are also concerned about ourselves. Our grieving can't change anything as far as the departed is concerned, but the death of this person may leave us with quite a bit to work through.

Our grief also expresses our fear about our own destiny. Facing the death of a loved one means remembering that we are accountable for our lives. This consoling passage of Scripture should not obscure the dimension of judgment. In this very letter Paul speaks of "the wrath to come" (1 Thess. 1:10 KJV), warns that it will come "like a thief in the night" (1 Thess. 5:2), with "sudden destruction" (1 Thess. 5:8).

Our society tries to keep us forgetting about death. And then someone we love dies, or maybe we have a close brush with death, and we realize then that we are not prepared. This is a hidden gift in our grief. It brings us face to face with death and eternity and beckons us to be prepared.

What is the answer to our grief? What are the sources of comfort?

The first source of comfort is that Jesus died and rose again. For those who are His, the day of wrath is transformed into the day of light and salvation.

The second source of comfort is that we have been, we are, and we shall always be, with our Lord. This is the overriding assurance of the Christian's life. Those who die in Christ remain in Christ.

The third source of comfort is that we shall be together. There will be a final homecoming as we, and every believer, will "meet the Lord in the air" (1Thess. 4:17). We shall be with our departed loved ones in Christ.

"Therefore, comfort one another" (1 Thess. 4:18). We thank God for Christian brothers and sisters who stand by us in our grief and know how to weep with those who weep.

Let us thank God that our grief experiences force us to pay attention to our deepest needs, and let us thank Him for comfort which is lasting, because it is based on a sure and certain hope.

Philip D. Needham, *The War Cry*

An Awful Day

John 14:1

Today, Lord, has been awful!
    It started badly.
Imps of depression sat on the bedposts
      waiting for me to wake,
      ready to pounce on me,
      to harry me
      and fill me with their gloom.

My head ached, my nerves were edgy
    and I felt irritable.

And then it rained ...
Not a decent sort of rain, soon over and done with,
but a penetrating, miserable, drooling kind of rain
that wet-blanketed soul as well as body.

There are days like that, Master.
Days when life is heavy, boring, meaningless;
days when no ray pierces the inward gloom,
    just plain bad days.

What is your recipe for such hours, Lord?
I am reminded of some words which were often on Your lips:
    "Take heart!"
They must have comforted Your followers many times,
You used them when they were startled,
    when they had lost their nerve,
    when they needed encouragement.

I need encouragement, Master,
So I quiet my mind and wait to hear You say:
    "Take heart!"
Thank You, Lord.

    Flora Larsson, *Just A Moment, Lord*

Reconciliation

2 Corinthians 5:19

Reconciliation is one of the Apostle Paul's great themes, one of his flaming certainties. "Now then!" cried he to the Corinthians, who dwelt in the center and seat of worldly wisdom, "We implore you on Christ's behalf: Be reconciled to God" (2 Cor. 5:20).

Reconciliation is both a message and a mystery. But because there is mystery in the heart of this great fact it is not therefore to be rejected. We dwell in the midst of mysteries, and we are ourselves mysterious creatures. Our unresolved interrogatives circle the globe and fill the skies, but we go on living, though we fail in knowing. So many facts must be accepted without explanation. This is true of spiritual as well as of material things.

Look with me at this lovely word reconciliation. It fills the mind with a healing color, like that of a golden sunset, closing with its quiet benison of a stormy day. It is as quiet and potent as a falling tear, when repentance and forgiveness meet, as sacred as the kiss that ends a quarrel and disperses misunderstanding, as strong as the renewed clasp of friendship when hands that have been separated are joined again in a touch warm and strong.

The initiative in reconciliation comes from God. Calvary is God breaking through to save us. There was no precedent for Calvary: there has been no repetition. It is unique and final.

Calvary cries aloud to men, "Come here, come near, and see what is God's mind toward you!" Stand at the cross and wonder and pray, for here was made possible the greatest moral miracle, divine forgiveness.

Luther said, "Sin is a knot which it needs a God to unravel." In Christ, the fact of sin and the fact of forgiveness are brought together, the legally irreconcilable are "made one" at the cross.

We are all hopeless moral and spiritual bankrupts. We face the tragedy of life's insolvency–our wasted capital, our disappointing or bitter dividends. Into this hopeless reckoning comes Christ, the Reconciler, compensating for our inadequacy, building again our wasted reserves, supplying the equation which balances and integrates the disordered life. He reconciles life's accounts and meets human deficit by divine forgiveness.

Never again can you hold yourself cheap, never again admit the inevitability of your own failure, if once you see human personality at Calvary's valuation. There stands at the cross, in the midst of our turmoil and sin, its loving and unchanging message to all mankind, "Be reconciled to God!"

Albert Orsborn, *The War Cry*

What Is Holiness?

2 Peter 1:4

~

A girl asked me, "What is sanctification, or holiness, that people are talking so much about?" She had heard the experience testified to and talked and preached about, until I thought that, of course, she understood it. Her question surprised me, but I rallied and asked, "Have you a bad temper?"

"Oh yes," she said, "I have a temper like a volcano."

"Sanctification," I replied, "is to have that bad temper taken out." That definition set her thinking and did her good; but it was hardly accurate. If I had said, "Sanctification is to have our sinful tempers cleansed, and the heart filled with love to God and man," that would have done, for that is sanctification—that is holiness. It is, in our measure, to be made like God. It is to be made "partakers of the divine nature" (2 Pet. 1:4).

A spark from the fire is like the fire. The tiniest twig on the giant oak, or the smallest branch of the vine, has the nature of the oak or the vine, and is in that respect like the oak or the vine. A drop of water on the end of your finger from the ocean is like the ocean—not in its size, of course, for the big ships cannot float upon it nor the big fish swim in it. But it is like the ocean in its essence, in its character, in its nature. Just so, a holy person is like God. Not that he is infinite as God is; he does not know everything; he has not all power and wisdom as God has; but he is like God in his nature. He is good and pure and loving and just, in the same way that God is.

Holiness then, is conformity to the nature of God. It is likeness to God as He is revealed in Jesus.

We are to be like Jesus in separation from the world. Jesus was in the world but He was not of the world. While He worked and associated with bad people to do them good, yet He was always separate from them in spirit.

The Apostle John, in speaking of those who expect to see Jesus in heaven says, "And every one who has this hope in him purifies himself, even as He is pure" (1 John 3:3). That is a lofty standard of purity, for there was no impurity in Jesus. He allowed no unclean habits. He indulged in no impure thoughts or desires. We are to be pure in heart and in life as He was.

We are to be like Jesus in love to God and to all men, especially to our brothers and sisters in the Lord. We are to be like Jesus by having God dwelling in us. We are to be like Him in our separation from the world, in purity, in love, and in the fullness of the Spirit. This is holiness.

Samuel Logan Brengle, *The Way of Holiness*

The Feast of Celebration

John 2:5

Jesus begins His earthly ministry in the company of two young lovers, and by His presence gives the pledge of God to marriage (John 2:1–11). It is His intention to be identified with people, and if with them in their sorrows, why not in their joys and legitimate pleasures?

But vexing problems can arise, even in the presence of Jesus. It is so on this occasion. The dilemma? There is no more wine. The celebration of life and love threatens to become the disaster of the empty cup. The cup is empty, and no human hand can fill it.

Is it not the same in the life of the soul. We allow the happiness of our first love for God to dribble away. The enthusiasm we once had for reading the Word of God vaporizes. The refreshment of prayer and meditation, which once seemed so necessary to growth in grace and in a deepening knowledge of the Savior, drains into dullness. The cup is empty.

The calamity of the empty cup brings a worried Mary to her son. After a brief exchange, Jesus leaves His mother and the celebrants. At the entrance are six stone pitchers. The instructions of Jesus are cryptic. "Fill the pitchers. Take a sample to the head of the house." The directions are followed, and the miracle happens. When the water/wine is tasted by the governor of the feast he announces rather headily, according to The Living Bible, "This is wonderful stuff!"

The presence of Christ makes all the difference. He changes the lower into the higher, the poorer into richer, the sour into sweetness, the spiky Mosaic law into the congenial law of liberty, the baptism of John into the baptism in the Spirit. The new wine of God's kingdom bursts the old wineskins of Judaism filled with the water of ritualism.

Perhaps Mary is our mentor. What she told the servants is the message we too should hear: "Do whatever He tells you" (John 2:5). If the poor water of our lives is to be transformed into the rich wine of love and service, and if the soul's cup is to overflow with a divine infilling, then entire obedience to Christ's will is required. "Whatever" means exactly what it says.

There must be not only entire obedience, but also exclusive obedience. It is "whatever He tells you." Other influences will try to trespass in the holy places of our heart. But it is what God in Christ by the Spirit says that must be obeyed. And obedience must be not only entire and exclusive, but it must be specific.

"Do whatever He tells you."

Arnold Brown, *With Christ at the Table*

Christian Faith in a Computerized World

Job 36:26

Voltaire, the avowed social critic and atheist, admitted, "The world embarrasses me, and I cannot think that this watch exists and has no watchmaker." Indeed, if watches must have a watchmaker, the incredible wonders of creation all about us, and within us, eloquently witness to a "world maker." Gerard Manley Hopkins, the poet priest, exclaimed: "The world is charged with the grandeur of God."

Recent discoveries, in both the infinite and the infinitesimal, open new revelations of the majesty and magnificence of the Creator's handiwork. The computer revolution has hit as a seismic force, collapsing time zones and national boundaries. Where does our Christian faith fit into this milieu of change? Gratefully, the church has long since emerged from the infamous Galileo episode where religion vigorously resisted and suppressed new advances in scientific discovery.

If you look for Christ on the Internet, you may find Him listed some 146,000 times. Even prayer receives momentum from the Internet, with prayer concerns daily posted by Internet and e-mail users.

But of course, technologies are not neutral. C. S. Lewis reminds us: "There is no neutral ground in the universe. Every square inch is claimed by God and counterclaimed by Satan." The church today is challenged by the widespread virus of cyberporn and cybersex with their anonymity and easy access. Christian families must vigilantly protect their young from the pernicious influence of salacious offerings on the Internet.

"Can you probe the limits of the Almighty?" is the penetrating question that comes to us from the ancient Book of Job (11:7). Man has an insatiable passion to explore how he fits into the grand cosmological scheme. The advanced resources from technology today can help us recapture an awareness and awe of the transcendent God. We want a God who is beyond the probe of our minds and satellites, a God higher than the utmost reach of our ultimate questions. Job reminds us that we have just such a God: "How great is God—beyond our understanding!" (36:26)

But the God of the Cosmos is also the God of Calvary. The God who holds the stars in their unerring courses also holds our frail and finite lives in His mighty hands. The God who knows the names of the incomputable billions of stars, knows us each by name and need. The God who flung galaxies into space condescends to hear our prayer, forgive our sin and accept us as His children.

Henry Gariepy, *The War Cry*

Making the Lame to Walk

Acts 3:6

⤳

I t has been well said that the "The story of the Book of Acts is of the Lord going up, the Spirit coming down, and the Church going out." At Pentecost the Holy Spirit came down and created a new instrument, the Church.

Peter, the once-cowardly fisherman, put out his net to catch souls—some 3,000 of them. They could not have been saved by Peter's preaching alone, but by the power of the Spirit.

Pentecost as a day had passed, but Pentecost as an era of the Holy Spirit had begun. The rushing wind was no longer heard, the tongues of fire no longer seen, but the post-Pentecostal church became visible where most the Church is needed: "in the common places and among the cripples" (G. Campbell Morgan). Faced with humanity's lameness, Spirit-filled disciples offered a new life and a new walk in the name of Jesus.

The world still needs religion that can put men on their feet, give power to overcome disability and send them "leaping and praising God" (Acts 3:8) into a place of worship. To such disciples the world, like the cripple, looks expectantly for a cure, but we can give only out of what we have.

The gate "Beautiful" where the miracle took place was, apparently, the best place for begging, and the vantage point the former cripple deserted as he held on to Peter and John. His first walk was to the Temple. The burning questions from men who could not accept the walking miracle before them were: "How did you do this? What power have you got or whose name did you use?" The authorities had simply given Peter an opening to reaffirm that there is no other name, nor power by which people may be saved.

> I know a life that is lost to God,
> Bound down by things of earth;
> But I know a Name, a precious Name,
> That can bring that soul to birth.
>
> (Author unknown)

The hardening opposition of the worldly Sadducees had but one result: the disciples spoke the word of God with increasing boldness. Earlier the authorities had noted that "these men had been with Jesus" (Acts 4:13). Behind the human events they saw the hand of a Sovereign Lord. The God who had healed the lame man would, if they remained faithful, heal many others.

Harry Read, *Words of Life*

On Practicality

Matthew 25:45

"Be practical" someone said,
"What can we do?
Don't get involved,
You might get hurt."

For the first time, I am practical
Because I am done with practicality.
Finished.

Didn't the Master say,
"Go into the highways
And the byways?"

For need is often dangerous,
Not safe nor simple;
It is vicious, or dirty, or sobbing,
Or threatening, or dreadfully repulsive,
Or, I suppose, running at the nose.

Away with practicality!
If you will, call me a Samaritan person—
Good or bad or otherwise;
I am done with the right side of the road.

Can't you hear the urgent callingness from other lives?
Walk with me where bloodied footsteps trail the wounded.
Where the hearts are cold.
Gray as granite, or broken, or crippled, or crushed.

The needy will be there,
And we shall care,
And share, each with each.
That will be sufficient.
And if pain comes, well, let it come.
Hurting will be preferable,
Under the circumstances, to not hurting.

Sallie Chesham, *Walking with the Wind*

Celebrating Pentecost

Acts 1:8, 2:1

The Feast of Pentecost marked the summer harvest, the second of the year. It concluded the growing season that had ceremoniously commenced seven weeks earlier on the Feast of Firstfruits.

While Pentecost was initially a joyful celebration of Israel's grain harvest, the festival also commemorated the giving of the law to Moses on Mount Sinai.

Passover falls in late March to mid–April, and Pentecost comes 50 days later in late May or early June. As many people attended the Feast of Pentecost as Passover. This accounts for the extraordinary list of countries represented at the Feast of Pentecost recorded in the second chapter of Acts.

For Christians, the most celebrated Pentecost in history was the one following the resurrection and ascension of Christ, when the Holy Spirit descended on 120 believers gathered in an upper room. During this extraordinary Pentecost, the Holy Spirit breathed transforming life into the followers of Jesus. At that distinct, divine moment, the church was born!

The fledgling church experienced staggering growth during and immediately following this festival of harvest. The Feast of Pentecost was truly a time of exceptional spiritual harvest. Within the first four chapters of the Acts of the Apostles, the church increased from the 120 gathered in the Upper Room to 5,000 throughout Jerusalem—an astonishing growth rate.

God's revelation to Moses on Mount Sinai was certainly in the minds of the disciples, when "suddenly a sound like the blowing of a violent wind came from heaven and filled the whole house where they were sitting" (Acts 2:2). This time, the turbulent elements were not heralding the Law, but the long awaited Lawyer—the Paraclete—the One who would serve as every believer's Advocate (1 John 2:1). The divine Advocate poured out at Pentecost, the Holy Spirit Himself, bestowed strength, comfort and victory to those who have been "set free from the law of sin and death" (Rom. 8:2).

The experience of Pentecost continues to be the great need of the church today. With prophetic discernment, Billy Graham laments: "The church today is powerless. We have no power because we do not have the Spirit of God in power and in fullness, in our lives."

Pentecost is a feast and an experience, a reminder of the past and an annual summons to fulfill the Great Commission: "Wait for the gift My Father promised. You will receive power when the Holy Spirit comes on you, and you will be My witnesses to the ends of the earth" (Acts 1:8).

William Francis, *Celebrate the Feasts of the Lord*

Give and Take

John 3:16

Give and take is the enduring message of Calvary: "For God so loved the world that He gave [gives] his one and only Son, that whoever believes in [takes] him shall not perish but have eternal life (John 3:16).

For three years, Jesus preached a "give and take" gospel. Now He gathers His disciples together and unloads a bombshell! "Where I am going you cannot follow now, but you will follow later" (John 13:36). They were obviously confused by this statement. Why does Christ have to leave? Jesus said: "And I will ask the Father, and He will give you another Counselor to be with you forever" (John 14:16).

There was a great void between Jesus' ascension and Pentecost. For a moment the disciples were prophets without power, followers without fellowship, men without a Master.

Why? So they might comprehend the limitation of their own humanity. So they might fully understand the transition from a self-centered life to a Spirit-centered life. So they might grasp the significance of a holy life.

God in the flesh was limited by flesh and blood. He could only be in one place at a time. He could only perform one miracle at a time. He could only relate to one person at a time. But God, through the indwelling presence of His Spirit, is capable of unlimited presence, unlimited miracles, unlimited relationships! This means that all—over five billion of us—can feel His touch anywhere and everywhere.

Unfortunately, for many there is still a great chasm between Calvary and Pentecost, salvation and holiness, self and others. There are many self-absorbed Christians who have not bridged the gap.

The material world advertises, "Take much and give little." Seminars on manipulation, motivation and meditation preach the message: "Take it any way you can get it, from anyone who will give it."

The Pentecostal message says, "You must give before you can take." How much? Everything!

Before Calvary, Jesus said: "Anyone who does not take his cross and follow Me is not worthy of Me" (Matt. 10:38). After Pentecost, the Holy Spirit inspired Jesus' followers to give "to anyone as he had need" (Acts 4:35). Give and take is the herald of holiness. Give and take—for goodness' sake!

Joe Noland, *A Little Greatness*

Holiness Defined

1 Corinthians 1:30

At conversion, we are "born of the Spirit," and from that moment the Spirit of God within us begins His sanctifying work. If we commit sin after conversion, He brings us under conviction and leads us to confess the sin and seek God's forgiveness.

The Holy Spirit not only convicts us of sinful acts, but convicts us of the sinful nature that lies behind those acts. He also gives the saved man longings after purity and likeness to Jesus. This work of the Holy Spirit may go on for years in the heart of the believer, until at last he comes to the place of full surrender and simple faith, whereby he enters into the experience of entire sanctification, being delivered from pride, unbelief and inbred sin.

Thus we may say that at conversion there is partial sanctification, and later on a definite second experience of cleansing from inward sin and the fullness of the Spirit, which we call entire sanctification. In this experience are included the entire cleansing of the heart from all sin (1 John 1:7,9), the entire surrender of the will to God (Rom. 6:19), and the entire filling of the heart with the Holy Spirit (Eph. 5:18).

William Booth defined holiness as the blessing of a clean heart, while John Wesley regarded it as an experience of perfect love. Spiritual power cannot exist without spiritual purity. An unclean heart brings condemnation and weakness, hindering our prayer life, robbing us of peace and weakening our witness. Purity and power must go together.

Above all, we must realize that holiness is more than a doctrine, or a theory or even an experience. It is Jesus Himself. "It is because of Him that you are in Christ Jesus, who has become for us wisdom from God—that is, our righteousness, holiness and redemption" (1 Cor. 1:30). How true it is that Christ is our sanctification.

Allister Smith, *The Ideal of Perfection*

Earthen Vessels

2 Corinthians 4:7

Indeed, as the Apostle Paul declares, "We have this treasure in earthen vessels, that the surpassing greatness of the power may be of God and not from ourselves" (2 Cor. 4:7 KJV). God is exhibiting His greatness within our weakness. The result of being Spirit-possessed is a series of contrasts and, to many, conflicts. It is well, then, for the believer to learn to recognize these tension points, their cause and their cure.

There are Christians who suppose that to be Spirit-filled is to be free from temptation. How manifestly untrue. Fresh from the creative genius of God and created in the image and likeness of that God, Adam was tempted. Retaining the divinity of the godhead, but clothed with vulnerable humanity, Jesus was tempted "in every way ... just as we are" (Heb. 4:15). And this immediately after His anointing with the Holy Spirit. The most holy of God's children face temptation.

"Earthen vessels" means physical limitations. Whether they mean merely physical weariness, fatigue, even exhaustion or failing health, a physical handicap—they all come to the Spirit-filled Christian.

And what about the emotions of a Spirit-filled man? Should they not be obviously spiritual? The answer is yes and no. Man is a creature of emotions. Love is one emotion. Love can be self-centered, grasping for attention, even judgmental. The unselfish, compassionate love of Christ is a hallmark of the Spirit-filled man. Anger is carnal when it is self-defensive. It is spiritual when it defends God, His purity and righteousness.

Man is also a creature of moods. It is when the moods get beyond bounds that they are distressing. But sorrow, joy, even ecstasy may come and go within the God-ordered life. And it is the Spirit who will keep these moods within bounds.

Possibly one of the most provocative tension points is that of Christian perfection. Jesus commanded, "Be perfect, therefore, as your heavenly Father is perfect" (Matt. 5:48 KJV). Now, perfection is that state which cannot be improved. Then how can the Spirit-filled man, who indeed is yet human, be perfect? Man's perfection lies not in accomplishment, but in spirit; not in performance, but in purpose. It is to Christian perfection that God calls us, not to sinless perfection. Sinless perfection says that one is not able to sin. Christian perfection declares that he is able not to sin. And therein lies a world of difference.

Milton S. Agnew, *The Holy Spirit: Friend and Counselor*

Don't Be a Dead Sea

Matthew 10:8

Aand here we are at the Dead Sea." Our guide pointed to the body of water on our left. From our bus window we could see what seemed like an ordinary fresh water lake. From a distance it looked inviting, especially with the blue of the sky reflected in it. The one incongruity was that the area around the water was desert, not the lush greenery one might expect.

Before we left the bus, our guide explained how the Sea is formed. Its primary water source is the snows of Mount Hermon, far to the north. The water flows down from there to the Sea of Galilee, from which the Jordan River is formed to feed the Dead Sea.

The same water that begins clear and pure becomes impure and stagnant when it settles in the Dead Sea. "The Sea of Galilee receives the water but then gives it out, making it a living body of water," he said. "The Dead Sea receives the water, but it settles there with no outlet and becomes stagnant and of no use."

We walked down to the water's edge. Like everyone else, we touched our fingers to the water and then to our lips. We wanted to taste the proverbial saltiness—and we were not disappointed.

As we left, my mind returned to the guide's words. We had seen the crystal clear waters of the Sea of Galilee. We had walked in the Jordan river. The water of the Dead Sea was unlike either of them. Water that had once been pure was pure no longer, because the Sea of Galilee disperses what it receives, while the Dead Sea hoards water for itself.

I thought of the rich man in Jesus' parable, recorded in Luke 12:16. He gave no thought for those around him but laid up treasure for himself. In the end, he was unable to enjoy what he had.

Contrast that with the widow of Zarepheth, described in 1 Kings 17:15. She was willing to share the little she had with the prophet Elijah. Not surprisingly, the meal and the oil continued to supply her needs and bless others as well.

I thought about my life and asked some hard questions. Am I self-centered so that my life may become stagnant? Am I neglecting to give myself in love to those around me? Do I keep from getting involved because it would make me vulnerable? Am I hoarding the blessings of God for myself instead of sharing with those around me?

"O God," I earnestly prayed, and continue to pray, "don't let me become a Dead Sea, but keep me a clear and living Sea of Galilee."

Joyce Winters, *The War Cry*

On Father's Day

Psalm 103:13

Last night I saw some lovely cards displayed,
And stopped to look, with others who would choose;
I paused, but soon I moved along the aisle;
The cards were not the kind that I could use.

I always sent them for this day in June
To say the things I seldom voiced aloud.
My father loved to read them; then he'd smile
And hold them as he sat with white head bowed.

I'm sure he thought of ice cream cones and toys,
Of lazy days on beaches, of games, and walks,
Of Easter clothes, of streetcar rides, parades,
Of family prayers, of light, and also deeper, talks.

I'm sure I know the reason for his smile:
He saw again the baby God had sent;
And then the searching child, the baffled teen,
Rebellious, questing, with such a selfish bent.

He would recall the day his heart was warmed—
The time I talked to him about God's call.
I still remember what he said to me,
"This means you'll never be your own again—at all!"

I'm glad I said my "thank you's" while I could,
And sent the cards that seemed the ones to choose.
Last night I left the lovely cards displayed:
The kind of cards I can no longer use

Mina Russell, *It's Beautiful!*

Real Men Do Cry

John 11:35

It isn't easy being male in our politically correct society. From early pre-adolescent manhood, we learn that real men don't cry and according to one book, real men don't eat quiche either.

Other unwritten rules create a false impression of manhood. Besides having an instinctive compulsion to channel surf, not cry and not eat quiche, real men never ask directions. They never admit that they are wrong. Mistaken, yes; misinformed, definitely—wrong, no way. And while Mom can cry, Dad is only permitted to get angry.

Like many kids, whenever I was compelled to recite a Scripture verse from memory, I relied upon John 11:35: "Jesus wept." As the shortest verse in the Bible, it's a lifesaver. But this verse also reveals part of Jesus' character that real men can emulate.

Artists have often portrayed Jesus in an almost too gentle, semi–effeminate way. But remember, He was a carpenter in the days before power tools and did the woodwork by hand. By the time He left Joseph's workshop to begin His ministry, Jesus probably had calluses galore, since much of His time was spent in hard work.

Perhaps we get the soft side of Jesus from the Christmas carol that speaks of "gentle Jesus, meek and mild." Let me assure you, there was no stunt double at the cross. The nails and spear were deadly and the agony real. Jesus carried a tree trunk across town while bruised and bleeding and was nailed to it. No one could challenge His manhood. When confronted by jeering accusers, He spoke of kindness and forgiveness in spite of the brutality He was facing. That beats anything a cinema tough guy can do.

Jesus went to the tomb of Lazarus His friend and, contrary to male myth, asked for directions. "Where have you laid the body?" (John 11:34). There He wept for the death of a friend, for the result of sin and for generations to come who would need a Savior.

I admit that I do mist up a bit at times when I am moved. But I can't ever approach the depth of feeling that Jesus experienced when He wept for me and my sin long before I was born.

Jesus was a real man and not the armor–plated, two–dimensional caricature of a Savior some would have us believe. He was tough and gentle, loving and strong. A man's man.

A. Kenneth Wilson, _The War Cry_

The Abiding Presence

John 14:17

᠅

God gave two great gifts to the world. He gave His Son, Jesus Christ, to be our Savior, and He gave the Holy Spirit to be our abiding presence. Consider Jesus' words about the Holy Spirit: "You know Him, for He lives with you and will be in you" (John 14:17).

Identify His person: "You know Him." The disciples already knew about the Holy Spirit because Jesus had told them about Him. We know about the Spirit because Christ revealed the Holy Spirit to us.

Acknowledge His partnership: "He lives with you." He is not a distant, obscure proposition. He is a present, familiar association. If we do not perceive him in continual partnership with us it is not because of His absence but because of our apathy. We sometimes think that if we have no manifestation of the Spirit, He is absent. The Spirit was not noticeably present with Jesus in those dark days of His temptation in the wilderness. But He was there. Whether you can feel or show any evidences of the Spirit or not, the important thing is to hold on to this truth: "He lives with you."

Accept His presence: "He will be in you." The Holy Spirit who is with us can be in us. The disciples realized this promise at Pentecost. The mention of that occasion causes some Christians to hesitate. Remember that the Holy Spirit is the Spirit of Jesus. There was nothing off-center about Jesus. Remember the list of the fruit of the Spirit (Gal. 5:22–23). There is nothing queer or peculiar here. The fruit of the Spirit is for all; the gifts of the Spirit are for particular persons for special purposes (1 Cor. 12:11). Claim this promise: "He will be in you."

The Holy Spirit is not a doctrine. He is a person. It is not our task to comprehend Him; it is our privilege to know Him in personal experience. He is better understood in action than in definition. Know Jesus and you know His Spirit. You have Him; let Him have you.

Bramwell Tripp, *Big Themes in Small Portions*

Living the Holy Life

Romans 12:2

Many of us have lived long enough to have observed a radical shift in moral attitudes in the western world that threatens the fabric of our society. However, there are those who constantly press for further changes that would permit greater laxity. They insist that all citizens should possess, as of right by law, the maximum possible degree of free choice for the exercise of sexual enjoyment in whatever form they desire, provided others are not directly harmed or unwillingly involved.

Such an arrangement strikes at the root of Christian ethics, typical of the insidious philosophy held in common by most advocates of "the new morality." Thrusting this line of thought still further, any individual should be free to create his own private criteria for conduct. Adoption of private moral standards eventually would lead to moral anarchy.

The argument also overlooks the inherent sinfulness of man. Our strong instinctual drives tend to get out of hand unless harnessed by a stronger power.

Another component in the philosophy on which modern moral permissiveness is grounded is that morals are derived from our culture and do not find their foundation in God. Christians are not blind to the influence of inheritance, custom and culture on the behavioral patterns. But they believe that God's Word, illumined by the Holy Spirit, reveals the basic moral pattern for men.

Not the times in which we live, but the Bible is the measuring rod for the Christian's practice as well as his faith.

Is it possible to maintain Christian standards of conduct and behavior in a world that stands in irrevocable opposition to the spirit of Jesus? The real answer is found in the biblical doctrine of holiness. The dilution or deletion of this doctrine would result in an emasculated gospel. Will you join me in fervent prayer for a revival of holiness teaching and holy living among God's people? Let us give the Holy Spirit's sanctifying work its proper place in teaching and personal experience.

Clarence D. Wiseman, *The Privilege of All Believers*

A Qwerty Question

John 8:12

"Y our keyboard a QWERTY?" asked the cyber techie with a sardonic smile. "Course it is!" I snapped back, hoping to mask my ignorance with an annoyed response.

I didn't want him to think that I didn't own the latest computer hardware, or that I had been napping at a rest stop on the information superhighway.

He left with a smug, self-satisfied look that said he had left me in a gigabyte of dust with no escape key in reach. I hurried to my dictionary of computing terms to see how badly I'd been had. As it turned out, every American's standard keyboard is a "QWERTY" —and has been since 1867!

"I knew that!" I yelled after him lamely, although he was long gone.

I discovered, too, in reading, that QWERTY—the first six keys on the top row of letters—were an inefficiency created by design. As typists got faster, they were constantly jamming the keys together at high speed. A leading manufacturer devised a new keyboard that moved the most common letters out of easy reach, intentionally slowing the typists down, instead of making the typewriter faster. Today, no typist can type fast enough to jam a word processor, yet the old keyboard design is still the well-entrenched standard.

There are plenty of people who view the gospel of Christ as an anachronism—out of date and out of step with life today. Jesus, however, remains the standard against which all others are judged.

While some feel He is superseded by more cosmic world views, those who accept Him marvel at His constancy. When we stay apace with Him, the document that is our life comes out right. Christ, although He is not new, after being tried, is always found true. Did you pass Him by? Perhaps it's time to put Him in your "active window" once again.

David Atkins, *The War Cry*

The Answer Before the Call

Matthew 6:8

D r. Ted Gabrielsen and his wife Jeannie were working at a small hospital in
Korea. Among their many problems was an acute shortage of medical sup-
plies. They prayed a great deal and often received practical help from Canada,
Britain, Australia and the USA.

Dr. Gabrielson, now a surgeon in the USA, takes up the story. "I was suffering from staph infections which had run rampant in our family during our first
year in Korea. During that period of time we had not established any reasonable
supply lines for the hospital and were using local fat-based soaps. I had con-
tracted recurrent boils. When one began to reside in the long finger of my left
hand it swelled to three times its normal size. As a surgeon the prospects of an
infected finger that was not coming under control despite available antibiotics
was daunting."

At the time Dial soap was manufactured with hexachloraphene, which was
subsequently removed from the general market in the United States because it
was found to cause problems in children or infants when they were bathed with
it. However, hexachloraphene was an effective germicidal agent that was mixed
with soap to lower bacterial counts on people's skin.

Dr. Gabrielsen telephoned his brother–in–law, Paul Rader, then in Seoul, and
asked if he had access to any Dial soap in order that he could institute the same
type of measures he had practiced previously. The then Captain Rader knew of
no source for the soap in Korea. However, in the course of conversation, Rader
indicated that a package had arrived in Seoul for him. Gabrielsen asked him to
look to see what it contained as he did not recognize the name of the sender.
When it was opened, it was a large box of Dial soap!

Dr. Gabrielsen reflects: "Before you call, I will answer" (Isa. 65:24) is the
important lesson here. In order for that box to be in Korea someone had to send
it at least six to eight weeks ahead of time. So, the Lord had spoken to someone's
heart to send that long before we knew we needed it, and the infection was
brought under control."

"For your Father knows what you need before you ask Him" (Matt. 6:8).

Wesley Harris, *Truth Stranger Than Fiction*

The Best Possible Start

Psalm 118:24

During the football game I am glued to the television on an afternoon to see how my favorite team is doing. But the editor in me can't help editing what the commentators say. I don't consciously do it; it's just that they say the most ridiculous things—regularly.

I appreciate that they don't have time to think about what they're saying, but they often come out with the same old cliches. One of the reporters will say that a team has gotten off to the "best possible" start. It may be a touchdown after just five minutes. But that does not make it the best possible start. A touchdown after two minutes would have been even better.

Or they might suggest that a team being down by two touchdowns after 10 minutes is off to the "worst possible" start. Well, it's not. They could, however unlikely, be down by three touchdowns after 10 minutes.

Sometimes it just isn't possible to find the right words to describe what's happening, not only on the football field, but also when something spectacular happens, or something affects us deeply. A commentator who saw the Hindenburg in flames above him knew all about that as he ran for his life.

Poets and hymn writers through the years have grappled to find the right way of expressing all kinds of moods and feelings—and they have done it with varying degrees of success.

When it comes to describing what it's like to discover the love of God, many people have found it hard to put into words. Some might say it has to be experienced to be believed. One songwriter expresses it this way:

> But what to those who find? Ah! This
> Nor tongue nor pen can show;
> The love of Jesus, what it is
> None but His loved ones know.

One last thing. To wake up knowing you are in God's love and care—whatever happens—does really give you the best possible start, every day.

Robert Street, *It's A New Day!*

A Call to Biblical Christianity

Ephesians 1:7

The Christian Message has a wonderful appeal. It is not first a demand with which we must comply. Do this! Do that! It is not a series of divine don'ts. It's God's generous offer of love—forgiveness, family and the Father's smile. He takes the initiative in seeking to embrace us in His love, beyond our deserving.

But surely there is more to the good news of the gospel than what it can give us. In the offer of the gospel lies a demand. "Gentle Jesus, meek and mild," could be tough in His demands for loyalty, sacrifice and obedience.

Futurist Tom Sine says, "We have reduced Christianity to a crutch to help us through the minefield of the upwardly mobile life. Our books, broadcasts and sermons encourage us to understand what God can do for us—help us get ahead in our jobs, color us beautiful. Biblical Christianity does not mean living the American dream with a little Jesus overlay. The big issue to be faced here is who is ultimately in charge of my life."

Most of us like a buyer's market. We want to contract for services of the Almighty on our own terms, sort of shopping by cable TV. No obligation, with a good return policy. Maybe that's why we like going to church on TV. All the people are squeaky clean and you can go out for coffee when they take the offering.

I read a remarkable testimony of a Salvationist in Sao Paulo, Brazil. Anna Maria was deep into spirit worship and witchcraft, communing with evil spirits, casting spells, and living between the cemetery and a spiritualist center. She came to The Salvation Army because she had seen a television program produced by the Army the year before. She heard the truth of the gospel. She found release from her bondage through the power of the risen Christ, and now she is living and working in one of our homes as a Salvationist in that country.

You may be enslaved and controlled by the powers of darkness and not even know it in our own current culture in this land. What was done in her life can be done in yours.

Paul A. Rader, *The War Cry*

Universal Culture in Christ

Luke 2:10

To view the Chinese as Asian is only half the truth. The term "Asian" lacks exact geographical boundaries. I am not a "minority" either, simply because I am not a quantity. Minorities in one place may become majorities in another. It suggests comparison instead of distinction.

I am a person in the family of man. I am Chinese by ancestry. The hard fact of sociology is not exactly what John Oxenham described in his song, "In Christ There Is No East or West." The song is the theology of the love of God, not the sociology of man. For in Christ there is East and West. And such distinction is absolutely essential and ethical.

I am writing this book in English but with my Chinese mind. I am a Chinese–American, an honorable term earned with much blood and tears.

The simple truth is, as long as our sociologists separate man's spiritual needs from his social needs everything will seem complicated. So our sociologists watching human perversity, political power plays and economic corruptions are totally helpless. They've reported the scene of disasters, but cannot redeem or reform.

Speaking of reform, that's where Christianity comes in. Jesus Christ, as the transformer of culture, introduces a universal culture in which each race maintains its own distinction. But the goals and treatments toward the optimum are the same.

Jesus said, "My commandment is this: love each other as I have loved you" (John 15:12). Dr. Lin Yutang regards this as "a natural, beautiful, new voice, never heard in history." On this subject Hudson Taylor, founder of the China Inland Mission, said, "If I have one thousand lives, I would not withhold even one, but give them all to China."

I have been asked which era of history I wished I could have lived in. I answered without any doubt, that time is now! For I am enjoying my journey which was paved with the blood and tears of the pioneers. Despite much disappointment, our endeavors have not been in vain, because God is so faithful to those who love Him.

Jesus is not the Savior of the East nor the West alone. He is the Savior of the whole human race everywhere. All who follow Him are walking in the Light where darkness is extinguished by a thousand rays!

Check Yee, *For My Kinsmen's Sake*

Our Alpha and Omega

Rev. 22:13

⤳

This magnificent title of our Lord comes to us in his final words to man as recorded in the last chapter of the Bible. Three times in this final chapter he declares, "I am coming soon!" (Rev. 22:20). The title, "Alpha and Omega," gives credibility and authority to the stupendous promise of His return. Deity alone could make such a claim as this title asserts.

Alpha and Omega are words for the first and last letters of the Greek alphabet. Their meaning is explicit in the amplification Jesus Himself gives. He is the Alpha, the Beginning, the First. What a staggering claim! First—before the empires of Egypt, Babylon, Greece, Rome. First—before the eons of time spoken of by geologists. First—before the Solar System, the Milky Way, the Pleiades.

He is the Omega, the End, the Last. What a blessed assurance.

"Father Time" is looked on as both a tyrant and a friend. Time will write wrinkles in our faces, turn our hair white (if it doesn't take it away altogether) and rob us of our vigor. But time can also be a corrector of errors, a confirmer of truth, a healer of sorrows and our best tutor. Our seemingly long history on earth represents only an episode in eternity.

But Jesus has no beginning nor ending. He is eternal. Even our calendars pay homage to His superiority over time.

There is another intriguing dimension to this title. The alphabet represents absolute wholeness, completeness. It is an inexhaustible resource for all of us to tap. The same 26 letters used by Shakespeare to write immortal lines have been used by lovers to express their feelings, by judges to pass sentences, by presidents to issue proclamations, by a parent to guide a child. Jesus Christ as our Alpha and Omega is our resource and inspiration for the whole realm of life and communication.

As our Alpha and Omega, He is also the Lord of our beginnings and endings. He is there at the thresholds of our lives—birth, growing up, when the young person goes off to college, at the marriage altar, at the start of a career, when the first child comes—all our important beginnings.

He is there in our endings—when we leave home, at the completion of a task, the end of a stay, leaving a place and friends behind, loss of a loved one, retirement, death.

We take comfort and courage from this title, with its assurance that our times are in the hands of the Eternal, our life becomes complete in Him and He is the Lord of our beginnings and endings.

Henry Gariepy, *Portraits of Christ*

The Conqueror

Luke 1:74

I want to see if there is not something said in the Bible about holiness of heart as definitely as we Salvationists say it, although in somewhat different phraseology. Now Zacharias was a good man; we read that he was "upright in the sight of God, observing all the Lord's commandments ... blamelessly" (Luke 1:6). Consequently, let us listen to what he has to say in his prophecy of Christ: "That we, being delivered out of the hands of our enemies, might serve Him without fear, in holiness ... all the days of our life" (Luke 1:74 KJV). God grant that may be your experience.

It is a charge brought against us by some that we make a hobby of the subject of holiness—that, like Paganini with his violin, we are always fiddling on one string. If it were so, I suppose he could have replied, or somebody for him, that he was able to bring more music out of his one string than his rivals could bring out of their four. And if it is true that we are too frequently engaged on this one topic, I think there are a good many who can bear witness that there has been brought out of it some music wonderfully enthralling, which music has been made a wonderful blessing to them, and to many who are round about them. But I take exception to the correctness of this charge. I say, varying the figure, we are running our "Hallelujah Express" to Heaven not on one line, but on three.

The first line of these rails we call pardon, and I am sure we very often talk about that. The second we term purity—a clean heart, with a clean life. The third term is sacrifice, or the giving up of all that we possess to the service of our great Lord and Sovereign.

That is, first, saved from hell and having the consciousness of it with our feet consciously on the rock of salvation. Secondly, saved from inward as well as outward sin. Thirdly, having been saved from the penalty and power of inbred sin, being enabled by grace to devote all we possess to the great work of leading to the Savior those who are around us.

We read that Jesus Christ came that He might deliver us out of the hands of our enemies. Our iniquities are the enemies referred to here. The whole teaching of the Bible can be brought to show that spiritual deliverance is the work which Jesus undertook, and which He wants to accomplish for us.

William Booth, *Salvation Soldiery*

The Conqueror (cont.)

Luke 1:74

Jesus Christ has come to you and to me, to deliver us from sin. No one would want to localize this purpose, or contract it, by saying He was intended to save a man from drink, falsehood, thieving—that is, to take the outworks, while the very citadel, the heart, is left infected with pride, selfishness, hatred, bad temper and everything that is bad and unlike God. Surely, to deliver him He must destroy those inward enemies and save us out of the hands of all that is devilish in our own secret passions, tempers, and dispositions.

Now, I think I hear you say, "How far can I be saved in this direction? Is there such a thing as an uttermost salvation? I am wonderfully saved already. I do now enjoy a wonderful salvation. A wonderful change has been wrought within me. I am not what I used to be by any comparison, but still I am conscious that there is sin within me."

For every man has two characters. He has a character with which the outer world is conversant, and an inward character which is only known to him and his Maker. Of this inner character many may say there are in it blots, much that is selfish, much that is devilish, much of which they would be ashamed to have the record transcribed on paper and read out before their fellow men. But there they are; evils spring up, continually grieving them and bring them into bondage. The cry often goes up to heaven from such hearts, "Can I be saved from these inward sins?" I answer in the words of this man, Zacharias, who spoke full of the Holy Spirit, "He came to save you out of the hand of your enemies" (Luke 1:74). That is, to make you free from their power, so deliver you that they shall have no hold upon you, in order that you may "serve God in holiness all your days" (Luke 1:75).

Now, mark the duration of this deliverance. Not merely for a few minutes just before you die, nor for an hour or two in a holiness convention. There is a deliverance—a deliverance from all sin—that can last all the days of your life, if you live to be as old as Methuselah. May the Lord save you properly and then people will be sorry when they hear about your funeral!

Do you hear? You never need sin any more. He's the conqueror. He can toss His enemies out of your heart. He will not only conquer, but He will annex your heart and make it His own territory over which He will reign absolutely. Thank God! He is Almighty to save and Almighty to keep.

William Booth, *Salvation Soldiery*

In The Secret of Thy Presence

1 Thessalonians 5:17

In the secret of Thy presence,
　　　Where the pure in heart may dwell,
Are the springs of sacred service
　　　And a power that none can tell.
There my love must bring its offering;
　　　There my heart must yield its praise;
And my Lord will come revealing
　　　All the secrets of His ways.

　　In the secret of Thy presence,
　　　　In the hiding of Thy power,
　　Let me love Thee, let me serve Thee
　　　　Every consecrated hour.

More than all my lips may utter,
　　　More than all I do or bring,
Is the depth of my devotion
　　　To my Savior, Lord and King.
Nothing less will keep me tender,
　　　Nothing less will keep me true;
Nothing less will keep the fragrance
　　　And the bloom on all I do.

Blessed Lord, to see Thee truly,
　　　Then to tell as I have seen,
This shall rule my life supremely,
　　　This shall be the sacred gleam.
Sealed again is all the sealing,
　　　Pledged again my willing heart,
First to know Thee, then to serve Thee,
　　　Then to see Thee as Thou art.

Albert Orsborn, *The Beauty of Jesus*

Image and Reality

Hebrews 1:3

Despite the counsel of the New Testament it is hard not to be conformed to this world—especially in what has come to be known in advertising circles as image building. Motivational research is now an industry of its own, employing techniques derived from psychiatry and offering in turn advice on how to present wares most attractively.

The image is all-important. According to this gospel, what sells an article—whether it be a cake of soap or a pair of stockings—is the image which speaks to the prospective buyer. Given the right image all things are possible.

The premise admitted, it is not a far cry to the deduction that a man's image can sell (or ruin) the man. But should image be our first concern?

We should remind ourselves that our fathers in the faith were not overmuch concerned about their image. If they had been, they would never have broken with the conventional religious practices of their day. They would never have set Great Britain by the ears had they kept one eye continually on the current public opinion polls. As for image, some of them in the most literal fashion made themselves of no reputation.

"Bramwell," said the Founder, "50 years hence it will matter very little indeed how these people have treated us. It will matter a great deal how we dealt with the work of God." So memorable a word puts this concern for image building in its place once and for all. Take care of the reality and the image will take care of itself.

A study of the model relationship between image and reality is found in Hebrews 1:3 where Jesus is described as "the exact representation of [God's] being." Here image and reality agree. Image is not a cunningly devised fable to hide the poverty of reality. Nor does reality need to be blown up to correspond with a larger than life image. What is found in the one is present in the other.

Hear the conclusion of the whole matter in a sentence written by William Booth: "Don't allow the world's praise to attract, or its blame to affright you from the discharge of the duty you owe to God, to yourself, or to the souls of those about you. God will take care of your reputation if you make His glory and your duty your sovereign aim."

Frederick Coutts, *In Good Company*

The Witness of the Spirit

Romans 8:16

How shall I know that I am accepted of God? That I am saved or sanctified? The Bible declares God's love and pity for sinners, including me, and reveals His offer of mercy to me in Jesus Christ, on condition that I fully repent of my sins and, yielding myself to Him, believe on Jesus Christ and taking up my cross, follow Him. But how shall I know that I have met these conditions in a way to satisfy Him, and that I am myself saved?

The Bible cannot tell me this. It tells me what to do, but it does not tell me when I have done it, any more than the signboard at the country crossroads, pointing out the road leading to the city, tells me when I have reached the city.

My religious teachers and friends cannot tell me, for they cannot read my heart, nor the mind of God toward me. How can they know when I have in my heart repented and believed, and when His righteous anger is turned away?

My own heart, owing to its darkness and deceitfulness and liability to error, is not a safe witness previous to the assurance God Himself gives.

How, then, shall I know that I am justified or wholly sanctified? There is but one way, and that is by the witness of the Holy Spirit. God must notify me, and make me to know it; and this He does. Says Paul: "The Spirit Himself bears witness with our spirit, that we are the children of God" (Rom. 8:16 NKJV). Unless He Himself assures me, I shall never know that He accepts me, but must continue in uncertainty all my days.

John Wesley says: "By the testimony of the Spirit, I mean an inward impression of the soul, whereby the Spirit of God immediately and directly witnesses to my spirit that I am a child of God; that Jesus has loved me and given Himself for me; that all my sins are blotted out, and I, even I, am reconciled to God."

When the Holy Spirit witnesses to me that I am saved and adopted into God's family as His child, then other evidences begin to abound also. My own spirit witnesses that I am a new creature. My conscience bears witness that I am honest and true in all my purposes and that this sincerity of heart is His blessed work in my soul and is a fruit of salvation. The Bible becomes a witness to my salvation.

The witness of the Spirit is not likely to be mistaken for something else, just as the sun is not likely to be mistaken for a lesser light.

Samuel Logan Brengle, *When the Holy Ghost Is Come*

Simple Secrets

Colossians 3:1–3

I recently saw a new patient in my office. During the course of the preliminary examination, he mentioned that he had lost over 100 pounds in the previous 10 months. Impressive by any standards!

I wondered which diet program he had utilized. "Jenny Craig or Weight Watchers?" No, he hadn't participated in any commercial diet program. "Was it the Fen–phen diet? Or did you use Redux, the new miracle diet drug?" He stated that he had not been to a doctor for several years, and therefore did not have access to prescription drugs.

Now I began to get excited. Here was a man who had lost 100 pounds in 10 months and was not part of any system. This could be revolutionary.

"So tell me, what is your secret? We could tell others and really help many people who are struggling with their weight. How did you lose so much weight in so little time?" He answered me in four words. His revolutionary new diet? "I ate less food."

This man had decided that he was tired of being overweight and had made up his mind that he was going to lose weight. In an area where so many people struggle year after year, trying every new fad and gimmick with little success, this man just did it. He wanted this more than anything else, so he set his course and accomplished his goal.

In the spiritual realm, I wonder why so many struggle with being holy. We try support groups, read new books and attend seminars. And yet year after year, we are disappointed by how little true progress we have made at becoming like Christ.

In his book, *A Serious Call to a Devout and Holy Life*, William Law suggests why we have not come as far as the early Christians. "If you will stop here and ask yourself why you are not so devoted as the primitive Christians, your own heart will tell you that it is neither through ignorance nor inability but purely because you never thoroughly intended it."

That's it. If we want to be holy, we must thoroughly intend to be holy, which includes rearranging our priorities in the light of God's Word. We must desire with all our hearts to please God in everything we do, at work, in our studies and with our leisure time. We cannot generate this desire, but must ask the Holy Spirit to give it to us.

Once again, we are drawn back to the simple truths. Want to lose weight? Eat less food. Want to become holy? Take time to be holy. Set your heart and mind on things above.

David E. Winters, M.D., *The War Cry*

God in the Shadows

Deuteronomy 33:27

Josef Korbel was imprisoned for ten years, often in solitary confinement. He was interrogated and tortured and half-starved for most of the time.

After his arrest, Josef's wife, Erna, used her skills as a nurse to support herself and her children, although often under the harassment of the communist authorities. In Brno she met an elderly woman, Mrs. Krejci, a widow who lived with her son who had a key position in a bank. Not being a communist, the son lost his job and endeavored to escape from the country only to be arrested and thrown into prison. The old lady had heard about the torture meted out to prisoners and also the inhumanity of many prisoners toward their fellow inmates. "If only they would put him in a cell with a decent man!" cried the old lady.

One evening, in the dead of the night, Josef's cell door was flung open and four guards pushed in a man. The newcomer standing unsteadily near the cell door was well dressed with a fur coat gaping open and a white shirt drenched with blood.

Josef lay the fellow down and taking a piece of wet rag pressed it gently to his battered face. In the morning Josef learned of the man's attempt to leave the country and of his arrest, then shared something of his own experience, saying, "My crime was my religious activity and preaching the Word of God. I was a Salvation Army officer in Brno."

The man lifted his head. "In Brno? In The Salvation Army? I am from Brno and I know a nurse there who attended my sick mother. This nurse also used to be in The Salvation Army before the organization was liquidated. She was a lovely and tender woman and my mother loved her."

Josef was intrigued. "Do you remember her name?" he asked. "Yes," the man replied, "It was Mrs. Korbel." "Then that was my wife," said Josef!

He hadn't known what had happened to Erna or his children after his arrest. Was she also in prison? Was she undergoing torture? He feared the worst even while he hoped for the best. Now he had news that she was still able to use her nursing skill and bring comfort to those in need.

There would have been thousands of inmates in prisons for political or other offenses. Humanly speaking, the chances of Krejci and Korbel being placed in the same cell would have been remote. But God was at work even in the midst of evil. While Erna was ministering to the mother, her husband was giving practical and spiritual assistance to the son. By the grace of God they both survived to tell their tale of answered prayer.

Wesley Harris, *Truth Stranger Than Fiction*

What It Takes

Matthew 5:13–16

During the 1920s, Mallory led a series of expeditions to conquer Mt. Everest. The first expedition failed, as did the second. Then Mallory led a third assault. But in spite of careful planning and extensive safety precautions, Mallory and most of his companions were killed.

When the remaining members of Mallory's team returned to England, they honored their fallen comrades at a banquet. As the leader of the survivors stood to acknowledge the applause, he turned his back to the crowd and stared at the enormous picture of Mt. Everest that hung behind the banquet table. The man addressed the mountain. "I speak to you, Mt. Everest, in the name of all the brave men living and those yet unborn. Mt. Everest, you defeated us three times. But, Mt. Everest, we shall someday defeat you, because you can't get any bigger and we can."

Remarkable courage.

The motto of the French Foreign Legion is little known but wholly consistent with the popular impression of that elite corps: "If I falter, push me on. If I stumble, pick me up. If I retreat, shoot me."

Extraordinary courage.

Acts of personal bravery and heroism never fail to thrill and inspire us, reaffirming as they do man's ability to rise above adverse circumstances or impossible odds. But courage is not simply a matter of doing, but being as well. Indeed, it may require more valor to be a certain person than to do a certain thing. After all, what does it take to preserve one's personal integrity day after day? It takes the courage to endure. And what does it take to rely on God? The courage to trust.

In the Sermon on the Mount, Jesus calls His followers to live courageously (Matt. 5:13–16). He challenges them to be the salt of the earth and the light of the world. He simply asks us to be what we profess to be—Christians. But that is no small order. In fact, it takes more courage than any mountain climber could ever muster. It takes a courage that has been born of a new life in Christ and nurtured by the Spirit of God Himself. Yes, that's what it takes to be a Christian.

Kenneth G. Hodder, *The War Cry*

What's in a Name?

Acts 11:26

The simple statement found in Acts 11:26 occurs almost casually in Luke's study of Christian origins, but behind the simplicity there is a fascinating and instructive history.

Antioch was a cosmopolitan city, as corrupt as any city had ever been. Its citizens were quick witted and quick tongued, notorious for inventing scurrilous nicknames for anyone disliked. That was so when Luke wrote.

It was the Antiochenes who openly mocked the Roman Emperor Julian in the streets of their city. Brought up in the Christian faith, Julian, a grandson of Constantine, who first made Christianity a state religion, abandoned it for the old pagan rites and, in imitation of the philosophers he admired, grew a beard. That was sufficient for the people of Antioch, who were clean shaven, to call him "the Goat."

There is, then, nothing strange in the fact that it was in Antioch that the disciples of Christ were first called "Christians." The word that Luke uses means "to transact business." In the ancient world, as in more modern times, a man who followed a certain calling very often took his name from his occupation: Baker, Potter, Smith, are examples with which we are familiar.

It is therefore allowable to translate Luke's phrase: "The disciples were, from the nature of their business, called Christians first in Antioch."

Does not that throw light not only on the keen, if slightly contemptuous, powers of observation of the Antiochenes, but on the manner of life of the early disciples? Their business was Christ. They talked Christ, in season and out of season. They lived Christ before the very eyes of their pagan, and often dissolute, neighbors.

Some years ago, the German critic J. F. Strauss shocked a somnolent Christianity by an article entitled, "Are we yet Christians?" He was clear-sighted enough to see that Christians who did not "live Christ" were unworthy to bear His name; that a Christianity which paid mere lip service to its Founder had lost all right to its ancient and honorable title.

But what about us? Have we any real claim to be called Christians? Is Christ the center and the circumference of our life? We might profitably spend more time examining the implications of the hallowed name we bear so easily and perhaps, so thoughtlessly.

Francis Evans, *Words from the Word*

Watch and Pray

Matthew 26:40–46

Surely by this stage the disciples could not be unaware that they were involved in something momentous. They had seen firsthand the buildup of tension between Jesus and the authorities; they had seen Judas depart and must have suspected that he was up to no good; they had heard Jesus talk at length about leaving them. And yet they just went to sleep in the open, lying on the ground.

In Gethsemane the disciples, even the inner group of three whom He took further into the garden, went to sleep not once but three times. Dropping off once might be understandable, but three times in these circumstances! We know from experience how easy it is to slip from prayer into mental wanderings and even into sleep, especially if we are physically and emotionally exhausted. But this was one occasion when prayer was most definitely required.

By neglecting prayer, they and we lay ourselves open to three dangers. First, prayer is necessary to cope with temptation: "Watch and pray so that you will not fall into temptation" (Matt. 26:41).

Second, prayer is helpful not only in present danger but in preparation for future situations. Regular prayer, whatever the circumstances, makes prepared people. If they had prayed harder the disciples might have been less likely to deny and desert. Their prayerlessness at this time showed them to be lacking in awareness of the critical spiritual situation they would soon face.

Third, they showed that they did not appreciate the place of prayer in supporting others. They slept in spite of Jesus' almost desperate pleas for support. "Get up and pray," says Jesus (Luke 22:46). He needed companionship; He needed supportive prayer. Here He was praying desperately about the most difficult situation of His life. Do not Christians sometimes leave the praying to those who minister to them, thus leaving them with an insupportable load?

Verse 39 in the Good News Bible says, "He went a little farther on." In spiritual terms this is a staggering understatement. Physically, He was only a stone's throw away; spiritually, there was an infinite gulf that separated them. But it was Jesus who found God in Gethsemane, and set His course according to the Father's will. When the disciples woke up, it was to hear Jesus say, "Rise, let us go!" (Matt. 26:46).

Clifford and Maureen Kew, *Question Time*

Love Conquers All

1 Corinthians 13:13

Love—the excellency of heaven! Was it not out of this very germ came the creation? Love was the beginning of all things, and love will rush in and throb out the final climax of all.

It seems, in order to show us how mistaken we can be in our judgment of our spiritual standing, that God reveals in the 13th chapter of 1 Corinthians a case of gems of highest worth—all that the heart could desire for this world—and shows that, while possessing so much, we can miss all.

In this case we find, first, the gem of oratory. Who could look upon it and not be impressed with its mighty value? "Though I speak with the tongues of men and of angels" (1 Cor. 13:1 KJV). What an overwhelming attraction there is in this supposition! Could a heart carry a burning theme and not covet that gift most fitted to voice its claims? Where God has thrown in a gifted tongue—skilled in swaying the mind as sky winds the foliage of the forest—convincing, convicting, converting the people by power of speech?

"Tongues of angels"—the tenderness of persuasion, fervency of entreaty, force of eloquence, depth of compassion of an angel's tongue. But while even so much possessing, if the one crown jewel of love be missing, then in the ears of God all the outward sounding has but the echoing emptiness, coldness and hardness of beaten brass, the irritation of battering cymbals. You can talk love without having it; you can expound its priceless beauties, with its rightful place in your heart filled with self.

We draw from our case our next treasure—the gift of knowledge. None but fools would think lightly of a gift so priceless. How much more to be treasured than wealth or sought for than fame. Its pursuit has made thousands oblivious to poverty or pain. But the Bible tells us that knowledge, grand and mighty as it is, without love, is nothing. To compare knowledge with love you may as well expect the raindrops to rival the ocean. One "vanishes away," the other is immortal.

We thrust our hands deeper into the case and draw from its clustering gems the pearl of sacrifice. "And though I give my body to be burned, and have not love, it profits me nothing" (1 Cor. 13:3 KJV). I could never say it, my pen dare not write it, were these not the words of Bible record. Only those offerings springing from the burning promptings of that love which to live must give, that in giving reckons not on gain, can bring eternal profit to the giver.

"God so loved the world" (John 3:16). This victorious power, this golden coronet for which there is no tarnish, this invincible force—Love—conquers all.

Evangeline Booth, *Love Is All*

The Army's Birthright

1 John 1:7

The Salvation Army was born not in cloister, nor in a drawing-room, but on a spiritual battlefield, at the penitent-form. And it has been nourished for spiritual conquests not upon speculative doctrines and fine spun verbal distinctions, but upon those great doctrines which can be wrought into, and worked out in, soul-satisfying experience.

One of the Army's central doctrines and most valued and precious experience is that of heart-holiness. The bridge the Army throws across the impassable gulf which separates the sinner from the Savior, who pardons that He may purify, who saves that He may sanctify, rests upon these two abutments: the forgiveness of sins through simple, penitent, obedient faith in a crucified Redeemer, and the purifying of the heart and empowering of the soul through the anointing of the Holy Spirit. Remove either of these abutments and the bridge falls. Preserve them in strength and a world of lost sinners can be confidently invited to come and be gloriously saved.

It is this holiness—the doctrine, the experience—that we Salvationists must maintain, else we shall betray our trust. We shall lose our birthright; we shall cease to be a spiritual power in the earth; our glory will depart. The souls with whom we are entrusted will grope in darkness and go elsewhere for soul nourishment and guidance. And while we may still have titles and ranks to bestow upon our children, we shall have no heritage of spiritual power, of burning love, of holy triumph to bequeath to them.

Our Lord still baptizes with the Holy Spirit and fire. He has given us a standard. He has given us a doctrine, and He waits to give us an experience that shall incarnate both standard and doctrine in heavenly and all-conquering life.

A Chinese man got full salvation and his neighbors said: "There is no difference between him and the Book." That should be said of you and me.

Samuel Logan Brengle, *The Privilege of All Believers*

Under His Wings

Matthew 23:37

One of the most vivid scenes in my memory occurred one lazy summer on my uncle's one-hundred-acre farm in Michigan. My brother and I were in luck because my aunt, who cared for the farm's poultry concerns, had just purchased 50 baby chicks to raise. These soft little balls of yellow seemed like dandelion fluff blown across the prairie in the summer wind.

By the hour we watched the tiny creatures peck grain and draw at the water tubes. On warm days they were confined in a chicken run where they could hop about and forage in the gentle sunshine.

Aunt Dina decided to leave the chicks in the run one afternoon when we went to town. While there, the clouds gathered with startling suddenness. Thunder rumbled down the valley, and the sky exploded with a vehement rain such as we had never seen before.

Aunt Dina drove home, her face drawn and grim. We knew she was dreadfully worried about the chicks. And her worry was not without cause, for when we pulled up the drive and raced to the chicken run, we saw the tiny yellow things in grotesque contortions, some struggling to get up, others still as death under burial sheets of rain. Two of the three hens nestled on the ground with glassy eyes and bulging sides—bulging because of the chicks gathered beneath their rain-soaked wings.

Aunt Dina lost 25 of the 50 chicks. Most of those sheltered beneath mamma's wings were still alive. We nursed them back to health under heat lamps in the living room.

The sight of the one desperate hen, her eyes wide and glassy with fright, wings scraping the ground as she chased the scattering chicks, is a memory as vivid today as it was then. For it is so like the scene Jesus described as He wept over Jerusalem: "O Jerusalem, Jerusalem, how often I have longed to gather your children together, as a hen gathers her chicks under her wings, but you were not willing" (Matt. 23:37).

Like my Aunt Dina's chicks, the people of Jerusalem who heard Jesus speak had no idea of the storm that was coming. They didn't believe that they needed Him, that their lives depended on Him in spite of the warnings of Jesus and the prophets before Him.

God does not offer us merely a shelter in the midst of turmoil. Revealed in the potent image of the hen with her chicks is the possibility of taking part in the very life of God.

Marlene Chase, *Pictures from the Word*

The Potter and the Clay

Jeremiah 18:1–10

God often uses the commonplace to teach His divine truths. He chose a common scene of Jeremiah's day for a classic parable on His sovereignty. "This is the word that came to Jeremiah from the Lord: 'Go down to the potter's house, and there I will give you My message'" (Jer. 18:1). Jeremiah went down as the Lord commanded. He watched the skillful hands of the potter knead the clay and form it into a beautiful vessel. But, before the prophet's eyes, the potter suddenly broke it.

Jeremiah observed that the potter did not discard the clay, but once more took the shapeless mass and kneaded and pummeled and shaped it on his wheel until he fashioned it into an exquisite vessel.

Then the Lord gives His message to the prophet. God, as the Potter, is the Sovereign of our lives. We are the clay, the vessel in the making. Clay has no intrinsic worth. It is not valued for itself but for its potential. We are but puny creatures on a pygmy planet that is but a speck in the universe. But in the hands of the divine Potter we can become a vessel of eternal worth.

The potter had a pattern, a design in his mind. But something went awry. The design miscarried. Perhaps a foreign substance got into the clay. Something went wrong with the clay of humanity. An impurity entered into mankind by the Fall of our first parents. God had destined humankind for holy living, but sin marred the design.

"So the potter formed it into another pot, shaping it as seemed best to him" (Jer. 18:4). What an eloquent statement of the indomitable patience of the divine Potter who has not cast us aside. At Calvary, the divine Craftsman atoned for our flaws and provided a second chance to be made over again.

The potter had to break the marred vessel before he could make it over. God has to break us before He can make us. He has to break our stubborn will, crumble our pride, shatter our selfishness, demolish our sin. God's fashioning begins with the difficult step of allowing Him to break down our resistance and reservations to His will.

The divine Potter dips into His palette and adorns life with the rich hues of His love, joy, peace, patience, goodness, and strength. After all the preparation, the pottery is ready to be put to use. It is created, not for itself, but to be put into service, where in Jewish homes vessels of pottery were extremely useful.

We too may become "an instrument for noble purposes, made holy, useful to the Master and prepared to do any good work" (2 Tim. 2:21).

Henry Gariepy, *Light in a Dark Place*

The Big Question

Matthew 27:22

In many ways the Roman governor Pilate is the most modern figure in the scenes that set the picture of the trial and crucifixion of Jesus Christ. He just did not want to get involved. Pilate's dilemma was that he had to make a decision about Jesus—a decision of which he tried to wash his hands. Evasion was the name of the game.

He did not want to make a decision that meant he would not be on the side of the majority. Hence his question, with its contemporary ring, "What shall I do with Jesus?" (Matt. 27:22)

This becomes a challenge facing every one of us. We cannot plead neutrality.

Our personal involvement in the death of Christ was recognized and acknowledged by the great painter Rembrandt in one of his finest paintings, *The Three Crosses*. It is a very dramatic scene of Calvary, and your attention is first drawn to the poignant figure of Christ hanging on the cross. Then, on the edge of the crowd, you catch sight of a figure almost hidden in the shadows. He is wearing clothes different from the Jewish spectators, clothes of a more modern age. This is the representation of the painter himself, for Rembrandt recognized that his sin had helped nail Jesus Christ upon that cruel cross.

A quite different painting of the crucifixion is that of the twentieth century painter Sutherland. It shows a stark modern cross as an instrument of torture. But there are no spectators. No curious crowd. No people at all. Why? Replied the painter when asked the question, "Because we are all spectators of the death of Christ. We are all involved."

This awareness is universal, as in the challenge of the Negro spiritual, "Were you there when they crucified my Lord?"

Yes, we are all confronted by the Savior on the cross. We all need to face the question, "What will you do with Jesus?"

The cross was not an incident in Christ's life, but the very purpose of it, the chosen path of God. St. Paul expresses the truth in utter simplicity: "[He] gave Himself for me" (Gal. 2:20).

He hung on the cross for my sin. He took my place, paid my debt, bore my guilt, died the death that I deserved to die, that I might find eternal life. This is the heart of the gospel. This presents you with the crisis of decision-making. What will you do with Jesus?

Eva Burrows, *The War Cry*

Covenant Renewal

Deuteronomy 33:27

When from sin's dark hold Thy love had won me,
　　And its wounds Thy tender hands had healed,
As Thy blest commands were laid upon me,
　　Growing light my growing need revealed.
Thus I sought the path of consecration
　　When to Thee, dear Lord, my vows were given;
And the joy which came with full salvation
　　Winged my feet and filled my heart with Heaven.

　　By the love that never ceased to hold me,
　　By the blood which Thou didst shed for me,
　　Whilst Thy presence and Thy power enfold me,
　　　　I renew my covenant with Thee.

But my heart at times with care is crowded,
　　Oft I serve with weak, o'erladen hands,
And that early joy grows dim and clouded
　　As each day its heavy toll demands.
Have I ceased from walking close beside Thee?
　　Have I grieved Thee with an ill-kept vow?
In my heart of hearts have I denied Thee?
　　Speak, dear Lord, O speak and tell me now.

By the love that never ceased to hold me
　　In a bond nor life nor death shall break,
As Thy presence and Thy power enfold me,
　　I would plead fresh covenant to make.
From before Thy face, each vow renewing,
　　Strong in heart, with purpose pure and deep,
I will go henceforth Thy will pursuing,
　　With my Lord unbroken faith to keep.

Will J. Brand, *The Salvation Army Song Book*

Burden Bearers

Galatians 6:2

About 2,000 years ago, Paul, with his big sympathetic heart, exhorted the Christians of his time to bear one another's burdens; that is, to help each other in the trials and difficulties they had to encounter as they fought their way through the world below to the world above. In doing this, he assured them that they would be carrying out the wishes of their Savior, the Lord Jesus Christ.

If we are to fulfill the law, that is, carry out the will of Jesus Christ and follow the example which He has left us in His own blessed life, we must do our part as burden bearers.

Look at Him lying a helpless infant in the manger. What does it mean? He has come to bear your burdens.

Look at Him contending with the devil in the wilderness. What does it mean? He is fighting for you and bearing your burdens.

Look at Him as He travels through the world in poverty, hunger and tears, being cast out, slandered and rejected of men. What does that mean? He is bearing your burdens.

Look at Him in Gethsemane's Garden. Oh, the burden is heavy on His heart! So heavy that it forces the very blood through the pores of His dear body. What does that mean? It is your burden that makes that bloody sweat.

Look at Him at Pilate's Judgment Bar. They are mocking Him, crowning Him with thorns, plucking the hair from His cheeks, and clamoring for His death. What does that mean? He is bearing your burdens.

Look at Him in the last dreadful agony, dying in darkness on the cross. What does that mean? He is bearing your burdens.

Look at Him lying in the grave, rising from the tomb, ascending to heaven, sitting at the right hand of the throne, showing His hands, and pleading with the Father. What does it all mean? He is bearing your burdens.

That is the rule, and there is the example He has left for you to copy. He says, "Go and do for your comrades, so far as you have the power, what I have done for you."

"Bear one another's burdens, and so fulfill the law of Christ" (Gal. 6:2 NKJV).

William Booth, The Warrior's Daily Portion

An Obstetrician's Point of View

Mark 10:14

In the book *Letters to Salvationists on Love, Marriage and the Home*, the Army's founder, William Booth, writes, "Children are, or ought to be, a great boon. It was the divine intention in the beginning that they should be the crowning blessing of a happy and useful life, and, beyond all question, that is the divine intention still."

On a Sunday morning while listening to the junior songsters at my corps, I was awed at God's handiwork. Each life, once a single cell upon conception with absolutely unique DNA, is now a trillion cells in the process of reaching full potential. These beautiful faces, some saved from the abortionist's curette, now sing to the honor and glory of God, each one touched in some way by the programs of The Salvation Army.

In the United States since 1973, one-third of the children antepartum (residing in the womb) have been sacrificed on the altar of human choice. Over 32 million lives have been summarily extinguished through elective in utero extermination.

William Booth has declared: "To possess children is a natural and all but universal desire. A society in which this is not the case is a rotten society. Where children are not desired, there is an unnatural perverted state of things, generally resulting from utterly selfish and worldly, if not devilish causes."

The gospel quotes our Lord as saying, "Let the little children come to Me and do not hinder them, for the kingdom of God belongs to such as these" (Mark 10:14). He entreats us to stand as children of the light, and we are admonished not to shed innocent blood. What could be more innocent than an in utero boy or girl in its amniotic maternal environment?

May we not consciously dehumanize the vulnerable or commit the sin of omission, standing by as children of all ages are persecuted, neglected and abandoned. May we truly be found faithful by those who follow in our footsteps, those tiny feet and tender hearts that are guided by our every word and example. May we not forget nor neglect our role to all, from the embryo to the grave, and all that is life in between.

Norman Raymond M.D., *The War Cry*

The Ascended Lord

Hebrews 2:18

Most folk prefer a story to have a happy ending and this is how Luke concluded the first section of his two-part account of the birth and growth of the early Church. "They returned to Jerusalem with great joy" (Luke 24:52).

For one thing, the first disciples learned that the Jesus who had conquered death and returned to the Father was the same understanding Lord whom they had known in Galilee, as the conversation on the way to Emmaus demonstrated.

The other cause for their joy was that no more would they be separated from their Master. Delivered from the limitations of space and time His word now was: "I am with you always" (Matt. 28:20). Whom seeing not, they could still love (1 Pet. 1:8).

We can also share this first century joy. First of all, the ascended Jesus never forgot what it was to be a man. What He learned by the things He suffered He never unlearned. We who are His followers can count ourselves blessed that He who returned to the Father shared our lot.

It pleased God as Man with man to dwell. Before that God was in heaven, "dwelling in the light which no man can approach" (1 Tim. 6:16 KJV). To Greek minds God was more remote still. They conceived God as impassible—that is, beyond or incapable of feeling. But with the God and Father of our Lord Jesus Christ there is no sorrow common to man which He has not shared.

A doctor may know what is the matter with me and yet not be able to effect a cure. My assurance lies in the title given to the ascended Christ of "Great High Priest" (Heb. 4:14). Our Great High Priest is both fully in touch with God and fully in touch with man. Jesus brings our multitude of needs to the plenitude of grace. Supply always exceeds demand! Seated "on the right hand of God" (Col. 3:1) is not a physical description of the place of Jesus but a theological statement concerning the power at His disposal from which He can meet the need of all who call upon His name.

So far as our earthly struggles are concerned Jesus has been here. He has passed this way before. He knew—and still knows—the way we take. And our Great High Priest also knows how best to help us hold fast our profession. "Because He himself suffered when He was tempted, He is able to help those who are being tempted" (Heb. 2:18).

Frederick Coutts, *In Good Company*

Breakfast on the Beach

John 21:12

Is the Christ adventure over for Peter? He is back at his fishing. Could it be that the great dream has evaporated? And now, empty nets and, without his Lord, an empty life.

Through the trailing morning mist something, someone, is dimly visible on the shore. With a strong voice He is calling across the water, asking about the catch. Learning that the night's work had been futile, He gives advice that immediately results in a harvest so great that the net is strained to the limit.

"It is the Lord!" The exclamation merges with the splash of Peter as he plunges into the water, anxious to reach the shore faster than any boat could take him.

Mercifully, thankfully, the first words of Jesus were not reproachful. Rather, Jesus had shown interest in their occupation; He had sympathized with them in their melancholy, and He had given them amazingly fruitful advice. When they came to shore, they saw a charcoal fire there.

The invitation is cordial and genuine: "Come and have breakfast" (John 21:12). Is not Jesus always calling us to communion with Himself? What He has prepared for us He wants us to share and to enjoy. If, in a spiritual sense, we have "toiled all night and caught nothing," (Luke 5:5 NKJV) He waits to provide the spiritual nourishment that will help us overcome our disappointment. If we, too, have been guilty of denial, if we, too, have "warmed our hands" at an alien fire, if we, too, have turned aside from a sacred vocation, He bids us "Come." The Master continually calls to those who spiritually hunger and thirst to "Come and dine."

The breakfast on the beach becomes a sacramental meal. There had been three denials by Peter. Now, for a triple sin there is a triple forgiveness. "Do you truly love Me more than all these?" (John 21:15). Three probing questions, three penitent avowals, and three binding obligations. The first, "Feed My lambs." The second commission: "Feed My sheep." And the third obligation: "Follow Me!" Forgiven, reinstated, commissioned. Once again Peter would be a "fisher of men," and by the grace of Christ he would follow to life's end.

"More than all else" love is the kind of love Christ expects in return for His gift of forgiveness. It was this kind of love that changed a denier into a devotee. As we seek to follow Christ, let us be sure that we are motivated by nothing less than "more than all else" love.

Arnold Brown, _With Christ at the Table_

Getting or Giving?

Matthew 25:31–46

~ॐ~

I read recently of a little girl who finished her prayer saying, "And now, dear God, what can I do for You?" The writer went on to say that, inspite of her years, the girl was spiritually mature enough to see the other side of prayer. Getting form God should be balanced by giving to God.

It is the nature and spirit of League of mercy members—those devoted Salvationists who regularly visit hospitals and institutions of all kinds where people are in pain or have problems—to demonstrate their gratitude to God for all IIis love by carrying that love to others. What they get from God they return to Him in loving service for others

The achievements of love cannot ever really be computed or adequately recorded. Done as they are in the name and power of Christ, every kindness shown to someone else is, as Jesus Himself said, a kindness done to Him. A smile, a handclasp, a friendly word, a prayer, are all tools of League of Mercy workers as they follow their rounds, bringing good cheer and perhaps a new hope to the lonely patient of the housebound aged. No one, however, can calculate the eternal results that flow from the use of such simple means when those means are invested with divine love. Perhaps there are others, like the little girl, who, in such a service, would find the answer to the question: "And now, dear God, what can I do for You?"

Jean Brown, *Excursions in Thought*

Why Me?

Isaiah 6:8

Why should a troubled world trouble me? Can't I close my ears and shut my eyes? After all, what can one person do? And anyway, why must that person be me?

Why me? That question was asked by Moses when God called him: "Who am I, that I should go?" (Exod. 3:11). He might have said, "I don't like the crowds and the clamor and the complications of Egypt. I like the peace of the desert. Why me?" It was the attitude of one who feels inadequate, even fearful. Why me? The answers are given.

First of all, Moses was a man with a cause. It was God's cause. The Lord said, "I have indeed seen the misery of My people ... I have heard them crying out ... I am concerned about their suffering. So I have come down to rescue them" (Exod. 3:7–8). God wanted Moses' help. It was already Moses' cause. He too had seen and heard and knew the distress of his people. He had taken his stand with the oppressed. Even though Moses had run away and hidden in the desert, his heart still cared about the slaves in Egypt. Moses was a man with a cause.

Then, Moses was a man with a call. God said, "So now, go. I am sending you to Pharaoh to bring My people the Israelites out of Egypt" (Exod. 3:10). It is not enough to recognize a great and worthy cause. There are many such in the world today. We must do more than see a need. We must sense and acknowledge a call which is positive and personal. Such calls seldom come with the dramatic vividness of Moses' revelation, but however a call may come, God has a task for you and me.

Finally, Moses was a man with a Companion. And that is the best part of it. God said, "I will be with you" (Exod. 3:12). And He was: through the Exodus and the wilderness, all the way and every day. From personal experience Moses would later say, "The eternal God is your refuge, and underneath are the everlasting arms" (Deut. 33:27). God's promise to every believer is the same: "I am with you always, to the very end of the age" (Matt. 28:20).

Moses was a man with a cause, a call and a Companion. He knew where he was going, what he was going for and with whom he was going.

What about your life? In the absence of a burning bush, will you face this burning question: "Who will help to heal the open sore of the world?"

Bramwell Tripp, *Big Themes in Small Portions*

The Perfect Heart

2 Chronicles 16:9

What is the perfect heart? It must be a different kind of heart to hearts in general. All hearts are not perfect toward God, or else His eyes would not have to be running to and fro throughout the earth to find them. They would be plentiful enough if they were the common sort of hearts. And another thing is evident on the face of the text, that these kind of hearts are very precious in the sight of God.

This cannot mean a merely natural heart; it must mean a renewed heart, because there are no perfect hearts by nature. It must mean, then, a heart renewed by the Holy Spirit, put right with God, and then kept right.

A perfect heart is one in its loyalty to God. It means a heart perfect in its obedience. That man or woman who has this kind of a heart ceases to pick and choose among the commandments of God which he shall obey and which not. He ceases to have his own will, though sometimes he may have a struggle with his own will and the way that God may call him to take.

The partial heart, so common, wants to serve God a little. It is willing to go a little way with God, but not all the way. Can it be expected that the Lord should show Himself strong in behalf of such people?

This perfect heart is perfect in its trust, and, perhaps, that ought to have come first, for it is the very root of all.

How beautiful Abraham was in the eyes of God; how God gloried over him. How do I know that Abraham had a perfect heart towards God? Because He trusted Him. I dare say he was compassed with infirmities, had many erroneous views, manward and earthward, but his heart was perfect towards God. Do you think God would have failed in His promise to Abraham? Abraham trusted Him almost to the blood of Isaac, and God showed Himself strong in his behalf, and delivered him, and made him the Father of the Faithful; crowned him with everlasting honor so that his name, from generation to generation, has been a pillar of strength to the Lord's people, and a crown of glory to his God.

Catherine Booth, *Godliness*

The Eleventh Commandment

John 13:34,35

Have we the right to assert that in the final hours of His earthly ministry Jesus added to the commandments of God? Yes, certainly, if we believe His statement that He was giving a new commandment. Obviously that must increase the number.

But was it really new? What was so novel about telling people to love one another? All great religions in the history of the world say something of the sort. The Old Testament certainly did, as Jesus was well aware. For, when asked to identify the greatest commandment He declared that it was the injunction to love God with all one's heart (Deut. 6:5). He went on to quote from Leviticus 19:18: "The second is this: Love your neighbor as yourself" (Mark 12:31).

Religious teachers have always inculcated the principle of benevolence or goodwill or love to one's fellows. What was so new about the words of Jesus at the Last Supper?

The novelty was twofold. First, Jesus added a cutting edge to an old ideal. If you preach about love no one quarrels with what you say—so long as you keep it vague and abstract. It is when you get down to the practical application of the idea that you provoke people. (He's getting personal now!) Everyone will agree that loving the human race is hugely desirable. It is loving the people next to us that we cannot stomach.

The command Jesus gives will not let us get away with that. It takes our eyes away from distant horizons and fastens them on the person next door. When we ponder these words we begin to see that there is certainly a new commandment because it is linked with the life of the new community which Jesus is beginning—His Church. They must love one another or the whole thing would be a sham.

But He did not leave it there. The greater novelty, indeed the essential newness, lay in the force of His personal example and the demand that they measure up to it. "Love ... as I have loved you" (John 13:34, 35).

In greater measure, this is a new commandment because Jesus gives His personal image to the ideal of love. "Love as I have loved you" must mean a costly, caring love.

This is the eleventh commandment. Orthodoxy is important; moral rectitude is a vital foundation for the Christian life; faith needs works and is dead without them. But above all there must be love for the brethren, for by this are Christ's disciples to be known.

David Guy, *The Eleven Commandments*

Impossible!

Acts 2:24

Death is final. Who has ever gone beyond the limits of life into the domain of death to return with word of what lies beyond?

Jesus died. There can be no question about that, in spite of current attempts to concoct tales of His swooning so convincingly as to persuade His practiced executioners that He was truly dead. The centurion detailed to hasten His death on the cross by breaking His limbs certified His decease before breaking a single bone. The greater miracle would have been the possibility that He might have still survived under such conditions. But it was not so. He died.

The executioners knew it. His mother knew it. His beloved friend and disciple John knew it. Joseph of Arimathea, member of the high court of Judaism, knew it, for it was he who laid His lifeless body in His own tomb. And for three days His corpse lay there, sealed under guard, lest friends, thinking Him less than dead, should try to revive Him or even to steal away His body in order to proclaim Him yet alive.

How can reasonable people conceive of the possibility of the dead coming to life again? Unless, of course Jesus knew what He was saying when He declared, "I am the resurrection and the life" (John 11:25). Could it be true? Was Jesus who He claimed to be?

Look closely at the man: His miraculous birth, the precise correlation of ancient prophecy with the unfolding drama of His life. Listen closely to His words of grace and truth, of hope and salvation. Hear the note of authority in His voice as it grips the hearts of His hearers. Watch Him still the storm, release the possessed, heal the sick, feed the hungry. Stand with the cynical crowd and see Him call His friend Lazarus to life, still bound in grave clothes. Hear from His lips as he hangs upon a Roman cross whispered words of forgiveness for His tormentors. This is the Jesus who says, "I lay down my life—only to take it up again" (John 10:17).

God raised Him from the dead. And in raising Him, He released life-giving, resurrection power into the life of our jaded world. The living Christ strikes off the chains of addiction, binds up the wounds of the abused and lightens the darkness of the despairing. He forgives the sinner and restores us to fellowship with the welcoming Father.

Impossible? "God raised Him from the dead ... because it was impossible for death to keep its hold on Him" (Acts 2:24). He is able to share that life with you and me. And with it, the possibility of a new and abundant life of fellowship with God. "The promise is for you!" (Acts 2:39)

Paul A. Rader, *The War Cry*

Called to be Saints

1 Corinthians 1:2

When a man receives Christ, he gets more than he asked for. Most of us, taking our first steps toward Him, are seeking simply for pardon and experience real relief when we are assured that our sins are forgiven. Becoming more fully acquainted with the Bible and its teaching, we learn of what happened to us on that red–letter day. We were regenerated (born again), adopted (placed in God's family), made heirs of God and joint–heirs with Christ and much more.

The blessings received at conversion, either present or potential, are so immense that I have a feeling it will take all eternity to learn how much we received when Jesus came into our hearts.

We are given a new title immediately; we are called "saints." It is one of the names for followers of Christ in the New Testament. Fellow believers, we are saints. What privileges the title implies, and what responsibilities!

There must be no downgrading of the greatness of God's initial work of grace in the soul. For if a Christian is, at the moment he becomes a Christian, called a saint, that implies momentous things. First, that he has begun to be holy. One cannot receive Christ sincerely, Christ in His purity and burning love, and deliberately hold on to sinful practices, or carelessly tolerate evil thoughts and words.

Just as the new Christian regrets any lapse into sin and longs to be holier, so the title "saints" which he bears is a promise that he will indeed be made more Christlike, by grace. For a saint is a person in whom the Holy Spirit is producing an ever-growing resemblance to Jesus Christ.

It was Chrysostom who said that parents should always give a new baby a great name; it would provide the child with an ideal after which to strive. Turning possibilities into actualities is the Holy Spirit's specialty! The God who sees the end from the beginning is the God who bestows a name that is a prophecy, and then proceeds to fulfill that prophecy.

Claiming us as His own, describing us as saints, our saving God sets our eyes on the heights. Let there be no doubt about it: God wants and intends to bring to completion the good work He has begun in you. He is faithful! (Phil. 1:6)

Edward Read, *Burning, Always Burning*

Writing the Last Chapter Well

Revelation 14:13

Death is inevitable for us all. Sometimes it comes suddenly, but most of the time it is a process, an important final chapter in our lives, critical to the meaning of our entire life story.

That chapter should be completed with an exclamation point, not a question mark. We should be affirming our faith, demonstrating trust, experiencing grace and receiving and expressing love. It is our time to pass on a legacy of courage and to witness that God is present in every circumstance of life and that His grace is sufficient for every crisis.

We are all too familiar with the reality that age takes a heavy toll on faculties and functions and that many people experience a terrible loneliness as friends die, families move away and strength abates. When such people face the prospect of unrelieved physical suffering as well, they may be seized with a feeling of desperation and loneliness. Some may even express a wish to die.

When patients see themselves as "an intolerable burden" or when they see life as "not worth living," should they have the right to enlist the support of physicians and end their lives? Besides medical, social and moral reasons, assisted suicide is inconsistent with a biblical view of life, death and suffering and accountability to God. Our role with our loved ones, when we cannot cure, is to care for and to comfort them.

Palliative care is a unique form of health care developed for the needs of people with terminal illness. As family members and friends of the dying, we need to understand that caring for such patients is a privilege. "We can foster a good death by repairing relationships, respecting wishes, helping the dying to live as fully as possible, reducing pain and allowing time and space for transcendence and for letting go," writes Dr. Ira Byock, president of the Academy of Hospice Physicians, in *Dying Well*.

When family is not available, faith communities can mobilize visitors and helpers to meet emotional, physical and spiritual needs.

Let us help our dying loved ones to write the last chapter of their lives well. Thus will people experience the love of God and the grace of God and the peace of God, and have the opportunity to affirm their faith and leave a legacy of courage in the face of suffering.

With the Apostle John, we affirm, "Blessed are the dead who die in the Lord from now on" (Rev. 14:13).

Herbert C. Rader, M.D., *The War Cry*

New Life in Christ

2 Corinthians 5:15,17

On a sandy stretch of the sun–baked Damascus Road Saul's life was radically changed so profoundly that he became a new man in Christ Jesus! He joined the sect he had been trying to exterminate.

There on the Damascus Road, his pockets bulging with the High Priest's deadly documents, he was beginning to grasp the significance of the Lord's death. Years later Paul was to write to the Corinthians, "And He died for all, that those who live should no longer live for themselves but for Him who died for them and was raised again. Therefore, if anyone is in Christ, he is a new creation; the old has gone, the new has come!" (2 Cor. 5:15,17).

Such a sublime perception in all its fullness could hardly have entered his mind as he lay prone on the desert road. It actually took years to be grasped by its full meaning, years of close communion with the Lord, of intellectual struggle, and of arduous experience in the service of the gospel. What Saul saw and heard that day became the secret of his inmost being. It constituted the most unalterable conviction of his soul.

So it is with every authentic conversion, when all life is opened to God's gracious healing pardon, cleansed by the blood of the Savior on the cross, regenerated by the power of the Spirit.

At a meeting in The Salvation Army's Mission compound at Chikankata in Zambia, I heard a mother from a very poor family living in a nearby village testify to her conversion. "The preacher preached," she explained simply, "and the Word of God attacked me in my heart." By divine grace, through faith, that illiterate mother and the erudite Saul found the self–same Savior. Saul too had been attacked by the Word of God. He too capitulated and became a willing captive; a slave was how he described himself in his epistles.

Indeed, conversion involves so radical a repentance that life is turned completely around. It involves so deep a faith that God in Christ becomes the supreme, most radiant reality of existence so that character, conduct and human relationships are all set moving in the direction of Christlikeness.

Clarence D. Wiseman, *The Desert Road to Glory*

The Unexpected Jesus

Luke 19:1–9

Zacchaeus was a wealthy Jew who lived in Jericho and made a handsome living as a tax collector for the Romans. Because of his occupation, he was viewed by his contemporaries as a sinner before God and a traitor to his country.

Despite his ostracization by fellow Jews, Zacchaeus was not void of spiritual sensitivity. When he learned that Jesus was coming to the area, he determined that he must see the much-heralded Teacher whose preaching, teaching and miracle-working were having such a profound effect.

Because he was short, he climbed a sycamore-fig tree in order to get a good view of Jesus. It must have taken a good deal of fortitude for this rich, sophisticated businessman to throw caution to the wind, to run ahead of Jesus and His entourage and to scamper up a tree as he probably had not done since boyhood.

Amazingly, when Jesus reached the spot, He took notice of the figure hidden among the branches, and He addressed Zacchaeus.

The mass of humanity crowding around the Master would not have expected Jesus to notice Zacchaeus, much less address him. But God Incarnate had thoughts that were not merely human thoughts. His ways, as the prophet Isaiah declared, are not our ways. So Jesus spoke to Zacchaeus.

Again the crowd was amazed. They might have expected Jesus to rebuke Zacchaeus for his traitorous ways, for serving as an agent of the Roman government, for seeking personal gain by charging more than the assessed tax. There is no way they could have been prepared to hear Jesus say: "Zacchaeus, come down immediately, I must stay at your house today."

It was an invitation Zacchaeus could not refuse. We can assume that the Holy Guest spoke lovingly and directly to the chief tax collector of the district. And we can assume that the divine Visitor outlined the plan of salvation. These assumptions are based on the results of their meeting. We know, first of all, that Zacchaeus found salvation, for Jesus declared, "Today salvation has come to this house" (Luke 19:9). We know, also, that a great transformation had taken place in Zacchaeus. This man, who had accumulated a fortune through dishonest means, now stated freely, "Look, Lord! Here and now I give half of my possessions to the poor, and if I have cheated anybody out of anything, I will pay back four times the amount" (Luke 19:8).

What a marvelous change came to the life of one who had an unexpected encounter with Jesus Christ. And such unexpected encounters are still happening!

Robert E. Thomson, *The War Cry*

A Divine Reveille

2 Corinthians 5:17

To some men and women there comes the rare experience when it seems, if only for a moment, that the barriers between God and the soul disappear and they find themselves in His very presence. Such an experience is often decisive in that life is never quite the same again; something new has broken into it, adding new vision, beauty and power. It is a new dawn, a divine reveille, which arouses one to action for God.

This is what happened in the life of Matthew the tax collector. As he sat at his work Jesus burst in upon his vision. For a moment a door opened into another world, and Matthew heard an authoritative voice calling, "Follow Me!" (Matt. 9:9). He closed his books, put away his money and followed Jesus.

This one supreme, quiet, insistent voice called him to a high vocation. It was the imperative command of a royal person.

Following Christ, like falling in love, is a mutual matter. It is Christ coming to man and man coming to Christ. Christ offers us a new chance, a new life—and from no one else can we obtain it.

Other religious leaders had frequently passed the tollbooth where Matthew sat at the receipt of custom, but they made no impression on him, nor did he on them. To them, Matthew was a traitor to the Jewish race in the service of the hated Romans, collecting taxes from the Jews for a foreign power. To them he was a social outcast.

But Jesus never looked upon men in terms of what they were, but in terms of what they might become. Jesus knew what potential lay dormant in the tax gatherer, and He stirred impulses that opened up vistas to a new life. Where the Jews saw a rogue, Jesus saw a potentially honest man. If Matthew's pen had been used for perfidy, a new Matthew could wield it to write a gospel. The crafty auditor could become, through Christ, a Christian author giving to the world a record of the immortal Word.

Is there a more inspiring thought to those who have failed, whose lives are blighted and broken, than that Christ always looks for the best in men? He knows the worst is capable of the best through divine grace.

To see in Christ a love which is not in ourselves, and to open our hearts to it, is the way of salvation. The real Matthew was awakened. The world becomes a different place when we follow Christ. Life vibrates with a new challenge: "Therefore, if anyone is in Christ, he is a new creation; the old has gone, the new has come!" (2 Cor. 5:17).

George B. Smith, *Meditations for the Ordinary Man*

A Happy Religion

Psalm 34:1

A happy religion is an attractive one. The bulk of the people around us are unsatisfied and unhappy, if not positively miserable. Nothing impresses them like the appearance of a glad and happy spirit in others. When they see it, they are apt to ask for the secret of the gladness and wonder whether they could find the same joy themselves.

All genuine salvation results in happiness and joy in the Lord. This is the experience of all truly converted souls. The first feeling of the newborn child of God is to sing or shout the praises of his Savior. Who is there that has not, at such times, felt heart and soul in harmony with the poet Watts when he writes:

> I'll praise my Maker while I've breath,
> And when my voice is lost in death
> Praise shall employ my nobler powers.
> My days of praise shall ne'er be past,
> While life, or thought, or being last,
> Or immortality endures.

Look at these two dear apostles, Paul and Silas, shut up in the deepest, darkest dungeon of the prison at Philippi. What a pitiable spectacle they present! Their feet are made fast in the stocks so that they can neither stand up nor lie down; and their poor backs are bleeding and smarting as the result of the scourging they received the day before.

How do they pass the weary hours? Let us listen. At midnight they burst out into prayer and praise—not a muttered, mumbled, melancholy sound, neither heard by man nor regarded by God. No, it is a glad song that rings out loud enough for all the prisoners to hear and, best of all, that reaches the ears of God.

To show His approval of this hallelujah kind of business, God caused an earthquake that shook the prison and liberated the prisoners. Then came the conversion of the jailor and the freedom of the Apostles, while thousands of people have been blessed through reading the story.

This joyful praise–God religion will help to keep depression, unbelief, and dissatisfaction away and will assist our growth in holiness.

William Booth, *The Warrior's Daily Portion*

The Bright Morning Star

Revelation 22:16

Immanuel Kant wrote: "Two things fill the mind with ever new and increasing wonder and awe—the starry heavens above me and the moral law within me." My favorite sight in nature is the spectacle of a star–bejeweled sky on a dark night. It fills the soul with reverence to contemplate not only their beauty but their fathomless distance and titanic size.

Enshrined in our archives of family memories is one evening when camping in northern Canada, after our evening campfire had died away we took our children down by the lakeside where we could view the open sky. It was one of those dark clear nights, and free of artificial lights the star–spangled sky sparkled in breathtaking majesty. Our son, then about seven years of age, looked up, and in a tone of awe and reverence said, "I never knew there were so many stars." It was a moment of prized discovery.

Every person of Christ's day had a picture in mind when Christ said, "I am the Bright Morning Star" (Rev. 22:16). The stars figured prominently in their lives.

The morning star heralds the dawn of a new day. Christ ushered in a new age. His life gave promise of a new and bright future.

At dawn, the stars gradually give way to the light until finally there is only one star shining. All other stars fade from view except for the morning star. Christ, as the Bright Morning Star, shines brightly when all other stars of our life fade away. Those things which now shine so brightly on the horizon of our lives will someday fade and vanish away. The stars of prestige, position, possessions and persons dear to us will one by one grow dim and fade away. But after everything else has vanished, Christ will still shine brightly and will radiantly beam over the horizon of life when the dawn breaks and the shadows flee away.

As the morning star is the brightest star in the sky, so is Christ the most radiant light ever to shine in our world. All other luminaries pale compared to the brilliance of His life. He is the peerless one of all history.

For many centuries man charted his journeys by the stars. Sailors navigated the seas with their eyes on the stars. The stars were the road maps, the directional signs for their times.

From Christ alone can we take bearings for our journey on the sea of life. Our compass needle will cease its oscillations when its directional point is turned toward the One who is the Bright Morning Star. Like a mariner, we may reckon all our decisions and directions from that Star.

Henry Gariepy, *Portraits of Christ*

A Christian in a Nuclear Age

Matthew 5:9

To contemplate a nuclear conflict within our lifetime is, for most of us, to think the unthinkable. What parent among us has not pondered his sleeping child and tried to guess whether that young life will end prematurely in instantaneous vaporization or, even worse perhaps, will drain away in the lingering throes of radiation sickness? But it is not only the parent who harbors secret thoughts. Today's child does not have to be very old before he becomes aware of the awful possibility of a world–consuming conflagration.

The Christian will not be fooled into thinking that the issues are political only. The Holy Spirit will guide him to a recognition of the deep moral questions at the heart of the matter. What can the individual Christian, who has no public influence or power, do to help?

Be as well–informed as possible. Be calm and at peace within your soul by daily walking close to the Lord who loves you. Remember that while missiles can be dismantled, knowledge cannot be uninvented, and so the human race has and will forever have the ability to destroy itself entirely in a short and measurable span of time. Pray therefore for the leaders of nations, for their military advisors, for the peace talks negotiators. Prayer means the individual Christian, without political power, may influence events in accordance with God's will.

Refuse to see the presence of nuclear devices on our planet as inevitable. Do not leave the thinking or the voicing of opinions only to the politicians. They need our Christian help to clarify the moral issues. Work on public opinion, not stridently but wisely, within your own circle of friends and contacts.

Living in the nuclear age requires courage to face up to the awful possibilities for the future. We can pray to be granted courage, but let us pray also for God to raise up men and women with obedient Christian hearts and able Christian minds to give us a theology for a nuclear age. God is alive. Jesus is risen. God is Lord of every molecule, every atom, every nucleus. We are God's appointed steward over the created order. The cross of Jesus speaks reconciliation.

Hope in an armed world? Only in Jesus can we find hope. Without Him, we are running out of time.

Shaw Clifton, *Strong Doctrine, Strong Mercy*

A Tribute of Love

John 20:21

In November 1910, we were ushered into the Founder's study, as he had expressed his wish of having a last word with us before we were sent forth to the Army's distant battlefield of India. Slowly feeling his way to where we were standing—his eyesight having become impaired—he sat down saying: "Come right near to me, my children."

Then, sitting quite close to him, his hands holding ours, he began, "You are going to India, and we are sending you to a very hard part of it, too, and I feel that it will mean to you hardship and sacrifice. I want you to be brave like unto that noble, heroic woman, Colonel Yuddha Bai, who has fought so brave a fight in that very part of India, and who has now laid down the sword."

And on went our grand old leader, speaking words of counsel and warning, comfort and encouragement, in accents of a father's concern and compassion concerning his two officers about to depart. Then he knelt in prayer, his hands still clasping ours, when he poured out his soul in yearning, passionate appeal for India, for "these girls, who were now going out to hardship and loneliness." One more long look at our grand old General standing before us as the prophet of God, yet so tender in the task entrusted to us, so buoyant in his faith for us, could we ever disappoint such trust? Out we went, our eyes blinded with tears, but in our hearts the fixed determination to go and carry out the sacred charge to our fullest ability.

It was far inland in India, in the land of Marashtra, a year or so later. We had left the great high road and were trudging miles and miles over the wild, barren countryside, leaving civilization and comfort far behind. How long the way seemed, how merciless the sun's rays over our heads.

At last we reached our longed-for destination of our weary journey. The question arose in my mind, whether it had been really worthwhile, wise too, to undertake such a hazardous, fatiguing journey to reach this village. I learned to look at the matter in a different light the following morning.

Great excitement of interest and joy was manifest on all sides among the villages, and a demonstrative welcome given us. What was the meaning of all this? Ah, we understood when we learned the story. Many years ago an English lady, the first that ever was looked upon by these people, had come to be one of them, teaching them of Jesus, caring for them in their sicknesses. And this lady was Yuddha Bai, and her memory was still fragrant and revered in spite of the lapse of time between.

Catherine Bannister, *The Practice of Sanctification*

The Secret of it All (cont.)

2 Corinthians 5:15

W ould we come and look where she had lived? They led us to one of the huts somewhat on the outskirts of the village. A simple mud hut consisting of two pieces, whereof the larger served for meeting place. The inner had been the Colonel's own little room.

Dismay took hold of me as I looked. Could it be possible for anyone to live and work in this small space, and that for three consecutive years? No room for table or chair or any other bit of furniture, just a raised mudbank in one corner which had served in turn as table, sitting and sleeping place. In this place Yuddha Bai had lived and toiled for the population of the village three full years, absolutely separated from all European contact, comforts, and habits. She—the lady of gentle birth, reared in a home of ease and comfort, surrounded by all the culture and refinement.

Considering all that and hearing so much more of her devotion, her abnegation day by day and year after year, how could we help being deeply moved? How my little bit of discomfort paled into insignificance beside her noble sacrifice. For me it meant just a few weeks out in the villages and back again to home and comfort, while this lady had given her life to that one village and district.

What was the motive for this life of self-renunciation, of sacrifice, conforming to the life and habits of these villages, down to dress and food, learning their language? Such came the insistent question—the motive, what the underlying secret? Could her rich gifts, her graces, her social position, her beautiful devotion not be used to better advantage in the home country? Were they not spent in vain in the lonely deserts of this barren land?

Only one answer is possible. Is it not because she had drunk deeply of the spirit of her Master and tasted something of "the joy that was set before Him, enduring the cross and despising the shame," (Heb. 12:2) in going after Him to seek His other sheep, for whom, too, He died.

Was it not because that love, that wonderful love of Calvary, had constrained her to count all things—all these earthly advantages—but "loss for the excellency of the knowledge of Jesus Christ" (Phil. 3:8).

And shall it not be found to be our secret too, of a joyous, blessed life with Him and spent for Him here in the days of our warfare and pilgrimage?

Catherine Bannister, *The Practice of Sanctification*

Moved With Compassion

Luke 19:41

The Savior of men came to seek and to save
    The souls who were lost to the good;
His Spirit was moved for the world which He loved,
    With the boundless compassion of God.
And still there are fields where the laborers are few,
    And still there are souls without bread;
And still eyes that weep where the darkness is deep;
    And still straying sheep to be led.

        Except I am moved with compassion
            How dwelleth Thy Spirit in me?
            In word and in deed
            Burning love is my need,
        I know I can find this in Thee.

Oh, is not the Christ 'midst the crowd of today
    Whose questioning cries do not cease?
And will He not show to the hearts that would know
    The things that belong to their peace?
But how shall they hear if the preacher forbear
    Or lack in compassionate zeal?
Or how shall hearts move with the Master's own love,
    Without His anointing and seal?

It is not with might to establish the right,
    Nor yet with the wise to give rest;
The mind cannot show what the heart longs to know
    Nor comfort a people distressed.
O Savior of men, touch my spirit again,
    And grant that Thy servant may be
Intense every day, as I labor and pray,
    Both instant and constant for Thee.

Albert Orsborn, *The Beauty of Jesus*

The Sacrifice of Stewardship

Romans 12:1

Stewardship, we have said, is a privilege more than a duty. Now I am saying that stewardship is sacrifice. Most people think of sacrifice as something done out of a sense of obligation or oughtness. Few think of it as a privilege. When is it a privilege? It is a privilege when we give up the old self-centered existence for the God-centered existence—when we deny ourselves and take up our cross and follow Christ (Mark 8:34)—when we put to death our self-absorption (Gal. 5:24). Sacrifice is a privilege when it opens the door to new life, when it takes us out of ourselves as we leave behind the lesser selves created by our sin.

Stewardship is the day by day living out of Christian privilege through the process of self-denial. The self-denial is essential because seeking that which is worthy requires the abandonment of that which is unworthy.

Stewardship is a sacrifice in two ways. First it is sacrifice in the sense of something given up. Second, it is sacrifice in the sense of something given.

The Apostle Paul appeals to the Roman Christians: "In view of God's mercy ... offer your bodies as living sacrifices, holy and pleasing to God—this is your spiritual act of worship" (Rom. 12:1). This presentation of ourselves is a twofold sacrifice. Yes, we become masters of dispossession in contrast to being bent on mastering the art of acquisition. But this "giving up" is an empty exercise if it is not the reflection of the "living sacrifice" of which Paul speaks. The all-important sacrifice is giving ourselves to God. This complete sacrifice triggers a life-offering of reflexive sacrifices as the offering of ourselves to God works itself out in daily offerings.

Our stewardship is the substance of our commitment. It is the sacrificial lifestyle of those who have sacrificed themselves to a God who sacrificed everything. It is the joyful practice of self-denial. The crazy thing about stewardship is that sacrifice is profoundly rewarding.

What is the one enduring treasure? It is the kingdom of God. Those who take this Kingdom seriously look at their own material treasures in an entirely different light. They cease being treasures and become resources. They become expendable for the kingdom.

Philip D. Needham, *The War Cry*

Our Father

Luke 10:22

⤳

All nations of this world, both civilized and barbarous, have a God of some kind, but their God is mostly a cold, hard, unloving force. The God of merely nominal Christians is no better than a stern magistrate, the author of a set of rules which they hate to keep. Our Lord states a general truth, attested both by the history and experience of mankind, when He says that no man can apprehend the nature of God by his intellect alone.

We are told as children that God made the worlds, and as adults we accept the statement because no other adequate cause for the daily marvels of the near earth and the distant universe can be found or suggested. But to accept God as Creator does not reveal Him to us as a Father. We can never know Him as Love, never understand His real nature and His feelings towards us, till we see Him taking our flesh upon Him, bearing our burdens, our sorrows, and our sins, living with us, dying for us, in the body called Christ Jesus. Only the Son can reveal Him.

Do you remember how, when you were little, your own father represented not only all power but all tenderness to you? If you were frightened, you sheltered in his arms; if you were hurt, you ran to him for sympathy; if you were lonely, he comforted you; and when your child's heart felt a thrill of love and tenderness, it found a full return from him.

God loves us more than that. Multiply the tenderest father's power of self-sacrificing love by infinity and that is how God loves. But how was He to make us know that unmeasured love and sympathy and every gracious quality which our hungry hearts demand?

Just as our fathers showed their love by stooping to our level, by becoming children with us, by incessant care and pains in all details of our need, so the Father of fathers has done for His children. He took our flesh, with its pain, hunger, temptation and weakness upon Him. He put himself into our possible circumstances—of poverty, homelessness, friendlessness; He came to the level of the outcast by law as well as by misfortune and ended His life with sorrow and suffering by the most horrible of deaths.

Love must always express itself by sacrifice. Whether it be the love of parent, lover or friend, sooner or later it meets and stands the test of sacrifice. The Lord high over all became a reproach of men, that we might understand His tender love for us.

Elizabeth Swift Brengle, *Half Hours with My Guide*

The God Who Hides Himself

Isaiah 45:15

Elizabeth Browning, with a poet's insight, said that every common bush was afire with God, but that the fact was unnoticed by the people who sat by it and just picked blackberries. In his poem *The Kingdom of God*, Francis Thompson says to the folk who think of God as dwelling "above the bright blue sky," that this world is so full of spiritual truth and heavenly beings that if we turned over a stone or looked behind a tree we might start an angel flying.

God never openly advertises Himself in His works. An attitude of reverence and effort of mind are necessary if we are to become aware of God in the things He has made. Unlike ourselves, who wait for applause when we have done something well, God does not bow about upon the stage where His works are shown, waiting for us to praise Him. He paints the wayside flower and lights the evening star and leaves them to be His silent witnesses. He places His song in the throats of singing birds, in the sound of waterfalls and streams, and in the crash of heavy seas against cliffs and hides behind them all.

If only He would do something dramatic and make us all see Him! When Jesus Christ was here in human form He said "No" to the temptation to win the people to His side by casting Himself down from the top of the temple, to be rescued by a company of angels, or by making stones into bread or by defying the strength of the spikes that fastened Him to His cross on Calvary and coming down from it. He does not work that way.

Men have always wanted a spectacular revelation of God. Even the prophet Isaiah seemed troubled about the apparent unwillingness of God to reveal Himself. "Truly you are a God who hides Himself," (Isa. 45:15) he said. In that expression, he brought out one of the deep mysteries of the Christian faith—a God who hides Himself.

Then came Jesus Christ, quietly, not in a great demonstration of power or majesty. Those with spiritual insight saw His glory. But a few years later He went away and was seen no more in physical form. Why does He conceal Himself? Because the Christian life is essentially one of faith, with lessons of trust to be learned which could not be gained in any other way.

When it is necessary God, standing within the shadows, will reveal His presence. Though unseen, all through life's journey He is near us.

James Morgan, *Nature Speaks*

Discovering Your Gifts

1 Corinthians 12:7

There is a trend today for questionnaires which are designed to help you discover which gift or gifts of the Spirit have been given to you. I sometimes wonder how we ever managed to know what God was up to before these questionnaires hit the market!

It takes time to realize what abilities God is placing within you. Remember that you have natural talents and abilities which will be enormously enhanced when used for God's purposes and the benefit of others. In addition, the Holy Spirit will gift you supernaturally with at least one spiritual gift. Be patient. Remain open. Stay humble.

Do not rush to conclude that a particular gift is yours. Allow yourself time and opportunity to realize with a steadily growing conviction that God has granted you something specific. Doors will open to you presenting situations in which you can be of service and calling for some ability or another. Take these opportunities and assess your progress for yourself. Did it go well? Did you feel at ease? How costly to you in nervous energy was the experience? Did anyone seem helped? Has anyone told you they were helped or encouraged by what you did or said? A sensible and prayerful consideration of questions like these will help you to know the direction in which the Lord is working in you. You would be wise also, once you have been able to experiment a bit, to talk things over with a mature Christian friend or leader.

Later years may bring a discovery of still further gifts and abilities. The Lord is always ready to surprise us and to do a new thing! He is also ready to remove from us that which has been received from Him but which has been selfishly used, for example, for personal glory or boasting. That is why, once we know the gift He has bestowed, we ought never to cease to thank Him for it and to plead with Him for grace to use it properly and in a spirit of Christlike love.

Shaw Clifton, *Never the Same Again*

Living By the Spirit

Galatians 5:25

This is the age of the Holy Spirit for the church. The energizing purpose of the Holy Spirit is continued under the New Covenant. With the baptism of the Holy Spirit, God promises and provides power (Acts 1:8). He is not satisfied with Christians who are weaklings.

Gifts are bestowed "to prepare God's people for works of service, so that the body of Christ may be built up" (Eph. 4:12). The Holy Spirit comes for the practical purpose of preparing men to be useful to God.

But, in a marked sense, He comes for the ethical purpose of developing Christlikeness, of cleansing, of baptizing the heart with love, of maturing character.

Paul wrote to the Corinthian church: "Do you not know that your body is a temple of the Holy Spirit, who is in you, whom you have received from God? You are not your own" (1 Cor. 6:19). The Holy Spirit comes to, and is now present with, all believers. As Paul expressed to the church in Rome, "If anyone does not have the Spirit of Christ, he does not belong to Christ" (Rom. 8:9). This is not surprising since the Holy Spirit, as the Administrator of the Godhead, has actively dealt with the person in bringing him to Christ.

There is a difference between the Holy Spirit being present with the believer and His filling him. God wants His temple filled! What does this say to the Church and to the individual Christian? It says that this sanctifying act of the Spirit is still today a blood-bought privilege, to them that ask, that Christ yearns to bestow the same experience of sanctification, that surely He even now continues His prayer before the Father for His children: "Sanctify them!"

Since we "live by the Spirit," we are exhorted also to practice a life of ordered holiness by the Spirit's very presence and power—"Let us also walk by the Spirit" (Gal. 5:25 RSV).

Believing in Christ for sanctification as well as for regeneration through the work of the Holy Spirit introduces one into a life of power and victory. Thus, to "walk by the Spirit" is to live one's whole life in accordance with the mind of Christ. Walking by the Spirit calls for a fellowship on the cross with Christ, a crucifixion of self. "May I never boast, except in the cross of our Lord Jesus Christ, through which the world has been crucified to me, and I to the world" (Gal. 6:14).

Milton S. Agnew, *The Holy Spirit: Friend and Counselor*

The Word Spoke

2 Timothy 3:15

It isn't by accident that the Salvation Army's first doctrine centers on the Word of God: "We believe that the Scriptures of the Old and New Testaments were given by inspiration of God, and that they only constitute the divine rule of Christian faith and practice."

Without the Scriptures we would be lost. The Scriptures give direction, correction, challenge, command, hope, explanation and foundation for living. Scripture is God's truth for His world. Its words bring life. Its pages confirm the possibility of forgiveness, salvation, renewal and empowering for living as God intends His people to live. Its messages are never exhausted. There is always more to find, more to take in, more to live by. To explore Scripture is to embark on an adventure that goes on and on, challenging both mind and heart and promising God's presence throughout the journey.

The psalmist was convinced of its value: "Your Word is a lamp to my feet and a light for my path" (Psalm 119:105). In the same psalm we read: "Your Word, O Lord, is eternal; it stands firm in the heavens" (v. 89). Writing to Timothy in the early days of the Church, the Apostle Paul declared that the holy Scriptures "are able to make you wise for salvation through faith in Christ Jesus" (2 Tim. 3:15).

With numerous translations of the Bible available to help our understanding, we may reflect on what William Booth said shortly after the Revised Version had been introduced in 1881: "I want to see a new translation of the Bible into the hearts and conduct of living men and women." If the word of God is to rule our lives we must study it, heed it—and live by it!

God sent His Son—the Word of God—to speak His words personally. We have some of those life-giving words recorded for our guidance and inspiration in the New Testament.

Life-giving though His words were and are, Jesus knew that words alone were not enough to meet the need of mankind. Ultimately He spoke supremely through His sacrificial death on the cross. The word was love—unconditional, total, self-giving love. The Word spoke with His life.

Robert Street, *Called To Be God's People*

First Things First

1 Timothy 1:5

꒖

Holiness was a passion with Paul. Reading what he wrote about it in epistle after epistle, it is impossible to miss the note of intensity. Addressing Timothy, the apostle impressed upon the young pastor that he ought to enjoy the blessing himself, and lead the Ephesian believers to the life of holiness: "The goal of this command is love, which comes from a pure heart and a good conscience and a sincere faith" (1 Tim. 1:5).

Paul challenged Timothy to lead the Church toward God's ideal. That ideal is love. It is powerful, making an immensely effective impact because it is the essence of holiness.

The divine love for the world—so immense, so unconditional, continuing to pour out its undeserved care even when rejected and answered by human hate—is to be reflected, and in some measure to be repeated, in Christian people.

Love like that glows through an evangelist of whom Billy Graham tells. At a university he had tried to reach the students with the gospel, but their reaction was hostile. One girl told him she didn't believe the things he had said. So the evangelist asked if he could pray with her. She replied, "Nobody ever prayed for me before, I guess it won't do any harm." He prayed, while she sat with her eyes open. But then she noticed something that amazed her. His tears were flowing as he prayed. She began to cry, too. "No one in my entire life has shed a tear for me," she sobbed, and then that young woman accepted Christ.

Anyone who imagines that sanctification sets you apart from sinners, aloof in your isolation, needs to take another look at the loving, approachable, healing Son of God. There is holiness incarnate.

To make His people caring and compassionate, resolutely willing to be Christlike in all their relationships, is the end toward which God's Spirit is always working. Only when a person lives lovingly does he or she demonstrate genuine Christianity.

Love and holiness, standing together in our text, are inseparable. Love, purity, a good conscience, sincere faith. Simple qualities all, but utterly indispensable components of the character of any who would serve in Christ's name. These are the elements of holiness, and that is surely first among first things.

Edward Read, *Timothy, My Son*

I Believe God!

Acts 27:25

～

Paul was a passenger on a ship about to be wrecked when he said, "I believe God!" Many of his shipmates had already given up hope of surviving the ordeal. But Paul told them of his faith in God and his certainty that, in spite of winds and waves, all on board would get to land safely. Said Paul, "I believe God!" (Acts 27:25 NLT).

This is a declaration of faith. Others stared in numbed despair at the fury of the elements, their voices muted in fear. Paul spoke, not to cry in terror, but to testify to his faith in God and God's promised deliverance.

Our world needs this kind of Christian witness. Fearful things may be happening; even more terrifying things may be forecast. The world that now is may be heading for certain shipwreck. But God and righteousness and truth will endure. Witness to this in the midst of personal turmoil or world confusion. Give voice to your faith and say, "I believe God!"

This is an attitude of expectation. Paul's reaction to varying situations was automatic and consistent because his dominant mood was faith. Attitude is much more important than circumstances. Real environment is created by the state or quality of our feelings. Situations are faced with faith or fear, thankfulness or complaints, cheerfulness or dejection, according to our prevailing attitude. Paul stood on the deck of that doomed vessel among a group of men who had already given up. They saw only dark danger. Paul saw God and bright expectation when he said, "I believe God!"

This is a realized experience. It was experiential—it reached back into the past. Active faith in God soon acquires personal precedents. Paul had "memory markers," and when he stood on that quivering deck and said, "I believe God," he was making a statement grounded in part in his own previous encounters and observations.

His experience was also experimental—it reached forward into the future. Paul had faith in God for the present and the coming emergency. His complete statement was, "I believe God, it will be just as He said."

Your private world may be shipwrecked. You may face discouraging, fearful prospects. Have faith in God. Say, "I believe God!" Make it an expression of an inner attitude, and it will become the declaration of a daily experience.

Bramwell Tripp, *To the Point*

When Tragedy Strikes

Job 13:15

⤳

The Book of Job lives because the heart of the world beats in it. Within its pages are enshrined some of the deepest questionings and yearnings of the human spirit. Time has not altered these, for the book could be written in thousands of homes today.

When a young wife dies leaving motherless children, or a husband is killed, robbing the home of the breadwinner, or disaster overtakes a business which took years to build, the same cries are wrung from the heart.

Added to life's tragedies are floods that drown, cold which freezes, earthquakes which smash cities to ruin, volcanoes which pour their boiling lava into homes. So Job seems to be right when he cries: "Yet man is born to trouble, as surely as sparks fly upward" (Job 5:7).

Job was a chieftain of immense wealth. He was wise and the spiritual father of his tribe. His creed was that God prospers and blesses those who trust in Him. But when calamity came to him, everything he believed about God was contradicted and his creed went to the winds.

In the story of Job, God accepted the challenge of the devil, and soon Job's life was turned into desperate havoc. Calamity after calamity befell Job. The Sabeans and Chaldeans slew his servants and cattle; lightning wrecked his house and slew his children. He became affected with a dreadful disease. Job did not understand what God was doing, yet he clung to the certainty that God would see him through. When Job said, "Though He slay me, yet will I trust in him," (Job 13:15 KJV) it was one of the most sublime utterances in the Old Testament.

Here lies the answer to the problem of suffering. Job moved from a belief in a creed to a trust in a Person. There is a difference in belief in God with the head and trust in God with the heart. Job won through, proving to the world that God is loved and trusted for His own sake alone.

Have the events of life made us cynical? Has suffering been too much for our faith? Our faith is that no ultimate harm can come to him who trusts in God. When the end comes the trumpets sounding on the other side will mean the final vindication of God.

George B. Smith, *Meditations for the Ordinary Man*

Adaptability

Hebrews 13:6–7

I sat somewhat disinterestedly in my window seat on the airplane as it taxied down the congested runway at Los Angeles International Airport, only to be jolted from my lethargy by a paradoxical sight. There, among the enormous lanes with their pulsating jet blasts and their furor to give gravity another "in your face" demonstration, a hawk hovered over a narrow strip of brown grass. She was fixed solely on the job at hand—to find a hapless field mouse for dinner. Now there's adaptability, I thought, for both the hawk and her prey. Such an inhospitable environment, but life must go on.

The hawk's forebears played out the same deadly drama long before the first Spanish padre surveyed the valley that tumbles down to the restless Pacific—long before the first clipboard gang decided that this was a good place for an airport.

I bear no ill will toward technocrats, or those who go giddy over the prospect of covering every vacant piece of earth with bituminous concrete. But I secretly hope that someday the predictable cycle of life will revert to its original design for Ms. Hawk's and Mr. Field Mouse's progeny, if they are lucky enough to survive.

Armchair philosophers muse that change is the only certainty. We look in the mirror and tend to agree. But what happens when a firestorm rages within, triggered by changing circumstances beyond our control? Do we perish or do we adapt?

Our first inclination may be to roll over with our belly up. But there's something fiercely noble about the other option—to persevere and even to prosper. That ability, I'm convinced, is borne from another realm. I've seen too many people of faith standing exultantly over their "Goliaths" to think otherwise.

The Christian commits not only his strength of character, but also his weakness and mortal fears to the preeminent figure of history. Christ sides with him and says, "I know all about it. I've been there. I've done that. Life goes on, and it even gets better."

I believe I can adapt to that! Or to say it another way—because you believe, you can adapt to that!

David Atkins, *The War Cry*

Forever Flowing Free

Psalm 77:19

The mighty oceans should not seem so ordinary. They should inspire awe and wonder. I know. I grew up by the Atlantic in a Maine seaport. When I stood at the shore in a storm, drenched with the thundering salt spray of crashing waves, I experienced the power at a primal level. To gaze from shore at the far horizon was to contemplate the unimaginable. To sail even a few miles from shore was to feel lost in the vastness.

The poet has written with the ocean swelling in his imagination:

> Praise to the Lord,
> Who, when tempests their warfare are waging,
> Who, when the elements madly around thee are raging
> Biddeth them cease,
> Turneth their fury to peace,
> Whirlwinds and waters assuaging.

Hymn writers have used the ocean as a metaphor in many ways. The Bible's main marine theme is the beauty, immensity and wonder of the oceans. In Psalm 139, David reflects on God's omnipresence and love which follows and surrounds us wherever we go, even when we try to run from Him. "Where can I flee from your presence?" David asks rhetorically. And then he answers his own question. If David tries to hide high up in heaven, or deep down in the earth, or out at the eastern horizon where the sun rises, God is there.

Then David looks one last direction, to the west, out over the seemingly endless Mediterranean. "If I settle on the far side of the sea, even there your hand will guide me, Your right hand will hold me fast." We, too, know the unceasing presence and unfailing comfort of God whose great love, boundless as the mighty ocean, includes us all.

John Greenleaf Whittier's timeless poem affirms God's mysterious, all-inclusive love:

> Immortal love, forever full,
> Forever flowing free,
> Forever shared, forever whole;
> A never-ebbing sea.

Kenneth Baillie, *The War Cry*

On Giving

1 John 3:16–17

꒦

God is the great Giver. It is not merely that giving is one of the great principles of action with Him, or one of the leading laws which He has laid down for His government; it is more than that—it is His nature.

We all know the difference. We can see it in a small way when we compare some of the people around us with each other. There are those who are selfish by nature, but who have, by force of will, or force of habit, or both, come in many matters to be kindly and generous in spite of their natural preferences and disposition. There are others to whom generosity is their natural element, of whom we can say they have a generous nature.

Thus it is with our God, only ten thousand times more so! His acts are generous. He gives because it is of His very nature to give. He gives regardless of the gratitude He may or may not receive. He gives as the eternal outflow of a loving heart. He gives because He just loves to give.

The moment we think of God at all we think of goodness, of one who is sending His rain on the evil and the good, feeding the wild beasts of the forests. The God our hearts need for the bestowal of our love and trust and service, the God for whom we could be willing to suffer and some even to die, must be the generous Being from whom there flows that loving stream of good toward all. Yes, this is the God we adore—the Great Giver.

Now we say that we are the children of God. Ought not the children to resemble the Parent? How can we consider ourselves to belong to His family unless, up to the measure of our ability, and so far as we have been entrusted with what can be bestowed, we are givers too?

When I speak of giving I am not thinking about material possessions only. I am thinking about influence. What a gift we can bestow there! I am thinking about kindness. What wealth every one of us may place in the hands and hearts of those who are around us by kind word and kind deeds!

I am thinking about faith. What a wonderful gift we can bestow upon others by our confidence in them, to their great enrichment! And I am thinking also of love, in the sense of goodwill, of service, of willingness to sacrifice for the good of the object loved. What riches God has bestowed upon us in giving us the power to love our fellows!

This also applies to our material possessions. "If anyone has material possessions," says the Apostle John, "and sees his brother in need but has no pity on him, how can the love of God be in him?" (1 John 3:17).

Bramwell Booth, *Life and Religion*

Christian Perfection

1 John 3:6

Spiritual health, or daily victory over temptation, should be taken as the Christian norm. In one sense "normal" is a totally inadequate word. It is "super-normal," one of the wonders of divine grace, that we should triumph at all over the sins which do so easily beset us. Yet we should not think of this life of daily victory as if it were reserved for the few who, by reason of disposition, could be described as naturally religious. The victorious life is not beyond the normal believer.

This does not mean that perfection in the final sense—nothing to learn, no further progress to be made—is for this life. To quote John Wesley: "There is no perfection which does not admit of continual increase." As the Army Mother used to say: "Sanctification is not final growth." It is not the same as complete attainment.

Glory will be required fully to crown what grace has begun below. But that does not mean that we cannot step out here and now on the highway of holiness.

With the Apostle Paul we do not think of ourselves as having already attained perfection or as being already perfect. It is no contradiction to say that part of the experience of Christian perfection is an awareness of one's own imperfections. So the Apostle Paul could describe himself as the chief of sinners. This is why our Founder could confess: "My great sorrow is that I have served the Lord so imperfectly."

The closer a believer's communion with his Savior the more keenly does he realize how far he falls short of resembling that same Lord. His self-reproaches arise from his nearness to the Master. Were he not so aware of the beauty of Jesus the less conscious would he be of his own shortcomings.

The first word in the Christian vocabulary is not struggle—but surrender; not one more try—but to yield to the divine will; not one more effort and this time you will make it—but to submit to Another.

Frederick Coutts, *The Splendor of Holiness*

The Sound of a Distant Trumpet

Ecclesiastes 3:11

The writer of Ecclesiastes gives us one of the sublime statements of the Bible about God's creative handiwork: "He has made everything beautiful in its time" (Ecc. 3:11).

It is mind–boggling to contemplate the beauty and majesty of God's creation. Our world is one of extravagant beauty and marvelous design. We live under star–strewn skies, are greeted each day with the grand spectacle of a sunrise, walk among the exquisite beauty of flowers and songs of birds and know the restless tides of oceans and the towering grandeur of mountains. These and countless wonders all about us render us fabulously wealthy with the endowments of our Creator.

The text also brings us one of the unexpected summits of this book: "He has also set eternity in the hearts of men" (Ecc. 3:11).

All around us God has put intimations of our immortality. He has planted within us an unrelenting intuition to see beyond temporal horizons and press beyond the limits of the finite. A sense of destiny haunts us. Eternal forces ripple in our blood. Immortal cadences echo in our ears. Sublime visions flash upon the screen of our imagination. Eternity beckons as deep calls unto the depths God has put in our souls.

With Francis Thompson, from his haunting "The Hound of Heaven," we hear the sound of a distant trumpet: "Yet ever and anon a trumpet sounds/From the hid battlements of Eternity."

Augustine summarized this longing and homesickness of the soul: "O God, You have made us for Yourself and our hearts are restless until they find their rest in You."

"Eternity is at our hearts," wrote Thomas Kelly, "pressing upon our time–torn lives, warming us with intimations of an astounding destiny, calling us home unto Itself. Yielding to these persuasions, gladly committing ourselves in body and soul, utterly and completely, to the Light Within, is the beginning of true life."

May we yield to this Light within who brings radiance and joy and fullfillment.

Henry Gariepy, *Wisdom to Live By*

Following Christ

Matthew 4:19

What is following Christ? It is not difficult to discover. Here a child can be on a level with the most learned divine. It simply means keeping His words and copying His example. Following means imitating. The children of Israel followed the pillar of cloud. They went in the same direction it went; they stopped when it stopped.

Now many make a common mistake with regard to following Christ, and it is a disastrous one. They think it means following Him to heaven, and that in the most comfortable way possible. Whereas the true idea, the idea which was taught by His example—and explained a thousands times over by His words—was that following Christ means following Him from heaven into a world of sin by paths of sorrow and suffering; indeed, just doing as He did. To be a Christian in reality is to be a Christ-man or Christ-woman.

Following Christ must mean having the same purpose. How is it possible without? How can the marksman hit the same mark if he does not take the same aim? How will a vessel reach New York if she does not steer for that port? How can a man follow Christ if he is not moved by the same purpose?

What was His purpose? The salvation of the world. Not the humiliation and suffering, and agony and death. These were only the means by which the end could be reached. He wanted to reach the dying millions, and by living a divine life before them, to make the salvation of all possible, to make the salvation of multitudes sure.

This was His purpose. To this every thought, and feeling, and effort was He offered up. His whole being was consecrated to its accomplishment.

Here is your pattern. What are you living for? What is the deep secret purpose that controls and fashions your existence? Let us watch and fashion ourselves with our divine Model.

William Booth, *The Warrior's Daily Portion*

Those Pop Quizzes
Romans 14:11–12

School was usually good, except for the dreaded pop quizzes. It was like the teacher had radar, for she always knew when we were most unprepared.

"All right, class. Put away your books and take out a piece of paper. We are going to have a pop quiz."

"It's not fair. We aren't ready. We haven't had a chance to study," we'd moan.

"You are supposed to know the material and be ready whether we have a test or not."

Since there was no reasoning with her and there were only so many times we could tell the school nurse that our malaria was flaring up again, all we could do was take the test and pray that we remembered the work.

It is important to be prepared, for living is one test after another. Some are multiple choice (good, better, best) while others are more true/false, right/wrong. Some are judgment questions—if a tractor trailer is doing 65 mph on the interstate and I have my old Chevy van with zero acceleration power, can I make the merge without being demolished? How can I relate to our teenage kids and still keep my sanity?

Still others are essay questions that test how well you know yourself and know the Lord as your Savior and guide. In those tests of integrity, when no teacher is looking and there is no answer key, it is important to be prepared. We will not receive a grade but will be called to explain what we have done with our lives on the final exam of life.

Scripture tells us that, "Every knee will bow before Me [Jesus] and every tongue will confess to God. So then, each of us will give an account of himself to God" (Rom. 14:11–12). And for that test, we never know the time or the day so we can't wait until the night before and cram for it. We must be ready at all times.

It also tells us that we should be ready to offer answers to those who are searching. "Always be prepared to give an answer to everyone who asks you to give the reason for the hope that you have" (1 Pet. 3:15). The hope that we have is in Jesus as our Savior and friend who saves from sin and has changed our lives. And if you ask me why, I'll tell you.

A. Kenneth Wilson, *The War Cry*

Our Place in the Son

John 14:13

Ⰶ

It was the hottest day on record in Washington, D.C. Few people ventured out on the blistering sidewalks that sent up a nearly visible steamy mist. Factoring in the humidity, the index reached 111 degrees.

Perhaps the weather heightened the odd appearance of the old man dressed in a winter flight jacket with fleece collar. He carried his belongings on his back and shuffled along the street.

Unfortunately, homeless persons are no oddity on our nation's streets. Although they have always been with us, we are becoming more keenly aware of their plight. Some two million people are homeless over the course of a year, estimates the National Alliance to End Homelessness.

If anyone understands the woundedness, the perplexity, the terror of the homeless, I suppose Jesus does. He left the splendor of heaven. He experienced the coldness, the hardness of life in a fallen world. He knew what it was to suffer loss, to bear rejection.

And how tenderly Jesus dealt with those who were beaten down by a power-conscious, materialistic society. He had nothing but censure for those who abused the poor, who contributed to the discomfort of others.

Close to the end of Jesus' Galilean ministry, the disciples witnessed Jesus' transfiguration on the mountain. In a moment of passion, one of them said, "Teacher, I will follow You wherever You go" (Matt. 8:19).

But Jesus knew they had not yet understood His mission or given their complete loyalty. They were not fully aware that discipleship must take precedence over material comforts, social duties, even family relationships. He reminded them that He didn't even have an earthly home: "Foxes have holes and birds of the air have nests, but the Son of Man has no place to lay His head" (Matt. 8:20). He was, essentially, homeless.

Or was He? Is homelessness only a matter of material dislocation or deprivation? "I came from the Father and entered the world" (John 16:28), Jesus declared. He knew exactly who He was and what He was doing. He is the welcoming hearth, the light in the window, the steaming bread prepared to give sustenance and energy to all who come to Him. He is the fixed compass point by which we can steer our lives. As we follow, we are led home to Him.

God is our home. We have only to accept His gracious gift of life, and of home, where we are open to the wind of His eternal Spirit nourishing, sheltering and loving.

Marlene Chase, *Pictures from the Word*

Hidden in Plain Sight

John 14:6

The truth is often hidden in plain sight; so close, yet so very far away. It can't be discovered in debate. It can't be realized in religion. It must be mastered through a personal relationship.

The first space walk actually occurred on Mars Hill. Stoic and Epicurean philosophers walked there every day, cogitating, ruminating and speculating about the truth. You might say they were spaced out on Mars Hill! Theirs was an impersonal God, out there, somewhere.

A foreign force, a remote ruler, a distant deity. They had even erected an altar with the inscription, "To The Unknown God."

Paul stood in the midst of the Areopagus and said: "What you worship as something unknown I am going to proclaim to you ... in Him we live and move and have our being" (Acts 17:23,28).

Paul is saying, "The truth is right there within your grasp. Come down to earth and enjoy a personal relationship with your Creator." Some elected to continue their lonely space journey while others "joined him and believed."

Pilate looked Christ straight in the eye and said, "What is truth?" (John 18:38). That's a legitimate question. We all struggle with it.

Lenin said, "Religion is the opiate of the masses." A brilliant scholar said, "God is dead." The Beatles said, "We are more popular than Christ." A well-known religious leader said, "I am the Messiah!" What is truth?

The truth was standing directly in front of Pilate in plain sight, and yet he couldn't see Him. Why? Because he hadn't experienced the Truth personally. Paul was standing before King Agrippa witnessing to the power of a changed life, and yet Agrippa could not see Him. Why? Because the Truth cannot be known through persuasion; He must be experienced personally.

Jesus said, "I am the way, the truth and the life" (John 14:6). Christ never hides. He is always in plain sight calling, "Ask, and it will be given to you; seek, and you will find; knock, and it will be opened to you" (Matt. 7:7).

"Then you will know the truth, and the truth will set you free" (John 8:32). Knowledge in this context requires an intimate personal relationship, one that is guaranteed to bring great joy and fellowship. He doesn't have to remain hidden. And that's the truth!

Joe Noland, *A Little Greatness*

Prayer for the Church

Ephesians 4:15–16

Father, we thank You for Your Church on earth. We praise You because Your Son Jesus is the head of the Church, and because the Church is His body, and we are empowered by His Spirit and commissioned to do His work and spread His gospel.

We thank You that everyone who acknowledges Jesus as Savior and Lord is part of the Church, and that each one has been differently gifted by Your Holy Spirit in order that Jesus should be glorified, that the fellowship of believers should be strengthened, and that we should serve the world in the name of Jesus Christ.

We pray for the different denominations which make up the one true Church. We praise You that this means Your work is done in many different places and that You are worshipped in many different ways. We ask You to forgive us for the fact that far too often we have allowed our denominational differences to become barriers between us and hinder the preaching of the gospel.

As we seek to work ever more closely with fellow Christians in various parts of the Church, we ask You to give us spiritual insight so that we can distinguish clearly between those spiritual truths on which we must never compromise and those things which are merely part of our human tradition.

Father, pour out Your Holy Spirit upon the Church so that we might march forward as a mighty army. Give us a holy intolerance of all injustice and oppression. Give us the courage to speak and act for the homeless and the hungry. Give us the wisdom to understand the complex moral issues of our age, and the authority to speak to the world with a prophetic voice. Give us the compassion of Jesus Himself so that, with loving hearts and in the spirit of self-sacrifice, we might bring all mankind to know the forgiveness and love of God.

Colin Fairclough, *My Father, Our Father*

A Summer Reverie

Acts 17: 27–28

God is near—so very near!
    I see Him in the rising of the sun,
    in the glow of an open fire,
    in the busy scurrying of a little mouse,
    in the radiant beauty of a wild flower.

God is near—I know He's near!
    I hear Him in the stillness of the early dawn,
    in the plaintive cooing of a dove,
    in the carefree laughter of a child,
    in the patter of the rain on parched ground.

It must be true that God is near!
    I feel Him in the companionship of many friends,
    in the unqualified love of my family,
    in the tender, prodding voice of conscience,
    in the inspiring wisdom of His word.

Yes, God is near—so very near!
    And yet, although His love I see,
    a timeless question puzzles me.
    With evidence like this about,
    how can it be that men still doubt?

Dorothy E. Breen, *It's Beautiful!*

All That I Am

Matthew 13:44–46

All that I am, All I can be
All that I have, All that is me,
Accept and use, Lord, As You would choose, Lord,
Right now, today.
Take every passion, every skill,
Take all my dreams and bend them to Your will.
My all I give, Lord, for You I'll live, Lord,
Come what may.

Often I come with my problems and cares,
Running to You when distressed;
But I must bring you the whole of my life,
Lord, I must give you my best.

All that I am, All I can be
All that I have, All that is me,
Accept and use, Lord, As You would choose, Lord,
Right now, today.
Take every passion, every skill,
Take all my dreams and bend them to Your will.
My all I give, Lord, for You I'll live, Lord,
Come what may.

Life has no purpose unless it is Yours
Life without You has no goal;
All that fullfills me is doing Your will,
Lord, I must give You my best.

All that I am, All I can be
All that I have, All that is me,
Accept and use, Lord, As You would choose, Lord,
Right now, today.
Take every passion, every skill,
Take all my dreams and bend them to Your will.
My all I give, Lord, for You I'll live, Lord,
Come what may.

William Himes, *Sing to the Lord, Vol. 1, Part 2*

Fellowship With Thee

Luke 24:32

Spirit of Eternal Love,
Guide me, or I blindly rove;
Set my heart on things above,
    Draw me after Thee.
Earthly things are paltry show,
Phantom charms, they come and go;
Give me constantly to know
    Fellowship with Thee.

Fellowship with Thee,
Fellowship with Thee,
Give me constantly to know
    Fellowship with Thee.

Come, O Spirit, take control
Where the fires of passion roll;
Let the yearnings of my soul
    Center all in Thee.
Call into Thy fold of peace
Thoughts that seek forbidden ways;
Calm and order all my days,
    Hide my life in Thee.

Thus supported, even I,
Knowing Thee forever nigh,
Shall attain that deepest joy,
    Living unto Thee.
No distracting thoughts within,
No surviving hidden sin,
Thus shall heaven indeed begin
    Here and now in me.

Albert Orsborn, *The Beauty of Jesus*

Hindrances to the Blessing

Hebrews 12:1–2

Holiness has not legs and does not go walking about visiting idle people, as a lazy Christian seemed to think who told me that he thought the experience would "come" to him "some day."

Be sure of this: it will not come, any more than a crop of potatoes will come to the lazy fellow who sits in the shade and never lifts his hoe, nor does a stroke of labor through all the spring and summer months.

Therefore, the part of wisdom is to begin at once, by a diligent study of God's Word, much secret prayer, unflinching self-examination, rigid self-denial, hearty obedience to all present light.

Before a watchmaker can clean and regulate my watch, I must give it unreservedly into His hands. Before a doctor can cure me, I must take his medicine in the manner and at the time he requires. Before a captain can navigate me across the trackless ocean, I must get on board his ship and stay there. Just so, if I would have God cleanse and regulate my heart with all its affections, if I would have Him cure my sin-sick soul, if I would have Him take me safely across the ocean of time into that greater ocean of eternity, I must put myself fully into His hands and stay there.

The second hindrance in the way of him who would be holy is imperfect faith. If you will be holy you must come to God "with a true heart in full assurance of faith" (Heb. 10:22 KJV).

Holiness is a great blessing. It is the renewal of the whole man in the image of Jesus. It is the utter destruction of all hatred, envy, malice, impatience, covetousness, pride, lust, fear of man, love of ease, love of human admiration, self-will and the like.

Is your soul hungering and thirsting for the righteousness of perfect love? Do you want to be like Jesus? Then, lay aside every weight, and the sin which does so easily beset you (Heb. 12:1). Present your body "a living sacrifice, holy, acceptable unto God, which is your reasonable service" (Rom. 12:1 KJV), and "run with patience the race which is set before you, looking unto Jesus the author and finisher of your faith" (Heb. 12:1,2 KJV).

Come to the Lord with the same simple faith that you did when you were saved. Lay your case before Him, ask Him to take away all uncleanness and to perfect you in love, and then believe that He does it.

Samuel Logan Brengle, *Helps To Holiness*

Achieving Tranquility

John 14:1

~

"Do not let your hearts be troubled," (John 14:1) said Jesus. Does anyone need this message? Of course we do. Just being alive makes us the target for countless fears and anxieties. We worry about ourselves and those dear to us because of the ever-present possibilities of accident and illness and death. Some of us are painfully aware of financial pressures, and some of us have private fears that we wouldn't care to name. As if our own personal cares were not enough, there's the threatening international situation. New alarms assault us every day. It's a frenzied world, and many hearts are troubled. The need for comfort is universal.

Before going any further, we ought to note the difference between being comforted and being comfortable. There are some things we ought not to be comfortable about. We should always be troubled about cruelty and injustice and corruption. When our Lord encouraged His disciples with these words of comfort, He was in the shadow of the cross. He would show by His death that He wasn't untroubled about sin and its eternal consequences.

We, too, must never be comfortable about sin in ourselves or in the world. The comfort we are talking about is not a sedative to dull us to the truth. There are some things we ought not to be comfortable about.

But in spite of the conditions around us, we can have a quiet heart. Jesus gave His prescription for a quiet heart.

First, the quiet heart is sure of the person of God. Jesus said, "Let not your heart be troubled, you believe in God, believe also in Me" (John 14:1 KJV). This is the indispensable foundation of a quiet heart. If we have faith in the unchangeable God, we have certainty in the midst of uncertainty.

The quiet heart is also sure of the presence of God. Death confronts us all with its fearsome suggestions of a solitary journey into a dark, cold unknown. Jesus has gone into that world beyond to prepare a place. He will come again and take us to be with Him forever. Faith in a God, whose presence will be mine forever, makes for a quiet heart. "Yea, though I walk through the valley of the shadow of death, I will fear no evil, for Thou art with me!" (Ps. 23:4).

These eternal certainties are the secret of a quiet heart, and they can be yours.

Bramwell Tripp, *To the Point*

Fireproof Faith

Daniel 3:1–23

≈

Its construction must have been the topic of conversation for months. The colossus made by Nebuchadnezzar was 90 feet high and nine feet wide and could be seen for miles. It surely was the talk of the empire!

The dedication of the golden image was an elaborate affair. The stern demand was proclaimed throughout the kingdom so that everyone knew that when the symphonic sound was heard, it was the cue to prostrate themselves before the golden image and pay homage to the king.

To forestall any rebellion, the king constructed a large furnace within sight of the image and his decree warned: "Whoever does not fall down and worship will immediately be thrown into a blazing furnace" (Dan. 3:6).

The orchestra struck the note, and as its symphonic sounds wafted across the plain, "all the peoples ... fell down and worshipped the image of gold" (Dan. 3:7). All the peoples, except for the three devout friends of Daniel. The astrologers were quick to report the defiance of the faithful three.

The three Hebrews acknowledged they had no claim on divine intervention, but had absolute faith in God's almighty power. The response of the faithful three served only to increase the rage of the king who ordered his furnace to be made seven times hotter.

The faith of these three men becomes enshrined in that Westminster Abbey of the Bible, Hebrews 11, with its roll call of heroes "who through faith ... quenched the fury of the flame" (vv. 33, 34).

The external setting may be different, but the inner truth abides. There are still many who know the experience of a fiery furnace, of a brutal force that seeks to destroy faith, and a Presence that enables them to survive the testing by fire.

The setting is no more barbaric than our own time. The distance from Nebuchadnezzar's furnace to the fiery furnaces of the Holocaust is not that great. And what about the "silent holocaust" of 1.5 million legalized abortions every year in our country?

This chapter may be as up to date as any in the Bible. Even as we read, devout Christians in certain countries are suffering in prison for their faith, some even facing death.

This great text reminds us that "the God we serve is able," (Dan. 3:17) and in our fiery furnace experience He will be with us and make us adequate.

Henry Gariepy, *Light in a Dark Place*

Christ's Last Beatitude

John 20:29

Scattered throughout the resurrection stories in the Gospels are wonderful statements of Christ. Shining among the words of the risen Lord is Christ's last beatitude.

We all know the beatitudes in our Lord's teaching in the Sermon on the Mount. No doubt, as He taught the crowds which followed Him wherever He went, He uttered other beatitudes. But His last beatitude, which we treasure for its contemporary relevance, was given in the Upper Room in Jerusalem one week after His resurrection.

Jesus had come to the Upper Room especially for the disciple Thomas, who has been labeled throughout history as "the doubter." Now, we should not be too hard on Thomas, because he wasn't much different from you or me.

He had given his support wholeheartedly to Jesus throughout His years of ministry. But his hopes had been dashed as he saw Jesus arrested and ignominiously hung upon a cross. His dreams shattered, he had gone off in despair.

In his sadness, he had gravitated back to the disciple band, to discover them in a state of excitement. They told him the staggering news that Jesus was alive, and had come to that very room.

Thomas was incredulous, unconvinced. Perhaps with bravado, with the air of one who doesn't lose his head in an emotionally charged atmosphere, he calmly says, "Seeing is believing. I have to see for myself the nail marks, the wounds. Even to touch Him, before I will believe He is alive."

When Jesus came for Thomas, the testimony of his senses was not needed. In that thrilling moment he believed, and from his lips came the joyous confession, "My Lord and my God" (John 20:28). A confession so deep that Thomas went on to do service in which he gave his life for the sake of Christ.

Looking at the kneeling Thomas, Jesus spoke His last beatitude. They were words for us today: "Blessed are those who have not seen and yet have believed" (John 20:29). What blessing has come to the multitudes of people down the centuries who, never having seen Christ, have believed and found Him to be their living, loving Savior and Lord.

Jesus understands us each one. He wins us, not by coercion, but by His steadfast love. And when we confess Him as Lord, the rich blessings of His presence follow us through all our days.

Eva Burrows, *The War Cry*

Fulfilling the Law

Romans 8:1–4

There is not a word, rightly understood in the Scriptures, in the whole New Testament that disparages or ignores or sets aside the Law of God. As the Apostle Paul comes to the climax of his argument, the great end and purpose towards which he has been advancing, he writes: "that the righteousness of the Law might be fulfilled in us" (Rom. 8:4). Jesus Christ shall destroy the work of the devil, restore man, and enable him to walk in the light.

What the law tried to do by a restraining power from without, the gospel does by an inspiring power from within. That is the difference. I could not keep it in the letter, but, united to my heavenly Bridegroom, I can keep it in the Spirit. He fills me with His love, and this enables me to keep the law, for love is the fulfilling of the law.

The apostle evidently considered this fulfillment of the law of righteousness in us as the highest end of our existence and of redemption; for he says, God sent His Son that the righteousness of the law may be fulfilled in us.

How? We shall be delivered from the reigning, condemning power of the law by virtue of an infinite, vicarious sacrifice punished in our stead, and then, married to Him, we shall serve in the newness of the spirit, and not in the oldness of the letter.

Now let us look at the fruit brought forth. Those people who are thus united to Christ fulfill the law in their affections. It is commonly said that if you get hold of the affections of a man or a woman you get hold of him or her. So you do. This is the touchstone. If you want to keep the precious things you have, hold them in subordination to Him. Oh, if Christ had your affections, how it would operate in everything!

This fruit will also appear in our family relations. When we have the fullness of love, it enables us to love God best and our neighbor as our self.

This fruit will also appear in our church relations. Is it not a fact that we are each other's keeper? Is it not a fact that God will require our influence over other souls? I believe it.

And now let us go down on our knees before God and ask Him to work this love in us and give us this spirit, that we may thus fulfill this law in all its relations.

Catherine Booth, *Aggressive Christianity*

Introduction to Greatness

Matthew 1:21

Wouldn't you agree that the word "great" is greatly overused and abused in the English vocabulary?

What would a sportscaster do without the word? No longer could he say: "What a great play ... great catch ... great throw ... great stop." Or the talk show host. No longer could he introduce "a great actress" or plug "a great book" or listen to "a great song" or watch "a great performance."

You get the point. The word "great" isn't so great anymore. Too bad. It used to be a noble word. It meant distinguished, preeminent, elevated, remarkable, of large scale and stature. The Greek word Luke uses to describe the angel Gabriel's word to address Mary, is *megas*, from which we get megaton, megalopolis, megabucks. Basically the Greek word means the ultimate of whatever it is you're talking about.

When the angel Gabriel made his startling announcement to Mary, he was talking about a person. "He will be great." Mary was not only to become great with child, she was to become great with a great child. Very few people in the world would deny the greatness of Jesus of Nazareth.

He was a great teacher. He had a mastery of simple parables to convey profound spiritual truth, and a phenomenal insight into the longings, fears, hopes and needs of others. He was a great healer and miracle worker. He was a great prophet, with the seer's insight into the times and course of events. He was a great lover of people, always with time for the individual and a special place in His heart for society's outcasts.

Wherein lies the greatness of a man? By accident or fortune of history some men rise to positions of importance, but they are not great men. Great men are men of simplicity and humility. They have the ability to see through the complex maze of life to the basic realities, and they live before those realities with great reverence and humility. Jesus was such a man.

But there is more to be said about Jesus' greatness. It was the greatness of God incarnate. He interpreted His own life on earth as an act of God.

In Jesus we see the greatness of a Savior. It seems that the parents of the Bethlehem Babe had no choice about their Son's name. As His destiny was fixed, so must His name be fixed to suit it: "You are to give Him the name Jesus, because He will save His people from their sins" (Matt. 1:21).

Have you in your life met this true greatness? If you haven't, make the acquaintance. Meet Immanuel—God with us. And you'll never be the same again.

Philip D. Needham, *The War Cry*

How Pure Must I Be?

1 Timothy 5:22

꙰

The pristine white brick building was evident from a block away. With the sun's rays bouncing off the walls, we sensed an air of spotless cleanliness about the Environmental Monitoring Laboratory where our son Doug works as an analytical chemist.

The guide who welcomed us began by explaining the work that went on in that facility. In short, he said it was their job to see that our drinking water is kept pure.

As technology progresses and as the population grows, new sources of pollution present challenges to pure drinking water. For instance, as landfills continue to grow in size and number, the possibility of ground water contamination also increases.

The guide explained how with computers and robotic equipment the chemists and technicians can identify the tiniest potential threat to our water supply and correct it before it becomes a hazard. "We are looking for one part per billion of impurity," he explained. "If you were to take an acre of sand, which is about 200 feet square, and try to find one impure grain at surface level, that would give you an idea of our task." He concluded by stating, "There is nothing so precious, so priceless, as clean water."

We left the laboratory, but I kept thinking of his words, "We are looking for one part per billion of impurity." Is it really so essential that our drinking water be that pure? If so, what kind of standard must God have for our personal purity? How pure must I be?

"Keep yourself pure," the Apostle Paul admonished young Timothy (1 Tim. 5:22). How can we live a pure life? It was the Apostle John who wrote the answer to that question. "The blood of Jesus, His Son, purifies us from all sin ... If we confess our sins, He is faithful and just to forgive our sins and purify us from all unrighteousness" (1 John 1:7,9).

There is nothing so precious, so priceless as a soul cleansed by the blood of Jesus Christ!

Joyce Winters, *The War Cry*

Why Sorrow?

Hebrews 2:10

Someone asks, "But why all this suffering—why should it be permitted at all? Is it not bad for the world, and so bad that God, if He be God, should prevent it?" Well, that is a difficult question. But it is, I admit, a fair one. It is, of course, a very old one. Many stricken hearts have asked it in all ages. Many fine minds in every age from the time of Job have tried to answer it. And the real difficulty about answering it satisfactorily is that there is no one answer. It is a subject on which we cannot generalize.

Nevertheless, two principal explanations of sorrow and suffering do stand forth in the history of mankind—two answers to that insistent inquiry, "Why should this or that agony be permitted in the scheme of a world created and governed by a wise and benevolent God?"

The first is that sorrow and pain are the first fruits of sin. By this it is not, of course, meant that every sorrow is a direct penalty for some particular wrong. No doubt some sorrows are. If, for example, a father neglects to train and discipline his boys and they grow up and rebel against him and break his heart, he is largely the cause of his own grief, and his neglect of his duty finds him out. Or if a woman neglects her health, or takes drugs or lives an unnatural life, she brings trouble upon herself.

It would, however, be absurd to say that all sorrow has this character. For it is evident that while much of it has, much of it has not. Suffering goes on its way to afflict many who have no responsibility for the wrong which brought it about. This is one of the most hideous facts about evil; but the responsibility for it is no more to be placed upon God than upon any other sufferer. He is one of the many who suffer from the consequences of sin—perhaps it will turn out at last that he was the greatest sufferer of all!

Why, then, is it all permitted? I answer not for punishment, but for discipline, for instruction, for warning, for training, and for turning men's hearts away from the earthly to the heavenly, from the human to the Divine. Unnumbered multitudes have realized in suffering a gift of priceless value, renewing the soul—refining character, and developing sympathy, humility, patience, strength—and bringing with it a revelation of God and His grace and power which had before seemed impossible. Suffering is permitted, not only to refine our spirits, not only to strengthen our faith, but to make us perfect for the work of saving others—of reaching other hearts, of carrying the heavy burdens of others, of healing the wounds and woes around us.

Bramwell Booth, *Life and Religion*

The Whole Duty of Man

Ecclesiastes 12:13

The writer of Ecclesiastes, presumed to be King Solomon, speaks of life as meaningless: "'Meaningless! Meaningless!' Says the Teacher. 'Utterly meaningless! Everything is meaningless'" (Eccles. 12:8).

He goes on to say that one can have wealth and fortune, power and prestige, pleasures and achievements, but then asks what they bring to life and what eternal value they have.

A popular philosophy today motivates people to grab all they can. Self-gratification. Survival of the fittest. The more we have, the more we want. There are bumper stickers which say: "Whoever has the most toys at the end wins!"

Is that what life is really all about? If so, then we have all come to the point where life has no real meaning. True, we must love ourselves as we love others. "Vanity" (the word used in the KJV) is thinking so highly of ourselves that nothing else really matters. We are number one. All else is secondary. And we must satisfy all our needs—at the expense of anything or anyone.

Solomon had everything, or so it seemed. He had wealth beyond measure, a kingdom to rule—he even had a thousand wives and concubines! Yet he was not satisfied. Something important was missing. He referred to his own life as meaningless and futile. There had to be something more.

People try to find meaning in life. Some find it easily. Others struggle for many years. Unfortunately, there are those who get tired of searching and settle for an easy way out. They may try drinking, gambling, drugs, crime or sex, but they don't find what they are looking for. The only true meaning to life is found in Jesus Christ.

Vanity? Meaningless? Yes, we can all get caught up in that. We have to look beyond ourselves to others, and then we must look upward—to our Lord and Savior.

"Here is the conclusion of the matter: Fear God and keep His commandments, for this is the whole duty of man" (Eccles. 12:13).

Beverly Ivany, *Teen Talk*

All Nature Speaks

Job 12:7

In Job's rebuttal to Zophar, he told him to look to nature and it will teach him of God. He cited three categories of fauna and the earth itself as a source of instruction about God (12:7–9).

First, "Ask the animals, and they will teach you" (Job 12:7). Ask a chipmunk, with a body barely six inches long, who made it able to carry and hide more than a bushel of acorns in just three days so he will be prepared for the long winter. Ask the snowshoe hare who turns its fur white only in the winter and the fawn who gave its spots to camouflage them from predators. Ask the sleek cheetah, the fastest land animal, who made it able to reach speeds of 70 miles an hour. Let the animals teach us of the marvelous endowments and providence of their Creator.

Job went on: "Ask ... the birds of the air, and they will tell you" (Job 12:7). Ask the millions of birds who endowed them with the marvel of migration as their feathered power takes them incredible distances, with the champion migrant— the small arctic tern—making an annual round trip of over 20,000 miles. Ask the ruby-throated hummingbird, weighing only an eighth of an ounce, who made it able to fly 500 miles across the Gulf of Mexico, its wings beating 50 times a second. Ask the birds and they will tell you who teaches them their solar and stellar migration, who planted their inbuilt compasses enabling them to span continents and oceans. Far more than Job ever knew in his day, the birds are able to tell us about the marvels of God's creative handiwork.

"Or speak to the earth," Job went on, "and it will teach you" (Job 12:8). What eloquence is spoken by creation in the miracle of seedtime and harvest, of the tapestry and wonder of a tree, the exquisite beauty of a flower, the spectacle of a sunrise that causes all the earth to blush at the extravagant beauty it is about to unveil.

"Or let the fish of the sea inform you," (Job 12:8) added Job. The infinite variety, the incredible fecundity, and the exotic creations of marine life testify to a God of unlimited imagination and creativity.

Annie Dillard, in *Pilgrim at Tinker Creek*, writes, "The extravagant gesture is the very stuff of creation. The Creator will stop at nothing. The Creator loves pizzazz."

May we pray to be kept open and aware to the wonder and beauty of God's creation and its untold blessings to us.

Henry Gariepy, *Portraits of Perseverance*

Fellowship Which Binds

Ecclesiastes 4:9–12

If fellowship is friendship with a plus, then Paul and Timothy enjoyed fellowship. Dissimilar in temperament and of different generations, they were nevertheless bound by a bond of affection. Paul once wrote of Timothy, "I have no one else like him, who takes a genuine interest in your welfare ... Timothy has proved himself, because as a son with his father he has served with me in the work of the gospel" (Phil. 2:20–22).

It is to Timothy that Paul can appeal for help at the end; he knows him to be the kind of thoughtful friend who will bring the cloak he needs, and his books—and hurry to get there before winter (2 Tim. 4:13,21).

But what is that plus in the friendship? It is, of course, the presence of the Holy Spirit. Unsaved people may be good friends, but only where both are Christians does real fellowship exist. In fact, our fellowship must first be with Jesus and then with those who belong to Jesus.

It is of the greatest importance for any man or woman in the ministry to appreciate the importance of fellowship. If our preaching leads men to Christ, it will surely lead them together. Let me aim at that, and let me foster and strengthen that fellowship—not by focusing on the group (for that can lead to unhealthy introspection), but by keeping Jesus resolutely in the center.

We need to be deeply impressed with the fact that Jesus is in the midst when we gather, to appreciate His presence, to love Him for it, and to let His love flow over our gatherings. The warmth and happiness of such groups will act like a magnet to the community in which we are set.

Men and woman are sinners, in need of a Savior. And that Savior is available, graciously near, ready to rescue. His name is Jesus—heaven's answer to earth's ruin and misery.

This Jesus has accomplished, once for all: the redemption of the lost. It is now for the lost to learn that and to be persuaded to respond to it in faith. Those who do will find Him strong to deliver, faithful to keep, and ready to enclose His own in a fellowship of wonderful love.

Edward Read, *Timothy, My Son*

Choose Wisely

Joshua 24:14–16

To be or not to be—those are the parameters. Even people who do not know any other Shakespeare quotations probably recognize this contemporary version of "To be, or not to be, that is the question" from *Hamlet* as he is deciding whether to live or die.

Simple choices are often the easiest to make, and the most profound. They can be evaluated, measured and decided quickly. When we have options galore, we have difficulty making up our minds. When I was a kid growing up in The Salvation Army, we always had a black car since that was the only color permitted. Now deciding the color of the car is as difficult as choosing the car itself.

We make simple choices each day: go or stay, up or down, in or out, yes or no, right or wrong.

There are times when simple either/or choices become more complex. When it comes to the big decisions—life or death, and most important of all, heaven or hell—the rewards or consequences of those choices are staggering. You have to decide one way or the other.

Joshua asked an either/or question of the rebellious, complaining, disobedient people of his day. They had often forgotten the Lord's provision and blessing while traveling from bondage in Egypt to freedom in their new homeland in Canaan. Joshua assembled the people and challenged them, saying,"Fear the Lord and serve Him with all faithfulness ... but if serving the Lord seems undesirable to you, then choose for yourselves this day whom you will serve ... as for me and my household, we will serve the Lord" (Joshua 24:14–15).

To be or not to be—to be in Christ or not to be in Christ, to be forgiven or not to be forgiven, to serve the Lord or not to serve the Lord—those are the parameters. When it comes to accepting God's way for your life and your eternal future, it is the most important decision you will ever make.

A. Kenneth Wilson, *The War Cry*

Evil Speaking

James 4:11

E vil speaking, or slander, is a very great evil and does an immense amount of harm. It is not necessary to say what is false in order to slander a comrade. Saying something about him in his absence, whether it be true or false, calculated to lower him in the estimation of others, can damage his influence with them.

Evil speaking does a very great deal of harm. To begin with it hurts the individual guilty of the act. We are so made that when we cherish a kind feeling, or do a loving action, we are benefitted thereby. On the other hand, we cannot indulge in bad feelings toward anyone, or perform any unlovable actions, without suffering ourselves in consequence. So that when a man slanders his neighbor, he injures himself as well. Bear that in mind; you cannot speak evil of anyone without having to suffer in your own soul.

Evil speaking grieves the Spirit of God, because it is contrary to the law of love. You are to love your neighbor as yourself. That is the standard of your love for your neighbor. But Christ said we are to love our comrades as He loved us, and He loved us better than He loved Himself. Now, if you love your comrades after Jesus Christ's pattern, you won't go about setting forth their faults and shortcomings to anybody who will listen to you.

Evil speaking hurts the feelings of the comrade slandered. It does, if ever he hears the story, and if he never hears about it, it is worse still because he never has a chance of defending himself.

By all that is sacred, my dear comrade, let us make a covenant with our tongues that we will not speak evil of any comrade, no, not even if we think that they have wronged us. Let us remember the example of our Lord, who prayed for the men who were gambling at His feet for His garments while their hands were clotted with His blood. Let us love one another.

William Booth, *The Warrior's Daily Portion*

While the Spirit Passes By

Acts 1:8

There are wants my heart is telling
    While the Spirit passes by,
And with hope my soul is swelling
    While the Spirit passes by.
O what prospects now I see,
What a life my life must be,
If Thy seal is placed on me,
    While the Spirit passes by.

There are sins my lips confessing
    While the Spirit passes by,
Treasures long my heart possessing,
    While the Spirit passes by.
All the world's delight and cheer,
All the things I held so dear,
Ah, how worthless they appear
    While the Spirit passes by.

Here I stand, myself disdaining,
    While the Spirit passes by;
Stand in faith, Thy mercy claiming,
    While the Spirit passes by;
Let Thy power my soul refine,
Let Thy grace my will incline,
Take my all and make it Thine,
While the Spirit passes by.

Herbert Booth, *The Salvation Army Song Book*

God's Ecology of Holiness

2 Peter 3:18

⤳

Ecology is that branch of biology that deals with the relationships between living organisms and their environment. Every living thing is immersed in a context or environment with specific characteristics.

Just as there are biological ecologies, there are social ecologies where individuals are immersed in social environments. It is not uncommon for us to be in and out of several social ecologies in one day: for example, home, marriage, work, the supermarket, church. Among my favorite social ecologies are Christian summer camps.

When Peter says "Grow in grace," (2 Pet. 3:18) he is speaking ecologically. He means that we should immerse ourselves in God's grace, in His loving kindness and in His presence. He provides a nutrient-enriched environment through our relationships with Him and others.

In the ecology of holiness, God's plan is that we first develop and progress. As we move ahead in our relationship with Christ, He does a deepening work. Often the work is done in a social/spiritual context of others and always in the context of God's presence in our lives. Second, at every stage of our growth and development, His love goes before us to help us move toward a restoration to His image and likeness. Third, He provides for us a nutrient-enriched environment to be the "means of grace," promoting our growth and well-being. This includes Christian teaching, fellowship, breaking of bread and prayer (Acts 2:42), and all the wholesome activities of small fellowship groups. God uses others to mediate His grace to us. It is this daily immersion in the means of grace that promotes this social ecology of holiness.

Brother Lawrence, a twelfth-century monk, understood the ecology of holiness when he practiced the presence of God throughout the day. In the wonderful book *The Practice of the Presence of God*, Lawrence tells how Jesus was experienced as present at all times, and with whom fellowship was immediately enjoyed and never ceasing. He was assigned often menial and mundane work in the monastery and yet he carried out his assignments in partnership with Christ, as his co-laborer, rejoicing and praising Him continually throughout each day.

Our lives represent the threads of the tapestry woven together to be both beautiful and functional for our Lord. To "grow in grace" is, like Brother Lawrence, to daily abide in Jesus Christ and to be immersed in the ecology of God's grace and holiness.

Jonathan S. Raymond, *The War Cry*

The Paradoxical Infant

1 Timothy 3:16

⤳

Billions of births have happened in the long course of human history. One, however, was unlike all others—the birth of the Man who was, and is, God. Concerning this birth the Apostle Paul uses the Greek word, _musterion_, meaning "a mystery." "Beyond all question, the mystery of godliness is great: He appeared in a body" (1 Tim. 3:16). But the word means more than just a mystery; translated, it means a mystery that is solved, a secret that is open to those who believe in Jesus Christ.

There are many profound paradoxes having to do with the birth of Jesus, four of them about which we may think with profit.

So Young and Yet So Old. Our Lord did not begin in "the city of David." His existence did not originate in a manger. Had we been present to watch Mary deliver her firstborn we might reasonably have assumed that we were witnessing the genesis of Jesus. But that assumption would have been wrong. The fact is that Jesus never had an origin, and the Bible states this clearly both in the Old and the New Testaments. The prophet Micah (5:2) declares, "But you, Bethlehem ... out of you will come for me one ... whose origins are from old, from ancient times."

So Poor and Yet So Rich. The New Testament makes no attempt to disguise the fact that Jesus was poor. He belonged to a peasant family. He elected to associate Himself with the "have-nots" rather than the "haves." It is not through His riches that we become rich, but by His poverty.

So Small and Yet so Great. It takes the breath away to think that the Lord of 30-trillion galaxies and constellations became the size of a tiny infant in order to enter the human race. But tiny as He was, "For in Christ all the fullness of the Deity lives in bodily form" (Col. 2:9). The Infinite became the infinitesimal while remaining the Infinite!

So Mute and Yet So Articulate. Here is an infant that is unable to say a single word. And yet John the evangelist says that "the Word became flesh and made His dwelling among us" (John 1:14). The divine being who named the myriad stars is incapable of articulating even the name of His mother.

Now, however, the words of Jesus have been translated into every human tongue. They have been studied in every age since they were uttered. They have meant more to humanity than all the words ever spoken by all the rest of humanity put together.

These four paradoxes leap out of the Incarnation: so young and so old, so poor and so rich, so small and yet so great, so silent and yet so articulate.

Arnold Brown, _Occupied Manger, Unoccupied Tomb_

God's Amazing Grace

Romans 1:7

I am among those authors who, when they set about the task of writing, have difficulty with beginnings and endings. Paul had no such problem. In his epistles he followed the stylized form of Greek letter writing. But though his beginnings and endings were written according to the transient conventions of his time, they were always filled with the eternal content of his faith. For example, almost without exception they contain the hallowed words, grace and peace, which ring through his writing like the melodious peal of a carillon.

The actual greeting which follows Paul's salutation in Romans is more than a mere greeting. It is a prayer of blessing containing a promise and a pledge: "Grace and peace to you from God our Father and from the Lord Jesus Christ" (Rom. 1:7). The grace of Christ was unveiled to Paul on the Damascus Road and remained the source of his achievements ever after.

When he speaks of the grace of the Lord, he means the unconstrained and undeserved favor and mercy of God toward needy, sinful man and the fact that Christ Himself is the sacrificial expression of that divine grace. (Eph. 2:4–9). Grace is the master word and key to Paul's theology. It appears 88 times in his writings and is actually one of the most significant words in the New Testament, for it indicates the nature of God and sums up all that He has done for us through Jesus Christ.

God's grace is not conditioned by the worth of its object. It is shown in His tender regard for the person who lives in sin.

Though grace comes to us while we are yet sinners through the convicting Spirit, it can be resisted and spurned. The dictionary gives eight different uses of the word grace, and among them is one that stirred my memory—"a short prayer of thanksgiving before or after a meal." As far back as I can recall, prayer at mealtime was an institution in my parents' home. This defense, available to every Christian family, helps to hold it together and protect it from hostile external influences. As a family altar, it is the heart of the home where the family gathers about God's Word and communes with the heavenly Father. There, children are taught the things of God and learn how to pray. A family at prayer is a sign of grace.

Clarence D. Wiseman, *The Desert Road to Glory*

The Priority of Love

Matthew 22:34–40

～

Jesus was asked to single out one segment of law as more important than the rest. Yet the Pharisees and Scribes regarded the law as sacrosanct, to be obeyed not only in its scriptural detail but also in subsequent interpretations.

This group of men would not normally condone any selectivity on observing parts of the law, considering that each part was equally valid. There is a danger, which we sometimes fall into, that we want to be selective about God's will, to obey Him in some things and be self-determining in others. So Jesus would have been on dangerous ground if He had said, for instance, "You shall not commit adultery" is more important than "You shall not steal" (Deut. 5:18,19). You can't pick and choose like that.

Jesus did not rise to this bait of discriminating between one specific commandment and another. He selects a verse that is the summing up of all other commandments (Deut. 6:5). He boils down religion to loving God with a total love: "Love the Lord your God with all your heart and with all your soul and with all your mind" (Matt. 22:37).

And yet, when Jesus has selected that verse, it is not quite all-embracing enough. So He expertly selects a second general statement, from Leviticus 19:18, which requires also love for one's neighbor, a love that is on a par with our own self-respect: "Love your neighbor as yourself" (Matt. 22:39).

Love must have a two-way thrust to satisfy Jesus but, when He has said that, He is content for all other laws to stem from it. Religion for Jesus is all about responses and relationships, both to God and to others.

To quote William Barclay: "To be truly religious is to love God, and to love the men whom God made in His own image; and to love God and man, not with a nebulous sentimentality, but with a total commitment which issues in devotion to God and practical service of men."

It has been said that while both the commands were known to His hearers, the new thing in what Jesus said here was to link "Love your God" with "Love your neighbor." Loving our neighbor means that we should be determined always to show genuine goodwill toward our fellow human beings and seek to bring out the very best in them; seek their highest good. We must show goodwill to others as we do to ourselves.

Clifford and Maureen Kew, *Question Time*

Threefold Sanctification

Ephesians 1:4

Sanctification carries the definition, "to make sacred or holy; to free from sin, to purify; to make Christlike." God had nothing less than this in mind when He created man in His image. "He chose us in Him before the creation of the world to be holy and blameless in His sight" (Eph. 1:4).

There can be no surprise, then, that Christ purchased our sanctification. "Christ also loved the Church, and gave Himself for it; that He might sanctify and cleanse it with the washing of water by the Word" (Eph. 5:22–26 KJV). He loved not only the sinful world (John 3:16), but also the believing Church. "Wherefore Jesus also, that He might sanctify the people with His own blood, suffered without the gate" (Heb. 13:12 KJV).

Conversion is becoming a Christian—the noun. Sanctification is becoming Christian—the adjective. Sanctification has three aspects, all under the administration of the Holy Spirit.

Initial sanctification is that cleansing of the outward sins of acquired depravity, largely the sins of the flesh. Writing to the unspiritual, carnal Corinthian church, Paul says, "But you were washed, you were sanctified, you were justified in the name of the Lord Jesus Christ and by the Spirit of our God" (1 Cor. 6:11).

Entire sanctification is complete, dealing with sins of the spirit, leaving no part of the personality untouched. This is expressed to the well–saved church in Thessalonica: "The very God of peace sanctify you wholly; and I pray God your whole spirit and soul and body be preserved blameless unto the coming of our Lord Jesus Christ" (1 Thess. 5:23 KJV).

Progressive sanctification is that growth, renewal, maturing, holy living and continual cleansing, which should be the unfolding life of every believer, but especially of those who are Spirit–filled. It is typified by Paul's statement: "We all ... beholding as in a mirror the glory of the Lord, are being transformed into the same image from glory to glory, just as by the Spirit of the Lord" (2 Cor. 3:18 NKJV). This is accomplished by the abiding fullness of the Holy Spirit in the life of the believer.

Milton S. Agnew, *The Holy Spirit: Friend and Counselor*

Extraordinary Love

Ephesians 4:32

We are living today in a post–Christian environment. Christianity may have been the "faith of our fathers," but we now live in a secular society where faith centers far more on bank accounts, insurance policies and the pursuit of transient pleasure. Love's meaning has shriveled to instant self–gratification.

The love we demonstrate must not be on the level of that which we see around us. Our love must be a transcendent love, which recognizes the supremacy of God, emulates the love of Jesus and seeks the enlightening guidance of the Holy Spirit. We are made for heaven, thus our love must transcend the secular and finite limits of this world. We must seek to saturate ourselves in Scripture and prayer, so that the love we bring to family life will have at its roots a transcendent, eternal quality.

In this "every man for himself" world, our love must be a tender love (Eph. 4:32). This must extend to the home where roughness and rudeness replace courtesy and respect. It may be difficult to be tenderhearted after a stressful day at work. We must not underestimate the struggles of our children as they grow to maturity—struggles of acceptance, struggles academically, struggles with peers and friendships, struggles with self–identity. This is the time for tender love, a clear demonstration of caring, understanding and support—a time for simply telling them that they are loved unconditionally.

If there is a place for tender love, there is also a place for tough love. Today there is a need for a return to Christian discipline, and parents must not ignore this important role. Tough love is neglected at peril. Often tough love is simply the courage to say "no" to a child's unrealistic wishes.

When I lived in Sri Lanka, where the two seasons are hot and hotter, I loved to walk along a particular road in Colombo. It was arched by trees which provided not only shade, but a significantly cooler temperature. I often thought how remarkable it is that without fanfare the trees absorb the intense heat of the day and transform it into a refreshing coolness.

How similar this is to God's purpose of a transforming love for each of us. He wants us to absorb hurts and anger and frustration and misunderstanding, and through His grace transform them into love, peace, forgiveness and harmony. This is the experience of holiness, the Christian lifestyle taught in Scripture, and the extraordinary love supremely exemplified by Jesus in every experience of His earthly life.

Dudley Coles, *The War Cry*

"Amen, God"

1 Chronicles 16:36

Lord, I've never talked with You about "Amen." It always seemed to be the end of my prayer. Today I suddenly, happily realized it is the beginning of my prayer.

Of course, I'm not going to start my prayer "Amen, God," but it really isn't such a far-out idea after all. Amen is such a full, rich word of assent or affirmation! I think this is why I was so thrilled when the songsters sang "Amen" fortissimo. So be it, God!

No questions, no "whys," no quibbling or challenging—only "Amen." So be it, Lord! Your purposes and plans, Your will and desires, Your answers to my prayers have my deep, glad assent.

Dear Lord, thank You for reminding me that my "Amen" is "Yes, God." I know that when the sun is shining it will be easy to say "Amen" clearly and loudly; but when it gets dark or if You say "wait" or "no," even though the "Amen" may be softly spoken, may it be a resolute consent to and acceptance of Your design for my life.

All the experiences I cannot understand—the circumstances which bring pain or anguish—so be it, Lord! All the joys, the dreams realized and all the fair blossoms of life—Amen, yes, Lord! Always yes!

"All the people said 'Amen' and 'praise the Lord'" (1 Chron. 16:36).

Virginia E. Talmadge, *Little Prayers to a Big God*

Linked Lives

Ecclesiastes 4:9–12

꩜

I have been watching the rainstorm outside my window that has been with us in terrific force for days. The 50 to 100 mph winds are very unusual for San Francisco, where I live. The tall eucalyptus trees are bowing down in slow motion, over and over, as they yield to the force of the wind.

When later I went outside I saw fallen, broken trees everywhere. I thought they had toppled over because the wind was too strong. But the newscaster said it was the incessant rains saturating the ground which caused the trees to uproot in the wind. The trees that fared better grew in close proximity to each other. You can tell I'm a tree-watcher.

God intends for us to grow together in close proximity with one another, so we can support each other when the storms beat upon us. Our spiritual roots intertwine, just as the tree roots do, and strengthen us when we would otherwise be weak. The Apostle Paul urges, "Bear one another's burdens" (Gal. 6:2).

God intends for us to help hold each other up amid the testings of life. The preacher in Ecclesiastes powerfully reminds us of this sacred truth:

> Two are better than one,
> because they have a good return for their work:
> If one falls down, his friend can help him up.
> But pity the man who falls and has no one to help him up!
> Also, if two lie down together, they will keep warm.
> But how can one keep warm alone?
> Though one be overpowered, two can defend themselves.
> A cord of three strands is not quickly broken (Eccles. 4:9–12).

Even the tallest trees can fall if their roots are not intertwined in a network of support with others around them. We were not meant to be loners in the kingdom of God.

May we, with linked lives, together grow stronger in Christ, intertwined by love's strong strands, and in love and support for one another hold each other up in the storms of life.

Keilah Toy, *The War Cry*

Love Story

Hosea 1–3

Hosea is the second greatest love story in the Bible, second only to the story of Christ. Hosea is the prophet of grace, the St. John of the Old Testament. This is the gospel according to Hosea.

God speaks to Hosea and humankind through the personal tragedy of the prophet. His grief becomes a doorway of discovery for the world to see a portrayal of the grace of God. The deeper insights and lessons of life are often given in the crucible of suffering.

Hosea is shocked as he walks into his home. His three children are unattended. He calls for his wife Gomer, but there is no answer. She is nowhere to be found.

He had been warned that this would occur. God had instructed him: "Go, take to yourself an adulterous wife" (Hos. 1:2). She would become symbolic of God's message to Israel. In response, Hosea had married Gomer and three children were born of their marriage.

Israel, like Gomer, had been unfaithful and said, "I will go after my lovers" (Hos. 2:5). They were bold and willful in their pursuit of sin. But God, after their needed chastisement, in unfailing love, tenderly renews His covenant with them: "I will betroth you to Me forever" (Hos. 2:19).

Hosea goes in search of his faithless wife who had abandoned her home, husband and children for a life of shame. He finds her where she has sold herself in adultery, and from the slave market he buys her back. In loving discipline and restoration to chastity, he reconciles her to himself.

When Gomer abandoned her home and family and went after other lovers, Hosea could have given her a written notice of divorce and been done with her. Or, according to the law of the land, he could have had her stoned to death as an adulteress. He did not seek his legal rights but instead paid the price for her redemption.

It is the love story of each of our lives. We have been called to be the bride of Christ, His Church, to be pure and faithful. But we have left Him in search of other loves. We have flirted with and gone after other gods. But God, the divine Lover of our souls, has searched to bring us back to Himself. He has paid the terrible price of our redemption on Calvary.

We are Gomer on the auction block of sin. Satan bids for our soul. But when all seemed lost, God sent Jesus Christ into the marketplace. He bid the price of His precious blood. There was no higher bid than that. He made the scarlet payment on Calvary for our eternal redemption.

Henry Gariepy, *Light in a Dark Place*

The God Who Is There

John 1:14

‿᷿

Thousands of families take to the mountains or the ocean when summer vacation rolls around. Some even leave their air-conditioned homes, pitch a tent in some chosen spot and live there for a period of time.

Nothing can quite test the endurance of a family like living together in a tent. Whether a two-room deluxe style or the one-person pup variety, camping means togetherness. You're together—cooking, eating, sleeping. A sudden thunderstorm threatens just as you unfold the tent and lay it out flat on the ground. You pour over the enigmatic symbols that sort out the short poles from the long poles. All the while the kids insist they're dying of hunger. Mom discovers that Dad must have slept through the entire Boy Scout program. As for Mom, she's been sweeter. Frustrations mount.

With patience, compromise and undiluted doses of love, the fun may come. There will be those delights of nature you left home for, those warm, fuzzy experiences that delight your heart. There may even be some unimaginable insight that explodes in the soul and changes who you are forever. But make no mistake; it will cost you something.

God promised Moses that He would pitch His tent and dwell in the midst of His people. It is a central theme throughout Scripture. From Exodus to Revelation we find the imagery: a holy God "pitching His tent" among His people. In the familiar passage in John 1:14, "The Word became flesh, and made His dwelling among us," the Greek work for "dwelling" literally means to "pitch a tent."

Talk about leaving the air-conditioned order and serenity of suburban living! God left the perfection and unimaginable beauty of heaven where legions of angels sang His praises, to pitch a tent among unholy people.

He is, in Francis Schaeffer's words, "the God who is there." He is personal and among us in a way that is extraordinarily reassuring but disturbing. We cannot avoid Him or revoke His claims upon us.

To bring us to the highest and best our souls can become He pitched His tent among us. Our Lord took the abuse we hurled at Him all the way to the cross. Yes, when He pitched His tent among us, He was in for the long haul. We can be sure that He has come to stay, even as Scripture reminds us: "Surely I am with you always, to the very end of the age" (Matt. 28:20).

Marlene Chase, *Pictures From the Word*

Walk As Jesus Did

1 John 2:6

A disciple who had known Jesus in the days of His flesh could give no better advice to Christian converts than to point them to His Lord. This counsel should not be written off as too generalized or too vague. Holiness is born of a relationship to God which will express itself in Christlikeness.

This definition, sound in doctrine, or if you like, in theory, is of the greatest possible assistance in practice. For the One whose example we are bidden to follow was touched with the feeling of our infirmities.

He was in all respects tested like as we are. To remember this will save us from writing off the life of holiness as unnatural, as if all it could do was to turn out a species of plaster saint in a stained–glass window setting. We do not have to cease being human in order to live the life of holiness.

No one should be fearful of the experience of holiness or deem it prudent to keep it at an arm's length. This state of grace will not deprive us of any worthwhile element in any of the relationships of life. This holds good of the boy/girl relationship which will be kept wholesome. The parent/child relationship will be included as well, for here we shall be given grace to be what we would have our children become. This will embrace the husband/wife relationship as well for this will be strengthened and enriched. Two people who truly love God and one another will forge a bond that cannot lightly be broken.

Nor can the man to man relationship be excluded, for in this we shall be able to manifest that personal integrity which is an incontrovertible sign of holiness of heart and life. For holiness is not primarily a matter of the emotions but the outworking of a Christian character which can ennoble every aspect of our lives.

Catherine Booth wrote to William before they were married: "The more you lead me up to Christ in all things, the more highly shall I esteem you and, if it be possible to love you more than I do now, the more shall I love you." Those two young Victorians knew that their affection for one another would not be diminished, but enhanced, by their mutual love for their Lord.

It must be said once again, no one is required to cease to be human in order to learn how to be holy. Rather is it as we grow in the experience of holiness that we learn how satisfying our human relationships can be.

Frederick Coutts, *The Splendor of Holiness*

Reflection

Psalm 139:13–16

My life
was in the mind of God
before I came to birth.
This dwelling place I call "myself"
was planned precisely, pleased
His purpose to fulfill.

My Lord,
the Architect Divine,
constructed by His power
an edifice with gracious scope
for righteousness and peace
reflective of His own.

How come
I do so often mar
the line and shape He gives
to life, the precepts which He sets
and which, within His will,
would hold me to His plan?

Oh, could
it be that ripples on
the surface of my soul
disturb the calm, disintegrate
the very shape of things
He had in mind for me?

Or, could
it be that wayward winds
of dire adversity,
encroaching on life's pleasant scene,
disturb the tranquil heart,
the soul's serenity?

O Lord,
restore Your calm to me
which once I knew within
Your perfect plan for life. I would
reflect Your purposes
well harbored in Your peace.

Lucille L. Turfrey, *The War Cry*

A Testimony of Salvation

Romans 5:1–2

It was in the open street that this great change passed over me. If I could only have possessed the flagstone on which I stood at that happy moment, the sight of it occasionally might have been as useful to me as the stones carried up long ago from the bed of the Jordan were to the Israelites who had passed over them dry-shod.

The entrance to the heavenly kingdom was closed against me by an evil act of the past which required restitution. In a boyish trading affair I had managed to make a profit out of my companions, whilst giving them to suppose that what I did was all in the way of a generous fellowship. As a testimonial of their gratitude they had given me a silver pencil case. Merely to return their gift would have been comparatively easy, but to confess the deception I had practiced upon them was a humiliation to which for some days I could not bring myself.

I remember, as if it were but yesterday, the spot in the corner of the room under the chapel, the hour, the resolution to end the matter, the rising up and rushing forth, the finding of the young fellow I had chiefly wronged, the acknowledgment of my sin, the return of the pencil case, the instant rolling away from my heart of the guilty burden, the peace that came in its place, and the going forth to serve my God and my generation from that hour.

I felt that I could willingly and joyfully travel to the ends of the earth for Jesus Christ and suffer anything imaginable to help the souls of other men.

One reason for the victory I daily gained from the moment of my conversion was, no doubt, my complete and immediate separation from the godless world. I turned my back on it. I gave it up, having made up my mind beforehand that if I did go in for God I would do so with all my might.

William Booth, *They Said It*

The Conquest of Worry

Matthew 6:34

It would seem that in these words—"Do not worry about tomorrow" (Matt. 6:34)—there is an exception to the rule; for is it not most improvident not to think about the future and prepare for it? This principle applied literally would mean the end of provident societies and insurance corporations. Bankers and brokers would go out of business. In this hard and brittle world one must look to the future, for the man who retires without having prepared for it will find that God is on the side of the provident.

We know that our Lord did not ignore the principle of preparing for the future, for His whole ministry was related to it. He urged salvation in the present to determine where we will spend eternity. On the cross He thought of His mother's future, and committed her to the care of John.

Deep in our Lord's injunction is advice against undue anxiety and worry. Jesus, in His Sermon on the Mount was advocating a living trust in the present that would make the future secure.

Worry is imagination run wild! We allow our thoughts to anticipate the worst, to build in our minds fearful images and situations which rarely come to reality. We cross our bridges before we come to them. We must be prepared to accept the worst if it comes, but must calmly devote all the thought and energy possible to improving the worst as it is now. If we reconcile ourselves to the worst we often find the worst never comes. Tomorrow will depend upon what we are today.

Victories can be won or lost in the mind. We rush to the chemist for tranquilizers when all we need is a right mental adjustment to life. Our Lord refused the sponge saturated with an appeaser on that day, showing that He would not die drugged. There is no external answer to the internal state of mind with which we face our troubles and tragedies.

When tire manufacturers found solid tires were cut to pieces by flinty roads, they invented pneumatic tires which absorbed the shocks of the roads. We need to learn that spiritual art which helps us to bend to resistant forces. The prayer of Reinhold Niebuhr is worth saying every day:

> God grant me the serenity
> To accept the things I cannot change;
> The courage to change the things I can;
> And the wisdom to know the difference.

George B. Smith, *Meditations for the Ordinary Man*

The Book

2 Timothy 3:16

The Bible is a very wonderful book. Its very name signifies this. It is The Book, the book which, above every other, a man should know, treasure and obey. It is valuable for many reasons.

God is its Author. He caused it to be written under His own special direction. The Holy Spirit put the thoughts into the hearts of holy men. They wrote them down. That is the reason we speak of it as the Word of God.

It tells us of God. We might have expected that our heavenly Father would not leave us in ignorance about Himself, that He would want to tell us of His power and love, and to declare what His feelings are towards us. And that is just what He has done in the Bible.

From it we learn all that we know about the birth and life and death, the resurrection and ascension of our Lord and Savior Jesus Christ.

The Bible tells us about the future state: of the resurrection of the dead, the Great White Throne, the heaven of delight, and the hell of misery.

It is the Bible that tells us of the merits of the precious Blood of our Savior, the possibilities of the forgiveness of sins, the purification of our hearts, the protection of God and the triumph of a dying hour.

Now, my comrade, what ought you to do with the Bible? I will tell you.

The very least that you can do is to read it. Read a few verses at a time; read them on your knees, when you rise in the morning, when you retire at night, in your spare moments. Read it in your families. See that you experience in your heart the blessings it offers. Fulfill the duties it commands. Publish the salvation of the Bible wherever you go.

Oh, my comrade, do not let the Bible rise up in judgment against you, as it surely will if you either neglect it, or if knowing about the salvation and victory of which it tells, you do not enjoy that salvation and experience that victory.

William Booth, *Religion for Every Day*

Depending on God

Psalm 121:1

In 1992 I was diagnosed with cancer. I received radiation and had multiple surgeries and chemotherapy for months. This was a very dark time of my life. Allan, my husband, was a complete source of strength and affirmation for me.

The cancer seemed to go into remission. But in 1994 it metastasized to my right lung. More chemotherapy didn't work. In November, a doctor told me to go home and plan my funeral. I got a new doctor!

Just as I was preparing for a bone marrow transplant, the most unfathomable thing happened. Allan was diagnosed with lung cancer.

I was stunned. And for the first time, I was angry. "Cancer in one parent is enough!" I said to the Lord. Plus, I loved Allan more than I loved myself. I was grief–stricken.

I was consumed with the idea that the Lord would call me home at any moment. But God chose to sustain my life and to take Allan home to be with him in October, 1995.

My life changed dramatically after that. I asked myself, "Who is Normajean? What kind of officer will I be? How do I raise three teenagers by myself?" My life was in fragments. God showed His purpose for me in Philippians 2:5, "Your attitude should be the same as that of Christ Jesus."

Just as I was feeling strong again emotionally, my cancer returned and penetrated my bone structure. My doctor told me I would be chemotherapy dependent for the rest of my life. I had to think really hard about that. But the Lord showed me I already was a dependent person. I was dependent on the Lord for His love and guidance. I was dependent on my children and family and friends for their love. So I figured I was just adding chemotherapy to the list.

I had to ask, "What does the Lord want me to do with the days He's given me? How can I show Christ in how I live through these days?" Opportunities have come that have been exceedingly abundantly more than I could ask or think.

People ask me if I pray for healing. I believe I am already healed. Not of cancer, but healed in my heart. Because after all I have been through, after all I have lost, after all I have suffered, I still believe in God, and I still trust Him for every day. I want Him to use my life to show He is faithful and trustworthy for the good days and the bad. And I want someday to hear Him say, "Well done!"

Normajean Honsberger, *Good News!*

The Kindness of God

Titus 3:4–5

Apart from the bold intervention of reconciling mercy, a spiral of violence may quickly accelerate even into furies of mass murder and ethnic cleansing. Witness the vain efforts of United Nations peacekeepers to hold opposing forces at bay long enough to find a path to peace.

This kind of thing can begin in ordinary human relationships, in families and marriages, as well as in communities and nations. The Bible states that the coming of God's own Son into our world was to break the cycle of angry reprisals in order to bring about peace with one another and with our heavenly Father. "When the kindness and love of God our Savior appeared, He saved us" (Titus 3:4–5). In loving kindness and tender mercy, God has moved toward us, risking our rejection and anger against His sinless Son, in order finally to embrace us in His love.

God's kindness was displayed in stark contrast to the meanness of the situation into which Jesus was born. Excessive taxation and the cruel exploitation of their Roman oppressors fed smoldering resentment among the common people. A petty king's paranoia sent ruthless goon squads into the surrounding countryside to brutally murder defenseless children in an attempt to destroy the presumed future heir to his throne. Before the drama of Jesus's birth was fully played out, His own parents found themselves homeless, poor and refugees fleeing for their very lives.

Sadly the world has not changed much over the centuries. Nineteen million people are currently acknowledged to be refugees on our planet. Frantic efforts are underway to stop the senseless killing of innocent civilians in ethnic clashes in Europe and Africa, while fresh violence breaks out elsewhere. Children have become the most numerous, as well as the most helpless, victims of such wars. Family violence is tearing communities apart. Children are abused, abandoned and aborted. AIDS claims ever more victims. The streets of some of the world's most sophisticated cities have become virtual battle zones. Into this cauldron of cruelty and human anguish stepped the kindness and love of God in the person of Jesus Christ.

We might have expected an angry God of judgment. But it was kindness, loving kindness, that appeared. God's kindness created a whole new world of possibility for every person, family, community and nation. "If anyone is in Christ, there is a new creation: everything old has passed away; see, everything has become new" (2 Cor. 5:17, NRSV).

Paul A. Rader, *The War Cry*

God in the Present Tense

Matthew 1:23

Many names and titles are ascribed to our Lord in the Scriptures. They describe not only what He has done, but what He is. Not only the spiritual benefits of the past, but what He can do in us and for us in the present.

Among the names and titles of God's Son is one of particular significance to His followers—Emmanuel—given centuries before His birth in the prophecy of Isaiah (7:14): "Therefore the Lord Himself will give you a sign; the virgin will be with child and will give birth to a son, and will call Him Immanuel."

The fulfillment of that promise is found in Matthew 1:23: "The virgin will be with child and will give birth to a son, and they will call Him Immanuel, which means, 'God with us.'"

"God with us"—now! The Present tense!

He is as close as the whisper of His name. Not in some far-off celestial computer center operating the machinery, but cradled in human hearts and minds.

He was Immanuel—God with us—in the cradle, eliciting the usual human expressions of adoration, love and admiration which come from any group looking upon a newborn baby. No doubt, He kicked and waved His little arms as if to invite doting visitors to take His pudgy little hand in theirs, and to speak in the high-pitched voice which uninhibited baby admirers are prone to use. There in a crude cradle in a Bethlehem stable He was God with us.

He was Immanuel—God with us—on the cross. There were those who recognized Him, even there, as "the Word made flesh" (John 1:14) who had "pitched his tent" among them for 33 years. Incarnational living comes through acceptance of the message of the cross, and the sacrifice of Jesus, our Savior.

He is Immanuel—God with us—as the Comforter. Our Lord's promise is still relevant: "I will ask the Father, and He will give you another Counselor to be with you forever. I will not leave you orphans; I will come to you" (John 14:16,18).

Jesus further reinforces the truth of his abiding presence in Matthew 28:20: "Surely I am with you always, to the very end of the age."

Robert A. Watson, *The War Cry*

The Love of a Broken Heart

Luke 19:41–44

⇗

If you have ever truly loved, you have known the pain of a broken heart. Just before leaving The Salvation Army's Hospital in Zambia to come home to America, my heart was broken unexpectedly.

I was called to the hospital to certify the death of a newborn baby, whose perfectly formed body had been extracted from a pit latrine. The mother was a teenage student who had hidden her pregnancy with loose fitting clothing, knowing that if she had been found to be pregnant, she would have been expelled from the school.

She went into labor in the dead of night, gave birth unattended in the bush, and in an act of desperation, had thrown her child into a pit latrine. The helpless infant, so flawless and vulnerable, had lived its few hours pitifully crying, before succumbing. Many days passed before I could hear a newborn cry without imagining this little one's pathetic cries alone and cold in the night. The image still haunts me.

My grief turned to anger against the one who had betrayed that most basic of trust relationships, a mother's love. I wanted her to know something of the pain she had inflicted on her defenseless offspring, this precious little lamb. (I discovered later that her fellow students attempted to beat her and were restrained only with difficulty by the school staff.)

The young mother was brought to the hospital soon after her child died, and she became my patient as well. Her look of wretched hopelessness made me quickly realize that my anger, although appropriate, was misdirected. The power of Satan had driven her to this heinous deed, and the powers of darkness were the proper target of my anger.

Jesus knew the love of a broken heart: "As He approached Jerusalem and saw the city, He wept over it" (Luke 19:41). Does your heart break over the sinfulness of man? As world events unfold, with countless atrocities, what is your response? Do you grieve over a lost and dying world?

Just before the police came to take the young mother to jail, I prayed with her. I asked God to forgive her for what she had done, and in silence asked Him to forgive me for my response. I took comfort in knowing her precious little one was already safe in the arms of Jesus.

We need to be angry and outraged at sin. But from this moral indignation must spring an even greater love for the sinner and the appropriate response of compassion for the wounded ones. God help us to stay tender enough to know the love of a broken heart.

David E. Winters, M.D., *The War Cry*

From the Mount of Beatitudes

Matthew 5:3–10

The Mount of Beatitudes rises above the ruins on the northwestern shore of the Sea of Galilee. This revered hill offers an awe–inspiring view of virtually the entire shoreline of the Sea of Galilee.

A narrow access road branches from the Tiberias highway and leads up the hill to the stately Church of the Beatitudes and adjoining hospice. Built in 1936, both facilities are now cared for by the Franciscan Sisters.

The renowned architect Barluzzi designed the distinctive octagonal–shaped church, utilizing the plentiful local basalt stone for the edifice and white stone from Nazareth to produce the unadorned, graceful arches surrounding the church's veranda. Each of the sanctuary's eight walls commemorates one of the Beatitudes pronounced at the beginning of the Sermon on the Mount. A lofty, elegant central dome symbolizes the ninth Beatitude. It reminds every believer that blessed (happy) are those who are persecuted because of righteousness, for theirs is the kingdom of heaven.

It is the concave southeastern slope, however, that makes this hill one of the most hallowed Christian sites in the Holy Land. Since the fourth century, Christians have identified this verdant crest as the place where Jesus escaped the pressing multitude to teach His disciples. He retreated from the large crowds that had followed Him and led His disciples to this secluded natural amphitheater, sat down and taught them. His subsequent summary of basic gospel themes is known as the Sermon on the Mount (Matthew 5–7).

It is important to note that on this occasion Jesus sat down to teach. When a Rabbi was formally teaching, or when the subject matter was of utmost importance, he sat down. The fact that Jesus sat down to teach His disciples indicates that what He was about to say was essential, fundamental and, in the paramount sense of the word, official.

The Mount of Beatitudes is also the traditional spot where Jesus chose His twelve disciples (Luke 6:12–16). The Sermon on the Mount, according to Luke's narrative, immediately follows the choosing of the Twelve. The Master's instructions may best be understood as an ordination address to the twelve apostles He had recently selected.

Jesus here introduces and summarizes guidelines and instruction for life and ministry that are unique, unprecedented and revolutionary. The Sermon on the Mount is, in fact, a distillation of the whole gospel message.

William Francis, *The Stones Cry Out*

A Mother's Religion

Ruth 1:16

Naomi is the mother's name and her story is told in the book of Ruth. Naomi, with her husband and sons, had been driven from her country by famine. Her husband and two sons died, leaving her bereft of kin and means of livelihood. She decided to return to Israel and advised her two Moabite daughters-in-law to remain where they were.

One took the advice. The other, Ruth, clung to Naomi and spoke the beautiful and memorable words: "Don't urge me to leave ... where you go I will go, and where you stay I will stay. Your people will be my people and your God my God" (Ruth 1:16).

Think of the life and faith of the woman who called forth those words. Ruth's life-altering decision was made because Naomi's religion had impressed her with its truth and hope.

This mother's religion was strong. It is quite easy to be religious in a favorable climate, surrounded by like-minded people. But Naomi kept her faith in a strange land and among alien people. She lived in Moab, but she didn't do as the Moabites did. For Naomi there was one God and she remained true to Him.

This mother's religion was attractive. We don't know how much Naomi talked about Israel's God, but there is little doubt that the way she lived for Him was impressive. It was a life so attractive in its faith and works that Ruth was willing to reject previous claims of country and religion and accompany Naomi to Bethlehem. We could all do with a religion that attracts.

This mother's religion was shared. It was strong enough and attractive enough to be conveyed from one person to another. Naomi's faith won the devotion of a daughter-in-law from another family to herself and from another religion to her God. How deeply and broadly it was shared is expressed in eloquent words and practical deeds. It included going and staying, new relationships with people and a whole-souled commitment to God. Naomi's faith was communicated and it became life-changing.

George Eliot is credited with saying that, "There are those whose celestial intimacies seem not to improve their domestic manners." Naomi was different. Her life with God had a healing, helpful influence on those about her and Ruth's words and actions are a continual witness to this mother's religion.

Bramwell Tripp, *The War Cry*

Songs in the Night

Psalm 77:6

Ultimately, a "night season" will come to each life. It is easy to sing in the sunshine when life flows along like a song. But at night the song must emerge from the shadows and come from the melody that the Lord puts within one's life.

But the night has its songs as well. The song of the nightingale is sweeter because it comes in the stillness of the night. The noises of the day are hushed and her notes float as sweet music through the night air.

God is the great Composer of the night songs. When darkness overtakes us, God gives a song. The Psalmist testified, "At night His song is with me" (42:8), and "I remembered my songs in the night" (77:6). In the midst of a crisis in Israel, God promised His people, "You shall have a song as in the night" (Isa. 30:29 NKJV). Out of the tragic story of Job's trials comes the radiant truth that "God ... gives songs in the night" (Job 35:10). Sorrow becomes the expositor of the mysteries of God that joy leaves unexplained.

This radiant truth has been confirmed in the experience of innumerable people who, when going through the dark valleys, have been encouraged and sustained by the song God gave to them. Many of our best-loved hymns were forged in the crucible of sorrow and suffering. "What a Friend We Have in Jesus" was written by the young Joseph Scriven when not long before his wedding day his fiancée was drowned. Fanny Crosby was blind and yet wrote over 6,000 hymns, many of them among all-time favorites.

In 1871 the ship *Ville du Havre*, halfway across the Atlantic, was rammed by a sailing vessel and cut in two. Mrs. Spafford saw her four daughters swept away to their deaths. When she and a few other survivors reached Wales, she cabled two words to her husband: "Saved alone."

Taking the earliest ship, he hastened to his wife's side, all the ache of his heart going out to her and to his Father God. When his boat reached the approximate spot where the *Ville du Havre* had met with disaster, God gave him the inspiration and courage to write the hymn that affirms: When sorrows like sea billows roll,/Whatever my lot, Thou hast taught me to say:/It is well, it is well with my soul.

There is a grace and strength from God that is not given in the everyday routine of life. But when trials come upon us, we may know His added grace, His increased strength, and His multiplied peace.

Henry Gariepy, *Songs in the Night*

Christ's Prayer for Us

John 17:17

W hen John Knox was dying and his wife brought the Bible to his bedside, she asked what she should read. "Read where I first cast my anchor—the 17th of John," he replied. Early or late, one may cast an anchor in these profound depths and be sure the anchor will hold.

Here we are permitted one of Scripture's rare glimpses of communication between members of the Godhead. Here we have the sinless Son of Man, who comes not by grace (as we must) but by right. A sacred hush hangs over John 17; one wants to take off his shoes on this holy ground.

The anguish of Gethsemane and the agony of Calvary will follow within hours, and Jesus knows it, but His peace is undisturbed.

But when a man has access to God, what shall he request? Sadly, some of us do not seem to know. Our prayers are, as a result, for things—a far cry from the praying in which our Lord engages.

For our sakes He "sanctifies" Himself (John 17:19). The term here means not to cleanse—Jesus did not need any cleansing—but to consecrate, to dedicate to the divine purpose. His coming was for us; His dying was for us; His praying is for us as well. To think—Jesus spent time in costly caring for me. Robert McCheyne said, "If I could hear Christ praying for me in the next room, I would not fear a million enemies. Yet distance makes no difference. He is praying for me."

The heart of this Calvary-eve appeal is that we believers might be sanctified (John 17:17,19). The "uttermost salvation" made available through such intercession is not only quantitative—salvation for all time and eternity—but qualitative—a complete salvation, a pervasive cleansing of the whole personality, a sharing in the wholeness of the divine nature limited only by the finitude of the man who receives it. Jesus is earnestly asking that for me, every day. The purpose of the cross is not only to pardon, but to purify.

If Jesus, in such an hour of crisis, asked the Father to sanctify me, ought I not to seek it for myself? May I not make His prayer my prayer, with assurance that God will answer?

Jesus' prayer, breathing out its blessing, is my assurance that this may be my experience, yes—shall be!

Edward Read, *Burning, Always Burning*

Get on God's Wavelength

Romans 8:16

The mosquito is best known as a pest, but if the sound of its wing beat is mechanically reproduced beside a planted kernel of corn, the kernel will grow to full ear in half the time the corn grows under optimal natural conditions. There is evidently a planned connection between the sudden emergence of buzzing hoards of insects each spring and the bursting forth of the vegetable kingdom in green glory.

A banana plantation in New South Wales, Australia, has discovered that bananas, too, grow bigger and better to music. To quote a portion of the news report, "It is giving results out of all proportion to the amount of fertilizer used."

Sir James Jeans, the English mathematician, physicist and astronomer, wrote: "Everything in the universe is in a state of vibration." Some of the vibrations are causative. Other sounds are results, called sympathetic vibrations. If two pianos are tuned perfectly alike, strike any note on the one and its counterpart on the other piano will instantly vibrate, but all the others remain silent and still.

For bridges, sympathetic vibrations can be calamitous. The Narrows Bridge in Tacoma, Washington was built by an idealist who carried the beauty of his mathematics too far. He tuned the cables of the bridge, and a 30–mile–an–hour wind played the tune and ripped the bridge apart. Newspaper accounts called the bridge "Galloping Gertie."

The Christian life is simply one of getting in step with God. It's tuning up to His standards. His great causative voice that once burst the summit of Mt. Sinai into flame can catch any honest heart willing to vibrate to His truth and make it resonate in perfect harmony with His divine will.

If you are out of tune with God, you have not availed yourself of the power that can be released in your life once God tunes you up. "Therefore, if anyone is in Christ, he is a new creation; the old has gone, the new has come! (2 Cor. 5:17).

Get on God's wavelength. "Anyone who believes in the Son of God has this testimony in his heart" (1 John 5:10). "The Spirit Himself testifies with our spirit that we are God's children" (Rom. 8:16).

Lyell M. Rader, *Romance & Dynamite*

Sons of God

1 John 3:1

Now are we the sons of God!
Unfinished, uncompleted;
But He who reigns within our hearts
Shall never be defeated,
Till by His Spirit He refines
The work He has begun,
And in our human faces shines
The beauty of His Son.

Now are we the sons of God!
Resembling in our fashion
The first–begotten Son of God
In purity and passion.
His holiness, His humbleness,
Sincerity serene,
Shall by His Spirit's presence
In our lesser lives be seen!

Now are we the sons of God!
In spite of human failing;
The pow'r of God at work in man
Is everywhere prevailing.
Imperfect samples of His grace
We still proclaim His story;
Incarnate in the sons of men
Are glimpses of His glory.

Now are we the sons of God!
The fam'ly likeness bearing
The foll'wers of the Son of God
His saviorhood are sharing.
Blind to their selfish wantings
And disdainful of disaster,
In selfless service they become
A little like their Master.

John Gowans, *O Lord Not More Verse!*

The Overcoming Life

Ephesians 6:10–11

You will have to fight the enemies of your soul to the end, if you are to make the glorious finish on which you are calculating. How you are to do it so as to be brought off "more than conqueror" (Rom. 8:37) is a most important question.

The first thing I advise is to find out the places in your heart and character where you are most in danger of being overcome. Every man, woman, or child has his or her most easily besetting sin, that is, some point in their thinking, feeling, or acting where they are weakest, and therefore likely to be most easily led into the doing of evil. You can be quite sure that the devil has discovered that place already, and you can be equally sure that that is the spot where he will be most likely to attack you.

Watch against unexpected attacks. Some of the most serious defeats in war have resulted from an insufficient lookout. "Taken by surprise" has been the reason given for any number of disasters. The same neglect of watchfulness will account for no end of defeats and backslidings in religion.

Resist the first beginnings of sin. The danger lies in the first glass, the first word, nay, often in the first look. The moment your conscience testifies to the presence of the tempter, stand on your guard, and resist the foe. With many temptations there is only safety in flight; arguments are useless, nay, dangerous.

Perhaps more people go wrong by dallying with the beginnings of evil than in any other way.

Keep out of circumstances, and away from places, in which you know you are likely to be tempted. Nothing can compare with the folly displayed by some who voluntarily associate with companions, relations and friends whom they know will tempt them to do, or allow things to be done which are wrong, or go into places where they know they will be tempted by the very things which have been their ruin in days gone by.

In the darkness and depression of temptation tell your case to the Savior. You can be sure of His sympathy. "Because He himself suffered when He was tempted, He is able to help those who are being tempted" (Heb. 2:18).

William Booth, *The Warrior's Daily Portion*

God's Day

Psalm 118:24

Today—this day—this very day
Is God's day!
Fresh from his hand,
And lent to me so graciously,
A day He planned.

Today, there's work for us to do
Together;
It is not mine.
The day, the work, and I are his,
At his design.

And if today some sorrow comes
Ere night fall—
Some pain or care—
Yet I will know he's with me still,
This day we share.

And in this day of ours I'll find
The gladness
He waits to show.
Some burst of joy, or quiet peace,
Today I'll know.

I will not wait tomorrow's
Golden hue
Or rosy way,
But with His joy I'll really live
In God's today.

Juanita Nelting, *It's Beautiful!*

Man's Continual Cry

Psalm 51:10

The remorse expressed in this penitential psalm is attributed to David after he had planned the murder of Uriah in order to posses his wife. Life compels men to acknowledge the existence of those inner self–contradictions which, apart from the grace of God, can be their ruin.

Because of these character flaws, it is man's nature to be dissatisfied with his nature, but how to shape it nearer to his heart's desire is beyond him. The Apostle Paul summed up man's continuing plight in the well–worn phrase: "For what I do is not the good I want to do; no, the evil I do not want to do—this I keep on doing ... what a wretched man I am!" (Rom. 7:19, 24).

The Christian diagnosis of human need is the truth also to which our children are introduced in their study of English literature, with the play *The Tragedy of Macbeth*, or *The Tragedy of Hamlet*, or *The Tragedy of King Lear*. That was how Shakespeare thought of these fated men—the essence of the tragedy in each instance that of a man of undoubted promise ruined by some flaw in his nature. Macbeth, for all his unquestioned physical courage, allowed ambition to become his master instead of his servant. Hamlet, of princely stock and of a thoughtful cast of mind, was the victim of his inner indecisiveness. And Lear's genuine affection, affronted by seeming gracelessness, exploded into wrath.

Nor are modern instances lacking of this interior civil war—as when a Dylan Thomas could say that "I hold a beast, an angel and a madman in me, and my problem is their subjugation."

What has the Christian faith to say to this? First of all, it recognizes that these are the facts of life. In the second place, it offers a remedy.

To Paul's plea "Who on earth can set me free from the clutches of my own sinful nature?" there is but one answer: God alone, through Jesus Christ our Lord.

Despair of ourselves is not a bad thing if it leads us to cast ourselves without reserve upon the saving power of God. The witness of the Christian gospel is that God waits to help the man who cannot help himself.

Frederick Coutts, *Essentials of Christian Experience*

The Abiding Holy Spirit

John 14:17

Jesus said to His disciples concerning the Holy Spirit that, "You know Him; for He lives in you" (John 14:7). The Holy Spirit had begun to work in them, but there was more to follow, for Jesus said, "and [He] will be in you" (John 14:7).

When a man is building a house, he is in and out of it and round about it. But when the house is finished, the owner sweeps out all the chips and sawdust, scrubs the floor, lays down his carpets, hangs up his pictures, arranges his furniture and moves in with his family. Then he is in the fullest sense within it. He abides there. Now, it is in that sense that Jesus meant the Holy Spirit should be in them.

The disciples had forsaken all to follow Christ. They had been commissioned to preach the gospel, to heal the sick, to cleanse the lepers, to raise the dead, to cast out devils. Their names were written in heaven. They were not of the world, even as Jesus was not of the world. They knew the Holy Spirit, for He was with them, working in them, but not yet living in them, for they were yet carnal, each seeking the best place for himself. They were fearful, timid and false to Him when the testing time came.

This experience of theirs before Pentecost is the common experience of all true converts. Every child of God knows that the Holy Spirit is with him; he realizes that He is working within, striving to set the house in order.

But often this work is slow, for He can only work effectually as we work with Him, practicing intelligent and obedient faith. Some days the work prospers and seems almost complete, and then peace and joy and comfort abound in the heart. At other times the work is hindered—and often almost or quite undone—by the strivings and stirrings of inbred sin, by fits of temper, by lightness and frivolity, by neglect of watchfulness and prayer, and the patient, attentive study of His Word, by worldliness, by unholy ambitions, by jealousies and envyings, by harsh judgments, selfish indulgences and slowness to believe.

The Spirit seeks to bring every thought into captivity to the obedience of Christ, to lead the soul to that point of glad, wholehearted consecration to its Lord, and that simple, perfect faith in the merits of His Blood which will enable him to enthrone Christ within.

Samuel Logan Brengle, *The War Cry*

Science and Faith

Psalm 8:3–4

I've never quite been able to work out why some people think science and Christianity don't mix. It's as if they think one disproves the other—and that's nonsense.

We've known for some time of the existence of black holes and that the galaxies of which we are aware probably form only one-tenth of the entire universe. But now we are being introduced to a new class of "black objects." Hydrogen and helium feature prominently in their makeup, but the number of these objects seems to be the most impressive piece of information. Apparently there are 10 million billion of them.

There's obviously a good deal more to learn about these failed stars, and there's a vast amount of speculation as to their value within the universe. But at least it gives the scientists something at which to point their telescopes.

No so long ago, two famous scientists set out to disprove the existence of God. As they examined the laws which govern our existence they amazed themselves by coming to the conclusion that evidence for a Creator was overwhelming.

Their research led them to issue a report which said that the chances of the world being an accident were a mere 10 to the power of 40,000. For those of us who don't know what this means—even with a calculator—they said it meant that the chances of the world being an accident were "so utterly minuscule as to make it absurd."

One of the professors said proof of a creator at work was to be found in "masses of evidence of designer activity that is continuing to sustain the universe."

Belief in a creator is one thing. The next step is to ask ourselves why He put us here and what do we mean to Him? To go through life without trying to get answers is to miss the best exploration (and discovery) of all.

With the Psalmist we exclaim, "When I consider Your heavens, the work of Your fingers, the moon and the stars which You have set in place, what is man, that You are mindful of him?" (Ps. 8:3–4)

Robert Street, *It's A New Day!*

A Faithful Witness

Acts 1:8

᠊ᡒ

Again and again the same vocation and commission is bestowed upon the apostles and disciples. To the ends of the earth and to the end of time this commission comes down to every one of the Lord's own: "Go and make disciples of all nations" (Matt. 28:19). That embraces us. And to every disciple who has preceded, or is to follow us, is promised His divine presence in this glorious work of testifying for Him.

God needs witnesses in this world. Why? Because the whole world is in revolt against Him. The world has gone away from God. The world ignores God, denies and contradicts His character, government and purposes.

He has had His faithful witnesses from the beginning until now. As the apostle says, "He left not Himself without witness" (Acts 14:17 KJV). Down from the days of Enoch, who walked with God, to this present hour, God has always had His true and faithful witnesses. In the worst times there have been some burning and shining lights. Sometimes few and far between, sometimes, like Noah, one solitary man in a whole generation of men, witnessing for God—but one, at least, there has been. God has not left Himself without witness.

Jesus Christ, the well-beloved of the Father, was the great witness. He came especially to manifest, to testify of and to reveal the Father to men. This was His great work. He came not to testify of Himself, but of His Father. He came to reveal God to men. He was the "Faithful and True Witness" (Rev. 3:14 NKJV). And when He had to leave the world and go back to His Father, then He commissioned His disciples to take His place and to be God's witnesses on earth.

Witnesses, you know, must deal with the facts, not theories, about what they know. Now God wants His people to witness to fact. And He wants us to be good witnesses, too. How much depends upon the character of a witness even in an earthly court! If you can cast a reflection upon the character or the veracity of a witness, you shake his testimony and take away its value. How important that Christ's witnesses should truly represent Him and His truth.

He wants us to be faithful witnesses. Every day I live, the more I am convinced that if God's people were to be in desperate earnest, thousands would be won. Witness! Witness! The Lord help you.

Catherine Booth, *Aggressive Christianity*

The Immovable Stone

Matthew 28:2

Every precaution had been taken. Having crucified Jesus, the authorities wanted absolutely no repercussions. People were still talking about the way in which Jesus allegedly had raised people from the dead. All of these reported incidents undoubtedly encouraged the authorities to forestall any possible fulfillment of the prediction that on "the third day He shall rise from the dead" (Mark 10:34 NKJV). If His disciples had forgotten, His enemies hadn't (Matt. 27:63).

The hitherto unused tomb of Joseph of Arimathea, as a resting place for the body of Jesus, would have suited the civil powers. A great boulder is rolled across the aperture. Not only can no one enter, but, perhaps more importantly in this particular situation, no one can get out.

Next, the seal is applied. Would anyone dare to tamper with it? All the authority of the Roman Empire is declared in that imprimatur. To see the seal of the Empire would be sufficient to scare off any of the Galilean's foolhardy followers intent on creating a legend.

The stone said "No Entrance!" It also said "No Exit!" The seal said "No Trespassing!" But, mused the authorities, what if the disciples of Jesus suddenly had a return of courage and banded themselves together to invade the tomb? Well, the legion could take care of that! Some well-armed soldiers could handle the followers of Jesus.

A stone ... a seal ... soldiers.

And then it happened! The angel of the Lord descended from heaven and came and rolled back the stone from the door and sat upon it. "The guards were so afraid of him that they shook and became like dead men" (Matt. 28:4). The seal was broken. From the angel there is a triumphant announcement. "He has risen! He is not here" (Mark 16:6).

Now, men need no longer march into the tomb without hope of egress. The stone is rolled away. The tomb is no longer a cavern without exit, but a corridor to a new and everlasting life! The law of mortality which says that every man who is born must die, gives place to a new law of immortality in and through the risen Lord.

Christ is risen! The grave cannot hold Him. Death is vanquished forever. And the truth of it, the fact of it, will echo again and again. Choirs will sing it. Trumpets will sound it. Bells will chime it, and millions of hearts will witness to it. He is risen indeed!

Arnold Brown, *Occupied Manger, Unoccupied Tomb*

Watching

Matthew 24:42

When I was a tiny child, my mother found me perched in a library window looking out intently at the distant road. "What are you doing there, child?" she asked.

"Watching for Papa," I said. "It is almost time for him to come, and I want to see him."

"But you are not ready," rejoined my sensible mother. "Look at your dirty hands and that soiled apron. Papa wants to see his little girl clean, and he likes your hair shining. Go and get yourself ready for Papa, and then take your papers and dolls' clothes off his table. I'm all ready for him, and so must you be."

It seems to me now that her advice is still good for older children in spiritual matters, and that her words show us exactly how we are to "watch" for our Lord. We are first to be ready ourselves, and then to make His earth ready as far as lies within our power. We have no business looking up to the clouds of heaven while our hearts will not bear the inspection of Him for whom we are looking. We have no leisure to study dates and times when the law of God for our daily lives is fulfilled in our hearts.

"Therefore, be you also ready," (Matt. 24:44 KJV) said Jesus. "Watching" can have no practical meaning but getting ready, if we are not so, and keeping ready, if we are.

It is explained in other parts of the holy Word how we are to be watching. "Watch unto prayer," admonishes Peter, "for the end of all things is at hand" (1 Pet. 4:7 KJV). Shall the end find us in fellowship with God?

"Watch thou in all things," (2 Tim. 4:5 KJV) Paul exhorted Timothy, just going into the work, and with great prospects before him. The young man was to watch Jesus continually, to test whether or not his life matched his Lord's.

Jesus himself said, "Watch therefore; for you know not what hour your Lord does come" (Matt. 24:42 KJV).

The eyes that so look for Jesus in all matters of the daily life will see Him. They will not have to wait for His appearance in the clouds of glory, but they will behold Him in the clouds of heaviness which may shadow their everyday life; they will find His healing balm on every thorn which would pierce them, His tears mingling with every drop of sorrow their eyes pour down, His form bending under every cross appointed them, taking its weight and pain and transforming it into a thing of joy. "Blessed are the pure in heart, for they [as they watch] shall see God" (Matt. 5:8 KJV).

Elizabeth Swift Brengle, *Half Hours with My Guide*

Sin, The Great Destroyer

Romans 6:23

❧

Sin is the great foe! Look at the destruction of the children and the young people for which sin is answerable. Look at the ruin of womanhood which goes steadily forward in every land. Think of the wives and mothers degraded or deserted, or both. Consider the moral and physical decay of manhood in the sinful sensualism of the day.

Oh, sin, thou archenemy of man, we hate thee. Sin, thou hateful monster, we challenge thy cruel and lawless reign over our fellows! But for sin there would be no war, no blight in the young people, no ruined womanhood, no corrupt men. Sin is the curse.

See the disorder it brings. Sin disarranges everything in men's souls. Lies come to look like truth. Virtue appears foolish and vice seems wise. Pleasure grows more important than duty. Self is preferred to God, time to eternity. It is a kind of upside-downism of the soul.

See how sin makes men try to be independent of God, their rightful Sovereign. Sin brought in this plague of the human spirit—pride—and we know how it destroys the very best of people.

What havoc sins works with faithfulness. Look at the children who promised to care for their parents, and don't. Look at the men and women who vowed to be faithful to one another, but have broken their vows. Look at the fathers who wrong their children, and at the prodigals who go off and break their mothers' hearts. And what of unfaithfulness to God? How sin inclines the heart to mistrust Him.

What a horrible effect sin has on the imagination, on all that belongs to the mind of man. It lights the fires of passion and filthy lust by unclean thoughts. And by and by the sinful mind becomes a dreadful infection to the whole man.

What rebellion sin brings about in men's souls. They get other rulers—self, money, degraded appetite, evil habit. These are among the gods sin substitutes for the great Father of Love. It is an awful exchange.

Yes, sin is the great destroyer. The fact is that nothing of the material order can do anything with sin. What is wanted is a Redeemer, a Deliverer, a Savior—a revelation which opens to the bad in heart a way to be pure in heart, which brings to guilt and despair and danger the assurance of pardon, of hope, of safety—or, in one word, of salvation.

Bramwell Booth, *Life and Religion*

The Sanctity of the Family

Acts 16:30–34

It was Felix Adler who described family as "the miniature commonwealth upon whose integrity the safety of the larger commonwealth depends." Pope John XXIII said simply, "Family is the first and essential cell of human society." The breakdown of marriages and, therefore, families has a cumulative effect on the larger society.

Our families shape our value systems, hand down a religious heritage, create our work ethic and model how we view marriage and raise children. It is because of this that Salvationists commit themselves to uphold the sanctity of marriage and family life.

We speak of "the family of God" as an image of the Church, and of a "bridegroom and his bride" as a picture of Christ in relation to His Church.

The greatest evangelical potential is found in communicating the gospel through the family. Paul knew this when he promised the Philippian jailer: "Believe in the Lord Jesus, and you will be saved—you and your household" (Acts 16:31).

By viewing marriages and families as a "sanctity" to uphold, we are saying that there is a holiness about these relationships. They are a gift from God and must not be profaned.

Our families are the communities of faith to which we first belong. Devotions, mealtime prayers and bedtime benedictions bind families together with spiritual strength. The International Spiritual Life Commission calls Salvationists to "restore the family to its central position in passing on the faith, to generate resources to help parents grow together in faithful love and lead their children into wholeness, with hearts on fire for God and His mission."

In a world of shifting values, it is good to be reminded that the witness of a family is not passé. As Shaw Clifton writes, "Happy and successful marriages outnumber those that eventually break down. Marriage is as popular as ever."

Fathers have a significant impact upon how their children will perceive God the Father, and mothers are without equal in influencing children to faith. Marriage and family life have a sanctity that must be protected.

If ever there is a fight worth fighting, this is it! This is the battle for the home. Let us fight the good fight with all our might.

Richard Munn, *The War Cry*

Dedicated to Truth

John 17:15–20

The depth and beauty of Christ's prayer for His disciples overwhelms, even startles us, while viewing the scene of our Lord's intercession before the ordeal of the Cross. At each coming we remain a little longer within the circle of those for whom Jesus prayed—Himself, His disciples, His Church, and us. It is a stupendous thought that in His prayer nearly two thousand years ago Christ included you and me. "I pray also for those who will believe in Me through their message" (John 17:20).

It is a passionately earnest prayer that God will save this group of men from the attachment to corruptible treasures that is the mark of the world. Christ pleaded with an intensity beyond our comprehension that His disciples should be consecrated to the real, the eternal.

The burden of Christ's prayer is that His disciples shall be sanctified by the truth. They are not merely to admire truth, or do no more than value it; they are to be dedicated to it. In the New Testament the word "truth" means more than merely true as opposed to untrue. It means genuine as opposed to spurious, perfect as opposed to imperfect. It is the property of substance as opposed to shadow.

We may say that our material possessions, our financial position and our properties are as a shadow compared with the only kind of position that really matters to God. Our rank or our position, even when and if deserved, is only as an imitation compared with the genuine qualities that make men great in the sight of God. Our intense activity is spurious unless it is a means to that great end for which we were called.

To be consecrated to the eternal means more than valuing incorruptible riches for ourselves. It means we shall desire eternal wealth for others. Jesus said, "For them I sanctify Myself" (John 17:19). This meant that He desired the sanctification, or dedication to truth, of His own people so much that He was willing to pay the extreme price to bring it about. For us, this means being drawn by something outside of ourselves so vast and irresistible that we cannot see ourselves at all. It involves a kind of caring of which we are not capable at all without Christ.

When we ponder the Lord's last prayer and through it know God's will for us, we would be discouraged did we not believe in the timeless words, "I have finished my work" (Rom. 15:23). He who saw the harvest in the seed of corn saw too the saints in the stumbling loyalty of the disciples. And so it is with us.

Catherine Baird, *Evidence of the Unseen*

Too Fast for Me!

Hebrews 13:8

In the early 19th century, railroads ran at what were considered dangerous speeds. After all, God never intended people to travel at 10 miles per hour!

Over the years life has accelerated to keep pace with transportation. In 1947 Chuck Yeager broke the sound barrier. Today military fighter planes fly at three times the speed of sound.

The year 1996 marked the 50th anniversary of the ENIAC computer. It was the size of a grade school gym and used enough electricity to light a major U.S. city. Now computers are sub-notebook in size. The computer you bought yesterday may become obsolete before the warranty expires.

Some industry experts calculate that computer performance and power will double every 18 months. If so, the one I am using now will soon be as antiquated as a quill pen.

Life is whizzing by at 100 megahertz (and then some) every minute of every day. Just yesterday we saw our kids watching "Sesame Street." Now we are wondering, "How can we pay for college?" Where did the time go?

If you feel things are speeding faster than you can control, you are right. Even when we are sitting still, the earth is zipping along on its solar orbit going 66,000 miles per hour.

Technology is not the only thing that is speeding ahead at a reckless pace. In terms of personal and spiritual ethics, things that used to be clearly right and clearly wrong are now relative and open to individual interpretation. Right is wrong and wrong right in many cases.

Is there something or someone in the entire world that is stable, solid and worthy of my trust that won't be obsolete in the near future? Yes! Scripture reminds us that the grace of God is eternal, secure and unchanging. It is never out of fashion. It never spoils or fades. It doesn't come with an expiration date. "Jesus Christ is the same yesterday and today and forever" (Heb. 13:8).

Those who know Jesus as their personal Savior from sin can count on His grace never changing. He is as powerful for their needs as He has been throughout generations.

A. Kenneth Wilson, *The War Cry*

Healing Waters

Psalm 147:3

When shall I come unto the healing waters?
    Lifting my heart, I cry to Thee my prayer.
Spirit of peace, my Comforter and Healer,
    In whom my springs are found, let my soul meet Thee there.

    From a hill I know,
    Healing waters flow;
    O rise, Emmanuel's tide,
    And my soul overflow!

Wash from my hands the dust of earthly striving,
    Take from my mind the stress of secret fear;
Cleanse Thou the wounds from all but Thee far hidden,
    And when the waters flow let my healing appear.

Light, life and love are in that healing fountain;
    All I require to cleanse me and restore;
Flow through my soul, redeem its desert places,
    And make a garden there for the Lord I adore.

Albert Orsborn, *The Beauty of Jesus*

The Therapy of Humor

Proverbs 17:22

To their pious claim of superior knowledge of God's ways with man, Job retorted: "Doubtless you are the people and wisdom will die with you" (Job 12:2). Andrew Blackwood calls this "the most humorous verse in the entire Bible."

This was a new Job taking the offensive. For the first time he reacted with sarcasm to the harsh judgments of his would-be comforters. In his three-chapter rebuttal, he called his contestants "quacks": "You are worthless physicians, all of you!" (13:4) And like the speaker of whom it was said that he could not have said less unless he had said more, Job satirized: "If only you would be altogether silent! For you, that would be wisdom" (13:5).

Job may have lost his possessions, but he had not lost his sense of humor. To be able to see the humorous side of a situation redeems many an otherwise hopeless predicament. Norman Cousins has written in *The Anatomy of an Illness*: "I was greatly elated by the discovery that there is a physiological basis for the ancient theory that laughter is good medicine."

The writer of Proverbs expressed this truth centuries earlier: "A cheerful heart is a good medicine" (17:22). The preacher in Ecclesiastes reminds us that there is "a time to laugh" (Eccles. 3:4). Learning to see the humorous side of things is one of the most serious subjects in the world to master. When life loses its humor, it is hard to be spiritual. Thomas Merton wrote: "The mark of a saint is the ability to laugh."

When Victor Frankl was in a German concentration camp, he made a pact with another prisoner. Every day they would find a joke in their experience in that hell that was Auschwitz. Incredible as it may seem, they were able to do just that, and it helped keep them sane and able to survive.

Are you going through a difficult experience? How instructive it is to note that the Book of Job, the saddest story of the Bible, contains some of the most humorous verses of the Bible. Stand back for a moment and capture a perspective that will enable you to laugh through your tears and trials. Humor and laughter are great gifts of God and can be a therapy in time of trouble.

Henry Gariepy, *Portraits of Perseverance*

The Music of God

Ephesians 5:19

Where did music start? In the heart of God Himself. The Bible is known and loved throughout the world as a book of laws, a manual of instruction for living, a literary masterpiece, the story of eternal salvation—the very Word of God. But it is also a book of music and song from beginning to end.

Its treasury has been inexhaustible and unsurpassed as a source for the most glorious music written through the ages. Georg Frederick Handel with his 21-day miracle oratorio *The Messiah* was not the first to be captivated by the music of the divine revelation, nor will he be the last.

When we lift our Sunday voices to sing, "Holy, Holy, Holy, Lord God Almighty," we are joining the mighty river of songs to God that has its head streams in the history of God's people.

For the people of God, there was party music for meaningful events. So Jacob's father-in-law scolds him by saying, "Why did you run off secretly and deceive me? Why didn't you tell me, so I could send you away with joy and singing to the music of tambourines and harps?" (Gen. 31:27).

Surrounding and infusing all this life-music was the music of God and His glory. God spoke to His broken but faithful servant Job about the day of creation when the morning stars sang together.

That song would be ever new, for in that great Psalm book that lay at the heart of worship, they and we are urged to "sing to the Lord a new song" (96:1). In that book are recorded songs of trust, despair, penitence and rejoicing. Only in the fullness of God's time would it become clear that the central theme of all the songs and all the music of God was then and is now the Lord Jesus Christ.

The music continued into the New Testament. Jesus told of the prodigal's elder brother hearing the music of the welcome-home party. On His last night before Calvary, Christ and the disciples sang a hymn before going to the Garden.

The mark of the new Christian church and the coming of the Holy Spirit was more music, "with psalms, hymns and spiritual songs. Sing and make music in your heart to the Lord" (Eph. 5:19). The joyful heart is an unmistakable sign of those who are born again.

Where does the music of God, which has gone round and round through all ages, come out? Around the throne of God where the redeemed play the harps of God and sing the song of Moses and the song of the Lamb.

Stanley Jaynes, *The War Cry*

I've Seen a Few Things

1 Corinthians 2:9

"Grandpa, were you ever young?" There were overtones of doubt in the voice of the five-year-old questioner. But the answer had a ring of confidence: "I sure was, Bobby!" The eyes that met the little boy's had both a twinkle and a far-away look. It was a long way back, but what was there was enjoyable to remember. "Young? Of course I was!"

The Psalmist said it too: "I was young and now am old" (Psalm 37:25). He wasn't answering a little boy's question. Rather he was looking at life's varied experiences from the vantage point of piled-up years. David lived a long time ago, but when he wrote those words he was writing for us. He is worth listening to.

David remembered his youth. We who are older sometimes act and talk as if we never had a taste of life's springtime. Recall it now and give thanks to God for it. There was a time when life was a succession of mountains to be climbed, and we had the strength and daring to scale them. Those years and those experiences were ours and we ought to recall them with gratitude.

David remembered his age. He had lived many years and he wasn't trying to kid anyone—least of all himself—about the calendar's uncompromising arithmetic. "I was young, now I am old." To say otherwise is a delusion. Age can be carried with dignity when it is worn proudly. It is never more pitiful than when it is cloaked in the ill-fitting, borrowed trappings of youth.

David remembered his God. He looked down the long vista of the years and said, in the preceding verse of that same psalm, "the Lord upholds," (v. 24) and in a following verse, "The Lord ... will not forsake His faithful ones" (v. 28) To have a faith in God and a trust born of experience is to have a strength greater than the best muscles and a vision sharper than the keenest eyes. Such a faith adds life to years, not just years to life.

Since David's time, God has revealed himself through his Son, Jesus Christ. His cross is the eternal evidence of divine love and the empty tomb is the triumphant symbol of divine power. So we go beyond David's words and say with Paul, "Eye has not seen, nor ear heard, nor have entered into the heart of man the things which God has prepared for those who love Him" (1 Cor. 2:9 NKJV).

I've seen a few things, but I've yet to see the best!

Bramwell Tripp, *To the Point*

Getting Past the First Step

Isaiah 41:10

It's like riding a bike, as the old saying goes. Once you've learned how to do it, you never forget. We've reached that developmental stage in our family. Our daughter Janine asked for a new set of wheels. After much scouring of newspaper ads and scrutiny of bank accounts, dad and daughter set off in search of a bike. Soon the journey ended, money changed hands and the secondhand bike became our firstborn's pride and joy. That was the easy part.

Janine's old bike had training wheels. Before that she enjoyed the stability of a toddler's tricycle. The old bike stood upright on its own. The trike didn't wobble. The new five-gear, drop-handlebar, fluorescent flamingo paint job, however, suddenly looked more like a nightmare than a dream machine.

A new world beckoned: a world of excitement, enjoyment and freedom. But this world of adventure could not be entered without pain.

During a morning that contained more spills than thrills, one thing was clear. While Janine could ride without help or hindrance from dad once she got started, the hardest step to take was the first. It was the initial push of the pedal that was proving so difficult. This rite of passage would have to wait for another day.

To be fair, it's not as easy as it looks. There's a lot to contend with. There's the weight of the bike, the coordination of the body, the dread of falling. After all, there's nothing so easy as falling off a bike.

To many people, living out the Christian faith appears just as daunting. Jesus offers us a world so new, so exciting and so different that He describes it like being born all over again.

Jesus offers us freedom. He promises a journey with a purpose, His company through life's ups and downs, and His comfort when we fall. But somehow that first step of faith is so hard to take.

We want to hold onto what we know and hand ourselves over to God at the same time. We're attracted by forgiveness, but held back by fear. We're afraid of missing out, yet afraid of messing up. We are going nowhere fast. We are in turmoil.

But we don't have to struggle alone. "Do not fear," God assures us, "for I am with you" (Isa. 41:10). In him we have a heavenly Father who holds us, guides us and encourages us to leave our fears and launch out in tandem with Him. After that first step, you'll be on your way!

Nigel Bovey, *The War Cry*, U.K.

What's For Dinner

1 Peter 5:8

A hunter who lost a prized hound dog in Blackwater State Park near Pensacola, Florida returned to the park hoping to home in on the hound's electronic tracking collar. Deep in the swamp he and several companions picked up a faint beep. It increased in intensity until they came face to face with a 10-foot alligator.

When an alligator catches its prey, it doesn't run it down like a lion and eat it in great pieces. Rather, it clamps down on the victim while dragging it into the water to drown. Leaving the corpse underwater, the gator can go back to finish eating at his leisure.

One of the most graphic images of Satan is found in 1 Peter 5:8: "Your enemy the devil prowls around like a roaring lion [or alligator] looking for someone to devour." He is not pictured in comical fashion—with horns and pitchfork—but as a beast looking for prey. People, not hound dogs, are the entree of choice.

Like a hungry gator, Satan does not swallow us whole. Instead he catches us with small sins that become patterns of rebellious behavior as he takes larger and larger bites. Finally, at his leisure, he finishes us, devouring all that we could have been, but now will never be.

Satan does not just want us humbled, humiliated, depressed or discouraged. He does not just want us beaten—he wants us eaten!

But the good news is "The One who is in you (Holy Spirit) is greater than the one who is in the world" (1 John 4:4). The believer whose sins are forgiven will experience a physical death, but will never again be subject to the spiritually carnivorous nature of Satan and sin.

"The sting of death is sin and the power of sin is the law. But thanks be to God! He gives us the victory through our Lord Jesus Christ" (1 Cor. 15:54–57). Let us stay close to the Savior for His forgiveness and constant protection.

A. Kenneth Wilson, *The War Cry*

Secular and Sacred

Romans 12:1

࿇

This call to present to God our bodies refers, primarily, to this body by means of which I have my being and earn my living—which is another way of saying that divine service is not limited to a particular hour on a Sunday, but covers all that takes place both in my work week as well as in my hours of leisure.

The purpose of the Christian faith is needlessly curtailed if its application is limited to special times and special areas of life. The redemptive purpose of God is as concerned with the way in which a man uses his time and spends his money as the way in which he says his prayers.

We all know that there is a plain difference between a place of worship and an industrial plant, though the balance of life requires our attendance at both. But to suppose that what goes on in the one—but not the other—is of interest to God, is to deprive man of his only hope of a salvation which can redeem the whole of his life.

The shoe repairer who helps to keep people's feet dry, the shopkeeper who serves wholesome food over his counter, the garage mechanic whose repair job is utterly dependable—and all others like them—can present their bodies, that is to say, what they do, to God as their acceptable service.

In the second place, we are to present to God not only what the body does but what the body is. We would miss an important part of the meaning of this command if we limited it to our physical and mental activities.

For what is the body intended to be? "The temple of the Holy Spirit" is the Christian answer. The body is more than a structure of flesh and bones. In this sense the body means the whole personality. "Your very selves," translates the New English Bible. This self or personality, presented to God, can be the temple or home of His Spirit, thus becoming yet another human instrument which God can use to accomplish His will on earth.

This is what holy living means—the dedication of as much as I possess to as much as I know of the will of God for me. And far from this total response cramping any man's style, it ennobles him who makes it and glorifies the God whose service is always perfect freedom.

Frederick Coutts, *Essentials of Christian Experience*

The God of Our Generations

Joshua 24:15

God loves to work across the generations. If you are the first in your family to come to Christ, God can start something brand new with you that is going to go far beyond you and touch generations yet to come.

Family life has never been easy. Most, if not all, Bible families were more or less dysfunctional, from Cain and Abel to Jacob and Esau to Joseph and his brothers to David and Bathsheba. Even Jesus' family did not believe in Him and apparently tried to persuade Him to give up on His mission. But God did not give up on the idea of family and neither must we.

One of the problems in our culture today is that families so seldom eat together. This can be one of the practical steps to take toward strengthening family life—determining that at least once a day, we are going to make the sacrifices necessary to touch base with one another—to sit down, pray and eat together as a family. More important even than talking about prayer is praying your way through life's crises with your family.

Our best devotional times were when we had an issue to deal with as a family. We'd look to the Word of God for guidance and we'd pull together in prayer to work our way through it. Sometimes it was after a sharp difference of opinion, and sometimes tears were shed on the way to a solution.

Our own personal prayer life is so important as we model our faith to our families. Our daughter Jennie sent my wife a beautiful Mother's Day note one year. She shared a number of memories of her mom and concluded with this: "My fond memory is of you praying and reading your Bible each morning, yet holding out your arms to me if I woke too soon and interrupted your time. I do the same with Beth (her daughter), because the greatest lesson you taught me is that loving your children unconditionally is prayer itself."

Devotional times with our families are invaluable because they give a pattern of spiritual discipline to our children that will strengthen them in working out that discipline in their own lives and passing it on to their children.

Keep believing for your children's salvation. God is faithful to His promise—for you and your household.

Paul A. Rader, *The War Cry*

Under Orders

1 Peter 1:15

Someone said that impression minus expression equals depression. The study of facts about holiness will do more harm than good unless we follow up with the right acts. We Christians are under orders: "But just as He who called you is holy, so be holy in all you do" (1 Peter 1:15).

You are a Christian; the call to holiness is always to believers, never to unbelievers. You are indwelt by the Holy Spirit and able to overcome temptation in His strength. In the popular phrase, you have a lot going for you. The pagan cannot help falling and failing and sinning, but there is no need for you to sustain defeat. Is this not what Paul implied by a sentence like this: "Our lower nature has no claim upon us: we are not obliged to live on that level" (Rom. 8:12 NEB).

Paul, after three chapters of Ephesians describing our wealth, makes a plea for a holy walk (Eph. 4:1). To the Corinthians he wrote about God indwelling His people, and then followed with the exhortation, "Since we have these promises, dear friends, let us purify ourselves from everything that contaminates body and spirit, perfecting holiness out of reverence for God" (2 Cor. 7:1).

When you set your face toward the sweeping transformation you need, you are ready to renounce whatever is wrong. Something of the old life must die (Rom. 8:13, Col. 3:5). This will probably be costly, and has been compared to a crucifixion (Gal. 5:24). In practice it means saying an unqualified and determined "No" to every action unworthy of a Christian. It means to reject all that stands condemned by the standard which Jesus sets for His people, that is the standard of Christlikeness. It means to make no provision in imagination or intention for anything less than holiness.

Accompanying the turning from all that is wrong will be an equally determined turning toward all that is right. Paul tells us what to "put off" and then what to "put on" (Eph. 4:22,24). Everything in our life must be either renounced or dedicated.

Christ is the pattern for His people. The little word "as" is potent: We are to "walk, just as He walked" (1 John 2:6 NKJV); to receive one another "as Christ received us" (Rom. 15:7); to "walk in the light as He is in the light" (1 John 1:7); to love one another "as I have loved you" (John 13:34). The same mighty monosyllable is on His lips in that solemn prayer of consecration: "As You sent Me into the world, I have sent them into the world" (John 17:18 NIV).

Edward Read, *Studies in Sanctification*

Dark Days

Romans 5:3–5

Jesus Christ said, "In the world you will have tribulation," (John 16:33 KJV) while Paul assures us that "All who will live godly in Christ Jesus will suffer persecution" (2 Tim. 3:12 KJV)

When you are a sufferer, when your burden of care and trouble increases, think upon the following. God has promised to support you in your trials while you walk in the light; that is, while you do His blessed will. Some of the most beautiful and precious passages to be found in the Bible describe the consolation He promises to His soldiers while they are battling with the difficulties, persecutions and sufferings of life.

He promises you the comfort of His presence. "When you pass through the waters, I will be with you, and through the rivers, they shall not overflow you; when you walk through the fire, you shall not be burned, neither shall the flame kindle upon you" (Isa. 43:2 KJV).

He promises you victory. "God is faithful, who will not suffer you to be tempted above that you are able; but will with the temptation also make a way to escape, that you may be able to bear it" (1 Cor. 10:13 KJV).

Tribulations are intended for your profit. "All things work together for good to them that love God" (Rom. 8:28 KJV). Rightly accepted, they will promote your holiness and usefulness, and help you to understand the struggle for the welfare of those around you. What is more, they strengthen faith and help the formation of that character which God desires His children to possess.

Dark days strengthen the soul. Perpetual and uninterrupted sunshine, soft and genial weather, make weak men and women. Frost and gloom and darkness make hard and vigorous people.

Dark days are instructive. There is no place like the school of adversity for teaching wisdom.

Dark days drive the soul to God. Nothing succeeds in throwing a man back upon his Maker like affliction.

Dark days increase the brightness of the bright days that are to come. What a magnificent background the sorrows of earth will form to the joys of heaven! How the tears and pains and crosses of this life will set off and render more glorious the songs and crowns and glories of the skies!

William Booth, The Warrior's Daily Portion, No. 2

Can You Say "I Know"

2 Timothy 1:12

"And the earth was without form, and void; and darkness was upon the face of the deep. And the Spirit of God moved upon the face of the waters" (Gen. 1:2 KJV). It is always the work of the Spirit of God to bring order out of chaos, light out of darkness, definiteness out of indefiniteness, certainty out of uncertainty, a clear experience out of a mixed state of the affections and will.

My comrade, does your spiritual experience somewhat resemble the primal earth? Is it shapeless when compared with the rounded, clean-cut life of some Christians you know, void of the triumphant experience of salvation which they possess, and with gloom and deep shadows where there should be an unbroken flood of light? The Holy Spirit is continually brooding over you, moving over the God-created depths of your heart, to change this unhappy state of things and to bring your experience to that condition of which even the Father Himself shall say that it is "good."

A man ought to be as sure of his salvation from sin as of his existence. There is no foundation in the Bible for a "hope-so" religion. "These things have I written unto you that believe on the name of the Son of God," wrote John, addressing Christians, "that you may know [not guess, or think, or hope, but know] that you have eternal life" (1 John 5:13).

Read the things that John says "we know" in his very positive epistles. "We know that we are of God" (1 John 5:19); "We know that the Son of God is come" (1 John 5:20); "We know that we dwell in him, and He in us" (1 John 4:13); "We know that we have passed from death unto life" (1 John 3:4); "We know that we have the petitions that we desire of Him" (1 John 5:15); "We know that we are of the truth" (1 John 3:19).

Have you this certain knowledge? Have you let God finish His fair creation of purity and peace in your heart? The Spirit of God is brooding over you always, to help you, to teach you, to carry you ever forward, to finish the work of your glorious salvation.

The Bible hope is a sure one. Make sure of yours by believing God till you can exchange its faint expression for that triumphant cry of Paul's, "I know whom I have believed" (2 Tim. 1:12).

Elizabeth Swift Brengle, *Half Hours with My Guide*

In the Sanctuary

Luke 12:6,7

Sanctuary is an interesting word. It is the term used for the central or primary room in a church—a place where people gather in corporate praise, worship and prayer. It is also a place where people can be alone, in a somewhat mysterious way, with their Creator. A sacred place to commune with God. A holy place.

Sometimes the lives we live are hectic, crazy. The treadmill keeps moving. Certain things on our agenda are important and demand immediate attention. But we need to stop from time to time to reflect on our lives, collect our thoughts, work through our priorities.

Many years ago, God instructed Moses to build and furnish a tabernacle for the Israelite people to worship and commune with Him. "Then have them make a sanctuary for Me, and I will dwell among them" (Exod. 25:8). God, dwelling with them. Fellowship and interaction with the Creator. Help in the time of need.

So often we feel lost, confused, totally out of it. We feel alone, as if no one else really cares. We're desperate because time is at a premium. It always is. As God gave a promise to Moses, He gives a promise to us: that He will be with us.

There's nothing spiritually wrong with escaping to a coffee place, either alone or with friends. In fact, a nice café may be a kind of sanctuary in the middle of a hectic day. A place to unwind, if only for a few brief moments. And it is important to enter God's house and to regularly worship in the sanctuary of a church. But above all, we need to enter into the sanctuary of God's presence. David poetically cried out: "My soul thirsts for You, my body longs for You" (Ps. 63:1). Why? What did he really desire in his heart? Only to see "[God] in the sanctuary and [behold His] power and ... glory" (Ps. 63:2).

David knew he could find ultimate rest and satisfaction in God's presence. Are we thirsty for meaning in life? Do we long to retreat from our fast-paced world and run into the presence of God?

David had experienced God's sanctuary in the past. Many today experience His presence through a peace of mind and heart that only He can bring. It simply takes initiative and a willingness of heart and spirit before Almighty God. Only then will we be able to cope realistically with life. Only then will we experience the fullness of His presence—in the holy sanctuary of the Lord.

Beverly Ivany, *The War Cry*

From Death to Life

1 John 3:14

Death is an inescapable fact. Euripides the poet called death "the debt we all must pay." George Bernard Shaw wryly wrote, "The statistics on death are quite impressive. One out of one people die." Death is the most democratic of all experiences.

No matter how we diet, how much we exercise, how many vitamins or health foods we eat, how low our cholesterol, some day, some way, we will die. The invincible reaper knocks ultimately at every door.

At some point each of us has felt the trauma of death. And in the poignant words of Tennyson, we have "a longing for the touch of a vanished hand, and the sound of a voice that is stilled."

God deals seriously with the topic of death. We find the word "die" or its equivalent more than 1,300 times in the Bible. It tells us that sin brought death into the world, but that is not its last word on the subject.

At Easter we celebrate our Lord's victory over death. His triumph over the grave vaporized all doubts among the believers in His day. The seismic significance of what took place on Easter is the epicenter of our faith. It is not a belief that grew up within the Church; it is the belief around which the Church itself grew up, and the "given" upon which its faith was based.

The resurrection forever negates the contrary arguments on eternal life—Feuerbach's "wishful projection," Marx's "consolation of the oppressed," Nietzsche's denial of the eternal and Freud's illusion theory.

In the radiant light of the resurrection, death becomes not a destruction but a metamorphosis, not a diminishing but a finishing. It is not a postscript or an appendix to our book of life, but rather reveals life on earth as merely the preface, with life in heaven as the full text—a text without end.

"We know that we have passed from death to life" (1 John 3:14). These words reverse the usual order of things. Conventional thinking says that we pass from life unto death. But John, who had heard the immortal words and witnessed the mighty life of the One who is the resurrection and the life, declares that the believer goes "from death to life."

The resurrection of Christ transformed the crucifixion into a coronation. And the truth that we affirm is that we have passed from death to life!

Henry Gariepy, *The War Cry*

A Saving Faith

Romans 10:9

I am going to speak of faith in the evangelical or saving sense—not faith as used sometimes to denote the whole of Christianity, or to represent a system of truth, but faith when it is used to set forth that act of the soul which translates it out of the kingdom of Satan into the kingdom of God—that living, powerful, transforming principle in the soul of the believer which enables him to live in obedience to God—the faith that saves.

What is this faith? It is not a mere mental perception or conviction of the truth. Saving faith is not intellectual perception of the truth. There are hundreds of drunkards who believe thoroughly in sobriety. I have known of many who have believed that abstinence was the finest thing in the world; nevertheless, you found them drunk every Saturday night just the same. Their faith in sobriety had no practical effect on their lives! This is an illustration of a mere intellectual perception and approval of a truth without any corresponding effect upon the heart.

Saving faith is not mere feeling on the subject of religion. But if it is neither intellectual perception nor conviction of the truth, nor mere feeling about the truth, what is it?

I like to let one Scripture explain another, so I want to remark that the word translated "faith," or "belief," as used in the saving sense, is, in several other places in the New Testament, translated "commit," or "committal," the giving of one's self to another.

What is faith? It is giving myself up to God, "risking" myself, risking my all, for this life and for the next, on the truthfulness and the goodness of God, and daring to live and act contrary to everybody around me, as if all that God has said were true!

Faith is, all through the Scriptures, represented as a voluntary thing. It is a thing you can do or leave undone. Faith must be a voluntary committal of your heart to Him. God wants your heart. Then He will enlighten your intellect. Faith is a thing of the heart, hence the philosophy of the Scripture, which says, "For with the heart man believes unto righteousness" (Rom. 10:10 KJV).

Dare you not pledge yourself to His throne and link yourself on to His almightiness? He waits for your choice. He knocks at the door of your heart. He woos your love.

Catherine Booth, *Life and Death*

The Gift of God

Psalm 127:3

Eighteen years ago, our son John was killed in an automobile accident. John, to his friends, was a real day-brightener; and to his family "fair as a star when only one is shining in the sky." Sixteen-year-old John, who enjoyed beating his old man at every game and in every race, beat his father to the grave.

Our own broken hearts are mending, largely thanks to many dear friends and co-workers. If in that year we relearned one lesson, it is that love not only begets love, it transmits strength.

We miss John very much. We wonder how he would look and what he would be doing these days if he were still alive. Indeed, John lives. Of that we are assured; he is with our Lord, and we will be there some day also.

When a person dies, there are many things that can be said, but the one thing that should never be said is, "It is the will of God." Our consolation lies in knowing that it was not the will of God that John should have died; God's heart was the first of all hearts to break.

We cannot confess that our lives have always been bright and sunny. Soon after the promotion to Glory of John, I could not pray as I used to do daily. I was angry that John's promising future had been taken away. I could not accept what had happened to him. This was the darkest time of our lives.

We were able to turn the corner by thanking God for John who was with us for those sixteen precious years, rather than theorizing on his unlived life. We started to pray together and to read God's Word together again. We later learned that comrades in Korea spent special times in prayer for us. Certainly the gift of the Spirit was there. We learned that there were countless friends around the world praying for us in those days. No wonder the Lord had been with us in the midst of the valley of the shadow of death, in those darkest days of our lives. We owe so very much to our Lord and to the power of prayer. We thank God for His deliverance of us, for through this experience we were able to prove yet once again, His love, His compassion, His goodness and His faithfulness.

Peter & Grace Chang, *The Gift of God*

Confession of Sin

1 John 1:9

The nature of man was not constructed to harbor evil. Sin is an intruder. Conscience, the fear of God, the capacity of memory, all want to acknowledge what is wrong, to expel it and to get rid of its sting. But men knowingly violate all this. They hide their sin. Thus they make untold misery for those about them and bring final ruin upon themselves.

The teaching of the Bible is perfectly clear on this matter. Confession is a good thing. It makes for pardon. It helps toward resisting temptation. It gives humility and vigor to the soul. And it is good, also, because it is the condition on which God grants forgiveness. "If we confess our sins," says the Apostle, "He is faithful and just and will forgive us our sins and purify us from all unrighteousness" (1 John 1:9).

Confession is important if only because, in the nature of things, unconfessed sin tends with terrible swiftness to destroy the soul. Evil grows worse by being hidden. Hidden fire—what a peril it is! Undiscovered disease—how awful! If the fire had only been uncovered, it might have been extinguished. If the sickness had been pointed out, a remedy might have been found in time. It is so with sin.

Without confession there is no salvation. The mercy of God is infinite toward men, and the sacrifice of Jesus Christ has provided a way of purity. But we must plead "guilty" before God if He is to pronounce us innocent.

And without confession there can be no peace of mind. The soul with unconfessed guilt upon it is like the troubled sea, it can never rest. The conscience with unconfessed sin upon it has a burden which nothing can take away.

Confession is an essential part of repentance; not merely the confession of sin in general, but the confession of particular sins. God will be no party to the covering-up business. Without confession there is no road to heaven. Without confession, no hope in Christ.

The solemn message of the ancient teacher is still sounding out its great warning: "He who conceals his sins does not prosper, but whoever confesses and renounces them finds mercy" (Prov. 28:13).

Bramwell Booth, *Life and Religion*

Transcendent Service

Matthew 19:19

During the Second World War a merchant ship on its way to Russia was torpedoed. Sixteen men were in a lifeboat when it capsized. Somehow they turned the boat right side up again but it soon became waterlogged. As they started frantically to scoop out the water with their hands, the captain, searching desperately for something better, suddenly remembered his briefcase stuffed with money for paying the crew. At once he emptied it and used it as a bucket.

When men are near to eternity their sense of values changes. Some things in life transcend all monetary value. Those who live for the material lose the spiritual. Of the shipwrecked man who had tied about his waist his bags of gold and went straight to the bottom, Ruskin asked, "As he was sinking had he the gold or had the gold him?"

The best work of the world, the noblest sacrifices, the greatest risks, are not done for money. What made Dr. Adrian Stokes, the English bacteriologist, go to Africa to study yellow fever, to catch it himself and to his last breath set down his symptoms, having his blood analyzed to supply data for future research? What could pay for that?

In the realm of clear moral vision, getting on, making money or winning fame profanes the noblest instincts. Kipling touched the ideal when, in speaking of celestial service, he said, "No one would work for money and no one would work for fame, but each for the joy of working!" It is the highest achievement of the human spirit.

To work only for wages destroys those finer qualities of character. Real life consists in developing our personalities and gifts by doing useful work for the joy of it and not for rewards. Materialism as a social force has its grip upon our civilization, and the only power that can break it is love expressed in transcendent service.

"Love your neighbor as yourself" (Matt. 19:19). These wise words of Jesus contain the motive force for genuine service to God and humanity. This kind of love through Christ is alone able to regenerate and unite society and is the answer to its international, national and domestic problems. The real test of our nearness to God is the way we feel and act toward one another.

George B. Smith, *Meditations for the Ordinary Man*

The Beatitudes

Matthew 5:1–12

The Sermon on the Mount is perhaps the best known part of the teaching of Jesus. It is also the least understood and certainly the least obeyed. Here we find Jesus giving instructions to the disciples. Many consider it the "Ordination Address" to the Twelve.

"His disciples came to Him, and He began to teach them" (Matt. 5:1–2). The Sermon on the Mount is a description of what Jesus wanted His followers to be and do. It describes an ideal that can never be reached by human strength alone.

Incorporated into the Sermon, we have what are commonly called "The Beatitudes." If you ask the general public to name the ingredients that make for happiness, you will likely hear such things as money, fame, success or popularity. J. B. Phillips paraphrased the Beatitudes as the world would render them:

Happy are the pushers, for they get on in the world.
Happy are the hard–boiled, for they never let life hurt them.
Happy are the blasé, for they never worry over their sins.
Happy are the slave–drivers, for they get results.
Happy are the knowledgeable of the world, for they know their way around.
Happy are the troublemakers, for they make people take notice of them.

How different was the response of Jesus. In the Beatitudes the word "blessed" is employed nine times. It is a translation of *makarios,* which refers to the bliss that belongs to the gods. It is thus an experience independent of outward circumstances. It is a joy which has its secret in itself.

The Beatitudes speak of a blessedness that exists in spite of events around us. The blessedness is completely untouchable and unassailable. In the Greek, there is no verb in the Beatitudes, thus they are not so much statements as exclamations. They are not promises of future happiness but speak of present bliss. In essence they are saying, "O the bliss of being a Christian."

In the Beatitudes we have a description of what human life and human community look like when they come under the gracious rule of God. It has been said that "rejoice" is the standing order of the Christian.

Bramwell H. Tillsley, *The War Cry*

Freedom From Fear?

Psalm 27:1

Fear is in the saddle. Individuals and nations—none have escaped its onslaughts or its subtle influence. The threat of nuclear war hangs over our heads. Economic pressures, terrorism and violence have led one analyst to indicate that many people today are "living scared."

The greatest saints have had their halos tarnished as they experienced negative fears. Abraham fled to Egypt when he faced famine. Moses tried to cop-out from God's call by claiming inability to communicate. David, the killer of Goliath, knew something of fear. Elijah towered among the prophets, yet when his life was threatened by Jezebel, he fled. Repeatedly we read of the strongly expressed fear of the disciples, in spite of having walked and talked with Jesus and having witnessed His many miracles.

Someone has said that fear prepares you for three Fs—flight, fight, or freeze. The negative type of fear disrupts the normal process of living to the extent that it can eventually destroy the individual.

It is never the intention or plan of God for His born-again children to move about with a fearful heart. From Genesis to Revelation God's message has been "Fear not!" From Paul comes the statement: "For God has not given us the spirit of fear; but of power, and of love, and of a sound mind" (2 Tim. 1:7).

In Psalm 27, the palmist is bold to testify of his trust in the Lord and his power to deliver: "The Lord is my light and my salvation—whom shall I fear? The Lord is the stronghold of my life—of whom shall I be afraid?" (v. 1). What a difference when fear assails if we have a strong sense of security, an assurance that we don't stand alone; that we have resources which are superior to our own and, more important, to our antagonist the devil. God is in control.

The force of David's confidence of freedom from fear is underscored by his use of the name Lord, the name that is written in many translations with all capital letters. This name of God, Jehovah, was so awesome among the children of Israel that for centuries they were forbidden to use it. David, in Psalm 27, uses this name 13 times. David knew wherein his strength and power and deliverance, even from fear, lay.

With David, we can confidently ask the rhetorical question, "Whom shall I fear? Of whom shall I be afraid?" The implied answer comes thundering back, "No one! Absolutely no one! He is in control."

Edward Deratany, *The War Cry*

I Come to Thee with Quiet Mind

Psalm 46:10

O Love, revealed on earth in Christ,
In blindness once I sacrificed
Thy gifts for dross; I could not see,
But Jesus brings me sight of Thee.

I come to Thee with quiet mind,
Thyself to know, Thy will to find;
In Jesus' steps my steps must be,
I follow Him to follow Thee.

O Love, invisible before,
I see Thee now, desire Thee more;
When Jesus speaks Thy word is clear;
I search His face and find Thee near.

O Love, forever claim my eyes!
Thy beauty be my chosen prize;
I cast my load on timeless grace
That my free soul may run the race.

Catherine Baird, *The Salvation Army Songbook*

The Lord's Loving Kindness

Psalm 103:17

It was late autumn 1969, as I climbed up to the very top of a mountain in the New Territory in Hong Kong. Below, the beautiful landscape was heavily surrounded with barbed wire. Signs everywhere warned that trespassers would meet serious consequences. This was the Berlin Wall of the Far East. The two worlds on each side of these wires had been fearfully separated for twenty years.

Before my eyes was an endless ocean of rice paddies. The grain was turning golden–brown, soon to be ready for harvest. On the muddy paths, two village boys were riding a water buffalo. Playing some game, their innocent laughter was a contrast to the armed guard in a hut, nervously watching through his binoculars to make sure no one crossed the border.

These moments flooded me with emotions. Just about 200 miles away lay the place of my birth. Twenty years ago I had voluntarily put myself in exile in pursuit of freedom. I left half my family behind at home. They, along with another 800 million people, had suffered in a cultural revolution, a manmade calamity, the most destructive in China's 5,000–year history.

For the first time I understood the sentiment of the Jews, who once by the riverside of Babylon lamented with the psalmist, "we sat and wept when we remembered Zion" (Psalm 137:1).

My family was denied the privilege of leaving the country because of their Christian faith. In the meantime, thousands risked their lives against gunfire as they fled into Hong Kong.

Chinese Christians often pay a higher sacrifice to keep the faith. They are accused by the Imperialists of abandoning traditions, and most seriously, of not rendering respect to the deceased ancestors. Our family was the first to become Christians in our village, and we were publicly ridiculed by our own kinsmen. So my parents decided to move to a small town northward.

A few years later, I visited that village and sadly found that most of the villagers had died of epidemics and starvation. The place was desolate. I stood in horror and was reminded of the precious promise of God we now claimed for His providential care of our family: "But the lovingkindness of the Lord is from everlasting to everlasting on those who fear Him, and His righteousness to children's children" (Psalm 103:17 NAS).

Check Yee, For My Kinsmen's Sake

The Good Fight

1 Timothy 1:18

On May 9, 1912, 7,000 Salvationists packed London's Royal Albert Hall to hear the Founder, William Booth. "And now, comrades and friends, I must say goodbye. I am going into dry-dock for repairs, but the Army will not be allowed to suffer, either financially or spiritually, or in any other way by my absence.

"And in the long future I think it will be seen—I shall not be here to see, but you will—that the Army will answer every doubt and banish every fear and strangle every slander, and by its marvelous success show to the world that it is the work of God and that the General has been His servant.

> While women weep, as they do now, I'll fight!
> While little children go hungry, as they do now, I'll fight!
> While men go to prison, in and out, in and out,
>> as they do now, I'll fight!
> While there is a drunkard left,
> While there is a poor lost girl upon the streets,
> While there remains one dark soul without the light of God,
> I'll fight—I'll fight to the very end!"

It was his last speech, perhaps his greatest. Three months later, on August 20, 1912, he died at the age of 83. Staff officers arriving at International Headquarters the following morning saw a simple message in the window: "The General Has Laid Down His Sword."

At a three-day lying-in-state, 150,000 persons filed past the old warrior's casket, and on the day of his funeral city offices of London were dark and shuttered. Around his grave lay wreaths from the king and queen and from titled heads-of-state throughout the world.

Unknown to most, far to the rear of the hall, sat Britain's Queen Mary. Beside her on the aisle was a shabby, but neatly dressed woman, who had confessed her secret to the queen. Once a prostitute, The Salvation Army had saved her. She had come early to claim an aisle seat, guessing that the casket would pass within feet of her. As it did, she had unobtrusively placed three carnations on the lid, and all through the service they were the only flowers on the casket. Queen Mary was deeply moved when the woman turned to her and said simply, in words which could stand as William Booth's epitaph: "He cared for the likes of us."

George Scott Railton, *General Booth*

The Decisive Experience

Romans 8:5

It is no accident that one story in the Acts of the Apostles is told three times over—that of the conversion of Saul. Yet though the story of the Apostle's conversion is repeated but three times in the New Testament, it could have been that he told it many times more on his thousands of miles of missionary journeyings—told it until his traveling companions almost knew it by heart.

Now this matter of personal testimony has its own difficulties for we Salvationists of the second and third generation. We may never have plunged catastrophically into sin. Nor have we ever wasted our substance in riotous living in a far country. We might even feel it to be an exaggeration to describe ourselves as brands plucked from the burning. Most of the commandments have we kept from our youth up. Must our testimony then be less effective than that of our fathers? In other words, must sin abound before an experience of grace can much more abound? As the apostle himself said in another connection: God forbid!

The experience called conversion can express itself in different ways for different people. No two human encounters with the grace of God are ever exactly the same. To some, conversion is a drastic change. But to others among us, we have always believed in such general truths that God is love, that in His mercy sin can be forgiven, and that by His grace temptation can be overcome. But there comes a moment when these truths to which we have long given passive assent suddenly become compellingly alive. They demand that we live by them.

Outwardly there may be little change in the externals of our living. But inwardly that moment of illumination and dedication is never to be forgotten. We do not need to have been very bad in order, by God's grace, to be made good—though at the crisis point we may doubtless feel bad enough. But while Paul called himself "the chief of sinners" gross habits had never mastered him. Like the rich young ruler he also had kept the commandments. And this is where many of us come in.

The new birth may well be that moment when, in an act of penitent self-surrender to Christ, the Lord becomes a living reality and His daily presence our all-sufficiency.

Frederick Coutts, *Essentials of Christian Experience*

God's Word To A Fallen World

John 1:14

The 1999 International Spiritual Life Commission of The Salvation Army stated: "We call Salvationists worldwide to a renewed and relevant proclamation of and close attention to the Word of God, and to a quick and steady obedience to the radical demands of the Word upon Salvationists personally, and upon our movement corporately." We need to affirm that the Word of God must be central in the life of every believer.

What is this book about? It is not a record of people desperately clinging to God by their fingertips. The Bible is, rather, the story of God's search for us. And as Christians we affirm that the heart of that search–story is the story of the life, death and resurrection of Jesus Christ.

Jesus Christ is the center of the Bible. The lasting value of the written Word is that it points to the enfleshed Word. The final Word is Jesus Christ. The true Word is Jesus Christ, He of whom the text itself bears witness: "The Word became flesh and made His dwelling among us. We have seen His glory, the glory of the one and only, who came from the Father, full of grace and truth" (John 1:14).

What impact is the Bible meant to have on us as Christians? The sure mark of the Christian is not spirituality—there are many people who appear outwardly spiritual, but who are not the children of God by grace. The clear sign that we are Christians is that we obey the Word of God.

Dietrich Bonhoeffer said: "Only he who believes obeys, and only he who obeys believes." God wants His book translated into the lives of His people.

But how do we ensure that translation will happen? Only by placing the Bible at the center of our common life through study, worship and preaching. Without this we languish and cannot be the people of God we are intended to be.

The Bible is indeed God's Word to a fallen world. It is His Word because of His work in the person of His Son Jesus Christ. The centrality of this Word made flesh comes alive as the Word is faithfully proclaimed, accepted by faith by sinner and saint alike, and acted upon in obedience to the Christ.

It is in this Word that we rejoice.

Roger J. Green, *The War Cry*

Judge Not!

Matthew 7:1–5

How often we are blind to our own faults while we are keenly aware of the faults of others. The "beam" in our own eye blinds us to our own failings. The critical people of Christ's day, so full of faults themselves, called Jesus "a gluttonous man and a wine bibber" (Matt. 11:19 KJV). What pain is caused by poisonous whispering. It is the besetting sin of many religious people and one of the cruelest sins in the world.

Gossip can be dynamite. Gossip is the uttered judgment upon another and, when unkind, is malignant, growing slanderous tissues which destroy members of "the body of Christ."

No human being can presume to judge another, because when we do we put ourselves in God's place. To judge another is to assume superiority. We all need to beware of the superior person who wants to tell us something about ourselves "for our own good." Robert Louis Stevenson reminds us: "There is so much good in the worst of us, And so much bad in the best of us; That it ill becomes any of us, To talk about the rest of us!"

Abraham Lincoln gave a fine word on this idea: "With malice toward none, with charity for all, with firmness in the right as God gives us to see the right, let us strive on to finish the work we are in, to bind up the nation's wounds, to care for the widow and the orphan, to do all that may achieve and cherish a just and lasting peace for ourselves and all mankind."

The world sees only the time a man falls; it takes little notice of the hundred times he may have conquered before he fell. Man who "looks on the outward appearance" cannot see the secret battle going on, the hidden struggle. We cannot know the causes of the faults we condemn. Many have secret sorrows that press upon them.

A man traveling in a railway car with another man nursing a crying baby said irascibly, "I wish to God you would take the whimpering child to its mother." The man burst into tears and said, "I wish to God I could, sir, but she's lying in a coffin in the luggage van."

The Christian's duty is to help men and women to rise out of their faults. Our attitude is like a boomerang; what we are to others rebounds again to ourselves. Said the quaint old Samuel Johnson, "Even the great God Himself does not presume to judge a man until he is dead."

George B. Smith, *Meditations for the Ordinary Man*

Jesus is Lord

Romans 10:9-10

W hat do you suppose is the most important word in the New Testament? Love? Forgiveness? Grace? Perhaps faith? Or hope? Author Calvin Miller suggests that the most important word in the New Testament is "Lord." Why? Because, "If you confess with your mouth 'Jesus is Lord,' and believe in your heart that God has raised Him from the dead, you will be saved" (Rom. 10:9–10).

Jesus is up front with the claim He makes on our lives and loyalties. This is what salvation is about—to be rescued from the dominion of darkness and brought into the kingdom of the Son, "in whom we have redemption through His blood, the forgiveness of sins" (Eph. 1:7 KJV).

If there is no king, there is no kingdom. If Jesus is not Lord, who is? Either Jesus is Lord of my life, or I come under the sway of something far smaller and more sinister. The devil has no brief for human autonomy. He doesn't allow us any freedom.

Jesus is Lord! Easy enough for us to say it. When the apostles said it, Caesar was Lord and brooked no rivals. Those who chose Christ anyway were in risk of their lives, and that is still true in many places around the world.

Mayor Kallelas, a committed Salvationist of Brazzaville in the Congo, was imprisoned nine times under the communist regime. Sometimes he was hung up by his feet. Time and time again he awoke in an emergency room of a hospital, all because of his commitment to Jesus Christ, his Christian testimony and his unwillingness to accept the dogma of an atheistic, communist government.

It's easy enough for us to say, "Jesus is Lord." But there may be a price to be paid. We must believe it in our hearts and enter into a loving, trusting relationship with God through faith in the Lord Jesus Christ. God wants us to experience His resurrection life and power. It's explosive. It's liberating. It's morally energizing. And enabling.

John MacArthur says the signature of saving faith is surrender to the Lordship of Jesus Christ. May we bear that signature.

Paul A. Rader, *The War Cry*

The Grace of Dependency

Luke 23:43

꒳

A reminder from St. Augustine guarantees to warm the heart yet chill the blood: "Two criminals were crucified with Christ: one was saved—do not despair; one was not—do not presume."

About these two, we know absolutely nothing, a fact that hasn't prevented pious speculation from building whole biographies about the one whose eleventh-hour discovery of Christ allows us to say of him, in the words of Shakespeare, "Nothing in his life became him like the leaving it."

But I'm not one to slight the other criminal. Perhaps he was an associate of Barabbas, the revolutionary hero released that same morning at the behest of the mob. Perhaps he was a freedom fighter, determined to see Israel's independence or to see Rome leveled by his attempt to gain it. In any case, in his harshest hour, he shows spirit. That's what his taunting of Jesus reflects—a defiant spirit similar to what Dylan Thomas wanted his father to show even as his life expired:

> Do not go gently into that good night,
> Rage, rage against the dying of the light.

He raged all right, this thief; no whiner, he was a fighter to the end. Frederick Buechner writes: "To grit your teeth and to clench your fists in order to survive the world at its harshest and worst is, by that very act, to be unable to let something be done for you and in you that is more wonderful still." The defiant thief could not be saved because a clenched fist cannot accept a helping hand.

The other criminal is also on a cross of isolation. He who is guilty hears the One, who of all people is the victim of injustice, pray for the forgiveness of His executioners. Such love proves too much. His own defiant heart breaks. He cries out, "Jesus, remember me" (Luke 23:42). And in his last hour, on a cross, Christ performs His last miracle.

In portraying the story of Creation on the ceiling of the Sistine Chapel, Michelangelo pictures the bond of love as it was first established. Surrounded by cherubim and seraphim, God simply reaches down His arm from heaven to touch Adam's extended hand. But the bond, once rent, is not easily restored. Sin has its price, and so has forgiveness.

Restoration takes place on two crosses when One in agony stretches out His hand and says, "Today, you will be with Me in paradise" (Luke 23:43). That is what atonement (at-one-ment) is all about.

Peter & Grace Chang, *The Gift of God*

Wisdom in Foolishness

1 Corinthians 1:21

Spiritual truth is often paradoxical. A paradox is a statement that on the surface appears contradictory, but whose truth emerges upon further examination. The Bible states that the key to being rich is being poor; the key to being strong is being weak; the key to being wise is being foolish. By exploring the paradox, we gain an appreciation for the breadth and depth of spiritual truth.

Obviously, complete understanding of the infinite will always remain outside the finite limits of human understanding. Enter the paradox: an attempt to phrase the unspeakable, to explain the unsearchable dimensions of God's truth, at least in part. Let us peer through the darkened glass to understand those things revealed to the probing mind of the believer.

"For since the wisdom of the world through its wisdom did not know Him, God was pleased through the foolishness of what was preached to save those who believe" (1 Cor. 1:21). What is this foolishness? How can something be absurd, yet true? What foolishness has God chosen to use to save those who believe?

It's right there in verse 23: "We preach Christ crucified!" To the Jew of Paul's day, a crucified Messiah was a stumbling block; to the Greek philosopher of Paul's day, a God who "so loved the world that He gave His one and only Son" (John 3:16) was foolishness.

But the Jews and Greeks of the first century do not stand alone in regarding the Christian gospel as incredible. In an age characterized by a crisis of faith, the simplicity of the Christian message is often cast aside as irrelevant to the issues of our day.

But is it really any wonder? The disciples themselves found it foolishness. Jesus told them what was going to happen to Him and they found it incredible. It seemed foolish, but it was the power of salvation. Once they had experienced it, it ceased to be foolishness. "The message of the cross is foolishness to those who are perishing, but to us who are being saved it is the power of God!" (1 Cor. 1:18). The foolishness of God is wiser than man's wisdom.

The key to being wise is being foolish. I'm foolish enough to believe that Christ crucified means my salvation. 'Tis a wise fool who believes!

Donald Hostetler, *The War Cry*

Things Possess Me

Matthew 6:19–21

Lord, I've made a disappointing discovery.
    Things possess me;
I've always tried to believe that I was the ascetic type;
    not the real ascetic, of course,
    facts were against that,
    but with tendencies in that direction.
Now I find that what is mine is very important to me,
    even if it is not of any great worth.

I don't want to be bound by things, Lord;
    to use, yes;
    to enjoy, yes;
    to lend, sometimes;
    but to hoard,
    simply to gloat over their possession, no!

Your Book tells us a few home-truths, Master.
It reminds us that even as we brought nothing into this world,
so we depart, empty-handed,
It makes one think.

There must be some secret formula to follow,
    to hold in trust,
    to use wisely,
    to treasure unpossessively
    and be ready to surrender.

I have a lot to learn, Lord;
please teach me how to hold lightly to this world's goods.

Flora Larsson, *Just A Moment, Lord*

The Trouble with Time

Ephesians 5:15–16

~

When I get to heaven, there's a thing or two I intend to ask St. Peter. Heading that list will be the question of time. I want to know what happened to it. When I was a child, the days between Thanksgiving and Christmas lasted longer than eternity. Today, I'm panicky if my Christmas shopping is not complete by October.

Time-saving devices now surround me. I can prepare a meal in minutes with my microwave oven. Dirty dishes get popped into the dishwasher. My giant-size washer and dryer make laundry a breeze. But a Murphy-like law of inversion is at work: the more time-savers I own, the less time I have.

Reluctantly, I am forced to admit that age might have something to do with the problem. Time no longer stretches endlessly in front of me as it did the summer I was nine. I've come to terms with my own mortality.

It's clear now that if I live to be a hundred, I will not finish everything on my "to do" list. I can no longer put off determining what matters most. Some things must be tossed out and the time has arrived to give up some of the dreams of earlier days.

What priorities remain? First, I plan to revel in the beauty God has lavished on us. As for music, I embrace everything from Salvation Army marches to hymns and those I sing along with in my car. My husband has expanded my musical appreciation to include the symphony orchestra, opera, even piano duet arrangements of Mozart. I hope to explore the riches of music until I join the alto section of the heavenly choir.

Then there's writing. I've gotten a late start, so I may have to seek immortalization somewhere else. No matter. Writing about people and subjects close to my heart brings me intense satisfaction.

Above all, relationships matter most—relationships with family, friends, colleagues, neighbors. I want to seize this day to tell people I love them.

I won't be satisfied relating to God in a superficial way, either. As far back as I can remember, His loving presence has been as real as my mother's goodnight kiss. At age 17, I made a personal commitment to follow Him. Now, just as I relish sitting down with a friend over tea, I look forward to frequent visits with Him. After all, we're going to be together for a long, long time!

Dorothy Post, *The War Cry*

The Test of Holiness

1 Thessalonians 4:7

Next to the word salvation the word most often on the lips of Salvationists is the word holiness. Even before there was a Salvation Army, the two people destined, under God, to be its founders were concerned with this second word. They knew it to be a biblical word and longed to make the experience which it represented their very own. Their mutual concern intensified rather than abated after their marriage.

Catherine wrote to her mother: "I spoke a fortnight since at Bethesda on holiness, and a precious time we had. William has preached on it twice and there is a glorious quickening among the people." Even within the limited context of Salvation Army life the word has had a lively past. What is of more concern: has it a future? For religious words and phrases can wither and die.

Are we to rate holiness as a word which aroused considerable interest in the past but lacks any future value? What is the difference, anyway, between a living word and a word that is dead? My own short answer would be that a word lives while it continues to answer a felt human need. The marks of a word that is alive is that it describes a present experience that is meaningful, purposeful and possible. How does this admittedly ancient word, holiness, stand up to these three tests?

There is in our bones this craving for rightness. I must get this chord right; this pattern right, this homework right. As the chorus says: "I want to live right"—another way of speaking of the experience of holiness. It is a meaningful word right enough.

And a purposeful word as well? Without any doubt! To enjoy the life of holiness is not a fancy of my own; it is God's declared purpose for me. What can give sure direction for my indecision, ballast for my instability, a definite goal for present uncertainty, is the truth that I can identify with the eternal will of God— which is my sanctification.

How does this word holiness pass the final test? Does it stand for an experience which is possible? Or are we tormenting ourselves with an unattainable dream? On this let two things be said. No believer should overestimate his difficulties and none should underestimate God's power.

Frederick Coutts, *The Splendor of Holiness*

Made Into Saints

Philippians 1:1

"The Scriptures give four names to Christians," wrote Andrew Fuller long ago, "saints, for their holiness; believers, for their faith; brethren, for their love; disciples, for their knowledge."

Saints—that was Paul's favorite term. Fifty-five times in the epistles you will find the members of the Church called that. To the Roman church, which included both slaves and citizens, he wrote, "To all in Rome, who are loved by God and called to be saints" (Rom. 1:7). To Philippi, where (as we know from Acts 16) one member was a cloth merchant and another a jailer, he wrote, "To all the saints in Christ Jesus at Philippi" (Phil. 1:1). Quite apparently, these were ordinary people, yet saints!

If the apostle were here today, would he address us as saints? There is little doubt that he would, although most of us might be quite uncomfortable with the title.

Saint means "sanctified one," and as in the Old Testament certain people had the right to be called holy because of their position, in the New Testament all true Christians are rightly called holy because of their position in Christ. After Calvary and Pentecost, no longer is it only selected office holders who are holy; the adjective is enlarged to include all God's people, for we have all become priests through grace.

It needs to be carefully noted that this is only the foundation of an experience of holiness, a description of status. The chief concern of the New Testament is not merely how a man may be called a saint, but how he can be *made* a saint. Having been given the title to holiness, how can we be given the experience of it?

Saints though they were, the early Christians were not perfect. That needs to be said, lest in our tendency to idealize the past we make them into spiritual supermen and give up all hope of being like them. They had their weaknesses, and all of Paul's 13 letters contain some rebuke. "The perfecting of the saints" (Eph. 4:12 KJV) was as necessary then as now.

But those first-century believers did have something the world had not experienced before. They had Jesus, and His promise: "I will ask the Father, and He shall give you another Counselor" (John 14:16). "The breathtaking claims of the New Testament in regard to holiness," writes W.E. Sangster, "is that while man is helpless and hopeless alone, by the power of the indwelling Spirit he can reach up to the dizzy height of holiness revealed by Jesus and scale the serene summit itself."

Edward Read, *Studies in Sanctification*

The Uses of Trial

2 Corinthians 4:17

Affliction occupies a large place in the economy of salvation, for though suffering is the result of sin, God takes hold of it and transforms it into one of the richest blessings of His own people. From whatever secondary causes the afflictions of the righteous may arise, whether from the sins of their forefathers, the cruelty of their enemies, their own mistakes, or the mistakes of their friends, or the malice of Satan, it is their blessed privilege to realize that the Lord permits and overrules all, and that He has a gracious end in every sorrow which He allows to overtake them.

There is a sense in which trial reveals us to God and makes manifest to Him what is in our heart. Thus Abraham by his obedience to the painful command made his love manifest to God. In nothing is love made so manifest as in willing, cheerful suffering for the sake of its object.

Trial also reveals us to ourselves. Does your heart chafe, fret and rebel? Are you saying, "All these things are against me?" If so, this is proof that the work of grace is at a low ebb in your soul, that your faith is weak and your spiritual perceptions dim. It is high time for you to awake out of sleep and cry mightily unto God for a sanctified use of the affliction which has overtaken you. If God sends the cross, it is to brighten the crown.

Trial also reveals us to the world. As the greatest manifestation of God to the world was by suffering, so the most influential revelation of His people to the world has been by suffering. They are seen to the best advantage in the furnace. The blood of martyrs has ever been the seed of the church. The patience, meekness, firmness and happiness of God's people in circumstances of suffering, persecution and death, have paved the way for the gospel in almost all lands and all ages. Patient suffering in affliction and anguish is the most convincing proof of the Divine in man which it is possible for humanity to give.

Sitting on a dunghill, apparently forsaken of God and man, and suffering the direst physical agony which Satan could inflict, Job attained his greatest victory and made that wonderful exhibition of trust in God which has been the comfort of God's people from that day to this.

Dear reader, how are your afflictions revealing you to those around you? Are you adding your testimony to that of the cloud of witnesses who are gone before, to the sufficiency of divine grace to sustain and comfort? Is your patient endurance saying to those who are watching you, "I can do [and suffer] all things through Christ who strengthens me" (Phil. 4:13 NKJV).

Catherine Booth, *Practical Religion*

Salvationist Sacramentalism

Hebrews 3:14

The Salvation Army does not practice sacramental rituals. This statement does not automatically lead to the conclusion that Salvationists therefore cannot possibly be sacramentalists. I advocate an understanding of sacramentalism that does not hinge upon any outward form or ceremony.

In 1883 in an article in which he addressed his officers, William Booth wanted to be clear that "No sacrament can rightly be seen as a condition of salvation." He wanted the Army to be free from "the grave dissensions" that sometimes were associated with the sacraments.

Minnie Carpenter, wife of General George Carpenter, described the transition of the Army from mission to church and mentions the influence of the Society of Friends (the Quakers) upon the Booths as an explanation for the Army's belief that the deep, inner experience of grace could be, and was, real without any external rituals. William Booth, she wrote, "pointed his people to the privilege and necessity of seeking the substance rather than the shadow."

Commissioner Paul Rader, before being elected General in 1994, spoke of the strangely ambivalent role of the sacraments in church history. He spelled out the Army's belief about the immediacy of grace: "We believe that the grace of Christ comes to us not through the act of partaking of small pieces of bread or drinking small cups of grape juice or wine several times a year as it is given to us by certain accredited ministers. We believe the saving, sanctifying, purifying and empowering grace of Christ is available to us here and now as we reach out in faith to Him. We believe that this grace is made real in our hearts by the presence and the power of the Holy Spirit through faith."

Then came the single most important sentence in his presentation: "When our hearts are made holy, all of life is a sacrament." Here then is Salvationist sacramentalism.

The authenticity of a sacramental life is not dependent upon ceremony. According to the Book of Common Prayer a sacrament is "an outward and visible sign of an inward and spiritual grace." Salvationist sacramentalism carries this to its logical conclusion and says that a person can be such a sign, derivatively from Christ, the one True Sacrament. You can be a sacrament. I can be a sacrament.

Shaw Clifton, *Who Are These Salvationists?*

The Sacrament of Life

Isaiah 63:3

My life must be Christ's broken bread,
    My love His outpoured wine,
A cup o'erfilled, a table spread
    Beneath His name and sign,
That other souls, refreshed and fed,
    May share His life through mine.

My all is in the Master's hands,
    For Him to bless and break.
Beyond the brook His winepress stands,
    And thence my way I take,
Resolved the whole of Love's demands
    To give, for His dear sake.

Lord, let me share that grace of Thine
    Wherewith Thou didst sustain
The burden of the fruitful vine,
    The gift of buried grain.
Who dies with Thee, O Word Divine,
    Shall rise and live again!

Albert Orsborn, *The Beauty of Jesus*

The Joy of Sorrow

Matthew 5:4

If you want to find a person's character, find out what makes him laugh and what makes him weep.

In this beatitude we have a real paradox, for it speaks of the "joy of sorrow" and the "gladness of grief." The word that is used for mourn speaks of a sorrow that pierces the heart, not just a passing sadness. This beatitude however embraces much more than mourning for the dead.

"I confess my iniquity; I am troubled by my sin" (Psalm 38:18). The way to God is always the way of the broken heart. We must be sure that it is sin and not the consequences over which we mourn. That does not mean we must wallow in self-reproach and condemnation. There is a place for genuine mourning for our sin and sins, but let us also remember that God forgives and forgets. Leslie Weatherhead reminds us that "forgiveness is the most powerful, therapeutic idea in the whole world."

We also need to mourn over the sin of the world, as Jeremiah wept over the sins of the people and as Jesus wept over Jerusalem. A church leader challenged his congregation with these words: "More than we need anything else today—more than money, better buildings, better choirs, social respectability—we need men and women who will tarry before God for a baptism of love. Then warmed by its fire and gripped by its passion, they will carry this love to a needy world."

"They shall be comforted." The word implies more than sympathy or the drying of tears. It includes comfort and consolation, summoning to one's side as an ally or helper and encouraging and giving strength. The word comfort comes from two Latin words meaning "with strength." Our God is the God of comfort and the Holy Spirit is referred to as the Comforter. "Weeping may remain for a night, but rejoicing comes in the morning" (Ps. 30:5).

Dr. Roy Allen translated this beatitude: "Blessed are they that mourn, for they shall be comforters." Paul wrote of "the God of all comfort, who comforts us in all our troubles, so that we can comfort those in any trouble with the comfort we ourselves have received from God" (2 Cor. 1:3-4).

Bramwell H. Tillsley, *The War Cry*

A Task for The Ordinary Man

Luke 5:1–11

G. K. Chesterton said, "When our civilization wants a library cataloged, or the solar system discovered, or any trifle of that kind, it uses its specialists. But when it wishes anything done which is really serious, it collects twelve of the ordinary men standing round. The same thing was done by the Founder of Christianity."

So it is that an important verdict, "guilty" or "not guilty," in a criminal trial involving a human life, is not entrusted to legal experts but to twelve ordinary citizens chosen at random. Every murderer knows that he gets a fair chance when his case is in the hands of "ordinary men standing round."

Jesus Christ chose the common people to share with Him a mission holding the issues of life and death. By intuitive wisdom He called twelve "ordinary men standing round" and entrusted them with powers transcending even the powers of the religious experts of His day.

Not in the whole of Palestine could one have chosen men more remote from the high vocation to which they were called. Unlettered and unknown, and yet the religious specialists—the Rabbis with their expert knowledge of the Scriptures— were passed by in favor of them. Christ's mission demanded the freshness of the unspoiled heart. Preconceived notions, hardened opinions and uncompromising prejudices were soils too hard and stony to receive the new seeds of Christ's teaching. He trusted love rather than education to carry on His work. He believed in integrity rather than intellect. He wanted not sophistication but simplicity of spirit.

He chose fishermen, ordinary folk. Let us take heart! Every ordinary person has something learning cannot give. If we haven't mind we may have muscle. If we haven't much in the head, we can have a lot in the heart.

But why did Christ choose fishermen? Because they were accustomed to cooperating with others. He wanted men who could work together as a team. He still wants ordinary people, willing to pull together in His cause.

Jesus called fishermen because they were men with a questing spirit, who would go out on to the high seas of the world to "rescue the perishing." Fishermen are men of action: resourceful, enterprising, adventurous, always seeking a new haul. Christianity can thrive only by capture. The high art of winning souls requires the dashing courage of the fisherman.

In every man and woman there is something Christ can use. This does not require high gifts and superior qualities, but simple faith, strong courage, and conviction that Christ is the answer to every need.

George B. Smith, *Meditations for the Ordinary Man*

He Who Laughed First

Luke 2:10

It took me a long time to hear God laughing. But then I began hearing some intriguing things. For one, I noticed the words of that time-honored confession of faith, the Westminster Shorter Catechism, concerning a Christian's "chief end" being "to enjoy Him forever." Now how do you enjoy someone who can't laugh?

For another thing, I began to see more laughter in the Bible. It was mostly a matter of letting texts come alive, which in many instances revealed God's humor and the sheer pleasure of life with Him.

And yet another observation: the Christians I found myself most drawn to were those whose love for God had a fresh sparkle and whose outlook had generous doses of humor. Their holiness was a joyful attraction.

All of this led me to take God's humor seriously and to realize that it invariably affected people who were in love with Him. That is why Tertullian, an early Church father, was right: the Christian saint is hilarious. He or she is sufficiently infected with God to join His laughter. The saint's God-given insight into life helps him or her see humor in new places.

The life to which the Scriptures point is suffused with good cheer, childlike delight and a certain carefree attitude. The New Testament message is a frontal assault on sadness and grim piety, and it offers a remedy for sinking despair.

From the very beginning of the salvation story to its end, joy emerges again and again. The birth of the Savior brings joy (Luke 2:8–20). His message and ministry elicit joy in the people (Mark 12:37). Near the end of His life He tells His disciples that the reason He has taught them is so that His joy might be in them and their own joy might be complete (John 15:11). Having met their resurrected Lord, the disciples are overwhelmed with joy (Luke 24:52). The early Church enjoys its life together (Acts 2:43–47); and the mission of the church brings joy to the recipients (Acts 8:8).

This is not to say that holiness is an easy road. For starters, it means taking up one's cross and dying to oneself. Nor should it be construed to suggest that tragic, and even horrible, things do not happen to God's beloved disciples.

The joy of the Lord is not a guarantee of perpetual happiness. Rather, it's something deep enough to sustain us through tragedy, a joy that neither person nor circumstance can rob us of.

Philip D. Needham, *He Who Laughed First*

Called to Follow

John 21:19

It is of interest to observe that the last command Jesus gave to Peter, "Follow me," corresponded with the first command He gave when He called both Peter and his brother Andrew from their nets: "Come, follow me" (Matt. 4:19). Then, of course, they were told they would become "fishers of men" whereas now Peter the fisherman was to be Peter the shepherd.

Following is a very personal business, insofar as Jesus calls us to become disciples. Time, however, does not weaken the need to follow; indeed, quite the reverse. Furthermore, experience teaches us that as we develop our skills and become richer in spirit, following Jesus becomes even more satisfying because we follow more thoughtfully and fruitfully.

In Peter's case, he was to follow Jesus to the cross itself (vv. 18,19). Not everyone is called to die for Christ. But Peter could not resist asking the Lord what would happen to John and received the reply that the pattern of John's discipleship was no concern of Peter. The fact is clear that just as we become believers on an individual basis so our discipleship continues to be distinctive, even though we are all members of the body of Christ.

God does not mass–produce or clone His disciples. There is a richness about our personalities which the Holy Spirit works to refine, reinforce and use in the Master's business. Consequently, there is an important place in the body of Christ for all kinds of gifts and potentiality. Peter was not John, and neither of them was Paul, but each had his own distinctive contribution to make to the building up of the Church. Our individuality ought not to make us difficult, proud and self–indulgent, but rather should make us part of the rich mosaic of the people of God.

> We know, Lord, we are wonderfully made,
> We differ in both gifts and personality.
> But with Your Holy Spirit's powerful aid
> His wisdom and originality,
> Within Christ's body we can take our place,
> And witness to Your all–sufficient grace.

Harry Read, *Words of Life*

In Life's Testings

Romans 8:28

Brengle's preaching was compelling, not primarily because he knew and believed the Scriptures, but because he was a living exemplar of what he preached. He often included himself, drawing from personal experience to emphasize his point. He knew that sorrow bowed many men tragically, and would often use such a Scripture reference as Revelation 21:4: "He will wipe every tear from their eyes. There will be no more death or mourning or crying or pain."

Looking straight into the eyes of his audience, for he used very few notes in later years, he would speak from his heart.

"From infancy my life has been punctuated by tragic losses, surprises and pains. I do not remember my devout father. He made the soldier's sacrifice during the Civil War when I was a very little child, and my earliest recollections are of a bereaved and weeping girl-mother, sighing, sad-faced and broken of heart.

"In my adolescent boyhood when a young fellow most needs his mother, I was away from home at school where I received my first telegram. It read: 'Come home quickly. Mother is dying.' When I reached home she was dead.

"At the beginning of my Salvation Army career, a Boston rough hurled a brick at my head and felled me with a blow that laid me out of the work for 18 months, and gave me a shock from which I have not wholly recovered in 35 years.

"In the midst of my Army career I was stricken with an agonizingly painful and dangerous sickness in a far-off foreign land, where I lay at death's door for weary weeks, returning home at last almost helpless, a mere shadow of a man. Some years later, lying helpless in a hospital, word was brought to me that the darling of my heart was dying."

"Oh, it is easy to preach in full and robust health about "grace," but the test comes in proving and practicing it in danger, in broken health, in poverty, in loneliness and in sore trial."

God does not make pets of His people. His greatest servants have often been the greatest sufferers. He assures us that "All things work together for good to those who love God" (Rom. 8:28 NKJV). Then He leaves us free to believe and prove it and be at peace.

Sallie Chesham, *Peace Like a River*

"A Great Cloud of Witnesses"

Hebrews 12:1

Imagine you're at the starting line in the most important race in history. You're in a great stadium filled with Olympic athletes watching your performance! That's the image the writer to the Hebrews presents to portray the Christian's journey. We're not wayfarers strolling leisurely along the byways of life or tourists returning each night to a fixed place, but we're contenders always on the move. We're heading for a particular goal—Christ Himself, His presence. It's the most important race ever run.

Not only is Christ the goal of our journey, He is also the companion of our way and our example. "For the joy set before Him [He] endured the cross, scorning its shame and sat down at the right hand of the throne of God" (Heb. 12:20). There, having reached His goal, He waits to welcome us when we reach the end.

Essential to the image is this "great cloud of witnesses." Our race is run in the gaze of the heroes of the faith who lived and suffered and died in their day and generation. They're watching, but what is more, they're cheering us on.

But how do we "catch a cloud and pin it down"? There's a sort of mystical quality about this cloud. How do we relate to people like Isaiah whom Jewish legend tells us was sawn asunder when he refused to take part in his country's idolatry? Or Jeremiah, stoned to death by his own fellow countrymen? Or more modern heroes who endured punishments so graphically cruel and insidious that our modern horror movies pale in comparison?

Even now, our world is experiencing a new wave of persecution that astonishes our modern tolerant sensibilities. Christians in China, Africa and other parts of the world are being imprisoned, beaten and murdered for no other reason than that they pledge allegiance to Jesus Christ.

Our task is to remain faithful now, in the little or large struggles of our lives. That, I believe, is all that the great heroes of the faith did. But it was enough. It was enough to see them through the most dramatic conflict, the deepest suffering, even death. And now they watch, this great cloud of witnesses, cheering us on. What a mighty applause that must be.

Marlene Chase, *Pictures from the Word*

Quick! The Bandages

Luke 10:36–37

He was lying in a ditch, blood oozing from several parts of his body. He had been beaten senseless. There was no one else in sight. The victim must have been traveling alone. That, in itself, was tempting danger. The descent on the unsuspecting was always swift and vicious.

The victim lay helpless and dying. There were some passers-by, but for various reasons they didn't stop to help. Then a solitary traveler saw the crumpled, wounded figure in the ditch and stopped to investigate.

The fact that the victim and rescuer lived on opposite sides of a traditional border didn't matter. There was a life to be saved.

Anything like a "911" call belonged to a distant future. Centuries would pass before an ambulance with life-saving staff and equipment would appear on a scene. Fortunately, there was some "oil and wine" in the saddlebag of this good-hearted "paramedic."

If he could get the victim to the next rest house, the sufferer might survive. The Samaritan had some money. He knew he could give the innkeeper two denarii—two day's earnings—as a deposit, and could settle whatever else was owing on a subsequent visit. But the immediate need was not money; it was for bandages! So many things are more important than money, and never more so than in the moment of crisis.

Bandages! Who has bandages? But, alas, there are no bandages in the saddle-bag. So, off comes the Samaritan's headdress, a piece of linen about a yard square. What had screened his eyes and protected cheekbones and neck from the hot Eastern sun become strips of cloth—improvised, blood-stanching, life-saving bandages! So "He bandaged his wounds" (Luke 10:34).

Did it really happen like this? We don't know, because it's only a story, a story told by Jesus (Luke 10:25–37), to a lawyer who was more interested in controversy than compassion. When he had asked, "Who is my neighbor?" Jesus tells him about the victim saved from death by a member of an ostracized race who doesn't pass him by on the other side. It is compassion in action, turned loose on anyone who lies helpless and bleeding in the ditches of life.

Helmut Thielicke suggests the decisive question is not: "Who is my neighbor?" but "To whom am I a neighbor?" It may be that there is someone, somewhere, who is pinning his hopes on me desperately hoping that I will not pass by on the other side. Beaten by life, I am his only hope of rescue. As Luther put it: "To whom am I to be Christ?"

Arnold Brown, *Reading Between the Lines*

Prayers Without Words

Romans 8:26–27

A perplexing part of Paul's theology of prayer is contained in the rather mysterious passage where he speaks of groans, which in reality were forms of wordless prayers: "The Spirit helps us in our weakness. We do not know what we ought to pray for, but the Spirit Himself intercedes for us with groans that words cannot express. And He who searches our hearts knows the mind of the Spirit, because the Spirit intercedes for the saints in accordance with God's will" (Rom. 8:26–27).

In solidarity with us, the Holy Spirit joins in our inarticulate beseeching, meeting us at the point of near despair; and He does so because "we do not know what we ought to pray." What Paul has in mind is the only solution left when we become conscious of our weakness, when our needs and unfathomable longings go far beyond anything our minds can grasp, beyond anything our language, even our groanings, can express. In such a crisis, only the Spirit can adequately intercede for us.

My father was a man of prayer. He was a Salvation Army officer and often faced agonizing problems as the spiritual leader and counselor of his flock. As a young teenager I recall occasions when he would emerge from his place of private prayer in our home, frustrated in mind and dejected in spirit. He had a saying at such times which expressed how he felt: "The heavens are as brass!" He had not "got through."

Though he may not have been aware of it, the Spirit was interceding for him. In God's time and in God's way the problem would be resolved. It was as though the Spirit simply took over when my father seemed to give up. It was then he learned that his "battering at the gates of heaven in prayer" was not in vain. And also then he learned how dependent he was on the Spirit who interceded for him with the Father.

My experience has been similar. So often I have prayed amiss. I have made an inaccurate assessment of the situation, or failed to perceive God's will for that particular crisis. But the Spirit interceded, in harmony with the Lord's prayer, "Thy will be done" (Matt. 26:42).

When we cannot read His thoughts aright, the Spirit comes to our rescue. When we lift empty and helpless hands because we know not how to pray as we ought, and our tongue is speechless, He stands by to support us.

Clarence D. Wiseman, *The Desert Road to Glory*

The Blessings of a Pure Heart

Ephesians 5:25–27

A pure heart will ensure a holy life, a life fashioned after the life of the Lord Jesus Christ. It will, at the best, be very imperfect, have many weaknesses, and be subjected to many mistakes; but still, according to the light possessed, it will be a holy life.

Such a man is honest and faithful in all his worldly dealings. He has an honest heart. His word is his bond. He has a true heart. He neither shirks his duty nor wastes his time. He has an industrious heart. He is loving to his wife, tender to his children, faithful to his comrades, gentle to the weak. He has a kind heart. He is compassionate. He pities the poor, yearns over the backslider, fights for the salvation of sinners.

A pure heart will give you peace. It is a condition of peace. You must not expect a life of uninterrupted gladness in the world. But the peace of God is your birthright and, with a pure heart, the treasure shall be yours.

Purity of heart is the condition on which God will enter and dwell in your soul. God wants to live with you, not only in your home, but in your very heart.

A pure heart will make you a blessing to those around you. A pure heart makes a good life. Goodness is attractive; men respect it and are drawn to it, for what it is in itself. So it is with the soldier who enjoys purity of heart and lives in harmony with the experience. A holy influence will be going out from him all the time, not only from what he says and does, but from what he is himself.

Now I affirm, on the authority of the Bible, that Jesus Christ your Savior is able and willing to keep you from doing wrong. First, you cannot doubt God's ability to make and keep you from sin. He who made you and sustains you in being, who redeemed you on the cross, can surely do this for you. He who will raise you from the dead and land you at last safely in heaven, is surely able to keep you from breaking His commandments all the rest of the short time you have to spend in this world. I am sure He can.

It may be a difficult task, perhaps, fixed as you are. But God will be equal to the undertaking. He has saved you from many sins already. Evil habits and passions that used to reign over you have been mastered.

And then, if God is able to make and keep you pure, you cannot question His willingness to do it. God tells us in the Bible in plain language that He wants to make you holy. Jesus Christ came into the world, lived and suffered and died that you might be made holy.

William Booth, *Purity of Heart*

A Letter of Recommendation

2 Corinthians 3:3

Ayoung boy walked into a drugstore and asked to use the telephone. "Hello, Dr. Anderson," he said after dialing. "Do you want to hire a boy to cut the grass and run errands for you? Oh, you already have a boy? Are you completely satisfied with him? Okay thanks, Doctor."

As the boy turned to leave the druggist said: "Just a minute, son. If you are looking for work I could use a boy like you!"

"Thank you, sir, but I have a job," the boy replied.

"But didn't I just hear you trying to get a job from Dr. Anderson?"

"No sir," was the reply. "You see, I'm the boy who is working for Dr. Anderson. I was just checking up on myself."

It is natural to be concerned about what others think of us. A good reputation is never achieved easily, and once gained, must be treasured as a valued possession. Indeed, someone once said that reputation is the only thing you take with you when you die. Shakespeare echoed that sentiment in *Othello* when he wrote:

> Who steals my purse steals trash ...
> But he that filches from me my good name,
> Robs me of that which enriches him,
> And makes me poor indeed.

For Christians, though, a reputation does more than simply reflect the person. It reflects the Lord we love. We must be living letters of recommendation for Jesus Christ.

The Apostle Paul reminds believers that they are "a letter from Christ ... written not with ink but with the Spirit of the living God" (2 Cor. 3:3). It is through the indwelling of the Holy Spirit that Christians become living testimonies to divine truth.

Jesus Christ was the "Word made flesh" (John 1:14). So we must make the gospel tangible to the world around us. It's our responsibility, and it is an essential part of successful Christian living. Through God's Holy Spirit, we must live our lives such that, when friends and acquaintances comment that they can "read us like a book," we're sure it's the right one.

Kenneth G. Hodder, *The War Cry*

The Fragrance of Prayer

Mark 14:32–52

It was the road of sacrificial prayer that led Jesus to the Garden of Gethsemane near the foot of the Mount of Olives. With only olive trees and sleepy disciples for companions, our Lord retreated to His favorite spot in the garden to spend the last agonizing hours before His betrayal and predawn arrest.

"Abba, Father," He prayed, "everything is possible for You. Take this cup from Me. Yet not what I will, but what You will" (Mark 14:36). The Son of God drank the contents of that fearful cup. "Thank God He drank it!" writes Harry Read (R) in *Words of Life*. "If He was free to reject it, and that freedom must surely have been His, then our salvation hung in the balance in Gethsemane."

During the years General Wiseman was away on war service, he sent to Mrs. Wiseman a bunch of dried lavender from the Garden of Gethsemane. She admitted to an initial sense of disappointment at seeing the shrivelled dry stalks. As she removed the stalks from the package, however, the scent of lavender permeated the air. She gathered a number of seeds from the stalks and planted them. With careful nurturing the seedlings became full-grown and eventually provided a fragrant welcome for her husband when he returned to Canada from war service.

For more than 40 years, wherever in the world their Salvation Army pilgrimage took them, slips of lavender were tucked away among their personal effects, to be planted in the next garden. Cuttings were shared with visitors, so that the fragrance of that strain of lavender has been released in many parts of the world.

When General Wiseman was promoted to Glory, a cutting of lavender was lovingly placed in his hands. The lavender, which derived its life and its fragrance from the Garden of Gethsemane, communicated its own special message: The fragrance of this godly life will linger on.

When Jesus prayed in that lavender-scented garden, "Yet not what I will, but what You will," He was yielding to the ultimate will of God. Even so, as the disciples of the Lord, may our lives be redolent with the fragrance of sacrificial prayer.

William MacLean, *The War Cry*

Have Courage

Psalm 31:24

We want a courage that will acknowledge Christ—the Christ of the New Testament—the Christ that was down upon shams, and hypocrisies, and luxuries, and selfishness, the Christ of the cross. We want a courage that will look the world—that hates Him still, and would crucify Him again—in the face, and say fearlessly, "I am on His side, and I glory in it."

We want a courage that will confess salvation. If God has spoken to a soul, if He has given it an inspiration, a forgiveness, an adoption, an inheritance, surely that is cowardice that would keep the soul from telling it forth for the benefit of the impoverished world about him.

We want courage to denounce iniquity, to call things by their right names. Having convictions of right and wrong, let us plainly tell them forth, whether we please or displease. We will not do it in order to create pain; but, surely, if God has shown us right from wrong, we should imitate Him, and show it to others.

We want courage to warn people of the wrath and ruin that are coming upon all evildoers. Why don't we speak out plainly and repeat it, and repeat it, until they say it to themselves, and wake up their slumbering souls and escape for their lives?

In short, we want the courage of our convictions. We want pluck and daring that cannot be abashed, that can stand up against the influence of a world in arms and risk everything to gain our holy ends.

This courage is often realized and manifested by naturally delicate timid souls—men and women who by nature would shrink from danger, but who, by grace, can face with unflinching calmness men and devils leagued in furious opposition.

There is plenty of this God-given quality in the divine storehouse. God gives it abundantly to those who seek. Courage, pluck, daring, heroism, whatever name this spirit may be known by, is not only a gift, but a growth. Cultivate it; stand up for God, and the spirit of the martyrs and holy prophets will come upon you.

William Booth, *The Warrior's Daily Portion*

Faith and Feeling

1 Thessalonians 4:3

God calls us to the heights: "Be holy" He says (1 Pet. 1:16). No one can do that, however hard he tries, until he realizes that God's commands are God's enablings. With the command we may have the endowment.

The psychologist Adler has pointed out how much insight lies in Jesus's first inquiry of the infirm man, "do you want to be made well?" (John 5:6 NKJV). The will is determination; it is decision; it is the direction of a man's desires. "It is God's will that you should be sanctified" (1 Thess. 4:3). The Christian is to bring his will into agreement with God's will in the matter.

John Ruysbroeck was a 14th century mystic of wide influence. One day two young priests approached him to seek his advice on Christian living. He is reported to have said to them, "You are just as holy as you want to be." It was profoundly true.

Perhaps any Christian movement that emphasizes experience, as The Salvation Army does, will need to take care to keep a sense of proportion. Our songs encourage us to expect religion to be heartfelt. Such an accent is legitimate, but let us not forget the divine order. It is (1) fact, (2) faith, (3) feeling. There is always the danger of reversing the order. Some Christians will believe when they "feel" convinced. But feelings were never intended to rule; we are to obey God whether we feel like it or not.

Our Lord's confidence in our capacity for holiness is amazing, almost incredible. But how encouraging! Even though what man is may be far from what he ought to be, Jesus is sure we can rise to it.

If that victory is ever won, however, it will be just that—a victory, over a thousand besetments and temptations. We encounter the same storms in which others have suffered shipwreck.

God looks upon His embattled child and says, "You can have victory if you really want victory, not with half your being but with every part of you." In the 19th century Kierkegaard said, "Purity of heart is to will one thing."

Holiness is wholeness, integrating the entire personality around one passion. Catherine Booth declared: "No man ever got this blessing if he felt he could get along without it." When it matters that much to us, command and promise, duty and privilege, will meet and mingle in the experience of sanctifying grace.

Edward Read, *Studies in Sanctification*

The Judgment to Come

Acts 17:31, Jude 14–15

～

Men in all ages have agreed with men of today in one thing—that in this life rewards are not proportionate to virtue, nor punishments to vice. That this is so is self–evident. The relation between conduct and condition is unequal. All around us we may see that the good and worthy are oppressed, while the bad and unworthy flourish. So manifest is this that it often appears as though there is no judge taking account of human action, or that if there be one, he judges unjustly. There is, however, another possibility. It is this—that judgment is deferred; that there is, in fact, "a judgment to come."

Sowing and reaping govern one another with inexorable certainty, as does everything in this life except as to doing good and doing evil. The exception has proved a terrible trial to men since the world was made. Out of those agonies has sprung a conviction that human existence does not end with the grave, but that in some other world, or in some other state, these inequalities will be rectified, the balance will be restored, and goodness will receive its fair reward, while bad-ness will meet its proper consequences.

The Bible fully harmonizes with reason and instinct in this matter. It declares from beginning to end that thus such a thing will happen as men's hearts have from the dawn of time either desired or feared. The first of the prophets, Enoch, only seventh from Adam, foretold it. "See," he said, "the Lord is coming with thousands upon thousands of His holy ones to judge everyone" (Jude vv. 14–15). And Paul, almost the latest of the great prophetic voices, with equal definiteness cried aloud, "For He has set a day when He will judge the world with justice" (Acts 17:31). What reason and instinct demand, therefore, revelation has clearly foretold. The judgment described in the Word of God meets this universal cry of the human spirit.

Look also at the universal sentiment as to hidden wrong. Is there not in every one of us a persistent anticipation, almost amounting to an earnest expectation, that sooner or later the secret will out, and the guilty will be brought forth? Is it not almost equally a conviction that unknown good ought somehow to be rewarded? The world has had innumerable examples of unselfish devotion to the well–being of others which have found no reward in this life. Is all this to be buried in oblivion for some, while trumpeted forth for others?

The pictures in which the Bible describes the Great Assize meet, with remark-able exactitude, these very demands.

Bramwell Booth, *Life and Religion*

Authentic in an Artificial World

2 Corinthians 1:12

We live and move daily among artificiality. We are growing tired of living with the cheap, the deceptive, the artificial. We want authenticity. We want to be real. We seek the truth. We want our lives to count for something.

What is the secret to living an authentic Christian life in this artificial world?

First, it is to know Christ. We share a faith which is rooted and grounded in Jesus Christ—a belief that one day God in Christ came to take away our sin and, through His death on Calvary, made us free. Free from the penalty of sin. Free from the power of sin. Our Bible tells us that we're just pilgrims here, and the journey shall not end until we see Him face to face in the place He is preparing for us.

The second requisite for an authentic life is Christ living in us. The old song says, "You ask me how I know He lives," and then affirms, "He lives within my heart!" The best proof of an authentic believer is one who every day lives out his faith in Christ. The desperate circumstances of people all about us require that we possess a real, living and vital relationship with Christ.

Finally, the authentic Christian in this artificial world is one in whom is the indwelling presence of the Holy Spirit. Our Lord informed those first disciples that He would be leaving them, but that He would send the Holy Spirit, the Spirit of Truth, whom He assured "will be in you" (John 14:17).

The Holy Spirit was instrumental in our redemption, working in us the miracle of salvation. But we don't have it all if the Holy Spirit has not brought full cleansing and complete freedom. That's what God wills for His children. We are not meant to stumble through life as carnal Christians. So let us rise up to the rich spiritual inheritance God has for us.

God wants us to be real, genuine, authentic. It will make a difference in our motives, relationships, deeds, attitudes and the way we affect others around us.

Thank God we can know Him, He can live in us and there take up His dwelling forever!

Israel L. Gaither, *The Salvationist Pulpit*

The Most Exalted Calling

Proverbs 11:30

Truly the profession of a soul–winner is the most exalted one spiritually, and therefore one which is surrounded by the greatest temptations. The higher the peak we climb, the greater our danger of wounds and bruises if we fall; and the higher the spiritual summit to which we aspire, the more awful our spiritual loss and disgrace should we prove untrue.

A soul–winner must be devoted to the salvation of souls. There must be something more than a mere enthusiasm which can shout through a hearty meeting and work like a slave by fits and starts when the Spirit's power is wonderfully manifest. There must be a devotion for souls.

Jesus Christ's pattern, described in the words, "My meat is to do the will of Him that sent Me," (John 4:34 KJV) is of a kind that will sacrifice time, rest, strength, human affections and even life itself. It is of a kind that has so completely achieved the mastery over self and pride in every form that it is willing not to hang back by reason of its unfitness. But, in the midst of others who excel in natural gifts and powers, it is willing to go forward and even have the appearance of foolishness if only it may have a share in giving forth the saving message.

Oh to remember to what a perilous height we shall have to climb if we are to tread in the footsteps of Jesus, the world's Savior. But if, having already become engaged in this great war, we do not yet see things in this light, what shall we do? First let us remember God will not suddenly make us fit for this work without any effort of our own. Just as for any earthly undertaking a man has to put forth his own determination, and study, labor and strain himself into fitness for it, so must we for this heavenly warfare. We must labor to bring our souls into sympathy—first with the awful need of the dying world, and second with the spirit, character, and message of Him whom we are trying to represent to those who know Him not.

For this purpose let us shut our ears to the earth, and listen to the despairing cries of the lost. Let us accustom our eyes to look into the darkness of the abyss of despair till earth's sights grow strange to us. Then let us kneel at Calvary's cross and look into the suffering face of Him who hangs there, until the burning unquenchable love of that Man of Sorrows flows into and fills our soul. Then indeed we shall need no spur to urge us forth to the most desperate needs for the world's salvation.

Catherine Bannister, *The Practice of Sanctification*

If It Weren't For Bad Luck

Habakkuk 3:17–18

We all go through times when everything on the horizon is bad. Every cloud contains a lightning bolt rather than a silver lining. Once I thought I saw the bluebird of happiness circling overhead ... but it turned out to be a buzzard!

I'm glad the Bible can relate to days like that. It gives us hope that God is still in control and knows what's best for us. We can be joyful in Him even if our circumstances are filled with gloom, despair and agony. Sometimes we are tempted to feel that prosperity is a right to be expected from God when we are obedient and faithful. But real prosperity means that God's plans will work out for our good–not necessarily for our financial benefit. (Romans 8:28 is not tied to the stock market index!)

Habakkuk 3:17–18 speaks of bad luck days when everything that should be working is falling apart. He has remembered the Lord although the outward signs of material prosperity are completely absent.

Habakkuk's calamities were disasters that might mean starvation and extreme poverty for a farmer and his family. Since I live within sight of a city skyline, I don't raise sheep, plant figs or herd cattle. What I can see is the complex and dangerous world. I guess I would say it this way:

> Though the promised promotion and the raise never comes,
> and we're not covered by flood or hurricane insurance,
> and my stock portfolio has gone belly up,
> and we don't qualify for food stamps,
> and my car has been stolen, the mortgage is due,
> and the doctor wants to see me about my latest EKG ...
> Yet will I rejoice in the Lord, I will be joyful in God my Savior.

Trust in God is based purely on knowing that God is in control and that He cares for me and my needs. I'm glad it doesn't depend on luck, for most days "if it weren't for bad luck, we'd have no luck at all."

A. Kenneth Wilson, *The War Cry*

The Mercy Seat

Romans 3:25

Over the years the penitent form has become an integral part of Salvationist identity. Countless seekers have found salvation at the mercy seat, and many more have found divine help and nurture. The mercy seat is situated between the platform and the main area of Army halls as a focal point to remind all of God's reconciling and redeeming presence.

"We expect people to get saved and sanctified in Army meetings," said General Paul A. Rader. He added: "Confidence in the power of the gospel and the saving and sanctifying work of the Holy Spirit is central to our faith and worship." Phil Needham states that it has value in a wider spiritual context: "The mercy seat should be utilized for any purpose involving prayer, including decision, confession, seeking guidance, rededication, thanksgiving, communion with God."

Shortly before His death, Jesus assured His disciples that it was to their advantage to leave them (John 16:7). Describing Jesus as God's provision for salvation, the Apostle Paul writes: "God presented Him as a sacrifice of atonement, through faith in His blood" (Rom. 3:25). Paul uses the Greek word *hilasterion*. The only other occurrence of the word in the New Testament is in Hebrews 9:5 (RSV) where it is translated "mercy seat." In effect, Paul is saying, "God gave Jesus as a mercy seat."

Through His life Jesus became the sign of God's appearance; through His death and resurrection Jesus became the means of God's atonement; through His ascension Jesus became the dispenser of God's grace. Our kneeling at a symbolic mercy seat energizes this three-fold truth into reality.

At the mercy seat we meet Jesus—the full expression of God, the Word become flesh, God in understandable terms. Here is where Jesus speaks to us. Here is where we can receive His Spirit in greater measure. Here is where we can become more like Jesus, better enabled to present Him to the world. With the poet, Doris Rendell, we would pray:

> We seek the healing of Thy cross,
> The mercy of Thy grace.
> Here at this sacred mercy seat
> May we behold Thy face.
> Here may we glimpse Thy holiness,
> Here on our souls descend,
> Here may we meet, and talk with Thee,
> Our Master and our friend.

Nigel Bovey, *The War Cry*

Why Should We Be Holy?

1 Peter 1:15,16

We should be holy because God wants us to be holy. He commands it. He says, "As He which has called you is holy, so be you holy in all manner of conversation; because it is written, 'Be you holy; for I am holy'" (1 Pet. 1:15,16). God is in earnest about this. It is God's will and it cannot be evaded. Just as a man wants his watch to keep perfect time, his work to be accurate, wants his friends to be steadfast, his children to be obedient, his wife to be faithful, so God wants us to be holy.

We should be holy because Jesus died to make us holy. He wants a holy people. For this He prayed. "Sanctify them through your truth" (John 17:17). For this He died: "Who gave Himself for us, that He might redeem us from all iniquity, and purify unto Himself a peculiar people" (Titus 2:14). He "loved the church, and gave Himself for it; that He might sanctify and cleanse it" (Eph. 5:25–26). Let not His precious Blood be spent in vain.

We should be holy in order that we may be made useful. Who have been the mightiest men of God of all ages? They have been holy men, men with clean hearts on fire with love to God and man. So long as there are any roots of sin in the heart the Holy Spirit cannot have all His way in us, and our usefulness is hindered. But when our hearts are clean the Holy Spirit dwells within, and then we have power for service. To be holy and useful is possible for each one of us.

Again, we should be holy so that we may be safe. Sin in the heart is more dangerous than gunpowder in the cellar. Before the disciples got the blessing of a clean heart and the baptism of the Holy Spirit they forsook their Master and fled.

Finally, we should be holy because we are most solemnly assured that without holiness "no man shall see the Lord" (Heb. 12:14).

I bless Him that years ago He awakened me to the infinite importance of this matter, sent holy people to testify to and explain the experience, enabled me to consecrate my whole being to Him and seek Him with all my heart, and He gave me the blessing.

Will you have it my comrade? If so, receive Jesus as your Sanctifier just now.

Samuel Logan Brengle, *The Way of Holiness*

Holy to The Lord

Zechariah 14:20

G od wills for His people an uttermost salvation. That has always been God's will. The meaning of the word holy was deepened by the prophets and altogether transformed by Jesus. Yet the New Testament can freely quote the Old Testament command, "Be holy, because I am holy," (1 Pet. 1:16) because that has always been the purpose of God.

The word itself comes from a root word meaning separated, and with Israel it was the divine will that God's people should be separate from their neighbors in faith and in practice. With the new Israel it is still God's will that we should separate from the world in habits because we are separate at heart.

Often "I have the desire to do what is good, but I cannot carry it out" (Rom. 7:18). But with God it is axiomatic that what He wills He can perform. So my sanctification, like my salvation, lies in yielding myself to Him with whom all things are possible.

Here then is ground which believers may feel firm beneath their feet. Here personal desire and scriptural teaching meet to provide the open door by which grace may fully enter. The experience of holiness is not merely one for which I long nor to which I am counseled by my teachers. This is that which God wills and which, with man's active consent, can be fulfilled in every life.

This is where we must give the life of holiness as exemplified by Jesus a fair chance. Some of us do not do that. We do not take the trouble to look long enough at Him. We pay more attention to a human interest picture in the daily paper. We gaze more intently at the television screen.

Ought we not to give this spiritual ideal at least equal time and attention? Sometimes we say of a person who may not have impressed us favorably at first blush: "He improves with knowing." Reverently we may say the same of the life of holiness as exemplified in Jesus.

Seize the banner, "Holiness unto the Lord," and make for the summit of the holy hill of God. Look to Jesus that He may quicken you with holy desire which, by the presence and power of the Holy Spirit, may find its fullest expression in holy—that is to say, Christlike—living.

Frederick Coutts, *The War Cry*

Peacemakers

Matthew 5:9

The Bible is a book about peace. It contains nearly 400 references to peace—peace of God, peace with God, peace among men both on national and individual levels. Peace is referred to 88 times in the New Testament and is found in each of its books. There is hardly an experience more sought after than peace. Paul begins each of his letters with a prayer that grace and peace may be upon the people to whom he writes.

Peace in the Bible is more than the absence of war. It is a positive experience and signifies the presence of all that is good and wonderful. The Hebrew word *shalom* contains in it the desire for all the goodness that God can give—a total well-being of body, mind and spirit. Peace is a creative force and a peacemaker is a person who releases this creative force to change his world.

The source of peace is God. Six times in the New Testament God the Father is referred to as the "God of peace." Jesus is revealed as God's peacemaker. "He Himself is our peace" (Eph. 2:14). John 14:27 has been called the last will and testament of Jesus: "Peace I leave with you; My peace I give you." The source of peace is God.

The enemy of peace is sin. People are at war with each other because they are at war with themselves. They are at war with themselves because they are at war with God.

This peace involves a man's relationship to himself. It also involves man's relationship to his fellow man. A false peace gives the impression that the problems have been resolved when they have only been covered over. The quieting of the surface when the depths are still stormy is no lasting solution.

In the Beatitudes, the people who are blessed are not the peace lovers but the peacemakers. You may be a peaceable man without being a peacemaker. The peace of this beatitude does not come from evading issues but by facing them. Dietrich Bonhoeffer spoke of "cheap grace." There is also cheap peace.

A Chinese proverb reads: "When there is righteousness in the heart, there will be beauty in the character. If there is beauty in the character, there will be harmony in the home. If there is harmony in the home, there will be order in the nation. If there is order in the nation, there will be peace in the world."

Bramwell H. Tillsley, *The War Cry*

God's Promise Is Kept

2 Corinthians 9:15

If ever there is a busy time, it is Christmas. I read about a woman who was busy buying Christmas gifts and preparing for her family's celebration. Suddenly, she realized that she had forgotten to send Christmas cards to her friends. She dashed off to a card shop, chose one with a picture she liked and in haste bought 50 of the same type. Hurrying home, she quickly addressed and posted them—just in time.

What a shock she received some days later when, glancing at the few cards that remained, she read the verse inside. It said:

> This card comes just to say
> A little gift is on the way.

All those disappointed friends are still waiting for that promised gift!

Fortunately, it wasn't like that with God's promised gift. He promised a wonderful gift to all mankind, and He certainly kept His promise. The gift was His Son, Jesus Christ, born in Bethlehem, given to the world to bring peace, justice, freedom and goodwill among men. He came to make the world a better place. To show men and women how to live life to the full. To bring reconciliation between man and God and between man and man.

God sent Jesus as a helpless baby born to an ordinary couple, Mary and Joseph. He grew up in a family, and shared our human life. He worked with His hands as a carpenter, and knew how hard it was to make ends meet. He understood what it was like to be poor. He faced all the trials and temptations that you and I experience.

Then, in obedience to God, He became the teacher of the good news, showing people that He is the Way, the Truth and the Life. But He was misunderstood, mocked, criticized, rejected, and His enemies hung Him upon a cross. This shining, sinless man carried our sins and opened to us a way of forgiveness, hope and peace.

But He rose from the dead and is alive today. By His Spirit He is with us. He helps us to be the men and women that we ought to be. He is Emmanuel, God with us.

God's promises about the Christ–child were more than fulfilled in Jesus' life on earth. And the reality in our own lives today when we claim those promises for ourselves is even more magnificent.

No wonder the Apostle Paul could cry out with a note of wonder and praise, "Thanks be to God for His indescribable gift!" (2 Cor. 9:15).

Eva Burrows, *Salvationist*

Send the Fire

Luke 3:16

Thou Christ of burning, cleansing flame,
    Send the fire!
Thy blood–bought gift today we claim,
    Send the fire!
Look down and see this waiting host,
Give us the promised Holy Ghost,
We want another Pentecost,
    Send the fire!

God of Elijah, hear our cry:
    Send the fire!
To make us fit to live or die,
    Send the fire!
To burn up every trace of sin,
To bring the light and glory in,
The revolution now begin,
    Send the fire!

'Tis fire we want, for fire we plead,
    Send the fire!
The fire will meet our every need,
    Send the fire!
For strength to ever do the right,
For grace to conquer in the fight,
For power to walk the world in white,
    Send the fire!

To make our weak hearts strong and brave,
    Send the fire!
To live a dying world to save,
    Send the fire!
O see us on Thy altar lay
Our lives, our all, this very day,
To crown the offering now we pray,
    Send the fire!

William Booth, *The Salvation Army Song Book*

We Ought to Pray

Luke 18:1

Jesus said "[Men] ought always to pray, and not to faint" (Luke 18:1 KJV). Commenting on that, Samuel Logan Brengle wrote, "That little 'ought' is emphatic. It implies obligation and is inescapable. Men ought to pray. They ought to pray always, and they ought not to faint or grow fainthearted and cease praying."

Why pray? Pray because you are a Christian. It is the very essence of a believer's being. Pray because your need drives you to your knees.

What evidence do we have that prayer is worthwhile? The only evidence that you need is that God commands it. Obedience is the hallmark of the disciple. To pray is simply to obey orders—and since our orders are urgent and unequivocal, it follows that failure to pray is inexcusable. Our prayerlessness is perhaps our greatest sin.

How does one learn the pursuit of God? Of all disciplines this must surely be the most demanding. And can we pray suitably, just because we are commanded to do so? It may seem a little like being ordered to fall in love! Should we not come to prayer eagerly, voluntarily, our hearts alight with longing for God? And like other disciplines it can become a delight. So much so that one comes to look forward to that little calm in the midst of much turbulence.

Praying is wide in its scope. It is broad in its caring, reflecting the fact that God loves every man, woman and child, all five billion of us. "If we have God-given compassion and concern for others," wrote Richard Foster, "our faith will grow and strengthen as we pray. In fact, if we genuinely love people, we desire for them far more than it is within our power to give, and that will cause us to pray."

"I want men everywhere to lift up holy hands in prayer" (1 Tim. 2:8). Pray then, because the Lord commands it. Pray, too, because you love the people for whom you intercede. Brothers and sisters, to prayer!

Edward Read, *Timothy, My Son*

A Conscience Without Offense

Acts 24:16

Conscience is that faculty of the soul which pronounces on the character of our actions. This faculty is a constituent part of our nature and is common to man everywhere and at all times. This office is to determine or pronounce upon the moral quality of our actions—to say whether this or that is good or bad. Conscience is an independent witness standing as it were between God and man; it is in man, but for God, and it cannot be bribed or silenced. Someone has called it "God's spirit in man's soul." It is something in us bearing witness against us when we offend its integrity.

The apostle labored to have always a conscience void of offense. But this implies systematic obedience to the dictates of conscience. Set on the throne of the soul to communicate the light and truth of God, and to witness impartially whether it is obeyed or not, of course there can be but one way to keep this conscience void of offense, and that is by so acting as not to offend, grieve, or incense it again.

To keep a conscience void of offense requires unremitting effort, exertion and determination. "Herein do I exercise myself" (Acts 24:16 KJV)—the whole man, soul, mind, body, myself. Here is need for "exercise" indeed. Here is "the fight of faith," the faith of the saints, which can dare, do, and suffer anything rather than defile its garments.

When inclination lures, when the flesh incites to that which conscience condemns, the will must say "No," and repel the tempter. Our first parents fell here. Their consciences were on the right side, but their wills yielded to the persuasions of the enemy, to unlawful self–gratification. Joseph's conscience thundered the right path, and his will acted it out. Pilate's conscience also thundered the right course, but his will failed to carry it out.

Do you resolutely say, "I will not do this thing and sin against God?" To keep a pure conscience requires great vigilance, lest by surprise or inattention we defile it. Our enemy lays many a snare to take us unawares.

A pure conscience is its own reward. No matter who condemns, if it approves, there is peace and sunshine in the soul. As a clean conscience is its own reward, so an offended conscience is its own punishment.

Catherine Booth, *Practical Religion*

By What Authority?

2 Timothy 1:12

A nyone who wants to join The Salvation Army is asked to sign the Articles of War (soldier's covenant), and to declare that he is "thoroughly convinced of the truth of the Army's teaching." But what is the teaching of The Salvation Army and where did it come from?

Eleven articles of faith sum up the beliefs, unchanged since 1878. Of course, the faith professed by Salvationists was not suddenly discovered in 1878. But why is it necessary to express beliefs in written statements—and why these particular eleven articles? Surely we cannot put God down on paper! Many of the ideas we find in later statements of faith are already found in Paul's letters. There have been various important statements of faith through the centuries, including the Army's eleven articles of faith.

By what authority? One could reply, firstly, "I know that what I tell you is true, because God has made it known to me personally."

But there is an obvious danger in the "personal inspiration" theory. How can you be sure that your idea is right and that your new truth has in fact come from God? Personal inspiration is of great importance; indeed we cannot have a living faith until we say, "I know in my own heart that it is true."

A second answer to the question is the appeal to tradition. Tradition plays a great part in all religious faiths. But we see at once two dangers in relying on tradition only. The first is the weakness of human understanding. Again, traditions become twisted by pride and greed.

We can reply to the question, "How do you know?" by saying, as Jesus did to the tempter, "It is written," or "Scripture says" (Matt. 4:4).

Here then are the three sources of authority for Christian doctrine: personal revelation, tradition and the Bible. All churches recognize them in some degree. All agree that personal faith is necessary for genuine religion, all have worthwhile customs and traditions handed down from the past, and all value the Bible.

We must apply both heart and mind to the study of the Bible. We use our brains but we also need humble hearts to receive what James Denney called "the Word of God, the revelation of God to the soul in Christ, attested by the Spirit."

John Coutts, *This We Believe*

God's Goal for Believers

1 Peter 1:15–16

The work of sanctification, of making holy, actually commences when a person repents and turns from sin, and is "born of the Spirit" by the grace of God through faith in Jesus Christ. The new birth, therefore, is the gateway to spiritual growth in the grace and knowledge of the Lord.

A careful reading of the New Testament makes it abundantly clear that holiness, which has to do with the dedication, cleansing and disciplining of human nature, is the goal toward which God calls all believers. "But just as He who called you is holy, so be holy in all you do; for it is written: 'Be holy, because I am holy'" (1 Pet. 1:15–16).

As defined in Scripture, holiness of life depends upon deliverance from the moral corruption and pride that infect heart and mind when the lower nature is cleansed and filled with the fullness of God's love. "The standard by which all requirements are measured," states *The Salvation Army Handbook of Doctrine*, "is not left in uncertainty: it is the standard of Christlikeness."

The Christlike life of holiness does not depend on the approval of others, but yearns for the approval of God. The holy life grows from within by the operation of the Holy Spirit in the heart, not by externally imposed rules, laws and disciplines.

If you examine a needle through a microscope of high magnifying power it will appear as rough as a piece of metal ore. But if you look at a thorn its surface will appear as polished and smooth under magnification as it does to the natural eye. The needle has been fashioned from without, the thorn from within. The needle was produced by man's ingenuity and skill, the thorn by the operation of God's natural laws. The life of holiness is the supernatural fruit of the sanctifying power of the God of peace Himself, working by His Spirit from within outward.

God is eager to bestow the blessing of full salvation on His children. Through His death on the cross, Jesus made this possible, for He purchased "our righteousness, holiness and redemption" (1 Cor. 1:30). God never commands what He cannot perform. Therefore, the rich, victorious, blessing–filled experience of the Spirit-filled life may be claimed by faith the moment you are willing to meet the Lord's conditions.

Clarence D. Wiseman, *The Desert Road To Glory*

Mount Purity

Isaiah 35:8

Let me illustrate the doctrine of holiness by comparing its attainment to the ascent of a lofty mountain. Come with me. Yonder is the sacred mount, towering far above the clouds and fogs of sin and selfishness. In the center of this unlovable and undesirable country the mountain of which I want to speak lifts its lofty head. Call it "Mount Pisgah" or "Mount Beulah" or, if you will, call it, "Mount Purity"—I like that term the best.

Those living on its lofty summit have glorious glimpses of the Celestial City. The atmosphere is eminently promotive of vigorous health and lively spirits.

But the question arises: "How can I get there?" There is evidently no mountain railway nor elevator on which you can be rapidly and smoothly lifted up to the blessed summit. Those who reach that heavenly height must climb what the Bible calls the "Highway of Holiness." And they will find it a rugged, difficult journey, often having to fight every inch of the way. But once on the celestial summit, the travelers will feel amply repaid for every atom of trouble and toil involved in the ascent.

The road to this glorious height passes through various plateaus or stages, each higher than the one that preceded it.

To begin with, there is the awakening stage, where the climbers obtain their first fair view of this holy hill. It is here that the desire to make the ascent first breaks out. A little higher up, and you reach the starting stage. Here those who fully resolve upon seeking holiness of heart first enter their names in the "Travelers Book."

But still ascending, we come to the wrestling stage. Here the travelers are met by numerous enemies who are in dead opposition to their ever reaching the summit. So, persevering with our journey, higher up, we come to the sin–mastering stage. Here men and women walk with heads erect in holy confidence, and hearts glad with living faith, for God has made them conquerors over their inward foes.

But there is one plateau higher still which, like a tableland, covers the entire summit of the mountain, and that is the maturity stage. Here the graces of the Spirit have been perfected by experience, faith and obedience.

What do you say to my holy mountain? Are you living up there? It is the will of God that you should not only reach the very summit, but that you should abide there.

William Booth, *The Seven Spirits*

O Boundless Salvation

Hebrews 7:25

O Boundless salvation! Deep ocean of love,
O fullness of mercy, Christ brought from above,
The whole world redeeming, so rich and so free,
Now flowing for all men, come, roll over me!

My sins they are many, their stains are so deep,
And bitter the tears of remorse that I weep;
But useless is weeping; Thou great crimson sea,
Thy waters can cleanse me, come, roll over me!

My tempers are fitful, my passions are strong,
They bind my poor soul and they force me to wrong;
Beneath Thy blest billows deliverance I see,
O come, mighty ocean, and roll over me!

Now tossed with temptation, then haunted with fears,
My life has been joyless and useless for years;
I feel something better most surely would be
If once Thy pure waters would roll over me.

O ocean of mercy, oft longing I stood
On the brink of Thy wonderful, life–giving flood!
Once more I have reached this soul–cleansing sea,
I will not go back till it rolls over me.

The tide is now flowing, I'm touching the wave,
I hear the loud call of the Mighty to save;
My faith's growing bolder, delivered I'll be;
I plunge 'neath the waters, they roll over me.

And now, hallelujah! The rest of my days
Shall gladly be spent in promoting His praise
Who opened His bosom to pour out this sea
Of boundless salvation for you and for me.

William Booth, *The Salvation Army Song Book*

"Fear Not"

Luke 2:10

～

Why is it that in the movies, whenever aliens come to Earth, they always announce to a wary populace, "We come in peace," even when they don't?

When the angels appeared on the scene in Bethlehem to herald Jesus' birth, Scripture records that they said to the shepherds, "Fear not" (Luke 2:10 KJV) Easy for them to say, since they were not the ones who had just been scared half to death.

The shepherds had no companions other than the sheep. No comfy sofa. No Nintendo. No ESPN. Theirs was a boring, thankless job: caring for smelly, stupid sheep. In the middle of one of those tedious nights, angels in gleaming white robes packed the sky singing, "Glory to God in the highest. Peace on earth!" Standing in front of them was an angel, dressed in a brilliant robe. Guess what he said? Right—"Fear not."

"Fear not, for I have great news and you are getting it first. In the City of David is born the Christ, the Messiah. Go and see this for yourselves. Don't mind the angel choir. They have been practicing for thousands of years and there is no holding them back any longer! Now go and see."

The shepherds immediately ran to see the Christ who came to save His people from their sins. There was no vote, no discussion.

At times we need to be careful and deliberate in our choices. But there are other times when we need to take a leap of faith into God's unknown adventure. What if the shepherds had said, "We don't have good enough clothes for a king," or "What will people think?" They wanted to see the Lord firsthand and didn't care about anything else.

Most people would have been content to hear the concert and go home, but not the shepherds. They seized the opportunity to know the Savior for themselves.

The angel came with news of hope and forgiveness for ordinary people. Perhaps this Christmas you will hear the message "Fear not" and discover Jesus' love for yourself. Unlike scheming aliens, the angels carry a message of love that is totally true and trustworthy.

Discover the Lord firsthand, with fear, reverence and excitement—just like the shepherds did.

A. Kenneth Wilson, *The War Cry*

The House of Bread

John 6:48, 51

Bethlehem—the very name floods the imagination and stirs the emotions. God chose this tiny village, annually revered in churches and homes around the world, as the cradle of celestial joy, hope and peace. Each Christmas, young and old contemplate the reality and significance of the manger, the shepherds, the Magi and the Holy Family under the star of Bethlehem. In this hamlet, one quiet, mysterious night two thousand years ago, an event took place that forever changed the course of history!

Modern Bethlehem is remarkably unchanged since the time of Jesus' birth. Its Hebrew name, "House of Bread," well defines this fertile parcel of land on the edge of the Judean desert. As they have through the ages, Bethlehem's fields still supply nourishing grain, the olive grove's distinctive oil, and the vineyard's succulent grapes.

At the time of Jesus' birth, shepherds were keeping watch over their sheep in a nearby field, and "an angel of the Lord appeared to them" (Luke 2:9). While no one knows the exact spot where the angel appeared to the startled shepherds, tradition identifies two sites.

In the second century, Justin Martyr wrote that Jesus' birth took place in a cave close to the village. At the urging of his devout mother, Queen Helena, the Emperor Constantine built a magnificent basilica over the site, richly decorating it with marble mosaics and frescoes. What had been a simple cave at the edge of an obscure village became the "heart" of the town of Bethlehem and the focal point of Christian thought and devotion throughout the world.

Descending into the grotto under the central altar, one follows a well-worn path. Numberless pilgrims have entered this cave believed to be the authentic site of Jesus' birth. The grotto's focal point is a fourteen-point silver star on the white marble floor, with the Latin inscription: "Here Jesus Christ was born to the Virgin Mary."

Here, in a hostel's basement cave in the village known as "the House of Bread" was born the baby who would one day declare, "I am the bread of life ... I am the living bread that came down from heaven. If anyone eats of this bread, he will live forever. This bread is My flesh, which I will give for the life of the world" (John 6:48,51).

May the Babe of Bethlehem's followers continue to respond as did His first century disciples: "Lord, evermore give us this bread" (John 6:34 KJV).

William Francis, *The Stones Cry Out*

Solitude

Psalm 130:5

Stress levels reach new peaks and blood pressures soar, all within a short space of time. We are told that solitude is mandatory for survival. But how? And when? Are we not already over-scheduled? It's a simple word—solitude—but can it become a reality in today's world?

An ideal setting would be a monastery or prayer center. Even a weekend away at such a facility could do wonders: silence, being in tune with one's soul, time to think, time to walk and time to listen. Time to read and to meditate with no noise other than the wind in the trees. Total bliss!

Even a short-term alternative can be beneficial. Being alone and simply thinking of a quiet, idyllic place can bring a sense of quietness and solitude and comfort.

But what about prayer? Have we forgotten about, or dismissed, prayer as a means of seeking peace and serenity? Prayers offered to God in solitude can bring healing and restoration to a frantic life. The yearning of the soul, the cries of the heart, the expression of thankfulness and joy, are all heard in prayer.

Seminars are not needed for personal prayer. Perhaps it's not the emptying of the mind that is necessary. Rather, the filling of one's spirit with thoughts of God, His creation, His blessings, His love. "But when you pray, go into your room, close the door and pray to your Father, who is unseen" (Matt. 6:6). At one with self and at one with God through prayer.

Prayer is no doubt the oldest form of meditation that has sustained and encouraged millions for centuries. It is dialogue between oneself and God: talking to God about extremely personal matters, sharing with Him all that is in one's heart, crying out to Him in anguish and thanking Him for all His blessings.

And then it is simply being quiet, listening to what He has to say to us. Solitude is a stirring of one's spirit, waiting upon the Lord: "I wait for the Lord, my soul waits, and in His Word I put my hope" (Ps. 130:5).

Is there anyone who does not need solitude? It is to be treasured as a precious gift, for it can be a means of communing with the Creator of the universe who is our Heavenly Father.

Beverly Ivany, *The War Cry*

The Colossal Event

John 3:16

Something colossal, inexpressibly great, happened in a nondescript stable among the wrinkled hills of Bethlehem on that first Christmas night. Imagine! The infinite becomes the infinitesimal! The God who created all things, from grass to galaxies, clothing Himself in the garb of humanity. The Creator of the cosmos shrunk so small as to become a fetus inside a virgin teenager!

The Babe of Bethlehem was the heart of God wrapped in human flesh! God became man, and each Advent season it takes our breath away. "God's infinity/ Dwindled to infancy" is the memorable phrase of the poet-priest Gerard Manley Hopkins.

We can gauge the size of a ship that has passed out of sight by the wake it leaves behind. The mighty life of Jesus Christ left a tidal wave of impact upon the world. His Advent became the hinge of human history.

Pope John Paul II, in *Crossing the Threshold of Hope*, poses a seminal truth and a rhetorical question: "In Christ the self-revelation of God in the history of man reached its zenith—the revelation of the invisible God in the visible humanity of Christ. Could God go further in His stooping down, in His drawing near to man, thereby expanding the possibilities of our knowing Him?"

Indeed, that Christ child, born in the feeding trough of Bethlehem's cattle shed, has opened for us the glorious possibility of knowing God—His presence, power, purpose and peace in our lives.

God, in Christ, became the Son of Man, that we might become sons and daughters of God. Christ descended the steps of glory that we might ascend with Him to worlds unknown. Beneath all the trimmings, tinsel and trappings of the season, Christ is its true treasure.

Because of the marvel of the Incarnation—God becoming flesh—we are more than a drop in the ocean of creation, a leaf in the vast forest of beings, an atom in the cosmos of existence, a speck on a pygmy planet. We are more than a cosmic accident, enchanted dust, a fortuitous concourse of atoms, the playing of an inscrutable fate, a slave to self and sin.

The miracle of the Advent continues for those whose hearts become a cradle for His birth, endowing us with the potential to become a child of God, with an eternal destiny.

Henry Gariepy, *The War Cry*

Just In Time for The Census

Galatians 4:4

We exist in a world of cybernetics. We are quite used to a periodic census, to polls that follow each other in interminable succession. We are accustomed to completing questionnaires that demand every procurable tidbit of personal history couched in terms of "when, where and how," but never "why."

Born "just in time for a census," we say of Jesus. The "where" we know: in Bethlehem, Joseph's ancestral city, where any family records would be kept. Joseph's genealogy showed him 27 generations in line of descent from the greatest of all Israel's kings.

The "how" we know. The Child arrives in unprepossessing circumstances. No accommodation in the lodge makes any emergency shelter, however rough, appreciated.

But for the "why" we must listen again to the Angel Gabriel's message to Mary and the reassuring one to Joseph: "You are to give Him the name Jesus, for He will save His people from their sins" (Matt. 1:21).

Only as the "why" is answered does the question of the "when" make sense— just in time for the first registration of its kind. A minor fact in the story, perhaps, but one with major significance.

God's indescribable gift is given in "the fullness of time" (Gal. 4:4 KJV). He is to be "numbered" among the children of men and, later to be "numbered with the transgressors" (Isa. 53:12). He is to be part of humanity's mass, under authority, subject to civil and magisterial powers, but brother to all. He is to be a cipher among millions of ciphers, classified by tribe and town, genealogically noted and inescapably recorded.

But that is not all. He is, thank God, as the Christmas carol reminds us, the "Brightest and best of the sons of the morning." Though "veiled in flesh," the Godhead is seen. He is, in the poetical words of Charles Wesley, "born to raise the sons of earth, born to give them second birth."

Because God included Jesus in the human census, the census of divine love will exclude none, for "Everyone who calls on the name of the Lord will be saved" (Acts 2:21). The One who was "counted in" during the Bethlehem census is the one and only Savior for those of us who, but for divine grace, would eternally be "counted out."

Arnold Brown, *Occupied Manger, Unoccupied Tomb*

The Incorruptible Christmas

2 Corinthians 9:15

༺

It would soon be Christmas again. With what anticipation we had watched the baking of sugared delights, the arrival of the mysterious packages from aunts and uncles, the unpacking of bright decorations that somehow never grew tacky from year to year.

Mother's gasp of horror upon entering the house and the impact of the ravished apartment struck with horrible suddenness. While we had been at church, someone had broken in and stolen what valuables they could unsheathe, including my mother's typewriter and my brother's rented accordion. But to our childish minds, what devastated us was the sight of the tree leaning crazily-wounded and raped of the bright packages that had once adorned it like jewels at the base of a crown.

We were shuffled off to bed and listened long to the subdued voices of the adults before we finally fell asleep. A kind of order was restored. The tree was righted, and the preparations for Christmas resumed. But in my heart, anger moved in like a predatory bird and nestled in stolid silence over my incubating dreams. Our Christmas had been stolen.

On Saturday morning before Christmas my mother dressed to go out. Mother never went away on Saturdays. I recall confronting her with this fact while frowning up at her from the bathroom door. "I'm going to the jail," she told me quietly. "I'm going to talk to the man who stole our things." The thief, known to the police, had been apprehended.

My mother scooped me up gently and smoothed back strands of dark hair that shadowed my eyes. "I'm going to tell him that God loves him and that he can be forgiven. I think if he knew that, he'd never want to steal again."

My angry tears overflowed. "But he stole our Christmas!" "Oh, no, honey," she said with a shining in her eyes that I remember with more clarity than her words. "No one could do that. Christmas cannot be stolen. It's here in our hearts where no one can take it away."

Of course, Christmas came again that year. Somehow mother managed to procure a few small gifts which she lovingly wrapped. There was the same indefinable warmth, the wonder that is Christmas. But in my heart lived a new awareness—a knowledge that I, like the thief, was loved and forgiven. That year I understood that whatever men may try to do to demean or annul this sacred holiday, Christmas cannot, will never be, destroyed. In all its sacred wholeness and light, it is incorruptible.

Marlene Chase, *The War Cry*

The Star in The East

Matthew 2:9–11

There's a light in the sky,
Though the sky be dark;
It's the light of the Star in the East.
There's a song in the storm,
Though the storm be long;
It's the song that my heart loves the best.

It's the song that broke over Bethlehem's hill,
The angels' song: Peace on earth, goodwill!
And the song made the whole wide world to thrill,
Lovely song of the Star in the East.

There's a thorn on the rose
That in fragrance grows
In the woodlands of friendship and peace.
Oft the flesh must be torn,
Ere the rose be born.
That will give to its sweetness release.

To bring joy to others my heart must mourn,
The worth of peace is best proved in storm.
'Twas the song in the night brought the Christmas morn,
'Twas the song of the Star in the East.

Oh, come to Jesus, bring Him your care,
Your sin He'll pardon, your griefs He'll share,
He's so tender, so strong, so true, so kind;
Oh, I love Him by far more than all.

Evangeline Booth, Carolers' Favorites

The Birthday of Joy

Luke 2:10–11

Christmas is the season of joy! Our hearts are filled with a warm sense of joy as we sing the carols, share in festivities, give and receive, and hear again the immortal Christmas story.

God knows that our world, filled as it is with sin, strife and suffering, longs to experience and sustain real joy. Christmas is the birthday of joy. The heavenly announcement that came to the shepherds on the Judean hillside that first Christmas sounds forth again for all who will hear: "Do not be afraid. I bring you good news of great joy that will be for all the people ... a Savior has been born to you; He is Christ the Lord" (Luke 2:10–11).

The magnificence of joy which Christ brought into the world can be the experience of every believing heart. In the Christmas story we cannot help but note how the shepherds were filled with great joy as they made their own personal discovery of Christ. From the humble birthplace of the infant Savior where they worshipped him, "The shepherds returned, glorifying and praising God" (Luke 2:20).

This experience is repeated every time a seeking soul comes in contact with Christ the Savior. An amazing joy is born within us to which we give expression in word and deed. The coming of Christ into one's life through personal faith is indeed the birthday of joy in the heart.

The momentum of joy is seen in the Christmas story: "when they had seen Him, they spread the word concerning what had been told them about this child" (Luke 2:17). The shepherds were carried by the momentum of their new-found joy back to their everyday tasks with a song in their hearts and a witness of good news on their lips.

How often have we heard expressed the wish that the spirit of Christmas might continue throughout the whole year! This is possible and, in fact, is one of the reasons Jesus entered human history. The deep joy He imparts continues and expands as He assures us: "My joy will remain in you and your joy will be full" (John 15:11 NKJV).

The magnetism of joy is inevitable when a person discovers Jesus Christ as their Savior. On that first Christmas when the shepherds spread the joyous good news about Christ, their obvious joy created interest among their hearers. "And all who heard it were amazed at what the shepherds said to them." (Luke 2:18).

This Christmas season can be the birthday of joy for each one who will make their own personal discovery of the Christ of Bethlehem's manger.

Robert Rightmire, *The War Cry*

What If?

1 John 4:9

Who has not played the mental game of "What if?" What if you had been born at a different time, in a different place? What if you were of the opposite sex? What if you were of a different race? What if you had been raised in a different country, by a different family?

Let's play our little mental pastime with the historical occurrence of Christmas. What if God, through the Holy Spirit, had not placed His sacred seed within the womb of His chosen handmaiden, Mary? No reference ever again would have been made of an innkeeper, still unknown by name. Shepherds in Bethlehem fields would have slept through another cool night, with no angelic chorus to startle the world with a *"Gloria in Excelsis"* to resound with grandeur through years yet unborn.

What if God had not sent a great shining star coursing through the sky? What if no "little Lord Jesus asleep on the hay," or holy child "born to be King?"

In my own heart, I know it's much too good not to be true. But what if Christmas had never happened, if Jesus had never come?

Peter would never have been heard of. Paul's Damascus Road experience would be unknown. No, it is really too good not to be true.

No cross would have found its sacred place in history, cherished, to be sung about and to be knelt before in worship of the figure hanging upon it. No "It is finished" (John 19:20) would have been spoken to make it possible for mankind to be freed from death and to enter into life forever with God himself. No empty tomb would announce victory over man's last enemy.

This season of the year would not be happening. No Handel's *Messiah*, no Bach's *Magnificat*, no singing of "Silent Night." No Christmas tree in the parlor, no children opening their gifts, no bells ringing their joyous carillon, no glowing candles splitting the darkness, no greeting cards from a myriad of friends, no sharing the thrilling announcement, "Unto you is born ... a Savior which is Christ the Lord" (Luke 2:11 KJV).

What if? Then, where would I go? To whom would I pray? How could I know that I am forever cleansed, redeemed, made holy and loved of God? Really and truly, it's all just too good not to be true!

But what if, in sad absence of personal faith, you choose not to believe it? Yes, what if?

Stanley E. Ditmer, *The War Cry*

There Goes the Neighborhood!

John 1:14

What a diverse and fascinating neighborhood we occupy on planet Earth in our little corner of the galaxy! Tribes and tongues and peoples and nations. This kind of wonderful diversity, this colorful mosaic of peoples and cultures, has moved much closer to home these days.

Sometimes people get nervous when a strange looking family from somewhere unfamiliar moves into the neighborhood. Who are they? Where did they come from? What are they really like? What do they believe? Someone fearful of change may mutter, "there goes the neighborhood!"

At Christmas, God came to us as a human person. "The Word became flesh and blood, and moved into the neighborhood" (John 1:14, *The Message*). He became part of our story. Part of our community.

He was born among us. He played in our streets. He worked there and laughed there. He was tempted and He taught there. We watched Him grow and get to know His neighbors—loving them with all their differences, caring for them, giving Himself to them in friendship and finally dying for them.

We saw the radiant glory of God in Him shining through His very humanness. It made our hearts sing for sheer joy. It means our human story can never be the same again. Having seen Him, anything is possible.

God has moved into our neighborhood. And all the dark forces of ignorance, prejudice, violence and fear are sent scurrying for the cover of night. "The Life-Light blazed out of the darkness; the darkness couldn't put it out" (John 1:5 *The Message*).

And the neighborhood? All its dark alleyways and dead end streets of despair must yield to the light of His presence. "There goes the neighborhood!"

Christmas has come for you, for me and for all in our dark and weary world. Light and promise are everywhere.

Paul A. Rader, *Young Salvationist*

Follow The Star

Matthew 2:9–10

The dark of deep December

Is pierced by light afar;

The mountain path to Bethlehem

Is illumined by the Star.

No darkness is so total,

No journey is so far

That man cannot be aided

By following the Star.

So in this hallowed season,

Let none our pathway bar;

For wise men still their life's way chart

By following the Star.

Edward Fritz, *The War Cry*

It's Time For Christmas

Galatians 4:4–5

A tyrant is loose in the world. It has everyone of us in its grasp. It controls every action and activity. It tells us when to get up, when to go to work, when to leave work and when to go to bed.

It is, of course, time. An unconquerable fact of life that cannot be expanded, accumulated, mortgaged, hastened or retarded. An anonymous author has written:

> I have just a minute,
> Only sixty seconds in it.
> Forced upon me,
> Can't refuse it.
> Didn't seek it,
> Didn't choose it.
> I must suffer if I lose it,
> Give account if I abuse it.
> Just a tiny little minute,
> But, eternity is in it.

God is conscious of time, and of timing. That is why we come upon a scripture verse like Galatians 4:4–5: "But when the time had fully come, God sent His Son ... to redeem those under the law."

So at just the right time God moved into this world through the gift of His Son. The arrival was not as man expected and certainly not as Hollywood or Madison Avenue would have arranged. But just when the right time came, God spoke through a baby's cry.

Emerson said, "This time like all times is a very good one if we but know what to do with it." It's time for Christmas because at the right time God speaks through men and women. Over the centuries God has raised up individuals to speak to their generation. Martin Luther, John Wesley and William Booth arrived on the scene when religion was at a low ebb. They, by God's grace and power, spoke to their age and altered the course of history. Billy Graham has been mightily used of God to speak to our day.

We are once again at the manger. The time is ripe for rejoicing, for renewal, for remembering and for responding. It's time for Christmas because "These are written that you may believe that Jesus is the Christ, the Son of God, and that by believing you may have life in His name" (John 20:31).

James Osborne, *The War Cry*

The Anonymous Innkeeper

Luke 2:6–7

This apologia shall be undisguised from the beginning. It is a plea for the re-evaluation of a man who has been unjustly condemned by preachers at Christmastime. I mean the Bethlehem innkeeper.

Our foregathers have draped around the innocent proprietor a shroud of innuendo that is libelous. The "no room in the inn" text has been overworked by hard-pressed pulpiteers frantically searching for a Yule topic, who chastise the innkeeper for deliberately closing his doors to Deity.

In no verse is there suggestion of a brusque refusal of admission. When the young couple arrived, the inn was already filled with dusty, tired travelers. They, too, had journeyed long miles to have their names placed in Caesar's census book. But then, as now, the rule was "first come, first served." There was no means by which a traveler could "wire ahead" for a room reservation.

Isn't that fair enough? Can we quarrel with such a policy? Suppose the innkeeper had knocked on the door of a slumbering traveler about midnight to report that a travel-weary young couple had arrived. Wouldn't he please vacate in favor of the newcomers?

Keep in mind the fact that the innkeeper did not know that the young woman was the Virgin Mary. Had the innkeeper known, surely there was enough chivalry alive to have provided the most comfortable pallet in the house for this divine Child.

Apparently he and his spouse sensed the situation. They saw the look of expectant motherhood in the face of a sweet woman. They did not urge that the couple continue to some distant hostelry. Rather, the innkeeper thought of the stable freshly cleaned for the cattle. There were the mangers and the bedding of fragrant new-mown hay. Here at least would be shelter and protection. The very thing in an emergency.

Follow the record to Luke 2:16. Shepherds came, and "found the Babe lying in a manger." Water would have been fetched for bathing. Oh, lovely gesture of sympathy! Blessed are the innkeepers who provide needed shelter.

Salute, then, the sympathetic innkeepers, and all their kith and kin. They are among all who merit the beatitude of the background.

To the Bethlehem innkeeper we make our apology and pay our respects this Christmastide. Some day we shall know his name, for he, at life's beginning, provided a manger for the little Lord Jesus.

P. L. DeBevoise, *The War Cry*

Mystery, Melody, Message of Christmas

Philippians 2:7

Only God could have thought of Christmas! It is a story of incomparable beauty. One finds a mosaic woven of stable straw and starlight, revealing to all humanity the splendor of the simple.

Its message is told and retold, yet it shines with added luster and beauty at each telling. It is repeated to the child who gazes in wonder at the sight of the creche, and received in awe by those who have entered the twilight of life.

It is a season that causes us to turn our eyes from around us to within us, from the material to the eternal, from the holiday to the holy day.

Christmas is a mystery revealed. John noted: "The Word was made flesh" (1:1). Who can comprehend the fact that the eternal Son of God divested Himself of His heavenly glory and "took upon Him the form of a servant, and was made in the likeness of men" (Phil. 2:7)?

On that first Christmas night, as angels anthemed His coming, majesty came to a manger, the Creator came as a child, the Omnipotent dwelt among the ordinary.

Had men choreographed such an event, there would have been the pomp and pageantry of Rome, with official proclamations and mass celebrations. One would have been overwhelmed by trumpeting troubadours, palatial surroundings and gilded carriages. Yet God unobtrusively made His own arrangements, and the mystery of the ages was revealed.

Christmas is a melody released. Luke records: "Suddenly there was with the angel a multitude of the heavenly host praising God and saying, 'glory to God in the highest, and on earth peace, good will toward men'" (Luke 2:13–14 KJV).

This was the long-awaited moment. Men from Adam to Malachi had searched the horizon, awaiting His coming. The heavens burst forth with this song of adoration. Musicians of succeeding generations have sought to capture the magnificence of His coming with pen and staff. What a proclamation so necessary to a world in constant conflict. And for all who are receptive to His mission, the melody lingers on in their hearts.

Christmas is a message relayed: "Unto you is born this day ... a Savior, which is Christ the Lord" (Luke 2:11 KJV). What a message to a weary world.

Willard S. Evans, *The War Cry*

Wrapped In Tinsel

Luke 2:10

Christmas is a remarkable time. It is an amazing institution around the world. The marvel and miracle of the Incarnation surpasses our capacity to understand. The Christmas story is the world's greatest miracle. Yet, the least of us, by faith, can experience its wonder in our hearts.

Christmas comes wrapped in tinsel and toys. The season is personified by a heavy-set obscure saint named Nicholas, popularly known as Santa Claus.

Some feel that this is a diversionary tactic by the world. The concept of Santa Claus, toys, gifts and sharing makes an economic occasion out of a great spiritual moment, detracting from its wonder and majesty.

Through many years I have seen the celebration of Christmas as a special gift of God. It is special in that it fulfills the angelic proclamation recorded in Luke's Gospel: "Fear not, for behold I bring you good tidings of great joy which shall be to all people" (Luke 2:10 KJV). Now, that phrase "to all people" is the operative word. Somehow Christmas should reach all people.

If the tinsel and the trappings, along with the enthusiasm of Santa's visit, make Christmas a marvelous time for all people, isn't it a magnificent communication tool for that greatest story ever told? How wonderful that this winsome way has been devised so that all people—those who believe and those who do not, those who know the glory of the incarnate Son of God and the transforming impact of His sacrifice and glorious resurrection, as well as those inured to any spiritual truth. All experience the celebration of the Christmas season. It must raise the question: "What is its real meaning?"

A youngster at home asks a mother or father, "What is the meaning of the star? Who was the Baby Jesus? What about the angels, and carols, and why do we give gifts to each other?" When those great carols are sung and their message aired by all the media, it would almost be impossible for anyone to live through a Christmas season without at least knowing it is about a Babe who came from heaven.

As we again ponder the Savior's entry into human existence, let us celebrate in gratitude for the opportunity presented to us to witness afresh in this special season of the year, to the indwelling presence of Christ in our hearts and lives. Let us pray, "Wrap it, Lord, in tinsel, amid the economic hustle and bustle, that others will see Christ in me."

Andrew S. Miller, *The War Cry*

On This Wise

Matthew 1:18

The 18th verse of the first chapter of Matthew's Gospel records, "Now the birth of Jesus Christ was on this wise" (Matt. 1:18 KJV). Then follows the wondrous story of Mary, and of Joseph, of the angel of the Lord, of the choice and conferment of the saving name—Jesus.

Matthew, one-time customs house officer in the dominion of Herod, here becomes the herald of Jesus as the Messiah of the Jews. Factually and precisely, in the manner of one trained to accuracy, he points the sequence of events. I appreciate the exact precision, the luminous accuracy of Matthew's history. The birth was "on this wise," and not otherwise; just so, as recorded.

Let the Christmas season take you right back to the beginning, the very source of this eternal splendor. And when you see how it happened, receive with simplicity the glory and the mystery of it. We know of the lovely legends and imaginative embellishments with which adoring saints have overlaid and even obscured the Bethlehem story. We do not need such fancies; the facts alone make heaven and earth to be filled with wonder.

Matthew is clearly concerned to emphasize the fact that the birth of Jesus was not according to the normal processes of human propagation, that His mother, Mary, was a betrothed virgin, that her just and devout Joseph was both fearful and ashamed, until the Angel of the Lord reassured him.

When we testify that the birth of Jesus was "on this wise," the divine Being revealing Himself in human nature and clothing Himself in flesh and blood, we mean a divine intervention.

There is a revelation of God in the order of the universe, and His ways are in the starry sky. But nature is an opaque medium, and she cannot show the God a sinner wants to know. She never goes out of her way to meet my need. She has no intimate touch, no saving healing word for me. Her rocks and mountains retain their dignity, and they call forth my wonder, but they frighten me. Her cascades and rivers flow on perpetually, but never wash away one of my shameful stains. Never, at any time, in any way, does the universe move toward me or draw me into forgiving intimacy.

I yearn to have someone "speak to my condition" in a way that the land and sea, and stars never can do. The Incarnation meets me there.

> He came right down to me,
> To condescend, to be my friend,
> He came right down to me.

Albert Orsborn, *The War Cry*

Home for Christmas

Psalm 45:8

"I'll Be Home for Christmas" is one of our popular Christmas songs heard often this season. Perhaps it is so popular because it strikes a responsive sentimental chord in each of us. It evokes the nostalgia of home and hearth and family gatherings at Christmastime.

Our family memories are rich with reminiscences of long journeys at Christmas where the holiday season would be blessed with loved ones and joyful reunion of children with grandparents, cousins and the extended family. The homecoming was always garnished with the tree (a real one), trimmings and tasty delicacies lovingly prepared. In more recent years, the "homecoming" has been to our house as children have grown and we have moved into the elite company of grandparents. "Home for Christmas" is one of the beautiful traditions that should forever be kept.

But let's look in on that first Christmas. A very interesting fact about it is that the event which is now associated with homecomings more than any other found the main characters in that historic drama away from home.

"And Joseph also went up ... out of the city of Nazareth" (Luke 2:4 KJV). Joseph and his wife Mary had to leave their home to comply with the decree of the emperor. They were away from home that first Christmas.

The shepherds under the starlit sky on a Judean hillside were away from home and their families. The wise men also had to make a long journey far from their homeland. And the herald angels left their celestial abode to bring the glad tidings to earth. They were all away from home that first Christmas.

But of course we have not made reference to the main personage in the drama, the protagonist of the "divine plot." What about the Babe of Bethlehem? He, too, was away from home. He had come from His Father's home, down from His splendor in glory, "out of the ivory palaces." Jesus was away from His home in that moment when He was born in the manger.

But there is someone else who was away from home that first Christmas. You were. I was. We were away from home. We were estranged from God because of our sin. The Son of God left home that you and I might come home—to God. That is what Christmas is all about—a great homecoming! Through the One who came in the miracle of the manger, we can "come home" to God.

Home for Christmas? In the deepest sense may it be so for each of us, through the grace of our Lord Jesus Christ.

Henry Gariepy, *The War Cry*

The Solitary Place

Isaiah 35:1

It would be my first holiday alone, following the death of my husband. "It will be a difficult Christmas," my friends told me solemnly, causing me to approach Advent with a kind of dread.

My friends were right, of course. There would be no secretive plotting of the children's gifts, no laughing over the tree that looked so perfect in the lot and so wretched in our living room. And on quiet evenings when the fire used to synchronize the tangled memories of a hectic day, I would know only the deafening roar of my solitary place.

Christmas seems to have been a solitary business for those involved in the first Advent. Consider Mary, alone with the poignant knowledge that her child, born of God, was destined to die. Consider the wise men, alone as they trudged across the desert without affirmation, and old Simeon, alone as he languished in the Temple, yearning to see the Christ before he died.

Each awaited Christmas in solitude of heart—the solitary place that begs all company but Christ. Each worshipped Him, accepting the miracle of the Incarnation, of God becoming flesh.

Martin Luther wrote, "Let him who cannot be alone beware of community. Alone you stood before God when He called you; alone you ... had to struggle and pray; and alone you will die and give an account to God."

If we attempt to substitute the so-called goodwill of Christmas, its mingled tradition and merriment, for the presence of God, we will only be more savagely aware of the emptiness of life. For without Him life is a desert and joy a series of mirages.

Why are the lonely more lonely at Christmas? Why are the despairing more desperate? Can it be that Christmas makes us more aware of our poverty without God? That all the merriment of friends and family, all the tinseled accompaniments fail to fill the void and leave us lonelier still? When holidays end, even though touched with human warmth, and no splendor has occurred in the soul, the end seems worse than the beginning.

"The wilderness and the solitary place shall be glad ... and the desert shall rejoice, and blossom as the rose" (Isa. 35:1 KJV). No place is so solitary that God cannot fill it with Himself. Indeed, we come in our solitude and discover in Him everything.

Marlene Chase, *Pictures from the Word*

The Power of The Spirit

Acts 1:8

Employers may know us by our commercial qualifications; sons and daughters know us as parents; neighbors and friends know us as single, married or widowed. But though we remain whatever designation fits us, we are more than that. We have a God–given task to fulfill. We are ambassadors for Christ, channels of divine grace, and the source of much encouragement and truth to those around us.

The gift of the Holy Spirit is the supreme gift. When we have Him, we have everything God has to offer us. The Spirit is the gift of gifts and, according to Jesus, the Father is more than willing to make the gift available to us (John 16:13).

There are certain things the Holy Spirit does for us all when He comes to us, some of which have been mentioned previously, but there are some personal things He does for us which He does not need to do for other people. This could be related to our personalities or to the task He wants us to do. Sufficient it is for us to say that there is no limit to His power to change and equip us. What a glorious provision this is!

The disciples would receive power after the Holy Spirit had come to them. We note the ordinariness of the disciples and conclude that this common characteristic is part of the divine strategy. God has always intended to work through ordinary people, knowing that His Spirit would make them extraordinary. The promise of power was made, therefore, because it was essential.

The Spirit's gift is unlimited. The Spirit imparts initiative, boldness, authority and powers of persuasion. We have only to compare the failure of the Apostle Peter in the courtyard when he was challenged about his relationship with Jesus (Luke 22:54–62), with his bold proclamation of the resurrection outside the Upper Room on the day of Pentecost to see the change the Spirit makes. How greatly we need the power, the fire of the Holy Spirit today!

> So often, Lord, I trust my own resources,
>   And work as though I labored all alone,
> Forgetful that Your Spirit reinforces
>   All I should do: all You desire to own.
> Remind me, Lord, that in my work for You,
> Your Holy Spirit's power will see me through.

Harry Read, *Words of Life*

Here At The Cross

Galatians 6:14

How can I better serve Thee, Lord,
    Thou who hast done so much for me?
Faltering and weak my labor has been;
    O that my life may tell for Thee!

    Here at the cross in this sacred hour,
    Here at the source of reviving power,
    Helpless indeed, I come with my need;
    Lord, for Thy service, fit me I plead.

Dull are my ears to hear Thy voice,
    Slow are my hands to work for Thee,
Loath are my feet to conquer the steeps
    That lead me to my Calvary.

Strength for my weakness, Lord, impart;
    Sight for my blindness give to me;
Faith for my doubtings, Lord, I would crave,
    That I may serve Thee worthily.

Bramwell Coles, *The Salvation Army Songbook*

The Gospel of the Second Chance

Philippians 3:13–14

New Year's Eve for me when I was a boy was overcast with solemn thoughts. My officer parents would see that the family attended the Watch Night service, where, after expressions of thankfulness to God for His mercies and exhortation to new resolutions to mend our ways, the crucial moment of the midnight meridian would approach as the seconds ticked away. Then the distant church bells would herald the dawn of a New Year, at which our hearts would be strangely awed by the magic of it all.

The service over, we would line up behind father and proceed to our home, where he would gravely open the door to the New Year, saying in sepulchral tones, "May the blessing of God be on this house through the coming year." It seemed as through the house had been exorcised of the evil spirits in the family circle through the past year, and that the angels of grace and goodwill had taken possession. It was all so mysterious, and in my childish fancy I thought the windows to a golden dawn had been opened.

Some time passed before I learned that divisions of time are artificial. Life is a continuous story, not a turning over of a new leaf in a book. I learned that "yesterday is tomorrow" and that our life is not in a calendar but in ourselves.

The past is not dead and done with on the stroke of twelve; it lives on in the present, moving into the future. For this reason the past may always be redeemed. To God no failure is final. He gives a second chance to all who will take it. The divine Potter never gives up. With infinite restraint and delicacy He toils to bring success out of failure. God's redemptive purposes are working for us.

A fallen woman brought to Jesus for censure received a new chance: "Neither do I condemn you; go and sin no more" (John 8:11). Her future was more important than her past. Jesus believed her capable of something better.

The past is redeemable. Tomorrow is still alive, pregnant with beauty, radiant with power, overflowing with glorious possibilities. We cannot relive the past year, but we can outlive it. After the martyrdom of Stephen, Paul gave himself a new chance: "But one thing I do: forgetting what is behind and straining toward what is ahead. I press on toward the goal to win the prize for which God has called me heavenward in Christ Jesus" (Phil. 3:13–14).

George B. Smith, *Meditations for the Ordinary Man*

Resolutions

Romans 13:11–12

I do promise—my God helping:

Firstly, that I will rise every morning sufficiently early (say 20 minutes before seven o'clock) to wash, dress and have a few minutes, not less than five, in private prayer.

Secondly, that I will as much as possible avoid all that babbling and idle talking in which I have lately so sinfully indulged.

Thirdly, that I will endeavor in my conduct and deportment before the world and my fellow servants especially to conduct myself as a humble, meek and zealous follower of the bleeding Lamb, and by serious conversation and warning endeavor to lead them to think of their immortal souls.

Fourthly, that I will read not less than four chapters in God's Word every day.

Fifthly, that I will strive to live closer to God, and to seek after holiness of heart, and leave providential events with God.

Sixthly, that I will read this over every day or at least twice a week.

God help me, enable me to cultivate a spirit of self-denial and to yield myself a prisoner of love to the Redeemer of the world.

Amen and Amen.

I feel my own weakness and without God's help I shall not keep these resolutions a day. The Lord have mercy upon my guilty soul.

I claim the blood; yes, oh, yes, Jesus died for me.

———————————

To live, to love, to serve my Savior Lord and meet His glad "Well done" at the finish of the fight is my highest ambition.

William Booth, *They Said It*

Contributor & Source Index

Contributors Awarded the Order of the Founder

Instituted in 1917 by General Bramwell Booth, this Salvation Army Order of Merit marks distinguished or memorable service such as would, in spirit or achievement, have specially commended itself to the Founder, William Booth.

Evangeline Booth (1930)
Catherine Bramwell–Booth (1983)
Samuel Logan Brengle (1935)
Robert Docter (1992)
William Himes (2000)
Josef Korbel (1990)
Lyell M. Rader (1984)
Mina Russell (1992)
Clifton Sipley (1996)
Gunpei Yamamuro (1937)
Check Yee (1997)

About the Author

In July 1995 Colonel Henry Gariepy retired as a Salvation Army officer, having served the last 15 years as its National Editor in Chief and Literary Secretary.

The author of 19 books, his *Portraits of Christ* has had a circulation of over 200,000 copies, and his *Portraits of Perseverance* has been published in several editions and languages. Commissioned writings include the authorized biography of General Eva Burrows and Volume 8 of the International History of The Salvation Army. The Colonel has also contributed chapters to 15 books, an article in the Wesleyan NIV Reflecting God Study Bible, and numerous writings in domestic and overseas publications as well as for the Army's international radio program "Wonderful Words of Life." He has published numerous photo-journalism features based on visits to Salvation Army programs throughout the USA and in Africa, South Asia and the Caribbean.

From 1969–1974 the Colonel pioneered the work at the Army's Multi-Purpose Center in the riot-scarred Hough ghetto of Cleveland, Ohio. It was a pacesetting program with over 10,000 members and 1,000 people a day coming through its doors for its many ministries. Upon visiting the Center, Billy Graham called it "Christianity in action."

During his career the Colonel also served as a corps officer and in positions of divisional leadership. He earned his Bachelor of Arts and Master of Science degrees from Cleveland State University and was honored by his alma mater with its 1994 Alumni Lifetime Leadership Award.

Colonel Gariepy's "active retirement" includes speaking engagements, teaching a weekly theology course at The Salvation Army's School for Officer Training in Suffern, NY, and serving as a literary consultant.

The Colonel is an outdoor enthusiast and jogger, being a three-time 26-mile marathon finisher. He and his wife Marjorie reside in Toms River, New Jersey. The "crown jewels" of their lives are their four children and 12 grandchildren.

Colonel Gariepy may be reached via email at hmgariepy@cs.com.